IMPEACHMENT
IN AMERICA
1635–1805

Peter Charles Hoffer and N. E. H. Hull

Some Americans came away from the impeachment proceedings against President Nixon fearing that the process was too cumbersome and too partisan to be effective or fair. Scholars and lawyers themselves disagreed on the grounds for impeachment and the procedures to be followed. This important book by Peter Charles Hoffer and N. E. H. Hull shows that impeachment has a long and honorable history in America, marked by substantial justice and procedural fairness.

Hoffer and Hull combine accounts of little known impeachment cases in our early history with broader observations on the role of law, politics, and personality in impeachment precedent. They find that impeachment and trial allowed colonial legislatures to punish misusers of power—even those protected by the crown—and that impeachments enabled the first state assemblies to prove that they would not tolerate corruption in any branch of government, including their own. Hoffer and Hull argue convincingly that the federal Constitution borrowed its provisions on impeachment and trial from the states, adopting the American variant of that process rather than the English methods. Subsequent state and federal impeachment cases, shaped by the inner dynamic that has always existed between power and precedent, embodied and tested republican ideals.

Peter Charles Hoffer is associate professor of history at the University of Georgia. *N. E. H. Hull,* formerly on the faculty at the University of Georgia and Vanderbilt University, is currently attending law school.

IMPEACHMENT IN AMERICA, 1635–1805

IMPEACHMENT
IN AMERICA,
1635–1805

PETER CHARLES HOFFER and N. E. H. HULL

YALE UNIVERSITY PRESS

NEW HAVEN AND LONDON

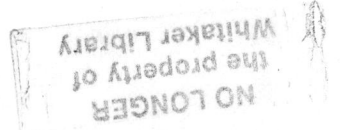

Designed by Sally Harris
and set in Baskerville type.
Printed in the United States of America by Edwards Brothers, Inc., Ann Arbor, Michigan.

Library of Congress Cataloging in Publication Data

Hoffer, Peter C.
Impeachment in America, 1635–1805.

Includes bibliographical references and index.
1. Impeachments—United States—History. I. Hull,
N. E. H., 1949–   II. Title.
KF4958.H63 1984   328.73'07453   83–19772
ISBN 0-300-03053-3

10 9 8 7 6 5 4 3 2 1

FOR WILLIAMJAMES BRANWELL PAINE HULL HOFFER

CONTENTS

Acknowledgments ix
Introduction xi

PART I The English Law of Impeachment and Its Transmission
to America 1
1 Criminal Impeachment in the Colonies, 1635–1699 15
2 Impeachment and Provincial Balance: *Vetch et al., Logan,
Trott,* and *Smith* 27
3 Revolutionary Impeachment: *Moore* to *Oliver* 41

PART II Impeachment and Republicanism, 1776–1788 57
4 State Constitutions and Impeachment Law 68
5 Impeachment and Trial in the States 78
6 Impeachment in the Federal Constitution 96

PART III Impeachment and Party Government, 1788–1805 107
7 Constitutional Impeachment, 1788–1795 116
8 The Politicization of Impeachment, 1795–1800 146
9 Impeachment for Cause, 1796–1805 164

PART IV Republican Impeachment Doctrines: "Dangerous
Tendency"and "Popular Will," 1801–1805 179
10 A Republican Script for Impeachment: *Addison,* 1801–1803 191
11 Dress Rehearsals: *Pickering* and *Shippen et al.,* 1803–1805 206
12 Power and Precedent: The Impeachment and Trial of
Samuel Chase, 1804–1805 228

Epilogue After *Chase* 256
Conclusion 264
Appendix English Precedent, State Cases, and the Origins and
Evolution of Federal Impeachment Law 266
Notes 271
Index 317

ACKNOWLEDGMENTS

THE ORIGIN OF THIS BOOK WAS A QUESTION DIRECTED AT ONE OF THE AUTHORS, for which neither she nor the interrogator had a ready reply. Ten years later, we can answer that impeachment was indeed common, and far more significant to contemporaries than historians have recognized. In the course of these years, we have contracted obligations that never will be discharged by mere "acknowledgment." Colleagues, teachers, students, and friends have taken time from their own books to help us with ours. Beyond this circle are scholars whose teaching and writing inspired our research and guided our thinking. Finally, the research could not have gone forward without the financial assistance of institutions—employers, grantors, and sponsors to whom our gratitude is substantial.

The following libraries, state archives, historical societies, and other depositories allowed us to use their collections and assisted in our research. We are grateful to the Maine State Archives and State Library, Augusta, Maine; the New Hampshire State Department of Archives, the Historical Society, and the State Legislative Library, Concord, New Hampshire; the Vermont State Library, Montpelier, Vermont; the Massachusetts State Archives, the Massachusetts Historical Society, and the Boston Public Library, Boston, and the Harvard University Libraries, Cambridge, Massachusetts; the Connecticut State Library, Hartford, Connecticut; the New York Historical Society and the New York Public Library, New York City, and the New York State Library, Albany, New York; the New Jersey Department of Archives and History and the New Jersey State Library, Trenton, New Jersey; the Historical Society of Pennsylvania and the Library Company of Philadelphia, Pennsylvania; the University of Delaware Library special collections, Newark, Delaware; the Virginia State Library and the Virginia Historical Society, Richmond, the Alderman Library, the University of Virginia, Charlottesville, and the Research Library of Colonial Williamsburg, Virginia; the Maryland State Library, Annapolis, Maryland; the North Carolina Department of Archives, Raleigh, and the Southern Historical Collection, University of North Carolina, Chapel Hill, North Carolina; the South Carolina Department of Archives and the Caroliniana Library, Columbia, and the South Carolina Historical Society, Charleston, South Carolina; the Georgia Department of Archives and History, Atlanta, the Georgia Historical Society,

Savannah, and the libraries of the University of Georgia, Athens, Georgia; the Tennessee State Archives, Nashville, Tennessee; the Kentucky State Archives, Frankfort, Kentucky; and the Library of Congress, Washington, D.C.

We are grateful to colleagues who read parts of the manuscript during its preparation: Michael Les Benedict, Bradley Chapin, Thomas Cogswell, Linda Grant dePauw, Richard Ellis, Harold Hyman, Herbert Johnson, Stanley Katz, Milton Klein, Forrest McDonald, Michael McGiffert, Richard B. Morris, Peter Onuf, Stephen Presser, Clayton Roberts, Joseph Smith, and Alden Vaughan. All their comments were extremely helpful; they are not responsible for any errors in the text.

Without grants of funds and released time the project would not yet be complete. We thank the American Bar Foundation, the Project '87 Committee of the American Historical Association and the American Political Science Association, and the Office of Research and the History Department of the University of Georgia for their support.

Last, but hardly least, we express our gratitude to Charles Grench, editor, Alexander Metro, copy editor, and the staff at the Yale University Press. They provided service beyond the call of duty. Editors in particular do not receive enough credit for the work they do. If this project is a success, it is because they would not allow it to be anything less.

INTRODUCTION

IN THE PERIOD 1635–1805, AMERICANS ADOPTED ENGLISH IMPEACHMENT LAW, AND in their turn, impeachment cases altered American political and constitutional experience. In colonial, early state, and federal impeachment cases and law, a tool used in Parliament to curb kings and punish placemen was molded into an efficient legislative check upon executive and judicial wrongdoing. The power of the English House of Commons to impeach anyone, for almost any alleged offense, was restrained; the threat of death and forfeiture upon conviction was lifted; and the interference of the Commons and the House of Lords with the regular courts of justice was limited. American impeachment law shifted, at first inadvertently and then deliberately, from the orbit of English precedent to a native republican course. Federal constitutional provisions for impeachment reflected indigenous experience and revolutionary tenets instead of English tradition.

Impeachments furthered the two central trends in early American constitutional history: the rise of representative lower houses and the emergence of checks and balances upon those houses. In the seventeenth century, impeachments and trials gave otherwise weak assemblies the power to uncover and punish crimes against the public trust by defendants too highly placed in government to be reached by the courts. In the eighteenth-century colonies, impeachment emerged as a method of checking the ambition of executive and judicial officers and, ultimately, the power of their English patrons. In the first blush of revolutionary state building, impeachment aided the lower house, often the only stable organ of government, to scrutinize and punish the conduct of disorderly, corrupt, abusive, and neglectful officials. By the later eighteenth and early nineteenth centuries, impeachment, mirroring state and national politics, afforded party leaders in the assembly an instrument to oust unpopular rivals. Impeachments expressed shared political values and enforced majority will. These threads of law and political exigency came together in the impeachment and trial of United States Supreme Court Justice Samuel Chase. With the Jeffersonians' failure to obtain his conviction, the heyday of partisan impeachments ended, but a more limited test for impeachable offenses survived and prospered. Impeachment continued in the states under a stricter construction of impeachable offenses; only the doctrines of "popular will" and "dangerous tendency," adopted by the Jeffersonians, were lost in the wake of Chase's trial.

We have attempted to recover these lost cases and case law because we believe that they constitute a neglected but important episode in American constitutional and political history. The importance of tracing the case law cannot be overestimated. Impeachments are proceedings in the lower house meant to end in trial. They may be brought to harass a political opponent or hobble an entire administration, but without some evidence of actual wrongdoing that might be tried before the upper house, efforts to impeach faltered. Unlike a motion to censure, an address to the governor or the king, a call for an investigation, or other related forms of public inquiry into malfeasance, impeachment implies the intention to prosecute the defendant in the court of the upper house. Impeachments are thus the beginning of court cases, entailing definitions of offenses, decisions on procedure, and formal defenses by the accused. In the Anglo-American legal system, case law—precedent— stands alongside statutes and constitutions as sources. Without a thorough knowledge of precedent of this type, our understanding of impeachment law in America must be incomplete.

In the absence of thorough recovery of American case law, students of impeachment in this country have fallen back upon English cases and commentary, assuming (by default) that American impeachment managers were familiar with and depended upon this body of materials. Such an assumption is misleading. The connection between American law and English law was real enough but always tempered by American conditions and ideas. Woe to the modern legal scholar, tutored by his or her own command of precedent, who substitutes hindsight and expertise for the inexact gropings of the historical principals.

Our only check upon the temptation to put more into our story than those who lived it could ever have known is to root our accounts in the political and legal circumstances of each case. We must not assume that impeachment takes place in a sort of legal ether, a pure substance which floats above the ordinary world of politics. Whether an impeachment was undertaken for partisan reasons or in response to a grave and obvious crime, all participants had some political relationship with one another. The framing of charges, the conduct of prosecution, and the arguments of the defense occurred in a political arena, not an empyrean realm of abstract laws existing in space without time. We wished to return impeachment to what it was in the hands of its American managers and defendants: a part of political and legislative as well as legal history.

But what broad legal precepts—what generalizations—can one derive from such a piecemeal approach? Can "rules" of law be extracted from such scattered cases as ours? Although episodes of impeachment may be similarly labeled and follow roughly parallel courses in early American history, are they in any way related to deeper common ideals and practices? In this instance at least, the answer is yes, there were "commonalities" in these cases—underlying conditions that fostered the development of law. Often legal forms express political and economic realities whose elucidation may in turn bring together or distinguish particular cases. The historical origins of rules of impeachment law cannot be fully comprehended without investigation of why particular cases were brought and sustained in particular courts at particular times; and when this is done, the patterns that emerge in American impeachment law reflect corresponding patterns in political conflict and constitutional growth.

The case law reveals that by 1805 a long gestation had come to an end. Over the course of 170 years, the Americanization of impeachment—fitting it to American needs, making it republican, defining its limits, experimenting with constitutional formulations, and prosecuting individual cases— progressed. Far more commonly used than legal historians realize, impeachment proved to be a valuable addition to American constitutions and an embodiment of republican ideals.

The process sketched above describes the domestication of impeachment but omits the great struggle within it between power and predecent: a tug-of-war between advocates of political impeachment and defenders of limited (though not necessarily criminal) prosecutions. By the end of the Revolution, the victory had apparently gone to the latter, but events proved the dispute very much alive. The rise of a two-party system gave renewed impetus to politicization of impeachment, under the guise of doctrines of "universal liability," "popular will," and "dangerous tendency." Against these extensions of strict constitutional language proposed in turn by Federalists and Republicans stood the weight of precedent. In our system, precedent can stand against power, expediency, and partisanship in the contest to explicate and administer law. While some lawyers joined the clamor for political removals, others, crossing party lines, cleaved to the restricted precedent of earlier impeachments. Against politicizers who would have distended the liability of officials, more conservative lawyers battled to limit the reach of legislative jurisprudence. Within these combats, advocates of legislative supremacy waged individual contests against upholders of judicial independence, and protodemocrats joined forces against political conservatives. This war of words was the inner dynamic framing impeachment law, limiting its application, and, in turn, reminding politicians of the importance of the rule of law in a republican system. Impeachment thus stands as an example of the larger dichotomy of power and precedent that has always shaped American politics and law. As Alexis de Tocqueville wrote almost 150 years ago, the influence of lawyers in American government has tempered the drive to power with an "implicit deference to the opinion of forefathers." In impeachment, precedent checked the impetuosity of partisan victors—an indispensable lesson for our times.

PART I

THE ENGLISH LAW
OF IMPEACHMENT
AND ITS TRANSMISSION
TO AMERICA

INTRODUCTION

IMPEACHMENT IN THE HOUSE OF COMMONS, WITH TRIAL IN THE HOUSE OF LORDS, originated in the fourteenth century. The seventeenth-century House of Commons, seeking curbs on corrupt ministers and councillors, revived and mastered impeachment practice between 1621 and 1641. Parliament had long functioned as the highest court in the realm, and its power to impeach rested upon this privilege. The Commons impeached for treason, trespasses, and other illegal acts in violation of statute, common law, or rulings of the king's courts of high commission. The House of Lords, to this day a trial court, sat as a body to hear the Commons' prosecution, then judged the accused. A criminal penalty was almost always attached to conviction. Prison, fines, along with forfeiture of lands and goods, and loss of office, were meted out to defendants. Capital punishment was rarely ordered. One seventeenth-century and a half-dozen eighteenth-century cases ended with death sentences. Anyone could be indicted in this way—officeholder and private citizen alike. It was the danger to the government or the public in the offense, not the official position of the offender, that led to the impeachment.[1]

Impeachments often had partisan origins and invariably had political repercussions. The simple fact that the case came to the House of Commons, a highly politicized body, rather than to a regular court of law exposed the defendant to his factional opponents. Both charges of treason, the most serious offense, and charges of "high crimes and misdemeanors," the most commonly alleged offenses for which impeachments were brought, could be politically motivated. Indeed any demonstrable breach of public faith could be "constructed" into a violation of the treason statute of 25 Edward III (1350), though the Commons did not often use this construction. The House of Commons found impeachment a potent weapon, exclusively theirs by precedent, to chastise, weaken, and—if the Lords would consent—penalize the king's ministers for corruption, infringement on parliamentary rights, misuse of power, and other abuses of public trust.[2]

The working relationship between the Commons and the Lords, while not always visible to those outside Parliament, shaped impeachment law. The Commons did not denounce a defendant but prosecuted him at a trial. In the earliest cases the king assented and executed the sentence, but by the end of the fourteenth century, the Lords judged the accused. Often in the seventeenth and early eighteenth centuries the two houses were at loggerheads. The Commons claimed a latitude in framing charges, which the Lords rejected. While the Commons used impeachments as practical tools to defend their privileges, rather than as precise instruments, the Lords—assisted by the royal judges—curbed the Commons' enthusiasm and corrected their pleadings. In point of fact, the seventeenth-century Houses of Lords tried very few of the cases brought to them and convicted only one in twenty of those impeached. On many occasions the Commons did not even prosecute—the impeachment itself was sufficient warning or inconvenience to the accused.[3]

Although impeachment periodically occurred after the 1370s, the explosion of cases in the reign of Charles I created the precedent for later impeachments in England. The Commons did not have to hear the defense of the accused or permit him counsel, but they were expected to undertake trial upon the charges. Laboring under this requirement, the Commons had to prepare the articles carefully, provide themselves with witnesses and counsel, take testimony, and arrange the whole under concise headings for the Lords. The Commons could receive information by common fame, the reports of its members, testimony at its bar, or messages from the Lords; but however the inquiry proceeded, the charges had to be drawn almost as tightly as any criminal presentment to have any chance of success.

As long as this practical consideration was observed, the Commons could impeach anyone in the realm except, perhaps, the royal family. As George Petyt reported in his *Lex Parliamentaria*:

> A Member of Parliament may charge any great Officer of State with any particular Offence.
>
> If any Lord of Parliament Spiritual or Temporal, have committed any Oppression, Bribery, Extortion, or the like: the House of Commons, being the general Inquisitors of the Realm (coming out of all Parts thereof) may examine the same; and if they find, by the Vote of the House, the Charge to be true, then they transmit the same to the Lords, with the Witnesses and the Proofs.[4]

Members of the Commons could be impeached.[5] When this happened, they were expected to step down from their seats. The most frequent targets of impeachment, however, were court officials, judges, and the king's advisors. These men might sit in the upper house as peers of the realm, or be commoners, as was Chief Justice Scroggs before his rise to power.[6] When a lord was impeached, he retained his titles but stood outside the House of Lords bar until the case was decided. He could not vote in his own cause.[7] Private citizens could also be impeached. Dr. Mainwaring in 1628 and Dr. Sacheverell in 1709 were impeached for preaching seditious libel from their pulpits. Both were ministers of the Church of England but had no other official posts.[8] The Commons was very sensitive to attacks upon its rights by private citizens. On November 20, 1660, William Drake, author of a pamphlet arguing that the Long Parliament of 1647 was still the legal one, was impeached, although he held no office.[9] In 1689 the Commons impeached Adam Blair and four other men for "high treason" in circulating a letter from the deposed king, James II.[10]

Curbing the great latitude of the Commons in bringing impeachments was the Lords' concern for legitimacy of charges, procedures, and evidence. The Lords granted the accused counsel in matters of law, allowed a full hearing of his defense, and permitted him to summon his own witnesses.[11] These privileges were similar to those a peer possessed when tried before the Lords for a common-law offense. The Lords gradually permitted counsel to speak for the accused at the bar, in defiance of the Commons' wishes.[12] The upper house even allowed a defendant's counsel to argue the legality of a pardon in bar of prosecution but dropped this allowance in 1700.[13]

The Lords preferred commoners accused of ordinary crimes to be tried before the regular courts but did hear impeachments upon offenses that could have easily been charged in King's Bench or the assize courts. Often the turning point in this decision was not the law but practical political matters. Although a majority of the Lords voted to send Edward Fitzharris, a minor character in the popish plot, to the regular courts for trial (perhaps fearing his disclosures would embarrass persons in high places), a minority of the Lords reserved their right to try anyone on an impeachment. The Commons, pushing for a trial in the upper house, protested "that it is the undoubted right of the Commons, in Parliament assembled, to impeach before the Lords in Parliament, any peer or commoner for treason or any other crime or misdemeanor; and that the refusal of the Lords to proceed in Parliament upon such impeachment is a denial of justice, and a violation of the constitution of Parliaments."[14]

Impeachments and trials invariably were surrounded by political questions. Through much of the seventeenth century the Commons and the Lords were enmeshed in political turmoil. The struggle for control of national government between king and Parliament could hardly fail to spill over into impeachment cases, particularly when the defendants were the king's ministers or advisors. "From the beginning, impeachment was associated with moments of political crisis and was often enough used as a weapon in factional rivalry."[15] Despite the political unrest, impeachment in the House became a bill of attainder in only two cases, and trial ended in bills of attainder in but three more. Aside from these, the Commons abided by the Lords' legal rulings (though on occasion with exceptionally bad grace).

The important point is this: if Stuart impeachments took place in a highly charged political arena, they were not merely political acts. Although the

House of Commons was rarely a disinterested finder of facts and framer of charges, impeachments could not proceed far without evidence of some wrongdoing, negligence, or betrayal of public trust. The Commons' periodic avidity for prosecution, seen in the political context of the era, takes on a less capricious and more disinterested hue. This was even true during the factional contests that led to the first seventeenth-century impeachments of Francis Bacon, Lord Verulam, and later, of Lionel Cranfield, Lord Treasurer Middlesex, and finally, of George Villiers, Duke of Buckingham. Bacon was a flagrant corruptionist and was duly convicted, as was Middlesex. Although the Lords were, as individuals and as a body, political, they were also the highest court in the realm. Their proceedings were more often than not fair, dignified, and learned. In this era of fevered political wars, impeachment trials in the House of Lords were among the least perverted forms of justice, striking a balance between political exigency and judicial restraint. After the Restoration the Lords generally remained unwilling to convict without evidence of willful wrongdoing. The Commons recognized this fact, and from 1626 to 1715, only five of the fifty-seven men impeached for "high crimes and misdemeanors" were actually prosecuted to judgment in the upper chamber.[16]

By the second half of the seventeenth century, impeachment came to stand for a justifiable concern among the Commons for misconduct in high places. Popular manuals and collections of parliamentary debates celebrated impeachment cases as "memorable matters" of parliamentary judicature:

By Parliament one Sir Giles Mompesson, a Moderne Caterpiller and pooler of the Common Wealth, by exacting upon Innholders, etc. was discovered, degraded from Knighthood, and banished by Proclamation.

By Parliament Sir Francis Bacon, made by King James Baron Verulam and Viscount St. Albanes, and Lord Chancellour of England, very grievous to the Common wealth, by bribery, was discovered and displaced.

By Parliament Sir John Bennit Judge of the Prerogative Court pernicious to the Common-wealth—was discovered and displaced.

By Parliament Lyonell Cranfield (Sometimes a Merchant of London) made by K. James Earle of Middlesex, and Lord Treasurer of England, hurtfull in his place to the Common-wealth, was discovered, and displaced.

By Parliament one Sir Francis Mitchell, a jolly Justice of Peace for Middlesex in the Suburbes of London, another notable Cankerworme of the Commonwealth, by corruption in exacting the penal Lawes upon poore Alehouse-keepers and Victuallers, was discovered, degraded from Knighthood and utterly disabled for being Justice of Peace.[17]

In this proparliamentary pamphlet, only impeachments (not bills of attainder) were raised as evidence of the lawfulness of parliamentary judicature. As John Selden, a leading parliamentary advocate, insisted, all impeachable offenses—extortion, violations of statute, deceitful conduct in office, violations of oath, misuses of monopolies and patents, and other corruptions— "oppressed the people" and merited punishment.[18]

The mixture of political venom and legal restraint that characterized Stuart impeachments persisted into the reigns of William, Anne, and George I. The first impeachment after the Glorious Revolution, against the Duke of Leeds for taking bribes, had the trappings of earlier cases. The Commons' real motive may have been to prevent Leeds from returning to the cabinet, but Leeds was also a corruptionist. Throughout the 1690s and 1700s Whigs sought to prevent Tories from entering government and Tories sought revenge against Whigs, resulting in articles of impeachment based upon the defendants' political miscalculations and mistaken policy. These charges never stood alone, however. Bribery, corruption, misuse of power, and willful neglect of duties were always added, and often proved. Impeachments "lurked in the shadows throughout William's reign to put fear into men's hearts."[19] In 1701, Lords Portland, Somers, Orford, and Halifax, Whig party leaders (though fallen from royal grace by 1700), were accused, respectively, of having misused their powers and given bad advice to the crown, misgoverned in Ireland, and delayed legal proceedings while in office. All were either acquitted upon trial or had their charges dismissed in the Lords, though their prosecutors, Tories aiming to deprive the four lords of office, wished otherwise.[20]

The most notorious of these political impeachments was also the most widely reported: the prosecution of Reverend Doctor Henry Sacheverell for seditious libels against the government. Sacheverell, a high Tory, used his pulpit to attack Godolphin and the revolutionary settlement of 1689. The government wished to muzzle him but doubted the effectiveness of a trial in Queen's Bench. Lord Somers, a member of the ruling ministry and himself a victim of impeachment, urged caution. Marlborough and Godolphin, allies of the Whig "junto," were more avid for prosecution. On Monday, December 12, 1709, the Whig leadership of the House of Commons began the drive to impeachment. Sacheverell's sermons were denounced as dangerous to the government and antipathetic to the Glorious Revolution. Ambitious Tories, including Harley, used the debate to jockey for office and embarrass the Whig government. Impeachment was voted but the outcome of trial was in doubt. Sacheverell had stirred deep currents of intolerance among high church supporters at large, who rallied to his aid. While the managers labored to prove that Sacheverell's words were sedition—a task Sacheverell's ponderous style and verbosity made difficult—the London mob interceded for the defendant. The Whig leadership finally carried on to a narrow conviction on party lines, but after four months of harrowing debate, maneuver, plotting, and anxiety the will of the government had broken. Found guilty, Sacheverell was only briefly imprisoned, and the offending sermons were publicly burned. He was barred from public preaching for three years. The Tories made great capital out of the trial and were able to topple the "junto."[21]

Tory leaders became the targets of impeachment when Queen Anne, their protectress, died. Robert Harley, whom she elevated to the earldom of Oxford, Henry St. John, made Viscount Bolingbroke, and Lords Ormonde and Strafford, all prominent Tories, fell prey to Whig-led impeachments in June 1715, the first year of George I's reign. The cases came to trial despite the weakness of the evidence and the misgivings of many in the Commons, but the two houses never agreed on procedure, and Oxford was acquitted. Strafford was not even prosecuted in the upper house. The other Tory lords fled. The charges against these men were that they had urged the queen to make a separate peace with France and had endeavored to secure the succession to the crown of the Pretender. The Commons lacked the evidence to prove that these ministers sought to bring in the Pretender and therefore had to press the charge of making a separate peace. The ministers parried this thrust honestly; they gave advice as they were sworn to do, under their commissions of office. And Parliament had accepted the treaty. How then could they be singled out for prosecution?[22]

With the dénouement of the trials of the Tory remnant, parliamentary fascination with impeachment flagged. Other political forms emerged to allow a quieter and more efficient test of ministerial popularity and influence. The cabinet system under Robert Walpole, though riddled with corruption and bewailed by ex-Tories and fringe Whigs, worked to ensure parliamentary confidence in the government. The few cases of impeachment which did arise fell into two fairly well-defined categories. Treason among the powerful still quickened the Commons' fears and led to impeachments of the Scottish leaders of the Stuart cause in 1717 and in 1746.[23] In a second category stood obvious cases of official malfeasance. Lord Chancellor Macclesfield was impeached, tried, and convicted for openly auctioning (for "voluntary" gifts) the office of master in chancery. He was stripped of office and ordered to the Tower until he paid his fine of £30,000.[24] With the exception of this handful of cases, the English experiment with impeachment was over. Even the notorious case of Warren Hastings, dragging on though it did for ten years at the end of the century, failed to reawaken the Parliament's old fascination for impeachment.

The timing of the explosion of parliamentary impeachment gave it a more central role in American constitutionalism than it ultimately had in English fundamental law. The colonies were settled during the century of impeachment in England. To the colonial lower house leaders, the spectacle of impeachment of the chief ministers of the realm by the vote of knights and burghers in the Commons carried a special message, gratifying to men so far from the source of royal power. Here was proof that the rights won at Runnymeade were not forgotten. One caveat disturbed this celebration of English rights in America: in purely legal terms, American assemblies had no right to bring impeachments. Practically, however, American men of affairs, concerned with the safety of their communities and with their own political advantage, did not constantly recur to constitutional principles or, rather, often ignored or refashioned rules of law to fit exigency and interest. Americans first adopted impeachment because they grasped its utility and were not told to desist, and continued to impeach even when proprietors and crown councillors explicitly told the colonists to stop.

Ultimately the colonists would fashion a theoretical justification for impeachment in the face of royal objections—but that would come at a time when such confrontation was open and widespread. In their first attempts at impeachment and trial, the Americans ignored theory and rationale. In this they actually followed the precedent of the Stuart Parliaments. The Commons arrogated to itself the right to impeach and to call upon the Lords for trial. The seventeenth-century parliamentarians found justification in the precedent of earlier Parliaments. No intricate theoretical rationale was needed, and despite the prolixity of political philosophers in that century, the right of impeachment was not emphasized in pamphlets and essays of the parliamentary party. To determine whether an offense fell within the bounds of impeachability, the Commons simply appointed a committee "to search for precedents."[25] When trial was before the Lords, they might similarly send a committee into the journals of Parliament to seek legal guidance.[26] The law of impeachment was no more or less than the accumulated exercises of impeachment by the Commons, with rulings on particular cases by the Lords. Any and every ruling on impeachment was legal because the root of public law was the pronouncement of Parliament.

Because the Commons did not need to spend an inordinate amount of time working out the theoretical justification for its impeachments, and, consequently, this subject did not appear at any length in the torrent of political and constitutional tract writing of the seventeenth century, it did not become obvious to American impeachment managers that they were usurping the powers of Parliament. When one examines the information that the colonial legislators had about impeachment and trial, one can see how the earliest colonial assemblies might simply neglect the exclusivity of the right of the Commons to impeach.

The seventeenth-century colonial lawmakers had a sketchy familiarity with the major impeachment cases. Word of mouth and a few books conveyed the substance of the prosecutions. Certain cases were much discussed in their time. Any visitor could hear about them at St. Paul's, in the Exchange, or in London taverns and polite drawing rooms. Later cases, notably Clarendon's, were discussed more thoroughly in pamphlet and newsletter. The first reliable printed sources on the Stuart cases were John Rushworth's eight-volume *Historical Collections* of parliamentary and royal documents (1659) and John Selden's posthumous *Of the Judicature in Parliaments* (1681). Rushworth, a pro-Commonwealth writer, gave full scope to parliamentary accusations of royal illegality. By the beginning of the eighteenth century Rushworth's and Selden's volumes reposed in many colonial libraries. The emphasis in the sources was on the definition of impeachable offenses, not upon the rationale for parliamentary jurisprudence. Selden reserved but a few lines for the constitutional basis for impeachment.[27] Texts and law dictionaries were just as terse on the subject. John Adams's copy of Giles Jacob's *A New Law-Dictionary* defined impeachment as "the Accusation and Prosecution of a Person for Treason, or other Crimes and Misdemeanors. Any Member of the House of Commons may not only impeach any one of their own Body, but also any Lord of Parliament, etc. And thereupon Articles are exhibited on the Behalf of the Commons, and Managers [are] appointed to make good their charge and accusation. Which being done in the proper Judicature, Sentence is passed, etc." Thomas Wood's equally popular *Institutes of the Laws of England* also mentioned impeachment. "The Commons," Wood noted, "have often Impeached several Persons before the House of Lords, and have prosecuted them to judgment. For the Commons, coming from all Parts, are the General Inquistors." Sir Matthew Hale's *History of the Common Law* (1713), on American lawyers' shelves by the 1740s, added his own taciturn message: the Commons, as the grant inquest of the nation, could impeach for illegal acts in the kingdom.[28] These reference works did not dilate upon the Commons' right to impeach, leaving, in effect, a vacuum for Americans to fill with cases of their own.[29]

In none of the early American cases does one find any attempt to justify the right of the colonial lower house to impeach. The right is taken as a given of English legislative jurisprudence. It was only after imperial authorities began to deny colonial legislatures this right that the provincials prepared elaborate justifications for impeachment, or tried to distinguish the case at hand from the class of cases estopped by the imperial rescript.

In the eighteenth century, colonial lawmakers were far better informed on English impeachment precedent, but each additional bit of knowledge about English impeachment, each reference to cases, ought to have reminded Americans that only the Commons in England could impeach. How were Americans to justify their own impeachments in the face of this knowledge? If, in the first cases, Americans borrowed impeachment because they were not explicitly barred from doing so; if seventeenth-century assemblies could have pleaded ignorance on this point, their eighteenth-century counterparts could not. From the time of the Vetch case, in 1706, whenever American impeachments came to the attention of the Privy Council, crown lawyers denied the assemblies the right to impeach anyone for anything. No document or decision, charter, regulation, act, or instruction that imperial officials drafted gave any colony the right to impeach. The positive legal provisions that mentioned impeachment, one in the Massachusetts judicial code used before 1684 and the other in the Pennsylvania Charter of 1682, escaped royal authorities for a time, but both loopholes were closed by the turn of the century. It is not clear whether these provisions were ever meant to sanction impeachment like that of the Commons. *Impeachment* always had the more general meaning of "indictment," which seventeenth-century colonial assemblies and councils, doubling as high courts, were permitted to hear.[30] For example, in March 1711 the North Carolina Assembly "impeached of high crimes and misdemeanors" former governor Thomas Cary and a number of his confederates in an ill-fated rebellion against proprietary appointee Edward Hyde. At the time the assembly acted, Cary was in Virginia, and his supporters were scattered throughout the Carolinas and the Old Dominion. There was no trial in prospect; Cary had escaped from the new governor's prosecution for high treason, not from charges made by the lower house. The assembly denunciation of the late governor stood midway in the law between an attainder and a reaffirmation of allegiance to the proprietors. When Governor Alexander Spotswood of Virginia returned Cary to North Carolina, there was no trial on the impeachment.[31]

Beyond the absence of specific grants of impeachment power to the assemblies, crown counsellors could raise a broader theoretical objection: the English borough was the model for colonial charters, and colonial legislatures had no more right to impeach royal officers than London's council had to impeach the lord chancellor. The Privy Council noted that the correct alternative to impeachment in America was recourse to executive or judicial authority in England. Appeal, petition, remonstrance, and address to the crown, Privy Council, or royal administrative officers were all courses sanctioned in imperial usage and statute. Colonial governments often followed this rule. A typical 1683 East Jersey "Address" indicates how different in form the proper appeal was from an impeachment:

To the Governor and Councill
   the Humble Addresse of the representatives of the Inhabitants of this province prsent Showeth
That whereas Captn Balcer of Elizabeth Towne from the first setling of this province to this Day hath approved himselfe to bee a man evill

principled not onely to the Govern^t Established in this Province but also in all his other Acc'ons wch as wee humbly conceive makes him verry unfitt for any place of Trust either Military or Civill Doe request that the said Balcer may bee Discharged from all and every such offices or places of Trust as hee the said Balcer holds now in this province[32]

An aggrieved private individual could always take his case to the assembly, which, if its members wished, could vote an inquiry into the conduct of an official. This was supposed to end in an address to the governor transmitting evidence, or even recommending removal. South Carolina lower houses were accomplished at the former, routinely bringing high officials to their chamber to explain themselves. On one occasion when executive affairs were in the hands of president of the council Arthur Middleton, the assembly demanded that Chief Justice Richard Allen explain why he had refused to issue a writ of habeus corpus to Thomas Smith. Middleton stepped in to force the assembly to "desist," a course they refused to follow on this occasion. They commanded the chief justice to appear before them, to no avail. Middleton prevented them from arresting Allen for contempt but could not block their expressions of displeasure.[33]

With the king's consent, the governors had the power to "depose" colonial officials. Should the governor fail to respond to the address, the colony could always petition the crown.[34] The colonies lay in the king's domain, whether they were charter, proprietary, or royal, and removal and punishment of his officers could be effected through the governor or the crown. As Massachusetts Chief Justice Thomas Hutchinson told a grand jury in 1768: in cases of official misconduct, "we must seek relief from Great Britain. If our Governor acts in an illegal Manner, we have a good King, and can easily have him removed. Upon a just complaint, we may have a Governor ordered to Westminster and there tried and punished." Other royal governors reiterated this rule.[35]

The colonial reply to Hutchinson's argument, implicit in every impeachment episode and explicit in the 1773 Oliver case, was that, as Englishmen gathered in representative bodies, the colonial legislators had the rights of the Commons in Westminster. The argument reduced to a "belief in a fundamental correspondence," as Bernard Bailyn writes, "between the English constitution and the separate colonial constitutions."[36] John Adams assumed this fact in Oliver's case when he argued, "But whence can We pretend to derive such a Power [to impeach]? From our Charter, which gives Us . . . all the Rights and Privileges of Englishmen: and if the House of Commons in England is the grand Inquest of the Nation, the [Massachusetts] House of Representatives is the Grand Inquest of this Province." It was a natural assumption—for the form and language of American legislative process paralleled that of Parliament—and hardly novel or naive. In the first place the American claim to the basic rights of English Parliaments, to wit, to inquire into the safety of their constituents, was enunciated as early as the first meetings of the Virginia House of Burgesses and the first sessions of the Massachusetts General Court.[37]

In the second place the colonists had before them the continuing English example, "the very definite and very bitter struggle . . . which parliament was carrying on . . . against prerogative. . . . It was not unnatural that the representative assemblies [in America] should have considered themselves heirs to much tradition of the High Court of Parliament." And even if the connection with the English constitution should fail, as it did in the final revolutionary crisis, the lower houses could argue that their right to impeach was embedded in the very nature of a popular representative government. Such a right need not be granted by imperial law or written in any charter. It was this right, apart from a specific grant of jurisdiction, that permitted colonial legislators to adopt parliamentary impeachment precedent.[38]

But why was impeachment so attractive to the colonists that they defied the Privy Council, labored at their own justifications, and surmounted obstacles to pursue it? The first obvious answer is that impeachment did assert the power of the lower house against objects over which it might otherwise have had no control. Impeachment was politically efficacious. A second answer is inferable: impeachment was a near-perfect symbol of the highest duty of a representative government. Impeachment thwarted corruption and protected the public. Both these answers are incomplete, for impeachment would not have been effective in practice or in theory if the upper houses and the governors of the colonies did not concede a certain degree of legitimacy to impeachment. This aura of legality of impeachment is the third reason why it was so attractive to Americans. In England as in America, impeachment and trial upon impeachment remained first and foremost legal proceedings, governed by known rules, proceeding according to set forms. In both England and America, respect for "law" was pervasive and genuine. Impeachment transformed public accusation and counteraccusation into prosecution and defense in a court of law. Precedent and statute (not ambition and innuendo), directed the framing of charges. When Parliament violated these limitations of the law, the impeachment fell, and the Lords simply refused to allow the case to be tried. The English love for law, the practicality of law, and the regularity of legal procedure made impeachment both workable and highly regarded in an era of great political uncertainty. These characteristics would naturally appeal to American colonists, who brought with them the English affection for law and faced at the same time great uncertainty about their place in the English imperial system. Impeachments would help to give order—to test and refine—that situation within the confines of established prosecutorial methods. By using impeachment against its enemies, the colonial assembly could claim to be the defender of law.[39]

While both the love of law and the autonomous urges in American legislatures ran throughout the colonial cases, colonial views of impeachment law changed greatly in the 138 years from Harvey's case (1635) to Oliver's case. This evolution can be divided into three periods or stages: criminal impeachments, provincial impeachments, and revolutionary impeachments. From 1635 to 1699, American lower houses engaged in impeachment of criminals as an alternative to trial in the regular courts. These first American impeachments may be characterized as experiments. With some vague idea of the procedure and a sharper idea of its great effectiveness, colonial lower houses "impeached" individuals for "crimes." The basic elements of English impeachment were present: violation of public trust, misuse of official power, or felony committed by someone in a position of authority could lead to prosecution by the lower house and trial in the upper house. From the first, however, the American cases showed pronounced departures from English precedent. The Americans accused were invariably officeholders; criminal penalties were not added to loss of office as punishment; trial often devolved into an "appeal" or petition for redress to executive authority. These deviations resulted from practical considerations; they did not represent conscious alteration of English precedent.

From 1701 to 1755 the colonists broadened the function of impeachment to include a primitive form of checks and balances against the executive and judicial branches. In this era the target of impeachment became seated officeholders who could not be controlled otherwise and whose conduct seemed, to the prosecutors, to endanger the colony. Finally, in a series of cases argued before independence, the colonists tested impeachment as a tool to resist imperial policy and assert the rights of the lower house as the representatives of the people. These cases differed from the provincial episodes in that they embodied a doctrine of actual, as opposed to virtual, sovereignty of the people. This watchword of the revolution-to-come would link impeachment with republicanism in the minds of American thinkers.

1

CRIMINAL IMPEACHMENT
IN THE COLONIES, 1635–1699

AMERICAN IMPEACHMENT PRECEDENT BEGAN ALMOST INADVERTENTLY, IN 1635, as a practical, local response to apparent misconduct in a high place. Royal Governor John Harvey of Virginia and his councillors "disagreed with one another, and there was no provision in the Virginia Charter for such disagreement."[1] The governor was accused of misfeasance in office, but what was to be done? There were precedents for handling similar offenses in recent English history: Chancellors Francis Bacon and the Duke of Buckingham stood accused of fiscal abuse of their offices in the lower house and were impeached.[2] In very similar fashion, after a stormy session with the General Assembly of Virginia, John Harvey was driven out of the colony and sent to England for judgment. This "thrusting out" of Harvey was called by his opponents a "petition of grievances," and by his friends a "mutiny." One hundred years later, William Keith, ex-governor of Pennsylvania, termed these actions an "impeachment," which in all but name they were.[3]

Harvey, formerly a ship's captain, had neither the personal magnetism nor the patience to deal with his rivals in the colony or their supporters in the home government. His policies regarding trade relations with Maryland, the Indian problem, and tobacco prices—added to his disdain for the leading councillors—fueled popular animosity toward him. By the spring of 1635, passions were boiling over. Jon Kukla has traced the final episode:

> Uncertain of how many councillors were united against him, but certain that some had had a part in the secret meetings and the petition, Harvey demanded that each councillor, without consultation, write his answer to the question, "What do you think they deserve that have gone about to persuade the people from their obedience to his Majesties substitute?"
>
> "I begin with you Mr. Menefie," Harvey said.
>
> "I am but a young lawyer," George Menefie responded, "and dare not upon the suddain deliver my opinion."

"That should be his answer under his hand," Harvey curtly replied. Nicholas Ferrar attempted to complain, but Harvey cut him off.

"I conceive this a strange kind of proceedings," Mathews interrupted. Harvey commanded him to be silent in the king's name, but Mathews continued: "There was no Precedent for such a command, But it was by a Tyrant, meaning that passage of Richard the third against the Lord Hastings."[4]

After two days of name-calling, the councillors arrested Harvey and chose a temporary successor. Kukla finds this episode a "coup," though he admits that the council apparently believed in the legality of its actions. Harvey was accused of crimes against the public interest. According to reports prepared by Mathews in Virginia and duplicated by his confederates in London, the governor had illegally suppressed letters from Virginia planters to Charles I begging renegotiation of tobacco contracts, plotted with Maryland traders against Virginia, and arranged a dangerous peace treaty with the Indians. These concerns had led to the assembly's "petition and letter" to the council. The council then asked Harvey to defend himself (just as the Lords would), and, when he refused, they called for a meeting of the burgesses and council in "James City" to hear the grievances. The General Assembly, with burgesses sitting for the counties, determined articles and resolved that they be sent, with Harvey, to England. There was no felony but a palpable case for abuse of public power.[5]

If this was a coup, the plotters struggled to conceal it. The calling of the General Assembly, the framing of charges by the burgesses gathered in the assembly, the submission of these to the councillors, and the councillors' efforts to prove their own legitimacy as judges of offenses under the charter, all point to an impeachment. While it may be true that the Virginia colony had a unicameral legislature until 1643 (the council and burgesses meeting together), in this case, if in no other, the functions of councillors and burgesses were very different from each other, and very similar to those of the Lords and the Commons in England.

Unwilling to risk the displeasure of the crown, the councillors did not subject Harvey to any criminal punishment in the colony. Although his prosecutors did not intend him to escape punishment (they sent him, in custody, to receive a sentence from the king), their actions reduced the penalty in the colony to mere loss of office. In a parliamentary impeachment conviction, a defendant could expect severe punishment, but colonial necessity forbade the literal adoption of English practice. The Commons and the Lords did not appeal to the judgment of the king in impeachment cases. To do so would have been to ask the crown to sit in judgment on its own placemen and advisors. The Virginians had no choice, however, for they lay in the "ancient domain" of the crown, with a patent from the king, government by his grant, and lands in his gift. In no document, charter, or law did the king give them the rights claimed through usage by his Parliament in England, nor could he. The General Assembly's assumption of a power very near impeachment was itself an act of lese majesty, which Charles's Privy Council answered by returning Harvey to his office in the colony.[6]

The first time the word *impeachment* was used in the colonies to denote a lower house charge leading to a trial came in 1657. On May 20, Roger Williams petitioned the General Court of Rhode Island, a body including both houses, to "impeach" William Harris for heresy and high treason. The attorney general investigated Harris and found that he had indeed written pamphlets critical of the colony's government. The assembly heard the case and decided: "Inasmuch as we being soe remote from England, [we] cannot be soe well acquainted in the laws thereof in that behalf provided [on treason]—though we cannot but conclude his [Harris's] behavior therein to be both contemptuous and seditious." The assembly sent Harris's writings, the charge, and his defense in the assembly to England for judgment. Williams's petition was for him uncharacteristically bitter, but Harris was a trying fellow—a man of temper, shrewd and litigious.[7] Harris was also land-hungry and used his knowledge of the English law to win suits in court over disputed claims. The assembly submitted his case to English authorities—in part to avoid involving itself in an essentially personal rivalry and in part to avert the displeasure of Harris's allies in England.[8]

Both Virginia and Rhode Island had turned away from the final step in trials upon impeachment: rendering judgment and punishing the guilty. The next series of colonial impeachments, all in Maryland, went to judgment. The first of these occurred in 1669 and concerned John Morecroft. He arrived in the colony in the 1660s, began legal practice during the later part of the decade, and was elected to the assembly from the parish of St. Mary's. He was impeached in the assembly by "the petition" (another English method of bringing impeachment) of Captain Robert Morris, one of the most powerful merchants and traders in the Chesapeake. When Morecroft sued Morris for libel in the provincial court, charging "false scandalous and opprobrious Words of and concerning the said John Morecroft then being one of the Attorneys of the said Court in the presence of the honorable the Lord Proprietary," Morris went to the assembly and demanded the "impeachment" of Morecroft, "a Member of this house."[9] During a stay in England, Morris might have learned of Bristol's attempt to impeach Lord Chancellor Clarendon, an affair that attracted national attention. Morris, who was not a member of the Maryland assembly, could have used the precedent of non-member Thomas Felton's 1610 "petition" against Commons member Henry Spiller, or, more recent, Bristol's attempt to force the Commons to impeach Lord Chancellor Clarendon, in 1663.[10]

Maryland charters, patents, and statutes made no provision for impeachment, but the assembly did not stop to consider this limitation upon its jurisdiction. The impeachment articles charged Morecroft with bringing the laws of "Westminster" to "St. Mary's"—an example of general colonial dislike for trained English lawyers—as well as with demanding exorbitant fees and simultaneously defending opposing parties in a suit. Morecroft held judicial office in St. Mary's, and these offenses were not so different from those charged against the Earl of Middlesex in 1624, especially the use of office to obtain personal gifts. Behind these charges was the political grievance that the assembly had against Morecroft for acting as the council's spokesman during an earlier debate over the charter. For these offenses the assembly could have disciplined him rather than impeach him for trial by the council. It is possible that they simply wished to embarrass the council and censure Morecroft by insisting on a trial in the upper house.[11]

When the assembly sent the articles to the council, it sent no prosecutors. This was a deviation from English precedent, though not entirely from English practice. Perhaps Morris advised this step. In any case Morecroft based his defense upon this and other lapses from proper procedure. He evidently had some impression of how the Commons went about impeachment, for he condemned the assembly action as "not any ordinary and just way of impeaching nor is it prosecuted to this honourable House in such Form and manner it is usual in matters of this kind to be observed and prosecuted." In addition to rebutting the specific charges, he insisted that the case belonged in the provincial court, where Morris could sue him for misconduct. The council concurred, acquitted Morecroft, and informed the assembly of its error. The council followed a course taken by the Lords in Clarendon's case: assisting the Commons to the "correct" interpretation of impeachment precedent.[12]

A more prominent defendant and a more significant crime made the second Maryland impeachment a fuller test of American divergence from English precedent. Thomas Trueman was an influential landholder. In 1676, while leading the militia in a disastrous attempt to besiege a Susquehannock Indian fortress, he ordered the execution of five sachems held as hostages. Partly for his bungling, partly to appease other tribes, and partly for an obvious felony, the assembly impeached him.[13] Using language very similar to "high crimes and misdemeanors," the assembly accused Trueman of "divers and Sundry Enormous Crimes and Offences." Morecroft may have suggested the language. Trueman had affronted the laws of God and man, and—equally important—the explicit instructions of the lower house. Buckingham in the New Rochelle affair, and Peter Pott and Clarendon facing the Dutch navy—all actions resulting in impeachment—had done no more to bring danger to England than Trueman had to Maryland. What was more, the murder of the sachems was an offense against the law of nations (the Indian chiefs representing foreign powers), if not under Maryland statute. Worst of all, Trueman had failed to require the Virginia militia captains to state their opinion (presumably strongly in favor of execution) in writing, "to be kept for Justification of himself and the people of this Province." This last charge, embarrassing the Maryland assembly while exculpating the Virginians, made impeachment more certain.[14]

Kenelm Chiseldyne, Trueman's lawyer, used Morecroft's line of defense. He insisted that the indictment of the lower house had been prepared without testimony from Trueman and was based upon an illegal petition, errors which a provincial court would not have permitted. Rejecting these arguments, on May 27, 1676, the upper house found Trueman guilty. The council then asked for a bill of attainder from the lower house, but the assembly wished only to fine Trueman. In the end, Trueman was fined and released under a bond for good behavior. Once more, the practical situation in the colony vitiated an honest attempt to follow English precedent. Trueman, although a holder of an executive post, was one of the class of landholders who made up the assembly. Moreover, he was not a king's man in the same sense as Buckingham or Strafford, and the offense, committed against Indians, was not deemed so dangerous to public order as an offense against English settlers. The council failed to act with the dispatch or independence of the House of Lords and reduced punishment to loss of office.[15]

This same sort of proceeding, beginning with a parliamentary impeachment and trial but ending with mere loss of office, occurred in a third Maryland case. In 1676 the assembly impeached Charles James, sheriff of Cecil County, for battery and perjury. In the continual tumult over land titles and the right to vote that landownership conferred, the sheriffs played a key role. The impeachment of James on May 27, 1676, for falsely swearing before a justice of the peace, inducing two other witnesses to follow his lead, and then assaulting another settler, Edward Pinne, led on June 1, 1676, to his removal from office by the council. No criminal penalty was assessed. James was a merchant and land speculator of some means and, like Trueman and Morecroft, a man whose interests were not different from the assembly's. His offense, like Trueman's, was indictable in a common law court but resulted in an impeachment in the English manner presumably because it was a "high" crime, and his punishment was mitigated by the social and political realities of Maryland life.[16]

The final Maryland impeachment was more complex in law and politics than its predecessors. Jacob Young, a Delaware resident employed by the

Calverts as an interpreter, had taken the side of the Susquehannocks once too often, and the proprietor finally asked trial and punishment for this "long Disturber of Our Peace and Quiet." From September 1681 to November 1683 the executive and both houses of the colonial assembly wrestled with the problem of bringing Young to justice. The issues raised in that long controversy suggest that the case against Young was no mere partisan squabble. The quasi-diplomatic role of the Indian interpreters and traders, with their powerful influence on the tribes, affected the security of the colony. The survival of Maryland, at least in the eyes of its government, depended upon the loyalty of these men, and Young appeared to them a would-be warlord of the frontier counties.[17]

The proprietor first sought to try Young before the upper house, under a special commission of oyer and terminer. This process was often used in the colonies to hear important cases speedily. Young's influence with the dangerous neighboring Northern Indians advised an expeditious proceeding. The charge was to be treason. The upper house, after some deliberation, declared itself inadequate for the task. English statutes forbade a trial for treason without two witnesses to the act, and as late as the fall of 1682 the prosecution could muster only councillor and Indian negotiator Colonel Henry Coursey to speak against Young. The council refused to permit the testimony of Indians against a colonist, disqualifying thereby a number of other witnesses. Instead of a treason trial, bound by statutory restrictions on the admission of evidence, the upper house suggested to the lower house that they impeach Young for "High Misdemeanors." After some jockeying between the two branches of the legislature, the lower house agreed. The assemblymen presumed that a crime had been committed and framed their "articles" of impeachment accordingly. Young was incautious enough to give them evidence of a general intent to do mischief, declaring, in a drunken moment, that he could do as he wished with the Indians. The assembly impeached him for bringing the proprietary into disrepute among the Indians, urging the "Northern Indians" of Maryland to war against the Piscataway tribe, speaking for the Indians at times likely to cause disorder, failing to mediate between the Northern Indians and other parties according to his instructions as an officer of the government, marrying an Indian, and—in a charge specified when the case came to the upper house—leading raids against the Piscataway. While not statutory offenses or constructive treasons, his acts were somewhat more serious than mere sympathy for the Indians. Young's extralegal power was substantial, for the Northern Indians had once before brought the colony to its knees. If, in the employ of the colony, he had violated his duties as an interpreter, he could be accused of malfeasance in office. In addition, the Maryland books were filled with statutes regulating commerce with the Indians, which Young seems to have ignored. Finally,

Maryland, like England, imposed stiff penalties upon rioters, and Young apparently was practiced in this occupation.[18]

Young's cause before the upper house was lost from the start. After Chiseldyne refused to speak for the defendant, Thomas Bland was named to assist Young in preparing a reply. On November 14, 1682, Young submitted a rambling, highly personal defense. He had lived in what would later be Delaware during the Trueman episode and argued that his friendships with the Northern Indians were normal conduct in his trade. After Maryland employed him, he had been loyal and done his duty to the province. He closed with the reminder that nothing had ever come of his supposed actions against the colony. He did not realize that in such cases conspiracy or advocacy was also an offense, whatever resulted from it. Young's witnesses were the Northern Indians, and though the upper house permitted a message from them to be read, they were not able to take the oath and testify for him. Without witnesses to prove he had not made disloyal speeches or given traitorous counsel, he could only fall back upon the eloquence of Bland. The upper house refused to let Bland speak, however, unless the "matter of law should arise upon trial." English precedent did not yet allow counsel to speak for a defendant except on purely legal matters. Young rested his defense with a petition for a speedy end to his sufferings, but, fearing Young's effect upon the Northern Indians, the council neither convicted him nor freed him until a year later. In October 1683 the lower house finally sent official impeachment managers to the upper house to prosecute Young. The upper house found him guilty and asked the assembly, as in *Trueman*, for a bill of attainder against him. The lower house again refused. Both houses then agreed upon a bill of punishment whose effective clause permitted Young's freedom upon recognizances for his good behavior. To this the legislators added banishment. Although imprisoned during most of the proceedings, Young's severest punishment in the end was loss of office and banishment.[19]

The next seventeenth-century case involved charges of judicial misconduct, behind which lay a fear of political corruption in a high place. The accused was Chief Justice Nicholas More of Pennsylvania. In 1681 More, a London physician and the husband of a wealthy Quaker, purchased 10,000 acres from William Penn. He also formed a joint stock company, the "Free Society of Traders," to capitalize Penn's venture in the New World. In return for More's assistance, Penn named him chief justice of the colony, clerk of the council, and provincial secretary. More had no legal training, and through ignorance, arrogance, and avarice he thoroughly mismanaged his high offices. His aristocratic taunts irritated the assembly, and his inflexible support for the proprietary interest made additional enemies. In the spring of 1685, at the climax of a debate on a bill to give more power to lower judges and reduce the prerogatives of his judicial office, More provoked the assembly once too often. The assembly began impeachment proceedings against him for high crimes and misdemeanors.[20]

Pennsylvania was one colony that could base its impeachments upon its charter (albeit upon an ambiguity of language). The nineteenth article of the Charter of Liberties allowed the assembly to "continue so long as may be needful to impeach Criminals fit to be there impeached." The assembly, led by speaker John White, interpreted the article as a grant of a privilege like that of the Commons: to indict for "illegal acts," for trial for the council. Its ten articles of impeachment against More included charges that he had issued an irregular writ, arbitrarily excluded a man from jury duty, refused to accept a jury verdict, changed a charge, bullied a witness, abused other judges, reversed a lower court decision, missed circuit in the lower counties during one session, and acted in contempt of the president and council. In presenting their case to the upper chamber, the assembly's prosecutors added an eleventh article asking that More be convicted of general disregard for his duties. Shortly before White had left Wales for the new colony, Chief Justice Scroggs was impeached at Westminster for abusing the juries and misusing warrants for election to the 1680 Parliament. The similarity of the two cases is striking but may have been coincidental.[21]

Responsibility for the trial and conviction of impeached officeholders was assigned by the Charter of Liberties to the council and governor, or the lieutenant governor in Penn's absence. A two-thirds vote was required to convict. When Penn left the colony in 1684 there was no lieutenant governor, and the council did nothing with the impeachment. The councillors were by now divided in their loyalty to the proprietor and probably failed to agree among themselves on how to handle the obnoxious judge. Instead, hoping that passions would cool, they found excuses to delay judgment. The frustrated assembly took its case directly to the proprietor in England. White informed Penn that "we have . . . impeached Nicholas More, a Member of the Assembly, of ten Articles containing divers high Crimes and Misdemeanors, and in the Presence of the President and Provincial Council, made very clear Proof of the said Articles." He assured the proprietor that none of the assembly's actions were aimed at him: "Altho' the Wisdom of the Assembly thought fit to humble that aspiring and corrupt Minister of State, Nicholas More; yet to you, dear Sir, and to the happy Success of your Affairs, our Hearts are open."[22]

Out of a mixture of loyalty to the proprietor, perplexity, and expediency, the Pennsylvanians ignored the Commons' firm rule against turning for aid to the executive in impeachment cases. The inability of the assembly to press the council to try More rendered the impeachment impotent. From London, Penn saw the danger to his power in the colony and replied to the assembly petition by appointing More to a different proprietary post. It may be that he pitied his old supporter, by 1686 a very sick man; perhaps he was not convinced of the validity of the charges.[23]

Confusion over the proper impeachment process within the assembly may have undermined its prosecution of More from the start. The assembly's impeachment managers needed More's court records to substantiate their case, but Patrick Robinson, clerk of the court and a close friend of the judge, refused to surrender them. For "Breach of Privilege" of the lower house Robinson was held by the sheriff in the assembly hall while the legislators voted him "a publick Enemy to the Province and Territories, and a Violator of the Privileges of the Freemen in Assembly met." The assembly then asked the council to make Robinson "incapable" of holding office in the future. Its action against him was a parliamentary imprisonment for contempt, ending in an address rather than a trial. Why the lower house chose this process instead of impeachment is unclear; perhaps More's conduct threatened the colony and hence could be seen as a "high crime," while Robinson's endangered only the rights of the lower house. In addition, already embroiled in one impeachment, the assembly might have been chary of a second. In England, abridgment of parliamentary privilege often led to impeachment.[24]

The next to last seventeenth-century colonial impeachment was deflected so astutely by Virginia Governor Frances, Lord Howard of Effingham, that scholars have mislabeled the episode.[25] On April 5, 1687, William Fitzhugh, a member of the Virginia House of Burgesses for nine years, was impeached by his colleagues. He had come to the colony seventeen years before, at age 19, and had established himself as a merchant-planter and lawyer.[26] In 1685 Fitzhugh was accused of overcharging the colonial treasury for his expenses as a garrison supplier. The lower house asked the governor to remove Fitzhugh from all his offices, and the governor directed the burgesses to hand the papers to Attorney General George Brent. Nothing further was done. On October 26, 1686, grievances from Stafford County were read into the lower house journal, charging Fitzhugh with illegally seeking 4,000 lbs. of tobacco as payment for his services in 1686, when in fact he had not sat in the house. The lower house appointed a committee to "manage the said charge" by investigating evidence and interrogating witnesses. The burgesses evidently had subpoena powers to call "what other persons they shall think fit." The governor, apprised of the inquiry, agreed to hear the case on November 4, 1686, at which time the burgesses might bring forward "articles of charge."[27]

A week later, the assembly "managers" came to the council, presided over by the governor, to prosecute the case. The assembly had styled itself "the grand inquest of the country," had called the offenses "articles," and had termed its spokesmen "managers." They sought to try Fitzhugh in the council. This was an impeachment but the governor quickly and forcefully parried its thrust. He replied that "[the council] were not then sitting as a

court of judicature—but that they will take so much notice of the presentment as to order the attorney general to prosecute."[28] Effingham misrepre-
sented the impeachment as a grand jury "presentment" before a superior
court. In truth, the councillors did sit as the colony's general court, but the
assembly was not asking the attorney general to prosecute before the general
court; it wanted to prosecute the articles itself, before the upper legislative
house. Governor Effingham nevertheless had taken the initiative away from
the assembly and placed the case in the regular courts. Fitzhugh understood
that he had been impeached; he told an English ally: "I speak knowingly Sir
though I did not belong to the House, yet was impeached formally by them,
and all methods pursued, as in an Impeachment by the House of Commons
in England, but it proved like all the rest of their Proceedings ill grounded
and worse managed, and in the end did me no farther damage than the
waiting upon them, till my triall was over. . . ."[29]

Behind the governor's sleight-of-hand lay matters of imperial politics.
Effingham was utterly opposed to broadening the privileges of the assembly
and had spent the previous three years of his term battling the burgesses. In
addition, Effingham and Fitzhugh were Tory supporters of King James II,
while the majority of the assembly were Whigs and did not trust the monarch.
Martin Scarlett, Fitzhugh's accuser, was a virulent party man, and Scarlett's
Stafford County was a hotbed of anti-Tory political activity.[30] Effingham
shielded Fitzhugh from harm, sending the 1685 charges to Attorney General
Brent shortly before Brent resigned to stand for the burgesses himself. The
1686 charge went nowhere, despite repeated inquiries from the burgesses.
The governor promised a trial "in due time," which never came.[31] Yet even if
Fitzhugh's accusers and his protectors had political motives, his alleged
offense was serious. Misappropriation of government funds could slip
through the common-law courts, and someone in Fitzhugh's position, without the availability of impeachment, might well escape all correction.

The last of the seventeenth-century cases resembled the first: a governor
was driven from his post by an angry legislature. The victim, or culprit,
depending upon whose account is credited, was Seth Sothel, one of the
Carolina proprietors. Sothel purchased Edward Hyde's share in the colony
and convinced the other holders to name him governor. Delayed five years en
route to his new post by the Turks, he arrived at last in the Albermarle in
1683.[32] Sothel tried to govern by fiat a population little disposed to autocracy
and soon found himself at odds with many. When the fall of the Stuarts
rocked England and undermined, for a time, the authority of the proprietors,
the assembly rose up against him. According to Francis Nicholson, lieutenant governor of neighboring Virginia, Sothel was "banished" by a mob, but
the assembly told a different story to the proprietors.[33] In their turn, they were
unwilling to admit to the new king their lack of control over the colony and

simply selected a new lieutenant governor, Phillip Ludwell. To Sothel they railed that "the people under your government have risen upon you" because of "injustice and oppression."[34] Though Sothel denied this, he refused to remain in the colony and would not return to England when summoned. Sothel's flight, the proprietors knew, would be taken as evidence of his guilt, and it was. The proceedings against him in 1689 were, in form, a hybrid of impeachment and address. The assembly had lodged charges against Sothel (which the proprietors termed "misdemeanors") at a session called for the express purpose of dealing with him. Assemblymen and proprietors apparently agreed that Sothel was guilty of illegal imprisonments, extortion, interfering with the regular process of the courts, receiving bribes, and seizing the estates of several men without any "due process" of law. The proprietors, however, later disallowed the acts of the assembly, refusing to permit it to oust their lieutenant. Instead, they regarded the entire business as a "remonstrance" to them.[35] By judging Sothel in England, they would answer the remonstrance. The assembly, for its part, did leave final resolution of the matter in the proprietors' hands but only after effectively removing Sothel from office. Again, loss of office was the only real punishment for conviction.

These first colonial cases are a single episode in American constitutional history, for in their most important aspects they were alike. They were directed by the assembly against the person named in the charges, not against another branch of colonial government per se or against authorities in England. Partisanship played a part in each case, but the lower houses were trying to protect the public against individual wrongdoing. If private malice motivated the accusations, evidence of illegal acts was required for the impeachment to proceed. The defendant might be accused of a recognizable common-law felony, as in Trueman's case, or of illegal conduct in office (with or without explicit statutory grounds), as in More's and Sothel's, or simply of some form of corruption, as in Morecroft's and Fitzhugh's. The colonists were hazy about the exact procedures to use in impeachment—no doubt because of the paucity of precise information on English law—but tried to follow parliamentary precedent.

Colonial variation from the English model followed the contours of local necessity. Prosecutions turned into appeals to higher executive authority when provincial councils, lacking the traditions and independence of the Lords, failed to take action. Convicted officials escaped punishment other than loss of office either because colonial legislatures could not risk offending the accused's patrons in England or because the accused were members of the legislature, and friends within colonial government cushioned the effects of prosecution. Defendants would have (and did) appeal more severe penalties to authorities in England, undermining the prestige of the colonial legislature. Only officeholders were impeached because they, in the absence of an established aristocracy, were the visible wielders of power. An uncooperative governor or council, or a weak prosecution following a successful impeachment could reduce impeachment from a criminal proceeding to a censure. Nevertheless, in all cases the impeachment managers were proud of the English constitution and insisted that it had journeyed with them to the colonies. Their use of impeachment exemplified their desire to affirm English legal and constitutional liberties in their new homes.

The colonists' admiration for English impeachment procedure was to have unexpected consequences in the next century. Throughout the seventeenth century the colonists groped down a dimly lit path toward full understanding of English impeachment law. The seventeenth-century lower houses do not seem to have grasped the large political function of impeachment in its English context: the Commons impeached ministers of the crown. The lower house of Parliament was the "Grand Inquest of the Nation," stalking evildoers and corrupt advisors where no other court could go: into the councils of the king. Colonial lower houses struck at one chief executive and two executive appointees, but not at executive power itself, and certainly not at the crown. When later eighteenth-century colonial lower houses fully examined the details of English impeachment, they soon grasped its power to extend the jurisdiction of the representative branch at the expense of its rivals.

2

IMPEACHMENT AND PROVINCIAL BALANCE: *VETCH ET AL., LOGAN, TROTT,* AND *SMITH*

THE LAST OF THE SEVENTEENTH-CENTURY IMPEACHMENTS TOOK PLACE IN 1689, on the eve of the Glorious Revolution. The next was not to occur until 1705. While impeachment in the colonies was hardly an everyday occurrence, this gap was no accident. The seventeenth-century cases grew out of domestic disorder, as one serviceable answer for official misconduct. The constitutional bar to this expedient—that only Parliament could impeach and try— did not deter colonial managers because the message was not brought home to them. They knew that the Commons impeached—who could miss this fact during the Restoration?—but they did not know that only the Commons could impeach. One of the first priorities of William III's administration was reorganization of the colonial offices. The Navigation Act of 1696 signaled tighter control of colonial trade; other steps limited and superintended the lawmaking powers of American assemblies. The message was received in America: in Massachusetts, for example, the new charter and the first laws under it were revised and revised again, until they met the approval of the crown. Elsewhere colonial lawmakers felt the weight of the new administration of the empire.[1] The "Englishing" of the laws entailed not only their emendation to conform to metropolitan practice but also the excise of novel colonial adaptations of English precedent. The "provincial" impeachments of the next half-century were no less acts of considerable license than their seventeenth-century predecessors, but unlike the latter, all the impeachments of the period 1700–50 ended in failure or appeal to higher English authority.

Nevertheless, within this narrowed compass, the provincial impeachments altered colonial legislative jurisprudence in a direction directly opposed to the intent of the new imperial strategy. Instead of aiming at the malfeasance of individuals, impeachment became part of a struggle between branches of government, ultimately expressing the independence of the lower houses. This trend (hardly confined to judicial proceedings in the assemblies) would

27

flow directly and irrepressibly into confrontation with the imperial authority itself.

This shift in objective paralleled events in England—though, again, with unexpected consequences. As the Commons gorged itself upon William's and Anne's ministers, impeachment became an instrument in the struggle between branches of government for supremacy. Impeachment, among other techniques, gave victory in this contest to Parliament, and, within that body, to the Commons, a fact transmitted to the colonies by the now well-developed organs of the English political press.[2] As though spurred by these events, the Vetch, Logan, Trott, and Smith cases in the colonies would involve broad interbranch struggle between locally elected assemblies and appointed royal or proprietary officeholders—conflict unseen in colonial impeachments except in *Harvey* and *Sothel*. Yet even as the colonial assemblies explored the capacity of impeachment to check and balance other branches of government, Parliament had moved on to a cabinet system. Without further guidance from contemporaneous English cases, the provincial assemblies were again freed to develop a native impeachment law and apply it to targets of their choice.

In the provincial cases, as in their American predecessors, particular political circumstances combined with suspected acts of corruption and misuse of power to produce impeachments. In the prosecution of Massachusetts merchant captains Samuel Vetch, John Borland, William Rouse, and Roger Lawson (1706), impeachment in America evolved toward a check upon the other branches. On the surface, the Vetch case followed the seventeenth-century guidelines. The charges had a clear criminal basis in a violation of laws against trading with an enemy in time of war. The Massachusetts General Court intended to try the impeachments before the council, as the Commons did before the Lords, and to punish the guilty with criminal penalties. At the same time, the lower house sought to check overbearing and corrupt Governor Joseph Dudley. Dudley's opponents in the assembly viewed the Vetch prosecution as an impeachment of the governor for avarice and abuse of the powers of his office. In this underlying effort, the most the anti-Dudley forces could expect was the governor's ultimate loss of office.

The affair began in 1691, when the second charter of Massachusetts Bay stripped the General Court of its judicial powers. Under the old charter the General Court acted as the highest bench in the province. In the earlier seventeenth century, Bay Colony law explicitly permitted the General Court to "impeach" criminals. The new royal charter forced the assembly and assistants to surrender their criminal jurisdiction to a separate court system, whose justices were appointed by the crown. The old Puritan country party in the General Court resented this loss of judicial power. The arrival of Dudley, a fierce partisan and soon the leader of a court party, further inflamed these animosities.[3]

Although Dudley was a native New Englander and as committed to the welfare of his colony as any other royal politician, he still expected to gain what he could from his post. Trade with the French in time of war was a treasonable offense but one widely practiced and very profitable. Dudley allied himself in this enterprise with Samuel Vetch, a Scots immigrant already established in the lucrative French Canadian trade. These ventures attracted a number of other local traders, including Borland, Lawson, and Rouse.[4]

In March 1706, assembly agents intercepted Vetch's ship, the *Flying Horse*, on its way to French Acadia and discovered incriminating documents and cargo on board. In June the General Court reported its suspicions to the council and detained Vetch for questioning. The council concurred with this step, asking the judges of the Superior Court to put Vetch under bond to remain in Boston. Even Dudley had to cooperate, sending search warrants to the lower house.[5]

Soon both the council and the lower house were scrambling for the lead in investigating the charges. The council created a committee of its own members (Superior Court Justices Samuel Sewall and John Leverett along with Elisha Hutchinson and Samuel Appleton) to pursue the case. The assembly insisted on representation on the committee and named four of its members to it. Before the committee reported to the assembly on June 22, two more assemblymen had been added. By the end of its deliberations, the committee had eleven delegates from the lower house, eager to join in the investigation. On the recommendation of the committee, the assembly voted to impeach Vetch and Rouse "for wickedly managing and carrying on an illegal trade" and giving "aid and comfort" to the king's enemies. Borland and Lawson were accused of "traitorously ordering and sending a sloop and goods" to New France.[6]

The lower house voted to vindicate the governor of involvement in the trade—faint praise if such a statement was necessary at all—to which the governor replied with brief thanks. Meanwhile, the assembly's net had caught more merchants; John Phillips and Andrew Belcher were implicated in the illegal trade. The inquiry was reaching the highest levels of Bay Colony society—potentially menacing too many of the assemblymen's own families. On June 12, 1706, the assembly decided to limit its accusations to Vetch and the three other captains. The lower house asked for a trial "before this general court" upon "a high misdemeanor."[7]

The case should have gone into the Massachusetts Superior Court of Judicature since the General Court of the colony no longer had the power to hear and determine criminal causes, and could not claim the right to impeach and try offenders in parliamentary fashion. The assembly may have inadvertently reached back for its lost powers under the spur of the wartime crisis or been so eager to uncover evidence of Dudley's complicity that it ignored the legal obstacles to its impeachment proceeding. For his own reasons Dudley did not desire the case to go into the Superior Court: a treason trial there might induce Vetch to reveal Dudley's complicity.[8] Under considerable pressure from the governor the council consented to sit as a court. The measure passed 9 votes to 8, over the dissent of Justice Sewall (who preferred trial in his own court).[9] The tortured reasoning of the council's resolution to take jurisdiction suggests that Sewall's objections, based upon the charter, were not easily overcome. The council finally decided that "the great importance, singularity, and difficulty" of the affair and its doubts about the Superior Court's jurisdiction in the case outweighed Sewall's reservations. To this was added the fact that Vetch and the others had already submitted to the authority of the General Court instead of requesting trial in the superior court. The council concluded that, as the 1691 charter permitted the General Court to impose fines and other punishments, the council could proceed upon the matter "by a bill of attainder" in the next session.[10]

Behind this far-fetched reasoning was Dudley's desperation to keep the case out of the regular courts. His enemies in the colony published the accusation that he preferred a trial in the council, whose members he might control. Cotton Mather, one of Dudley's most outspoken antagonists, accused Dudley of conspiring to keep the case away from a trial jury. According to Mather, Dudley persuaded the captains to submit to the assembly. Other anti-Dudley pamphleteers blurted out that Dudley led the cover-up, "using all imaginable Artifices to vindicate himself," and reminded readers that the Superior Court could order capital punishment of the captains if a jury found them guilty—while the council could only fine and imprison them.[11]

Nevertheless, the assembly, knowing that it could not try Vetch and his cohorts without the council, acceded to the council's jurisdiction. Although the council termed its hearing an "attainder," the case was really a trial upon an impeachment. The defendants received copies of the charges, had counsel, were prosecuted by the attorney general on "articles of high misdemeanor," and were permitted to defend themselves. In impeachments, attorneys general often joined the managers' side. The trial dragged on through August 1706 and ended with a guilty verdict from the council. They then passed "a bill of punishment"—another misnomer, for unlike the parliamentary "bill" of the same name, the case was not brought to a regular court at any time—fining all the merchant captains and barring them from public office. Disqualification from officeholding was not a sentence upon attainder or "bills of pains and punishments" but invariably followed conviction upon an impeachment.[12]

Frustrated in their pursuit of the merchant captains, the leaders of the assembly belatedly made the flag-of-truce trade into a statutory treason. On August 31 they voted that "a traitorous correspondence with any of her majesty's enemies during the continuance of the present war with France," as well as an unlicensed embarcation "in or upon any vessel or vessels with an intention to go into" New France, would be regarded as "high treason." These acts came within the broad scope of "levying war against the king," already forbidden in the treason statute of 25 Edward III (1350). The "intention" to travel into enemy waters without official permission was far more difficult to prove than the actual exchange of goods in a Canadian port. In effect, boarding the ship became a constructive treason, a conspiracy to levy war. The assembly excepted from its proscription legal exchanges of prisoners and licensed supply of prisoners, commissions the governor could dispurse—but only with public knowledge. All in all, one must regard the statute as an ex post facto thrust at suspected miscreants who were apparently slipping through the fingers of the angry assemblymen rather than a considered and lucid aid to the regular courts in matters of illegal trade with the enemy.[13]

Sewall, though a member of the council, dissociated himself from the verdict. After speaking with Borland nearly a year later, Sewall concluded that Dudley was involved in both the crime and subsequent shielding of the ship captains. When, in November 1707, Dudley urged the council to condemn the pamphlets accusing the governor of conspiracy, Sewall refused, saying: "I fear this censure [of the anti-Dudley pamphlets] may be of ill consequence to the province in time to come, by discouraging persons of worth and interest to venture in appearing for them [the authors] tho' the necessity should never be so great."[14]

In England the Board of Trade, confronted with Dudley's report, Vetch's testimony, and pamphlets by Dudley's antagonists, suggested a new trial in the regular courts. The Privy Council, acting in its capacity as the appellate court for the colonies, invalidated the bill of punishment and freed the defendants. The Privy Council had seen danger in colonial lower house use of impeachment.[15] The episode ended in the Massachusetts Superior Court of Judicature's Boston sessions, held on November 30, 1708. Quit of the bill of punishment, the merchant captains were indicted by a grand jury for trading in contraband. Attorneys for Borland, Vetch, and their comrades argued that the court had no jurisdiction in the case (the position of the council two years before) but the justices overruled this contention. In the space of a single day the petty jury disposed of issues which had disrupted the General Court for three months. Unconcerned with checking Dudley's power, the assembly's aim, the jury found the captains not guilty.[16]

While the Vetch case may be viewed as a seventeenth-century impeachment case, a criminal act handled in the General Court under its remembered, judicial powers was a transitional episode as well. The prosecutors impeached and tried the captains to check corruption in the executive branch of government. The Privy Council dismissed this step out of hand, a command to which some in the Bay Colony appeared to bow. On January 18, 1732, the lower house addressed Governor Jonathan Belcher: "The Representatives who raise the money [for the colonial treasury] and whose constituents pay it, have no sort of remedy [for misuse of funds] . . . for we cannot impeach, as is the usage of the House of Commons in such cases."[17] Despite their abjuration of the power to impeach, the General Court regarded itself as having the same higher duty as the Commons: protection of the public weal from malefactors. The Privy Council decision in *Vetch* notwithstanding, the General Court's view of itself kept alive the possibility of impeachment to control and punish the executive branch of government, as in the Vetch case. In the middle 1760s Thomas Hutchinson, lieutenant governor, chief justice, and foremost historian of the Massachusetts Bay Colony, judged that *Vetch* remained a precedent that any loyal crown official must reject. The General Court had not only contravened the power of the governor but had also questioned the basic structure of imperial rule. The revolutionary potential of the precedent was not lessened because the General Court had failed to follow the logic of its lese majesty to its ultimate conclusion.[18]

The second eighteenth-century impeachment fell upon William Penn's protégé James Logan, Pennsylvania's provincial agent and secretary of the colony's council. As in Vetch's case it became a struggle between branches of government: one representing locally elected officials, the other, proprietary executive appointees. When Penn returned to England in 1684, he left Logan in charge of the key executive offices of proprietary finance. Logan plunged into his responsibilities with tactless vigor. In so doing, he clashed with David Lloyd, a Welsh lawyer whose talents induced Penn to appoint him attorney general, councillor, and clerk of the provincial court in 1686. Amity between Penn and Lloyd dissolved by 1688, and in 1693 Lloyd entered the lower house as a leader of the antiproprietary party, shortly thereafter becoming speaker of the assembly.[19]

Animosity between Lloyd and Logan flared into a broader contest between the legislature and the executive during debate over the Judiciary Act of 1706. The crux of the dispute was the prerogatives each branch claimed for itself. On November 28, 1706, Logan fumed: "The Case is short and plain: The Assembly requests several Things to be granted away from the Proprietary and Governor, which are now his Right, and to this he will not agree." The day after receiving the governor's veto of the courts bill and Logan's explanation, the legislature resolved unanimously that it had the right "to address and advise the Governor to turn out or displace for Misdemeanour, any Magistrate or other Officer constituted by the Governor." It further asserted without dissent that "if any such Magistrate or Officer shall be impeached by the Assembly for official Misdemeanour, such Magistrate or Officer, upon

Proof made of such Charge, ought to be removed or displaced at the Instance of the Assembly." The house, led by Lloyd, correctly assumed that Logan's "pernicious Counsel" induced Lieutenant Governor John Evans, a young Welshman, to threaten to constitute the courts himself in the absence of an acceptable courts bill. It resolved finally "that an humble Address be made to the Governor, to remove the said *James Logan* from his Council and presence." When Logan, replying on behalf of the lieutenant governor, ignored the assembly's charges, the house voted "that a Committee be appointed to draw up certain Articles of Impeachment against *James Logan*."[20]

With this step, the assembly turned from an "address" to the executive for removal of an erring minister to the wholly distinct process of impeachment. Although the two were entirely different, it is possible that Lloyd believed impeachment to be the logical sequel to an ineffectual appeal. He knew that the bringing of impeachment charges unified the lower house in defense of its privileges against the executive, and had before him one clear precedent—the impeachment of Justice More in Pennsylvania—and perhaps a second—the Vetch case. In Pennsylvania the lower house's right to impeach appeared in the original charter, saw use in the More case, and was reaffirmed in 1688; it reappeared in the new 1701 charter, although no provision was made for trial. One might infer from the assembly's boast that "the People of *Massachusetts*, in *New-England*, could not pretend to greater Privileges than the Proprietary granted to the Purchasers and Adventurers here" that information on the Vetch affair had reached Philadelphia.[21]

Did the actions of the Massachusetts General Court have any legal bearing upon the Pennsylvania Assembly's course? Knowing that the lower house of another colony had impeached merchant captains did not create precedent for Pennsylvania. English and proprietary law were the only correct sources, in theory, but then, in theory, the Pennsylvania lower house did not have the right to impeach Logan at all. The Massachusetts example must have encouraged Lloyd and his forces. If nothing else, the reference to the impeachment of Vetch and his coconspirators indicated that the colonial lower houses were beginning to take an interest in one anothers' activities. Hardly a precursor for the Committees of Correspondence, the exchange of information nevertheless taught Pennsylvania legislators that they shared common problems with their colonial neighbors. The formal citation of the Massachusetts case in the assembly report went beyond simple communication of information to the lieutenant governor. Though the Vetch case could not be legal precedent, it was a legal pretext. If Massachusetts, presumably under its charter, could impeach and seek trial of malefactors, so too could the Pennsylvania Assembly. The "Privileges" of one colony under the English constitution were the privileges of another. Here was one faint glimmer—not yet fully explored, for there was no need—of an "American" law of impeachment based not on explicit delegations of privilege from England but upon the inherent rights American lower houses shared.

The assembly prepared thirteen "articles of impeachment" against Logan. The first accused him of using his influence with the proprietor to "insert a certain Salvo [that is, a rider] . . . in the Proprietary's Commission to his Lieutenant-Governor, whereby the final Assent to all such Bills as he was to pass into Laws in this Province, is absolutely lodged in the proprietary." The second also objected to a clause in Evans's commission that gave him the power "to call Assemblies, and . . . to prorogue or dissolve" them at his pleasure—a clause, the assembly maintained, that had been inserted at Logan's behest. The next four articles were indictments of Logan's performance as land commissioner. The seventh article accused Logan of deliberately concealing from the assembly various objections of the Board of Trade to the earlier version of the courts bill, leading the assembly to write new bills that would be equally and embarrassingly unacceptable to the Board of Trade. There followed other objections to his conduct in land transactions. The twelfth article charged Logan with "a wicked Intent to create Divisions and Misunderstandings between him and the people." The last accused him of interfering with the election of Sheriff John Budd.[22]

Dissatisfied with the brief reply Logan issued in the council, the assembly insisted on its right to prosecute him and requested that the lieutenant governor act as judge and jury (the Frame of Government of 1701 having abolished the legislative power of the upper house). Evans scheduled trial for May 12, 1707. The speaker and assembly arrived en masse—literally following English precedent whereby the Commons prosecuted as a body— presented the articles of impeachment, and asked Logan to plead. The lieutenant governor now demurred that his powers were not comparable to those of the House of Lords in England, repeating a consensus reached only that morning in the council. Lloyd retorted that the charter gave the assembly the power to impeach and that although it did not spell out the trial procedure, there was the precedent of the More case to follow. The lieutenant governor conceded the point by ordering the trial to continue. Logan admitted his ignorance of the law and gave a graphic demonstration by asking to hear the evidence against him before pleading to the charges. Caught between the secretary, whom he wished to protect, and an implacable assembly, Evans declared an adjournment until the next morning.

When the trial reconvened, after Evans and Logan met in serious conference, the lieutenant governor returned to his initial aversion to presiding over an impeachment trial. He informed the lower house that "the Governor and Council have declared their Opinion fully to the Assembly, that they are not qualified to hear and judge of the Articles of an Impeachment exhibited against the Secretary, according to the parliamentary Proceedings of *England*;

and being no judicial Court, they cannot oblige him to plead in any Form." The lieutenant governor offered to receive any complaints against Logan in the usual fashion, that is, as an appeal to the judgment of the executive. Public opinion in the colony soon shifted to Logan's side, and Lloyd lost his seat in the assembly. Yet precedent had been created which, when the venerated William Penn no longer lived, would be used in a more sweeping assault upon proprietary rule.[23]

In the Carolinas, as in early eighteenth-century Massachusetts and Pennsylvania, factions in the assembly saw impeachment as a tool to check the power of externally appointed executive and judicial officials. During the spring of 1719 the assembly of South Carolina waited anxiously for the proprietors to assent to four bills intended to give it greater control over land grants, Indian policy, elections, and prices. When the proprietors vetoed the entire package, the planters who led the lower house correctly suspected that Chief Justice Nicholas Trott had undermined their case in England. For covert political opposition to the assembly, no less than for the malfeasance in office named in the charges against him, Trott was impeached.[24]

Trott's uncontrolled power in the courts of the colony invited legislative scrutiny. He had been trained at the Inner Temple and had served in South Carolina as attorney general and judge of the vice-admiralty court before his elevation to the council and appointment as chief justice in 1703. Once an ally of the assembly, by 1703 he was firmly in the proprietary camp. Although Trott performed genuine services for the bench and bar in the colony, he was an autocratic and avaricious political operator. Holding multiple positions as chief justice, sole judge of common pleas and king's bench, and leader of the vice-admiralty and chancery courts, Trott stood almost above the law. He could not be charged with being the proprietors' pawn but he could be accused of misusing his judicial powers. In April 1719, thirty-one articles of impeachment were presented in the assembly, charging that Trott "had been guilty of many Partial Judgments" and "that he had contrived many Ways to multiply and increase his Fees, contrary to Acts of Assembly, and to the great Grievance of the Subjects." Trott was accused of creating new fees for himself, delaying cases and giving legal advice in court, and drawing up legal documents while acting as a judge.[25]

The assembly impeached Trott but could find no way to try him. He insisted to his accusers that he held his commissions at the pleasure of the proprietors. In 1707, when Trott stood on friendlier terms with the assembly, the council had asked that he be impeached for judicial misconduct. At that time the assembly had replied that the council "were not a House of Lords nor a proper jurisdiction" before which the assembly could prosecute a case. Twelve years later, Trott used the assembly's old ruling against its new leaders. The assembly, reversing its position, asked the governor and council

to try him, but the council, advised by Trott, decided that it had no power to
try an impeachment case. When the assembly pressed the council to take the
issue to a higher authority, Governor Nathaniel Johnson refused to shield the
defendant. Instead, he sent councillor Francis Yonge to the proprietors with a
"letter of grievances" against Trott, along with the assembly's "remonstrance" against the veto of the four acts. The assembly, governor, and
council recommended that Trott be either removed or at least limited to one
of his offices. What began as an impeachment had temporarily become an
appeal.[26]

For three months Yonge pleaded for an audience before the proprietors.
When at last the proprietors heard his petition, they found the presumption
of the assembly alarming. Yonge returned to the colony bearing the proprietors' praise of Trott and instructions for the formation of a new, pro-Trott
council. The assembly refused to accept this mandate. Johnson called for new
elections, and the proprietary party was overwhelmed at the polls. In the
chaotic weeks that followed, an ad hoc "Association" replaced the assembly
and chose a council to its taste, which then tried and removed Trott from
office. Political considerations—the proprietors still theoretically ruled in
South Carolina—prevented a more sanguinary punishment. The Trott impeachment became entangled in the larger contest between the assembly and
the proprietors, though it had not originated as an attack upon the proprietary. As he fell, Trott reached out for support from England and, like Logan,
ended by threatening to topple the men whom he served. Penn's stature in his
own colony, compared to the weakness of the remaining Carolina proprietors, had much to do with the contrasting outcomes of these two impeachments.[27]

Two decades later a futile attempt to impeach the chief justice of North
Carolina, William Smith, proved that political support in the colony and
able political maneuvering by the accused could prevent impeachment in the
assembly. Smith, an educated English lawyer, received appointment as a
councillor and chief justice shortly after arriving in the newly reorganized
royal colony. He got along famously with Governor Gabriel Johnston, and
with the governor's aid set about establishing himself as a landed squire. By
the end of the decade he had over 7,000 acres in the colony and an annual
income of £550. Smith wished to incorporate his holdings into a township to
be called Wilmington, but families already established in the region resisted.
Led by the Moores, influential landholders in the south of the colony,
anti-Smith forces tried to prevent the council's confirmation of the incorporation of Wilmington. The chief justice would not permit his dream of
landed nobility to be shattered so easily. With Johnston's consent, he declared
himself the possessor of a double vote in the council and there blocked
opposition to incorporation.[28]

In the fall of 1738 Smith's opponents in the lower house, led by Sir Richard Everard, Samuel Swann, and Maurice Moore, proposed seventeen articles of impeachment against the chief justice. They believed they had a chance of success in the assembly, though Smith's influence in the council and with the governor would have rendered the trial verdict a foregone conclusion. Even nominal victory over Smith was denied by another of the chief justice's stratagems. According to depositions collected in 1749, Smith and Speaker John Hodgson managed to convince northern county assemblymen to absent themselves from the November 1738 session. North-south rivalry within the colony was lively, and Smith had earlier defended the interests of the northern counties. Without these members, the assembly lacked a quorum and had to adjourn. The newly elected assembly that gathered in February 1739 to weigh the evidence against Smith was, according to Smith's enemies, packed with his supporters.[29]

The journal of the lower house recorded a brief and unsuccessful impeachment attempt. The whole process, from the reading of the seventeen articles through the issuing of warrants for evidence and witnesses to the final vote, took only three days. According to the journal, every assistance was afforded the complainants by the speaker, and the dismissal of the charges by a majority of 6 votes exonerated Smith. The chief justice informed the council that the assembly had fully vindicated him. "After nine hours of debate," he wrote in 1740, the assembly "were so sensible of that Gentleman's Integrity and faithfulness in the discharge of his Office [and] were so fully convinced of what was at the bottom their design to put in a tool of a Chief Justice in order to get the Supreme Court of Justice and consequently the whole property of the province under their own management . . . [that] the fullest House that was ever known . . . Rejected . . . their infamous accusation."[30] Unlike Trott, Smith maintained some support in the lower house, and, equally important, the royal authorities in England, unlike Trott's patrons among South Carolina's proprietors, gave Smith powerful backing. These internal and external friends insulated Smith from his partisan opponents.

After their defeat, the anti-Smith faction prepared *A True and Faithful Narrative of the Proceedings of the House of Burgesses of North Carolina* to vindicate their case. They accused Smith of using illegal tactics to prevent a quorum in the fall 1738 session of the assembly. The authors also attacked the speed of the 1739 inquiry, engineered by Speaker Hodgson, for preventing the complainants from gathering all their witnesses and materials. The journal neither specified the charges nor printed any of the evidence, an omission which the *Narrative* corrected. The first article was a general condemnation of the "violent, arbitrary, and illegal manner" with which Smith rendered judgments. The second argued that he swore to call juries by ballot but was actually calling them by "venire" (*venire facias juratores*, that is, bidding the

sheriff select a jury and bring them to court, rather than by random selection
of eligible jurors by ballot). The third and fourth articles accused Smith of
holding courts where he pleased and executing criminals when he pleased,
contrary to assembly laws and common-law precedents. The next three
articles detailed incidents in which Smith imposed penalties without regard
to the law or the rights of the defendants, and articles eight, nine, and ten
documented the chief justice's appetite for extorting fees. In the next two
articles, the legal chicaneries Smith employed to funnel court fees into his
own pocket were revealed. The last five articles found him guilty of bad
temper and violent personal feeling against anyone who dared chide him for
errors—among whom was Sir Richard Everard.[31] Great discretion was conferred on magistrates from local justices of the peace to high court judges in
the common-law tradition. If these allegations were true, Smith had overextended the bounds of magisterial authority. What emerges from the *Narrative* might, perhaps, include some evidence of felonious activity, but primarily it is a portrait of the creation of a powerful, unscrupulous, and self-serving
political machine. Unable in the council to prevent Smith's political empire-
building, his opponents brought an impeachment in the assembly on
charges of malfeasance.

Although the provincial impeachments of proprietary and crown officials
challenged the exclusive privileges of the Commons, the provincial assemblies did not intend to weaken the imperial connection. Even as colonial
assemblies applied this check upon crown appointees, they drew consciously
and respectfully from parliamentary impeachment precedent. Without the
assumption that the English constitution traveled across the Atlantic, impeachment would forfeit its legitimacy. In addition, all these cases involved
or ended in some form of appeal to the crown.

Provincial precedent nevertheless diverged still further from   English
guidelines than had the seventeenth-century colonial cases. Vetch's case, ad-
mittedly transitional, to one side, Logan, Trott, and Smith were impeached
solely to remove them from office. All were incumbents accused of misusing
their power when their impeachments began. No criminal penalties were
sought—a departure from both the English and the earlier colonial cases. Of
course, it may be argued that many early eighteenth-century English impeachments aimed to remove or bar mistrusted or overbearing politicians
from office, but in Parliament, criminal penalties were still sought and some
of the accused held no office at all when they were impeached.

It required little imagination to note, as Hutchinson and the Privy Council
did, that with or without a trial and conviction, impeachment could make
life miserable for a royal official and disrupt colonial government. As yet,
removal from office could not be forced by an impeachment, for the power to
accomplish this lay at the seat of empire. Too lax, too corrupt, or, contrarily,

too efficient an imperial official was safe if the king willed it. For impeachment to directly challenge this imperial connection would, in effect, stand the provincial precedent on its head: attacking the authority of England rather than seeking English help to discipline a local official. The lower houses had no reason to embark upon this course, but, again ironically, dependence upon England planted the root of future struggle.

In all the provincial cases—despite the growing divergence of procedure from English precedent—a fear of corruption tied American managers to English predecessors. Fully half the multitude of English impeachment prosecutions in the seventeenth century and Queen Anne's reign alleged extortion, bribery, peculation, and other misuse of public funds. The same sort of charges were leveled against Logan, Trott, and Smith. Impeachment in England had been a popular and an effective remedy for such avarice, as Jonathan Swift sarcastically noted in one of his newspaper pieces: the most cunning of official malefactors "can tell how to go within an inch of impeachment, and yet come back untouched. They know what degree of corruption will just forfeit an employment. . . . How much to a penny you may safely cheat the queen."[32] There was certainly occasion in the "Age of Walpole" for many impeachments. From the speculative bubbles at its start to scandals at its end, Walpole's tenure was disfigured by fiscal irregularities. An alliance of old "country" Tories, radical dissenters, Scots reformers, and Whig "Commonwealthmen" poured out volumes of exposé. From France, Lord Bolingbroke excoriated those who put self-interest above public interest, and avarice above principle. In London, John Trenchard and Thomas Gordon filled the newspapers with the letters of an angry "Cato," censor of the "ridiculous, dishonest, and narrow notions of selfish and inconsistent men." All the hangers-on and graftsmen about Walpole were Cato's targets. Sworn to the defense of a mixed constitution, these Commonwealthmen and their political allies hurled abuse at Walpole, but to little avail. Parliament, itself corrupted, would not pursue the corruptionists.[33]

This stream of newspaper articles, pamphlets, and books may not have swayed Parliament, but the indictment of official corruption did influence the thinking of colonial legislative leaders. To their eyes, corruption lay in royal patronage. They welcomed the efforts of the anti-Walpole alliance to purge self-interest from the imperial system, and eagerly read the materials sent across the Atlantic by the Commonwealthmen. In New York, for example, Governor William Cosby's attempts to capitalize on his office were condemned with slogans that Lewis Morris and his opposition party lifted from anti-Walpole publicists in England. In other colonies, similar attacks on the patronage demonstrated the impact of the campaign against corruption.[34] *Cato's Letters* and other tracts found their way into every major colonial library. From the mid-1720s the words of "Cato," the "Craftsman," and the "Old Whig" were read, quoted, copied, and remembered throughout the colonies. They tutored Americans, already disgusted by their own experience with English placemen, to the "threats" liberty faced from within government.[35] And American legislative leaders took action, when they could, against this germ of corruption, with attempted impeachments. Only four cases actually came to trial, and not one was fully successful, but all of them showed that Americans took seriously a set of civic virtues which England's rulers seemed to spurn.

Looking ahead to a financially ruinous war for empire and the ministerial exactions which followed, one will find that this American capacity to discern and expand upon English radical critiques of government, illustrated in the provincial impeachments, was to have momentous consequences across an entire range of issues. Fear of fiscal malfeasance by the ministry in London would remain the theme, but the object of suspicion would shift from corrupt agents of the crown to the corrupting influence of the imperial tie itself. Impeachments mirrored and energized colonial aspirations as the crisis of empire approached.

3

REVOLUTIONARY IMPEACHMENT:
MOORE TO *OLIVER*

THERE ARE EPISODES IN THE HISTORY OF THE LAW WHEN A FEW CASES SIGNAL THE rise of a new doctrine, and the doctrine heralds a new epoch of constitutionalism. The last colonial impeachment cases fit this description. The impeachments and near impeachments of Chester County Judge William Moore in Pennsylvania (1757–58), Chief Justice Charles Shinner of South Carolina, New Jersey Treasurer Stephen Skinner, and Chief Justice Peter Oliver of Massachusetts (1773–74) introduced two momentous novelties into American precedent. First, these cases were ultimately directed against English authority over the colonies. Second, they rested upon an assumption of the supremacy of the peoples' representatives, assembled in colonial lower houses, over other branches of government.

The rights of lower houses in the colonies were never firmly settled. English law made these bodies subordinate corporate councils, called into session under the king's instructions to his governors or under charters he granted, and dependent upon his final assent for their legislative powers. Such a view was repugnant to the leaders of American assemblies, and in practice they found ways to wrest power from royal governors, proprietors, customs officials, and vice admiralty judges.[1] The often uneasy provincial balance between obedience and independence in these legislatures was shaken during the French and Indian War.[2] The colonial assemblies did not wish to deny the authority of England in protest against these incursions but sought some remedy in the English constitution against excessive or corrupt misuse of power by imperial agents.[3]

During the war years and the crisis which followed, three colonies whose impeachment precedent was well established, Pennsylvania, South Carolina, and Massachusetts, would employ impeachment to force concessions directly from England. New Jersey legislators would go almost as far. Impeachment, which in colonial hands had already moved so far from its English progenitor, changed its shape once more in these last colonial cases. From a tool of provincial assemblies to chastise corruption in other branches, it became a method for expressing the people's grievances (as enunciated in their assemblies) against imperial rulers. As in the provincial cases, politics played the catalyst—thrusting impeachment into situations which changed impeachment law even when impeachment did not lead to trial, conviction, and removal.

The impeachment of a Pennsylvania county judge introduced the new pattern. From the first it was an assault upon the powers of the proprietor in England and his supporters in the colony. By the mid-1750s, confrontation between the proprietor in England and his provincial assembly over the war was continuous. Defeats in western Pennsylvania added new urgency to the old hostilities. From 1755 to 1756 the war party—the proprietary forces led by Lieutenant Governor Robert Hunter Morris, the western settlers, and the Anglican establishment—fumed while antiproprietary forces in the assembly fussed.[4]

The bitterness of political infighting became apparent in the estrangement of Benjamin Franklin and the Reverend William Smith, leading in tortuous fashion to the impeachment of William Moore. With Franklin's assistance, young Smith had founded the Philadelphia Academy and become the first provost of the College of Pennsylvania. Wartime partisanships separated the patron and his protégé. In the winter of 1755–56 Smith championed the proprietary cause and Franklin advocated the assembly position. When Franklin journeyed to England as colonial agent, his defense of assembly rights was maintained by his lieutenants in the lower house. In 1757 the assembly struck boldly against Smith and proprietary government, using Moore as a tool.[5]

Moore was a Chester County landholder, militia leader, and justice of the peace. He strongly supported the war effort, for which he was rewarded on February 22, 1757, with a proprietary commission as chief judge of the Chester County court. In the summer and fall of 1757 the assembly received petitions from Chester County plaintiffs declaring that Moore had set aside jury verdicts, delayed executions of judgments, and refused to pay his personal debts. Moore regarded these petitioners as "Inhabitants of little or no reputation" and denied the jurisdiction of the assembly in bringing any charges against him.[6] When the assembly called Moore to account for his behavior, he refused to appear. The assembly could not force him to resign because his commission was at the pleasure of the king. On September 28, 1757, it sent the first of many requests to newly arrived Lieutenant Governor William Denny that Moore be removed from his offices.

Unwilling to give the assembly cause to upset the delicate negotiations over the war supply bill, Denny convened a formal inquiry. On October 20, 1757, Moore testified to his opposition against the assembly's war policy and denied that he had ever been formally summoned to appear before the assembly. Moore vowed that the "groundless and scandalous papers [and] petitions most shamefully procured against me by some of the members [of the assembly]" had no truth to them. The judge was a feisty advocate indeed. Satisfied with Moore's account and hoping that inaction was a safe course, the lieutenant governor permitted the matter to rest without a decision. Moore was not so sensible. When the assembly adjourned for the winter of 1757–58, he published an accusation in the *Pennsylvania Journal* that the lower house had manufactured evidence against him. Although Moore had secured permission from outgoing Speaker Isaac Norris to print the defense, the new assembly took official umbrage. The first order of business for the new speaker, Thomas Leech, was to arrest Moore for libel.[7]

To embarrass the assembly and assist a political ally, Smith published Moore's defense in a German language newspaper. Though Smith prudently waited until the *Journal* and the equally prestigious *Pennsylvania Gazette* had published similar accounts, his caution was unavailing. He was detained for contempt of the assembly at the same time that Moore was arrested. Joseph Galloway, Franklin's chief aide, directed the prosecution. Galloway intended the indictment of Moore to lead to the suppression of the far more dangerous Smith, and on January 5 the latter was duly convicted of contempt of the privilege of the assembly.[8]

The trial became a cause célèbre. As Edward Shippen, Jr. told his father, "The affair of Will Moore and W. Smith put everything into a flame." Moore had admitted all, while Smith denied everything. The "solemn" trial which followed ended in the conviction of both men, "but the evidence was agreed by everybody out of doors to be very lame." When Smith made an "elegant and pathetic closing speech to the assembly," about 100 people "joined in a general clapping of hands in the face of the house. This you may believe gave great offense." The members started from their chairs, closed the doors, and arrested a few of the applauders. One of them, Thomas Willing, publicly admitted that he joined in clapping for Smith.[9] A proud and resolute Moore and a dismayed Smith were led away to the Philadelphia jail, to be held at the pleasure of the assembly. The jailer was instructed to disregard the orders of any other official save the speaker of the lower house, lest the prisoners seek their freedom upon a writ of habeus corpus from the colonial supreme court. When Smith applied for this writ, Chief Justice William Allen refused to interfere in the assembly's business.[10]

Smith's struggle to free himself on bail led ultimately to England, where, at liberty during the adjournment of the assembly, he sought the aid of the appeals committee of the Privy Council. Armed with briefs from prominent attorneys William Livingston and William Smith Jr. of New York, he obtained concurring opinions from the king's attorney general and solicitor general. The Privy Council shortly thereafter ordered him freed from jail and warned the assembly not to assume the judicial powers of the Commons.[11]

While Smith wriggled free of the clutches of the lower house, Moore languished in the Philadelphia jail. Unlike Smith, a private citizen accused only of a breach of the assembly's privilege, Moore could be impeached on charges of corruption in office. In contradistinction to Trott's case, in which both sides appealed to England, Moore was a pawn in a struggle between the proprietary government and a popular faction. Lieutenant Governor Denny was trapped with Moore in the assembly assault upon proprietary government. Denny deposed to the assembly that he was surprised that the new house had pursued the libel against its predecessor. But more was at stake than two libel charges, as the assembly would demonstrate in the scope of its arguments demanding trial of Moore in the council.[12]

When Denny refused to remove Moore on the petition of the new assembly, the lower house formally impeached the judge. If criminal impeachment, followed by trial, was its aim, the assembly had before it an impossible task: to convince Denny to disregard his own inquiry, in effect to repudiate his power to hold such investigations, and instead to sit as judge and jury in an impeachment trial. In the process he would also have to render a formal decision on Moore's guilt. Galloway and the assembly party were too experienced to expect such a turnabout. From the first, their aim was not to convict the defendant but to challenge the proprietary system itself. They therefore placed their argument on the high ground of the English constitution. The assembly told the lieutenant governor that its power to impeach was "strictly agreeable to the Usage of Parliament, and Customs of our Mother Country," as well as "incontestably in the Assembly, by the Charter of Privileges, and an established Law of the Province." It warned Denny that any attempt by him to circumvent the impeachment would be "an Innovation in the Constitution, as it would be erecting a new Court of Judicature, unknown in the Government before."[13]

Although Denny knew that the assembly sought to embarrass the proprietary, he still hoped that it would assist the war effort. He had to find some reason to bar himself from sitting in judgment on the impeachment, while avoiding an open feud with the legislature. He too cited parliamentary principle: an executive did not have and could not assume the powers of a House of Lords or council. Denny adopted Evans's argument, which he had read closely. In England the impeachment trial always took place before this "middle branch"—the Lords—but in Pennsylvania, Denny wrote, the legislature was unicameral. The lieutenant governor had no power to stand in the stead of the council or upper house. "No such jurisdiction is given him by the Words of the Charter, or elsewhere, that I can find, on the strictest Scrutiny." He added that this was a wise precaution, for should such a power fall upon one man, he might overthrow the rights and liberties guaranteed by the English constitution.[14]

On January 17 the assembly rebuked Denny for rejecting a basic charter right of the lower house. The assembly had re-read the Logan case and took a very different view of Lieutenant Governor Evans's refusal to try impeachments. It found Evans "a Gentleman remarkable for being destitute of every Virtue, either moral, political, or religious. The Government was in a continual Ferment during his whole Administration: The Rights of the People in perpetual Jeopardy by his arbitrary and unjust Invasions." The assembly then broadened its arguments to include the entire range of political issues in contention. "The principal Powers of our Assemblies are, those of making Laws, granting Aids to the Crown, and redressing the Grievances and Oppressions of the People. The first, you well know, is highly invaded, and greatly diminished, by arbitrary Proprietary Instructions, now in your Possession. . . . The second has been greatly violated by the frequent and constant Amendments in our Money bills." The third of these grievances was the Moore case, and it was the effect, not the cause, of the larger breach between the governor and the lower house.[15]

Untried and fearful of renewed custody when the assembly reconvened in the fall, Moore again took a hand in his own defense. On August 28, 1758, he petitioned the king to deny the assembly the right to impeach him. The tone of his plea was very different from his newspaper article:

In all moral Probability your petitioner must be obliged to fly from his Country or be a prisoner for Life, unless he will submit to give up his Right of tryal in the Common Courts of Justice . . . thereby contributing to establish in a Body of Representatives here a *Power* above *Law*.

Moore prayed that the king would not permit the assembly to "erect themselves into an extraordinary . . . court of judicature."[16] In 1759 the Privy Council, ruling on the Moore case, denied the assembly the right to imprison for a libel against a previous assembly and also denied that the assembly possessed parliamentary privileges, including the power to impeach. Moore was fully exonerated and restored to his offices the same year.[17]

Despite this, the Moore impeachment broadened the assembly's own conception of its authority and made it more jealous of the powers of the lieutenant governor. The assembly had expressed the difference between its interests—conceived by its leaders to be identical to the interests of the people—and the interests of the proprietors and their agents. The proprietor fully recognized this threat—nothing less than rule by popular vote. Proprietor Thomas Penn, writing from London in the spring of 1758, apprehended "an attack from the assembly" against the lieutenant governor, proprietor, and government itself.[18]

Moore was a straw in the wind, tossed by proprietary politics, but it served notice of conflict to come at the end of the war. In the writs of assistance cases in Massachusetts and the suits for damages arising out of Virginia's Two-Penny Acts, colonial lawyers were undermining the appellate jurisdiction of the law lords in the Privy Council. The same men who acted as counsel in these cases, James Otis, Jr. and Patrick Henry, would use the provincial assemblies as forums for expanding their assault on the lawmaking powers of Parliament. While no move was made to reinstate proceedings of any kind against Moore or Smith, the issues which led to their plight were exacerbated in 1763 and 1764 by rumors of new parliamentary taxes. Again the colonial legislatures became the fulcrums for American protest. The Sugar Act, the Stamp Act, and the Townshend Acts gave substance to the "tendencies and possibilities" of English corruption feared in America. The result was a subtle shift in the long-standing competition between royal governors and their lower houses. The obstacle to autonomy in the assemblies was no longer the instructions of the governor, but his master's prerogatives. Out of this struggle came a number of near impeachments that embarrassed the governors and weakened royal government.[19]

In the spring of 1766, with the business of the court of common pleas of South Carolina at a standstill for want of royal stamps, the bar petitioned Governor William Bull to reopen the courts without the dreaded stamps. The chief justice, Irish immigrant Charles Shinner, was adamant: no stamps, no official business. Governor Bull bent to the petition of the lawyers and appointed new associate judges. On March 3, 1766, they came to the opening of the court and took their seats to hear members of the bar argue the first case on the docket. Lowland notables John Rutledge, Charles Pinckney, and Peter Manigault at the bar and, on the bench, newly appointed justices Rawlins Lowndes, Benjamin Smith, and Daniel Doyley agreed that the case could be heard without stamps because there were no stamps; necessity prevented compliance with the Stamp Act. Shinner would have none of it. He dissented from the opinions of the new judges: the law was clear, and no man might profit from its violation. The attorney general, Egerton Leigh, and court clerk, Dougal Campbell, as well as the council, joined the outvoted chief. Encouraged, Shinner refused to concede. At last, in April 1767, the assembly asked the governor to remove Shinner for incompetence. After Shinner replied to the charges at length, Governor Charles Montagu, newly arrived in the colony, put the matter to his council. They now supported the assembly unanimously, and the chief judge was "suspended" pending instruction from the crown. While this was no impeachment, it came close to becoming just that. Only Montagu's compliance (and prudence) and Shinner's death staved off the Pennsylvania experience.[20]

Near impeachments of this type had a cumulative effect. The lower house and the governor of South Carolina were not reconciled by the Shinner affair.

In the early 1770s a series of thrusts and parries ended with irreconcilable differences over obedience to parliamentary demands. Lower house leaders' assumption of the parliamentary privilege of investigation, capped by the threat of impeachment, could paralyze a royal government. The progress from simple inquiry to a near impeachment aimed at imperial authority was evident in a series of New Jersey cases. On June 18, 1767, the assembly, sitting in committee of the whole, reported that Chief Justice Frederick Smyth sought special compensation to hold a second session of oyer and terminer (criminal) court in Salem County. The allowance set by statute was not enough to induce him, he later admitted to the lower house, to travel from his home all the way to Salem "in the hot season." He did maintain that he only broached the matter of extra allowances in a private letter, for which presumption the assembly chided the judge. There was no charter or statutory authority for the assembly to call the judge to account in person before its members in the first place. He was named by the king and held commission during royal pleasure. Parliamentary custom alone afforded a precedent (which, of course, the assembly's responsibility for paying Smyth's salary reinforced). Two years later the assembly officially investigated John Forman, a Monmouth justice of the peace, for encouraging "many litigants' suits at law before him" and receiving exorbitant fees thereby. After hearing his testimony, the assembly only admonished him for holding court in a tavern. Sheriff Samuel Tucker fared worse. Though he was a member of the lower house, his conduct was censured. Fortunately, he overcharged his clients in his capacity as a lawyer, not an official. Thus far, the lower house had done nothing but censure, requiring no action from royal governor William Franklin. Assembly relations with Franklin were tense but not disruptive through these episodes; he had pulled together a council of able and influential New Jersey merchants and landholders that protected him, and the royal interest, from direct attack. But not for long.[21]

In a direct extension of its self-arrogated investigatory powers, the assembly voted an inquiry into the robbery of the eastern treasury office. In July 1768 a gang had taken more than £6,000 from under the nose of Stephen Skinner, treasurer for the eastern district. The assembly heard testimony on the case in its fall 1769 session and did not accuse Skinner of anything, but a year later, when he refused to restore the missing funds, they accused him of negligence. For four years, from 1770 to the spring of 1774, the assembly lobbied for his removal upon charges of negligence and loss of public trust. The uproar drowned out ordinary business, drove the governor to despair, and ended with victory for the lower house. The leader of the movement was James Kinsey, a popular party spokesman. His motives (and those of the nineteen men who consistently voted for the treasurer's removal) were various: they represented a new element in Jersey politics and wanted the assembly to name its own treasurer and to control its own funds. In the end, Franklin had no choice but to accede to their demand for removal, though Skinner saved his patron loss of face by resigning on February 24, 1774.[22]

The assembly and the governor knew that the proceedings verged on an impeachment. While the lower house at first petitioned the governor to determine the manner of inquiry and removal (if Skinner failed to make up the lost funds), they soon turned to investigation and indictment. Franklin viewed this change in direction as a thrust at his own authority, and it was. When Kinsey and others demanded that he and the council hear the case upon the indictment of the lower house, he recognized the outlines of an impeachment. His reply, in a moving (and exhaustive) message read in the lower house on September 23, 1772, reminded the lower house that any order for removal of an official must show "sufficient cause" to be acceptable to the Privy Council. It was not in the authority of an assembly to demand removal, or they might "turn out any officer of the government." The harassed governor could not maintain this bold restatement of long-standing Privy Council doctrine: no business would be concluded unless he made some concession. He conceded the growing autonomy of the popular branch and begged the lower house to act in a parliamentary way. If they were a minia- ture House of Commons, they must proceed by correct steps. Even Parlia- ment would not allow executive (that is, royal) censure of an impeached official without a trial and conviction. He knew that Kinsey and his allies, by an unshakable series of 19 to 7 votes, aimed at removal of Skinner. By granting to the assembly leadership what it already claimed for itself, he meant to be reasonable, but his plan backfired. The assembly would not be deterred. When the gang responsible for the theft was captured and confessed, Franklin rushed a minutely prepared and torturously pleaded account of their actions, exculpating Skinner, to the lower house. They voted it unsatis- factory. When Skinner, after conference with Franklin, asked the lower house for permission to remain in office until a jury trial could determine his guilt, the assembly retorted that he could show his good faith only by resigning first, then submitting himself to trial. When the governor reported to the lower house the Privy Council's judgment on the affair, ordering him not to remove Skinner, the lower house formally "resolved" their own "opinion" that Skinner was negligent, and that this was "sufficient reason . . . coupled with general dissatisfaction of the people" for removal. With some in the assembly arguing for a petition to the king and others pressuring the gover- nor privately, Skinner resigned.[23]

Though Skinner was never formally impeached, the motions against him and the call for a removal by the council and governor were more than an address. The lower house never did concede to the governor sole jurisdiction for removal, because they would not allow him to hear and determine the case himself. Kinsey and his allies in the assembly were well acquainted with

Pennsylvania politics; they took the Pennsylvania newspapers and had deal-- ings in the Pennsylvania courts. They allowed Franklin none of the leeway the Pennsylvania managers accorded Denny. For his part, Franklin knew that he was not being addressed or appealed to but told to remove the eastern treasurer. Although he must have recognized that control of finances was one of the assembly's motives, he did not consider it the major issue. Instead, in all his many messages to the lower house on the Skinner case, he battled against the implied insult to his judgment, his jurisdiction, and his place in the system of colonial government. He perceived the threat to be a judicial one, concerning control over appointments and tenure, not one of a fiscal nature, over treasury accounts, liability, and security of funds. In this, the coming dissolution of his government by the revolutionary committee of safety would prove him correct.

In 1773 a similar struggle between the lower house and the governor propelled the Massachusetts General Court into its second impeachment effort. The target was Chief Justice Peter Oliver, but the object of attack was royal control over the superior court of the colony. When, in the early 1760s, Thomas Hutchinson criticized the General Court's encroachment upon the king's courts in Vetch's case, he was battling his own General Court for control over the judicial branch. The lower courts were increasingly unresponsive to the nominal supremacy of the governor, representing the king. Hutchinson wished to Anglicize these lower courts and told the Suffolk grand jury repeatedly that the bench must be modeled upon and responsible to English authority. But rival politicians in the General Court suspected a hidden design in Hutchinson's plans for the courts: the corruption of an independent judiciary by a combination of royal patronage (including royal salaries) and Hutchinson family alliances. Hutchinson's appointment of his in-law, Oliver, as chief justice of the superior court ignited the legislators' fears and led to the impeachment of Oliver.[24]

When, in 1770, Hutchinson was elevated from the lieutenant governorship to replace Governor Francis Bernard, he needed a loyal replacement in the chief justiceship. He turned first to Benjamin Lynde, Jr., who accepted, but, sensing the coming storm over royal salaries, soon resigned. Hutchinson next offered the post to Oliver, recommending him to the home government as "the man most likely to resist popular pressure." Oliver, the youngest son of a great mercantile family, fit easily into the colony's elite officialdom. He was related to Hutchinson by marriage once in his own generation and twice in the generation of his children, and his brother, Andrew, Hutchinson's brother-in-law, was Hutchinson's lieutenant governor as well. Although Oliver had served as an associate justice of the superior court for almost twenty years, he preferred to remain at home in Plymouth County tending his lands, his library, and his iron works rather than ride circuit. The status of the chief justice's office, the promise of an increased salary paid out of customs receipts, and his unswerving filial devotion to Hutchinson finally led him to accept the higher post, where he became a weak pawn in the power struggle between the royal governor and the rebellious assembly.[25]

Hutchinson and the General Court were deadlocked on the judiciary issue until the rumor that the English government might fund the salaries of the superior court justices from customs duties gave the assembly a popular rallying cry. Hutchinson advocated royal salaries to bring order and dignity to the court, but the legislature feared that with the end of its own grants to support the judges would come the end of the court's sensitivity to local needs—a crucial issue when so many political disturbances now ended in the superior court chamber. At the opening of the 1773 term the General Court made crown salaries for the justices the focal point of its assault, warning the governor that "the people without doors are universally alarmed" about the threat. When Hutchinson reported that Lord North's ministry had ordered that the justices be paid from customs receipts, the lower house bellowed: "We conceive that no Judge who had a due regard to Justice, or even to his own Character, would chuse to be placed under such an undue bias as they must be under, in the Opinion of the House, by accepting of and becoming dependent for their Salaries upon their Crown. Had not his Majesty been misinformed with Respect to the Constitution and Appointment of our Judges by those who advised to this Measure, we are persuaded he would never have passed such an Order."[26] The governor was safe from the General Court as long as he did not displease his English masters, but the superior court judges might be brought to heel. This was the assembly's next move.

The assembly baited its trap for the justices by voting a grant of £300 to Chief Justice Oliver for a year's service already passed, and £200 to the associate justices for the same term. The treasurer was to determine whether the justices accepted and used the General Court salary. In June the treasurer reported that Oliver and associate justices Foster Hutchinson, Nathaniel Ropes, and William Cushing had used only half the grant. The General Court then changed its warning into an ultimatum: should the justices accept a crown salary in lieu of the assembly grant, they would violate the "most important Clause in the Charter," whereby the assembly was empowered to pay for the services of government. That was on June 25; three days later, the assembly told the justices "without Delay, explicitly to Declare" whether they would accept a crown salary.[27]

Behind its confident facade, the assembly searched for some legal method to force Oliver to accede to its wishes or surrender his office. The method they chose was impeachment (in retrospect an appropriate and effective choice), but where had the assembly obtained this plan? The Vetch precedent was well known to Hutchinson, and his historical account of it was already in print.

Strange to say, though Hutchinson's work was widely read by his political opponents, none of them resuscitated the Vetch case.[28] Closer to home, Josiah Quincy Jr. had discoursed at length on impeachment in 1768. His *Boston Gazette* article dwelt upon the elevated political duties of the lower house. Quincy, one of the leading legal authorities among the anti-Hutchinson faction, noted that "a short attention to the following extracts [from Rushworth and Selden] will convince every intelligent mind, that, while the first principles of our constitution . . . are adhered to, no subject . . . is beyond the reach of a strict examination into his conduct, or out of Danger of a scourge for his crimes." The remedy was simple: "A peer of the Realm may be impeached in Parliament," and so, by implication, might a malefactor in the colonial lower house. Adams, many years later, claimed that it was he who had suggested impeachment of those justices accepting royal salaries. In his autobiography he recalled that he had dined with members of the General Court and other gentlemen during the salary crisis and had agreed with them that royal payment would be the ruin of the liberties of the country. "I believed," Adams recalled, "there was one constitutional Resource. . . . Several Voices at once cryed out, a constitutional Resource! what can it be? I said it was nothing more nor less than an Impeachment of the Judges by the House of Representatives before the Council. An Impeachment! Why such a thing is without Precedent. I believed it was in this Province: but there had been precedents enough, and by much too many in England."[29]

The origin of the impeachment plan remains unclear despite the superabundance of claimants for that honor. Hutchinson knew of Quincy's essay, for the lieutenant governor explicitly rejected colonial impeachment in his 1768 Suffolk grand jury charge,[30] but Adams, who probably did mention impeachment to Hawley and others, did not credit Quincy, Hutchinson, or the Vetch case, though Adams had read Hutchinson's history and had worked on criminal cases with Quincy. What is more, according to his autobiography, Adams first urged Hawley and others to seek redress in "written instruments" rather than in "less manageable rights" like impeachment.[31] Nevertheless, in an 1817 letter to William Tudor, Adams insisted that he had immediately sought to convince Justice Edmund Trowbridge and Hawley of the legality of impeachment: "that the power of impeachment was essential to a free government; that the charter had given it to our House of Representatives as clearly as the constitution, [that it existed] in the common law as immemorial usage, [which] had given it to the House of Commons in England." Adams was never shy about claiming his due in bringing on the Revolution, but in the present case his own role seems to have grown with time.[32] Assuming that Adams did not draw upon Hutchinson's history or Quincy's newspaper articles, what brought impeachment to his mind?

Throughout January and February 1773, Adams had engaged William Brattle, a supporter of the crown, in a war of words. Brattle warned that the General Court's hectoring and curbing of the judges using the instrument of salaries would rob the judiciary of its independence. Adams disagreed. From English history and custom, parliamentary debate, and legal commentary he elicited evidence that the pleasure of the king was the goad of the judges. Often, he admitted, this had broken the courts of law beneath the will of the king, but Adams had no brief to defend the crown or its courts. The commissions of the American superior court judges rested similarly upon the pleasure of the king, and their offices could be removed summarily at his order. Adams urged that the governor and council remove those Massachusetts judges who did not obey the laws and customs of the province (by which he meant accepting a salary from the General Court alone). If judges could be removed at pleasure, there was no need to try them for misconduct upon an impeachment. Only when Adams's arguments seemed to fall on deaf ears did he begin to cast about for an alternative manner of removal. One was at hand from his exhaustive search into English precedent during his debate with Brattle. Adams had encountered repeated impeachments of English judges — precedent for a similar course in Massachusetts. Adams referred to this research in his autobiographical note on impeachment when he recalled the extent of the English cases: "precedents enough, and by much too many."[33]

Oliver was tried by public opinion long before the impeachment was voted. Stirred by their representatives to the General Court, the grand jurors along the superior court circuit refused to serve if Oliver sat. Edmund Trowbridge, one of the associate justices of the Superior Court, remembered the effectiveness of the impeachment investigation in a September 1775 memorandum:

At Boston Court in August 1773. My Brothers Hutchinson and Cushing were very zealous for supporting the Honour of the Court, by immediately fining everyone returned to serve on the Jury, that should decline taking the Oaths because the Chief Justice was Impeached by the House, and committing him to Gaol until he paid the fine. I told them that I thought we should be far from supporting the Honour of the Court by such a procedure. That I believed the persons so committed would be soon liberated by the people, and that we should not be able to do the business of the County. But finding they disregarded what I said, and grew warm upon it, I determined to know Governor Hutchinsons mind therein and if he disapproved of the measure proposed, to desire him to let his Brother [Oliver] know it [.] On the Saturday before the Superior Court was to be held at Worcester in September 1773, I waited upon the Governor at Milton, laid the matter before him, and told him plainly

what I thought would be the Consequences of such fines & imprisonments. . . . The Governor said "I don't see how the Court can well avoid
fining such jurymen as do, *merely* on account of that Impeachment,
persist in their refusal to take the Oaths, but there is no need of comitting
them *presently* for the fine and it will be better not to do it." I desired his
Excellency to let his Brother know that [was] his opinion; & by his
conduct at the Court suppose the Governor did. While I was at the
Governors ['] Commodore Loving & Joseph Scott came in, and gave the
governor a letter from Judge Oliver [;] while the Gov. was reading it, I
asked them if the Chief Justice intended to go to Worcester Court. Both
of them said he did and was to set out Monday. After they were gone I
told the Gov. I was afraid Judge Olivers going to Worcester would be
attended with bad Consequences, that there would be no court held
while he was there; and proposed his Excely^s sending an express to
prevent his going. The Gov. said, "There will be no need of that, I don't
think he will go [.]" I told the Gov. that Loving and Scott also said he
would, upon which the Gov. gave me the letter they brought him,
wherein the Chief Justice wrote the Gov. that he should not go to
Worcester Court.[34]

While the other justices waited for Oliver to take a decisive step, the
revolutionary leaders kept the fire burning under Oliver and Hutchinson.
Trowbridge had not exaggerated the popular response to impeachment.
From Boston, in September 1773, Samuel Adams spread the word of Oliver's
travails:

The [Superior] Court is now sitting here; and the Grand Jury have
presented a Memorial to them, setting forth as we are informd, the
Contempt with which the Grand Juries of the province have been treated
in the Letters of Govr Hutchinson & others; asserting the Independence
of Grand Juries as being accountable to none but God & their own
Consciences for their Conduct. . . . They have also represented to the
Court, the great Uneasiness in the Minds of the people of this County &
as they conceive of the whole province, by reason of the uncertainty that
yet remains, respecting the Dependence of the Judges on the Crown for
Support, & their own Doubts & Difficulties on this Account; & they pray
that the Court w^d come to an explicit & publick Declaration thereupon.[35]

Through the fall and winter of 1773–74 the *Boston Evening Post* kept the
story of the grand juries' refusals to sit on its front page. Wenham town
demanded that the General Court seek "constitutional remedies" against the
chief justice and the governor.[36] On January 24, 1774, correspondents to the
paper defended jurors fined for not serving when Oliver sat. One correspon-

dent claimed to have witnessed Oliver's "harsh" conduct against jurors and warned, "The time approaches, sir, when this exertion of your power, with the foundation it was intended to support, will come under the enquiry of the guardians of public liberty."[37]

On February 14, 1774, the General Court voted the impeachment against Oliver, "an enemy" to the "constitution," and asked his removal. By the twenty-fifth this had turned into an impeachment for "high crimes and misdemeanors." The assembly charged that he had permitted himself to be bought by a salary "unjustly and unconstitutionally levied and extorted from the Inhabitants of the American Colonies" and that he had acted "against the known Sense of the Body of the People of this Province." For these alleged abuses the assembly asked the governor and council to try Oliver and, if found guilty, to remove him without delay from his judicial offices. Asking Hutchinson to sit as a judge in a case against his handpicked successor and political supporter was a perversion of impeachment—it would make trial a mockery—but the request forced the governor to either defend the unpopular chief justice or accede to the demand for a trial.[38]

Caught in the storm, Oliver was reduced to pleading that "I can with the strictest truth assert, that I have suffered since I have been upon the bench of the Superior Court, in the loss of my business and not having sufficient [funds] to maintain my family."[39] To Trowbridge he would later write:

I had fully determined to go to Barnstable Court where I always went with pleasure as I imagined I was among a set of [men] virtuous & well affected to government, but I cannot bear my part of the Burden of this term with you[;] my reasons are these, three or four days since one Dr. Freeman of Sandwich was at a tavern in this Town, and before several of my neighbors was asked whether I intended for Barnstable Court He was told yes. He then said that there was an high insult designed me at Barnstable if I went there, and sent his compliments to me to call at his house if I went, as I knew where he lived. This last I took as the beginning of an insult, for his person I did not remember I ever saw: but his character I am sufficiently acquainted with, for I was informed that he left money at a tavern at Plymouth to treat a set of infamous villains who destroyed some of my property in Plymouth last Winter. I am quite willing to attend my duty at every Court, but if I cannot without danger to my person, I think myself excusable. From the general character I have had of that Freeman, and from what I have seen of a writing said to be his, and from what I have of his treatment of a stranger, who traveled thro Sandwich last winter, I apprehend that his mind is so callous to every sentiment of virtue that I should not dare [go] without defensive weapons to guard me, which are not proper at all times to ride with, to pass within ye reach of that malevolence which I think he is possessed with.[40]

Hutchinson, for his part, told the General Court that he could not try the chief justice because "if I should comply with your request or take any steps in order to the Removal of the Chief Justice, from this place, merely for receiving what is thus granted him by the King, I should make myself chargeable with counteracting his Majesty and endeavoring to defeat his Royal Intentions expressly signified to me."[41] Hutchinson did not dare permit the council to hear the case, because many of its elected members seemed too eager to try Oliver. Francis Walett has told the story:

> When the Council asked Hutchinson to name the time of the trial and requested his presence, the governor impatiently reminded the councillors of the constitutional limitations on this purpose. Bowdoin replied for the Council that the governor's statements tended "to take away or lessen the jurisdiction of the Governor and Council" for these officials "have always been esteemed the proper judicature before whom officers appointed by them have [been] triable for crimes or misdemeanors." The message further asserted that a denial of the rights or remonstrance and impeachment would "have an unhappy tendency to encourage the executive officers of the government to deviations from their duty," and would be "incompatible with the safety and happiness of the people."[42]

Frustrated, Hutchinson averted the trial by proroguing the General Court.

The pleading of Oliver and the legalisms of Hutchinson could not detract from the victory of the assembly. Their indictment of Oliver was tried in the court of public opinion. While the majority of the patriot faction was not yet ready for violent resistance, impeachment of the chief justice was an effective weapon against royal government. Typically, when the Suffolk grand jury refused to meet, its jurors declared that the rights of Massachusetts men and women were "not the gifts of kings."[43] John Adams, following the circuit of the superior court in York County, Maine, reported to Abigail that Oliver did not appear for the June 1774 session. The foreman of the grand jury told Trowbridge, acting chief justice, that if Oliver presided, the jury would disperse, impeachment trial or no.[44]

Behind the partisan effort to check and balance royal government stood a larger constitutional achievement. Consensus among the legislators and their constituents upon the appropriateness and the force of the impeachment of a public official for violation of a public trust bespoke commitment to certain constitutional assumptions. Bound to an ideology of the supremacy of representative legislatures, impeachment moved from an expeditious tactic toward becoming a fixture of American government. The origin of colonial impeachment lay in the colonists' understanding of English precedent, but its American unfolding had led to a new meaning for impeachment. The people, through their own representatives, not virtually through the Commons in England, had the right and power to oust wrongdoers in office. The adoption of impeachment in the salary controversy led to this conclusion.

The impeachment of Peter Oliver was the last colonial case but hardly the least. Though a singular event, its impact upon the minds of other colonial leaders was both direct and indirect. In a direct sense, the impeachment helped to doom royal government in Massachusetts. The governor and his council could no longer work smoothly together, and relations with the General Court were wrecked. The regular courts sat if and only if Oliver absented himself, and then under a cloud. Had the Boston Tea Party occurred before the impeachment crisis began, that is, before the government was hamstrung by the threat of impeachment, royal officials on the scene might have been able to move more effectively against the rioters. The door to the reorganization of Massachusetts' government would not have been opened. When the crown recognized the impotence of the old form of government—driven to distraction by the impeachment—it overreacted. The Boston Port Act might have been passed even had the provincial government been in working order, but the other acts, giving virtual dictatorial powers to new governor Thomas Gage, would not have been necessary. The severity of the parliamentary response set off protests in the other colonies. While local conditions and long-standing controversies undergirt these protests, the closing of the Port of Boston was on all the patriots' lips. In every county of Virginia whose voters met to register their sentiments that summer of 1774, for example, the fate of Boston was pointedly cited as a cause of alarm; thirty-one of the thirty-one counties that recorded instructions to their newly elected burgesses protested Massachusetts' plight. But for the impeachment of Oliver, the royal authorities need never have awakened this dragon.[45]

The impeachment of Oliver had an indirect influence upon the revolutionary crisis as well. Because the man who instigated the prosecution—John Adams—became one of the chief and most persistent advocates of independence, and because he operated at the center of colonial protest—in the Continental Congress—impeachment became familiar to revolutionary leaders from other colonies. Adams's role in the adoption of impeachment by the new states is documented below, but this role would not have been played without the Oliver impeachment.

PART II

IMPEACHMENT
AND REPUBLICANISM,
1776–1788

INTRODUCTION

OLIVER'S CASE PIT THE MASSACHUSETTS GENERAL COURT AGAINST ROYAL AUTHOR-
ity. Oliver had done nothing averse to English law; indeed, he was impeached
for obeying a directive from the crown. Nevertheless, with his impeachment
the superior court of the colony was hamstrung, and the governor was forced
to dissolve the assembly to forestall the council's demand for a trial. While
Hutchinson and the popular party brayed defiance at each other, royal
authority collapsed. Impeachment had toppled a government—but could it
also preserve governments, new state systems far weaker and more experimental in form than the Bay Colony?

The next impeachment that occurred in the North American continent
had a totally different character from *Oliver*. Two years after independence
was declared, in the beleaguered little state of New Jersey the assembly voted
an impeachment against a county judge. The executive council heard the
prosecution managers from the lower house, then the defendant in his own
defense, and voted to acquit him. The proceedings disrupted neither the
assembly nor the council; the state's business went on as usual. In the next six
years, impeachment cases followed against officials in New Jersey, Pennsylvania, Virginia, Massachusetts, Vermont, North Carolina, and Connecticut.
These impeachments did not dislocate the new state governments, nor were
they designed for disruption. They did not challenge the legitimacy of
executive or judicial power, and they were not resisted by governors or judges.
Impeachment had become common in America and was to become even
more familiar in the next two decades. Somehow the Revolutionaries had
absorbed impeachment into a republican system.

The problems involved in domesticating impeachment had been immense. First, impeachment was an expression of the vast inherent power of
the House of Commons, and the Revolutionaries had stood aghast at those
powers during the crisis. Could the liberties of subjects be so easily swept
away by an all powerful Parliament? Evidently so. As Samuel Sherwood, a
minister in Fairfield, Connecticut, warned in August 1774:

> If the parliament should once take it into their heads, that it is expedient,
> or for the general good, that all lands in America should revert to the
> crown . . . what will hinder their carrying it into execution? And indeed

59

the Boston port act doth actually afford us a precedent of the exercise of this power.... Now what is this but a vote of parliament to take away our landed property. And that power which hath been once exercised have we not all reason to fear will be exercised again.[1]

Impeachment entailed this immense, uncontrolled power. The House of Commons could impeach anyone in the realm for offenses its own members deemed dangerous to common safety. There was no reason the colonists should not be subject to this power, although it was far more efficient to try them in the king's courts at Halifax or even in London than to have a full dress impeachment and trial in Westminster. Still, a John Adams or Thomas Jefferson legally could be arrested, carried to England, and impeached by the same Commons that both men abused in print.[2] In this context, who among the Revolutionaries would wish to see impeachment privileges of the English type (of anyone, for any offense, with forfeiture and capital penalties upon conviction) lodged in American lower houses?

In addition, impeachment was linked by theory and practice with monarchical government. Impeachments, both colonial and English, were methods of bringing charges against men so close to the crown that indictment in the regular courts could not touch them. Without impeachment, only assassination or revolution could topple such men if the king wished them to remain in power. Both had been used in England, in addition to impeachment, as Benjamin Franklin facetiously remarked.[3] But there would be no kings in America—George Washington laid that ghost to rest—and aristocracy was barred by law. Mixed government would not rest on hereditary "orders" in society but on functional branches of government.[4] Without a king to shield wrongdoers in office, without an aristocracy to protect their own from public outcry, was there any need for impeachment?

Third, there was no guarantee that impeachment would work in American republics. The effectiveness of impeachment as a legal process (as opposed to a purely political act) depended upon the legal expertise and fairness in the House of Lords. The Lords had turned away all but a handful of the Commons' impeachments during the heyday of English impeachment, either preventing purely personal or political cases from coming to trial or dismissing the charges when no proof of wrongdoing emerged. With the Lords sat the most experienced and learned judges in the realm. This mixture of judicial and legislative functions in the House of Lords was not to be found in American upper houses. There would thus be no informal juridicial safeguards that a man prosecuted before an American council or senate would not be hounded to his death by his political enemies.

Finally, impeachment and trial inevitably mixed judicial and legislative functions of government, in violation of the principle of separation of powers. Parliament in England had great judicial powers because it emerged from the king's *curia regia*. In addition to impeachments, the House of Commons could exercise its own quasi-judicial powers to investigate the conduct of its own members, to attaint or punish men who had fled justice in the regular courts, and to create committees to oversee the execution of justice in the courts. The House of Lords was the highest appeals court in the realm and remained a court of first instance for peers accused of felonies. The Revolutionaries were not content with this mixing of functions. Multiple officeholding had left a bad odor in colonial government. Typically, Hutchinson's position as lieutenant governor, chief justice, and council member was not unique in the colonies and invited the anger of revolutionary leaders. Almost all the state constitutions forbade multiple officeholding, particularly offices in different branches of government. Trial of impeachments in upper houses seemed to violate this rule.[5]

In only one area of theory did impeachment fill a gap which "classical" republican thought left glaringly vacant. If the Revolutionaries believed conflict between virtue and corruption was inevitable in republics, there could be no guarantee that republican magistrates in America would escape the temptations that destroyed liberty in England. Human nature, not monarchy, was the root cause of decay. Whether one accepts the thesis that early American republican thought was based upon Florentine concepts of civic virtue, upon Lockean ideas of contract, or upon native legislative experience, the problem of the corruptibility of magistrates troubled the rebels. As John Adams wrote to Mercy Warren in April 1776, "Public Virtue cannot exist in a nation without private [virtue], and public Virtue is the only Foundation of Republics." Checks and balances, limited grants of power in fundamental constitutions, and bills of rights were partial solutions but none of them could save republicanism from the concerted attack of corrupt ministers of state. In England, impeachment in the Commons house had curbed the appetites of rapacious politicians, and, as we have noted, colonial impeachment advocates understood and applied the lesson: corruption and conspiracy to corrupt were also grounds for bringing charges. This powerful check upon personal interest in public officials would have as much use in a republic as it did in a monarchy.[6]

The experience of the first revolutionary congresses and committees of safety reinforced the teachings of theory: no government, however purely conceived, could escape the dangers of corruption, misuse of power, and outright criminality. In the last year before independence, cases of this sort had to be handled by the provincial assemblies or their designated agents because the royal courts no longer operated. Local committees of safety, working in conjunction with the assemblies, visited summary justice upon innocent and guilty, dissenter and criminal.[7] Typical was a case in the New

Jersey provincial assembly: on February 6, 1776, William Steele confessed to charges of Loyalist agitation. He paid the costs of his prosecution and put up £50 in colonial currency as a bond for his good behavior.[8] Acting as high courts, the assemblies monitored county judges' conduct: the Pennsylvania Convention, for example, directed the judicial functions of regular courts by legislative act. On September 25, 1776, the assembly ordered all justices of the peace to arrest and hold anyone whose speech or writing opposed the Revolution.[9] As the crisis led to open war, and then independence, legislatures reached for even more potent judicial weapons against their political enemies. In a few states, mass bills of attainder permanently excluded Loyalists from citizenship. The attainted were deprived of lands and goods by legislative fiat unless they came forward and swore allegiance to the new government. In Georgia a 1778 Act of Attainder convicted 119 individuals of "high treason," confiscated their lands, and warned them that "if" they came into the state they would be tried for treason. In a true attainder the bill replaced a trial and gave a judgment in the absence of the accused; this act was thus more a confiscation law than an attainder.[10] Individual bills of attainder were also passed. In Virginia, Josiah Phillips, a notorious Tory raider, was attainted, although when he was captured, the assembly permitted a regular criminal court to try him.[11]

Such sweeping assumptions of judicial power by assemblies might be expeditious but could not continue. Lower houses had other, more important business than hearing cases of petty crime on their merits. Wholesale condemnations of suspected traitors by legislative enactment denied individuals the procedural rights which, in quieter moments, the Revolutionaries wished to expand. Many of the state constitutions explicitly guaranteed the rights of trial by jury, defense counsel, and cross-examination to their citizens.[12] The judicial branches of the first state governments soon made inroads into the summary jurisdiction of the lower houses. Courts resumed regular operation in most of the new states during the war and gradually assumed control of the criminal prosecutorial functions of the government.[13]

Although the assemblies ceded their powers of prosecution of common crimes to the courts, the handling of wrongdoing within government remained a vexing question. The gradual increase in the volume and specificity of the criminal statutes might allow prosecution of officeholders in the ordinary courts, but the bulk of official malfeasance would never amount to criminal conduct. What then was to be done with those who misused their offices? At first, Revolutionaries had proposed that free, frequent, and regular election of all officers of government would solve the problem. They believed that the English system owed part of its corruption to the number and authority of nonelective officers in the realm, and the irregularity of election for Parliament. In Virginia the Revolutionaries hoped to avert this danger by "frequent, certain, and regular elections" in order that all officials, "at fixed periods, be reduced to a private station, return into that body from which they were originally taken." The drafters of the Pennsylvania Constitution were even more explicit about the connection between election and malfeasance, and promised that "those who are employed in the legislative and executive business of the State, may be restrained from oppression, the people have a right, at such periods as they may think proper, to reduce their public officers to a private station, and supply the vacancies by certain and regular elections."[14]

While the concept of electoral control of corruption was widely espoused, it had inherent shortcomings. There was no provision for curbing corruption or misuse of power between elections. While in cases of tampering with their own elections, the lower houses already had the power to refuse to seat disputed members, corruption and misuse of power in other branches might be so severe—so threatening to the existence of the new, weak republics—that they could not wait for the next election. A second problem arose when the electors refused to unseat a palpable wrongdoer. This was not inconceivable: he might have included them within his peculations, and corrupted his constituents. In the alternative he might have so cowed them by previous misuse of power that they dared not remove him. Finally, there were a few officials who did not hold office at the will of the people. The threat of electoral removal did not touch these incumbents.

The practical defects of reliance upon electoral removal of wrongdoers to one side, the revolutionary legislators and constitutionalists had already recognized that the lower houses must retain certain quasi-judicial powers. The right of the lower house to punish those who contemned their authority, and to investigate public affairs in general, conferred jurisdiction over the person of suspected offenders, whether or not regular court proceedings were instituted against the same person. In addition these assemblies assayed two other methods of removal. The assembly might dismiss, after hearings, any of its own appointees to lower government posts. This was regularly done in a number of the states, during and after the war.[15] Grounds for dismissal included all manner of misfeasance but did not imply guilt of any crime. Intention to subvert the public interest was not a required element of these charges, for they were administrative, rather than judicial, proceedings—firings rather than convictions. More formal charges might be brought in addresses to the governor seeking removal of an official. This practice derived from colonial precedent and was written into a number of state constitutions. For example, Maryland made removal by the governor, upon address of both houses of the legislative branch, an alternative to electoral removal and removal upon conviction of a felony in the regular courts.[16]

The drawbacks of this proceeding were two. First, the legislatures had to go hat-in-hand to the executive branch, the very same sort of dependence upon the royal governor, Privy Council, and crown that the colonial lower houses had resented. Even when the two houses determined to follow this course, the address did not have to allege willful or criminal misconduct. It needed only a favorable vote by both houses, not an investigation or trial. These addresses, therefore, did not establish motive, intent, or knowledge of supposed wrongdoing. For this reason, disqualification was not added as a penalty in the states that formally incorporated address as a form of removal.

Only impeachment and trial in the upper house demanded a full investigation, required trial, and allowed the suspect the rights of counsel, cross-examination, and subpoena. Only through impeachment and trial could a malfeasor be convicted of willful, knowing misconduct. This was the practical experience of colonial impeachment managers and led to the inclusion of impeachment in republican constitutions. The Revolutionaries were, above all, practical, and colonial experience with impeachment influenced state constitution writers. The connection between colonial precedents and state provisions is inferable from the pattern of state adoption. Among the states including impeachment in their first constitutional drafts, that is, Massachusetts, Pennsylvania, North Carolina, Virginia, New York, Vermont, New Jersey, and Delaware, all except New York had colonial cases or modeled their constitutions upon states with colonial precedents. Vermont, not one of the colonies, copied its constitution from Pennsylvania. Delaware and New Jersey were also influenced by Pennsylvania. Among those states not immediately including impeachment in their constitutions—Connecticut, Rhode Island, Georgia, South Carolina, New Hampshire, and Maryland—only South Carolina could claim eighteenth-century precedents, and South Carolina added provisions for impeachment in 1778. If prior experience with impeachment made no difference in its adoption one would expect no difference in the percentage of those colonies with and those without prior experience adopting impeachment. The difference between the random distribution and the actual distribution argues that colonial experience with impeachment was a factor influencing impeachment provisions in state constitutions.

One does not have to depend upon statistical relationships to trace the chief conduit for this influence. In terms of constitutional theory, impeachment could be retained as an extension of the legislative right to inquire into public wrongdoing, or discarded with attainder as a relic of parliamentary jurisprudence. Someone had to remind the revolutionary framers of the utility of impeachment. The earlier American cases did not speak for themselves, but they did find voice in the ubiquitous, insistent, and often brilliant garrulity of John Adams. Adams regarded himself as a tutor of the principles of government to his generation, and he rescued the first American impeachment precedent from oblivion. Though not familiar with the scope of impeachment in the colonies, he correctly transmitted the essence of that precedent.

He was enamored of an uncorrupted English constitution and believed that impeachment prevented corruption. He was well acquainted with impeachment practice from his role in the Oliver case. During the deliberations of Revolutionaries at the Second Continental Congress, he pronounced a republican blessing upon impeachment. His *Thoughts on Government*, widely circulated in April 1776, included this passage on public officials:

> For misbehaviour the grand inquest of the Colony, the House of Representatives, should impeach [officials] before the Governor and Council, where they should have time and opportunity to make their defence, but if convicted should be removed from their offices, and subjected to such other punishment as shall be thought proper.[17]

Adams's thoughts on impeachment spread to other provincial capitals. One can trace his direct influence in Virginia, the first state to include impeachment in its constitution. As early as November 1775, Adams shared his notions of representative government with Richard Henry Lee, one of Virginia's delegates to the Second Continental Congress.[18] Lee and George Wythe, another Virginia delegate, asked Adams to expand upon his views, an effort leading to publication of *Thoughts on Government*. Lee sent copies of the *Thoughts* to Williamsburg, where they circulated.[19] George Mason, the collator and drafter of the original Virginia Constitution, was influenced by Adams's work.[20] The twelfth article of Mason's first draft reflected this influence:

> Let the Governor, any of the Privy Counsellors, judges of the Supreme Court, and all other officers of government, for maladministration, or corruption, be prosecuted by the Lower House of Assembly. . . . If found guilty, let him, or them, be either removed from office, or forever disabled to hold any office under the government, or subjected to such pains or penalties as the laws shall direct.[21]

The language of Mason's work—including all officers and defining punishment (removal, disqualification, and "such pains or penalties as the laws shall direct")—was almost identical to the Adams's proposal.

Adams's suggestion also found its way into the thinking of Thomas Jefferson, albeit by a more circuitous route. Though Jefferson and Adams worked together on the Declaration of Independence, Jefferson did not rely on Adams's *Thoughts* in drafting a constitution for Virginia. Sometime before June 13, 1776, Jefferson set down an outline of government for Virginia. Although Mason's draft was already public and Jefferson had access to Adams's pamphlet—documents urging the incorporation of impeachment and trial procedures—Jefferson did not include impeachment in his original plan. In mid-June he prepared a clean copy of the draft, at which time he added a section on impeachment. The Virginia Assembly was already considering adoption of the Mason draft with impeachment in it; Jefferson probably followed their lead on this point. A clue to the fact that Jefferson did not assign the same importance to impeachment as had Adams and Mason lies in the way Jefferson added it to his draft. Instead of directly stating that the lower house had the power to impeach or, alternatively, that all officers of the new government could be impeached, Jefferson tacked impeachment onto the last words of a section he inserted on the composition and powers of the state supreme court. He specified that the supreme court was to have five members appointed by the lower house and tenured upon good behavior. They would determine appeals. Finally, in what reads as an afterthought, Jefferson added that the court would "try impeachments by Representatives."[22]

The Virginia draft provisions on impeachment differed from Adams's model in one significant respect: trial was not held in a council or upper house but before the supreme court. Adams favored a strong upper house to balance and check the excesses of the popular assembly. In Virginia the executive council was a shadow of Adams's proposal with few powers and little influence. The Virginia deviation from Adams's plan was thus a practical matter.

In more indirect fashion, Adams's ideas moved next door, to the Pennsylvania state convention. The first Pennsylvania Constitution made far more concessions to common people than Adams thought proper, and explicitly ignored his defense of bicameralism. The document was an experiment in popular government.[23] George Bryan, Arthur Young, and the other drafters reduced the council and the president of the state to an advisory capacity, leaving the initiative to a popularly elected house. Impeachment, an expression of the Commons' authority, complemented this experiment. Section 22 allowed the impeachment of "Every officer of the state," with trial before the "president or vice president and council."[24] This was Adams's language, particularly the stipulation for trial in the upper house. In impeachment trials, the state council had more power than in any of its otherwise very circumscribed activities.

Where did this clause originate? Pennsylvania had a colonial impeachment tradition which the leading radical spokesman, Bryan, tacitly recognized in his widely read *Genuine Principles of the Saxon, or English Constitution*. He wrote that the council "should take cognizance of high crimes; such as mal-administration of justices in their offices; being the proper inquest for this purpose" but continued that the governor and councillors themselves should be tried for misgovernment in the regular courts.[25] Pennsylvania's colonial impeachments were aimed at seated judges and a colonial secretary; Bryan's program reflected this experience. His exclusion of gover-

nors and councillors was dismissed by the convention in favor of impeachment of all officers, Adams's idea of impeachment. Adams's *Thoughts* circulated in the city of Philadelphia and may have been added to the
Pennsylvania document by one of the more moderate convention members—
Thomas McKean, for example, one of Adams's friends.

Adams had asserted that impeachment need not be surrendered by republican constitution makers; it could be made republican. The price of adoption
and incorporation was self-denial by the legislative branch. States had to
renounce the uninhibited power the Commons possessed in impeachments.
If American lower houses could impeach anyone, as the Commons could, for
any offense, as the Commons could, and ask any penalty upon conviction, as
the Commons could ask in the House of Lords, then the power of the state
assemblies would be very great indeed. Adams's restriction of impeachment
to those in office, for official misdeeds, limited the judicial power of the
assembly. Private persons' acts would be safe from prosecution in the lower
house. The regular courts' exclusive jurisdiction over common crimes was
preserved. That done, impeachment in the new republics would express not
the extension of the unchecked power of the lower house but balance between
the power of the lower house and the courts, an example of the limitation of
government so prized by the framers.

Under the impetus of revolutionary movement, deviations from British
practice forced upon colonial American impeachment managers by political
exigency—confinement of charges to officeholders, for offenses while in
office, with punishment limited to loss of office—had become essential
ingredients of a new impeachment procedure. This republican impeachment
law was then included in state constitutions. Under the English precedents
which guided colonial prosecutions, these deviations were accidents; under
republican impeachment law they would become the very heart and soul of
the process.

4

STATE CONSTITUTIONS AND
IMPEACHMENT LAW

THE TRANSFORMATION OF IMPEACHMENT FROM A CHECK AGAINST MONARCHICAL misdeeds to an instrument of republican government was first explored in state governments before 1787, and fully realized in the federal Constitution. Between 1776 and 1787, state politicians drafted and tested various provisions for impeachment. Delegates to the federal convention—Madison, Randolph, Paterson, Mason, and Hamilton—supported by the voices and votes of other knowledgeable state leaders, fashioned national impeachment provisions along lines laid down in the states' constitutions.[1]

Incorporation of impeachment into state constitutions proceeded swiftly. Pennsylvania, Vermont, New Jersey, Delaware, New York, North Carolina, Virginia, and Massachusetts included impeachment provisions in their first constitutions. Before the 1780s had ended, New Hampshire, South Carolina, and Georgia adopted impeachment. Alone among the original states, Connecticut, Rhode Island, and Maryland waited until the early nineteenth century to add impeachment to their laws.[2] From the first, all state constitutions rid impeachment of its unrepublican provisions. In Pennsylvania "every officer of state" could be impeached. No official was above impeachment, and the ordinary citizen was safe from it. The only impeachable offense Pennsylvania specified was "mal-administration," which implied that common and statutory law crimes were to be handled by the regular courts. Trial upon impeachments in Pennsylvania was delegated to the president and executive council, with the advice of the state supreme court. The nature of punishment was not indicated, except that the "punishments" for impeachment could be mitigated only by an act of the General Assembly.[3] Perhaps the use of the plural referred to removal from office and disqualification; perhaps it recalled the variety of punishments the House of Lords meted out in impeachment trials.

Vermont adopted the Pennsylvania provisions word for word, including an innovation seen nowhere else in Anglo-American law. Pennsylvania and

Vermont created "Councils of Censors," special bodies which would meet at multiyear intervals to "inquire" into the propriety of taxation, disbursement of public monies, execution of the laws, and possible revision of the constitution itself.[4] In addition these councils had the power "to order impeachments."[5] The Council of Censors could subpoena papers, persons, and evidence, all of which presumably was turned over to the assembly when the censors directed an impeachment. It is not clear whether the assembly had to vote on the impeachments or merely prosecute them. In Pennsylvania the censors met only once and had no impeachments on their agenda. In 1785, the Vermont censors ordered the assembly to prepare and prosecute an impeachment against Matthew Lyon, but the case came to naught.[6]

Other states' original constitutions defined impeachable offenses and provided for trial in a manner consistent with republican tenets rather than English precedent. The 1776 New Jersey Constitution permitted impeachment of judges and other officers for "misbehavior." Trial for these cases was held before the executive council.[7] The council had the option of finding the accused guilty but declaring that the offenses did not warrant removal from office. This form of mitigation, finding the facts true but insufficient under the law to punish the suspect, was used in four New Jersey cases.[8] In Delaware's first revolutionary compact, the state president and other officers "offending against the state by maladministration, corruption, or other means, by which the safety of the commonwealth may be endangered" could be impeached within eighteen months of leaving office.[9] Obviously the penalty for conviction in cases prosecuted after the suspect left office was disqualification. Conviction of an official in common-law courts during tenure of office could also lead to immediate removal. The Delaware provisions were the first to spell out specific categories of impeachable offenses. As in the vaguer formulas in Pennsylvania and New Jersey, the crucial element for an impeachable offense, as opposed to a common crime, was danger to the public good.[10]

Pennsylvania, Vermont, Delaware, and New Jersey followed Adams's rule in placing the trial of impeachments in the upper house of the legislature. In the first three of these states, the councils were quite weak and, perhaps for this reason, the constitution makers did not fear abuse of the power to try to punish impeached officers. The authors of the New York, North Carolina, and Virginia constitutions conformed impeachment laws to republican theory but created unique arrangements for trial. In New York's fundamental laws, impeachment lay against all officers for "mal and corrupt conduct" in office.[11] Counsel was explicitly permitted, a step taken sixty years before in England. Impeachment required a two-thirds vote, an impediment to hasty action. In provision for trial, the framers placed a second bulwark against the misuse of legislative jurisprudence: a special court for hearing impeachments which consisted of the president of the senate, the senators, the chancellor, and the supreme court bench.[12] The new court satisfied the doctrine of separation of powers, since it was separate from the senate. The creation of the new court also guaranteed the participation of learned judges in impeachment trials. The compromise was far from ideal, however, because two branches of the government, the legislature and the judiciary, were mixed.

North Carolina's constitutional framers identified impeachment as a fundamental right, bracketing it with grand jury presentments.[13] In North Carolina, impeachment did not arise from the powers of a branch of government but from the more basic right of the people to be protected from evil or corrupt officers. Accordingly, section 23 of the 1776 North Carolina Constitution provided for impeachment of any official violating any part of the constitution, for corruption and maladministration. While these provisions were quickly settled, procedure for impeachment trials was debated in four consecutive sessions of the North Carolina lower house. At the end of these debates, representative William Blount proposed that the state supreme court try impeachments at its regular session in the district where the offense occurred, with the verdict given by a local jury. When a judge was impeached, the governor, the speakers of the house of representatives and senate, and three lawyers would preside. Blount's proposal, his part in an effort to impeach the superior court judges, failed passage, though its provision for lawyers sitting in judgment on the highest judges remains unprecedented in Anglo-American law.[14]

In Virginia, too, the right to impeach was readily conceded but the manner of trial was disputed. Mason's draft limited impeachments to officeholders suspected of maladministration or corruption: offenses against the office or public trust, not common-law crimes. Trial was to be held in the supreme court.[15] The final version of the constitution made the governor (when out of office) and others "offending against the state, either by Mal-administration, Corruption, or other means, by which the safety of the State may be endangered" impeachable in the House of Delegates, with trial in the general (supreme) court.[16] A vagueness had crept into the definition of who might be impeached between Mason's first draft and the approval of the constitution. The "others" might be ex-officers or even private citizens, an idea that originated with Jefferson. His draft had arrived in Williamsburg before last revision of the constitution and was influential in the final debates.[17] Jefferson proposed that the court of appeals try impeachments of "high offenders" lodged "by the House of representatives for such crimes as shall hereafter be precisely defined by the Legislature, and for the punishment of which the said Legislature shall have previously prescribed certain and determined pains."[18] Whereas offenses would be precisely delineated, defendants were simply "high offenders"—a category which might include anyone.

Jefferson's loose terminology was influenced by Virginia's wartime experience. The new republic was constantly in danger from within as well as from without. The very necessities which herded lower houses such as Virginia's into the adjudication of criminal causes blurred the lines of this jurisdiction. The boundary between cases heard as impeachment and cases heard under general, unwritten assumptions of judicial power in emergencies was never clear so long as the war raged. In 1778 the lower house moved to extend the peacekeeping powers of the governor, allowing him to remove any justice of the peace after investigating the charges against the justice and consulting with the council. In 1783 the council explicitly rejected its commission as a star chamber and found the summary removal power unconstitutional. Governor Benjamin Harrison concurred, but the passage of the act showed the grave anxiety of the lower house about "misconduct" of all types, anxiety which Jefferson betrayed in his groping formula for impeachment liability.[19]

Jefferson tried to be too precise on the place of trial of impeachments. To be sure, he was not alone in his concern for the proper tribunal. The question of where to try impeached judges evidently embarrassed a number of Virginia's leaders. If trial were in the highest court, judges accused of impeachable offenses would be tried by their brethren on the bench. There was no question of exempting judges from impeachment, quite the reverse; the problem was to find an impartial tribunal. Unlike the constitutions of Pennsylvania and New York, which merely made "all officers, executive and judicial" impeachable, Virginia fundamental law spelled out the liability of judges in a wholly separate clause: "If all or any of the Judges of the General Court [the supreme court of the state] should on good grounds, (to be judged by the House of Delegates) be accused of any of the crimes or offenses abovementioned, such House of Delegates may, in like manner, impeach the Judge or Judges so accused, to be prosecuted in the Court of Appeals. . . ."[20] While the delegates satisfied themselves with this statement of good intentions, Jefferson was not impressed. He wanted special arrangements to ensure that impeachment trials would be above collusion between the defendant and his judges. In 1783 he included a revision of impeachment trial procedure among his general proposals for constitutional reforms.[21] His impeachment court was to be a blend of all branches and bodies of state government, an insurance against hasty decisions and partisan convictions:

There shall moreover be a court of IMPEACHMENTS to consist of three members of the Council of state, one of each of the Superior courts of Chancery, Common law, and Admiralty, two members of the House of Delegates and one of the Senate, to be chosen by the body respectively of which they are. Before this court any member of the three branches of government, that is to say, the Governor, any member of the Council, of the two houses of legislature or of the Superior courts may be impeached by the Governor the Council, or either of the said houses or courts for such misbehavior in office as would be sufficient to remove him therefrom: and the only sentence they shall have authority to pass shall be that of deprivation and future incapacity of office. Seven members shall be requisite to make a court and two thirds of those present must concur in the sentence.[22]

Jefferson, a trained lawyer and passionate rationalist, recognized the inherent difficulties in trials on impeachments: trial in the upper house violated strict republican separation of powers; trial in the lower courts was subject to the vagaries of politics; trial in the highest court was open to collusion when the defendants were supreme court judges. Jefferson's solution blended logic and arithmetic. Each of the three branches was to be represented in a special court of impeachments, under a numerical formula so complex that even Jefferson's facile pen faltered in the effort to describe its composition. In theory, the numerical design checked the influence of any one branch and ensured that defendants were not tried solely by co-workers. To counter the additional privilege he had given the lower house by permitting it to have a part in the trials, Jefferson proposed that the governor, council, and even the superior courts could bring impeachments, a step which has no precedent whatsoever in impeachment law. The prospect would have unglued any government, though it fit, in extreme form, the republican injunction to check and restrain power at every turn. One wonders if Jefferson did not intend to hamstring impeachment by the scheme. To protect the defendant whose office hung in the balance, Jefferson required that the special court could convict only upon a two-thirds vote. Massachusetts and New York already required two-thirds margins for conviction. The two-thirds requirement made conviction more difficult and did not fit the republican preference for majority decisions. Although Jefferson's addition of this rule seems prescient in the light of the federal provisions four years later, it cannot be explained in the same way as his tripartite court of impeachments. The latter was a literal exercise in republican theory, while the two-thirds rule was an aberration. There is an explanation which does fit both parts of Jefferson's plan. After his own disturbing brush with impeachment as governor in 1781, Jefferson grew to dislike the ease with which it could be brought and the simple majority with which the defendant could be convicted. Perhaps, he may have reasoned, if the governor himself could bring impeachments, the legislature's appetite for impeachment might be curbed. The two-thirds rule made any conviction harder, his other objective.[23]

Jefferson's plan was never approved—its sheer complexity would have discouraged the most determined impeachment managers—and the problem of what to do with the erring judges remained. Legislators could unseat one of their own without using impeachment. Executive officeholders could be tried upon impeachment in either the upper house or the courts without causing special problems. Complicating the thorny problem of trial of judges was the fact that judges, unlike legislators and executives, generally were not elected officials. The independence of judges was an exception to republican electoral theory, which theoretically permitted them to rise above demagogic clamor and partisan movements.[24] In the struggle to obtain tenure during good behavior, instead of at the pleasure of the governor or legislature, advocates of judicial independence conceded that incompetent and malicious judges could be impeached. But the practical questions of how to try judges on impeachment was not easily answered and controversy over this flowed into the assault upon Justices Pickering and Chase. In the heat of impeachment of the former, Jefferson told Senator William Plumer, Pickering's ally: "This business of removing Judges by impeachment is a *bungling way*."[25]

The controversy over impeachment trials in the state did not close with Jefferson's suggested revisions to the Mason plan. James Madison made his contribution to the debate in 1788. By his sponsorship of the federal Constitution a year earlier, Madison almost stood equal in reputation to the drafter of the Declaration of Independence. John Brown of Kentucky thus sought Madison's opinion of Jefferson's program for trial.[26] Madison replied that Jefferson's impeachment proposals invited a republican version of Thomas Hobbes's war of each against all. Always frank in his criticism, he did note that Jefferson wrestled a tenacious opponent:

A Court of Impeachments is among the most puzzling articles of a republican Constitution; and it is far more easy to point out defects in any plan, than to supply a cure for them. The diversified expedients adopted in the Constitutions of the several States prove how much the compilers were embarrassed on this subject. The plan [Jefferson's] here proposed varies from all of them; and is perhaps not less than any a proof of the difficulties which pressed the ingenuity of its author. The remarks arising on it are 1: that it seems not to square with reason, that the right to impeach should be united to that of trying the impeachment & consequently in a proportional degree, to that of sharing in the appointment of, or influence on the Tribunal to which the trial may belong. 2: As the Executive & Judiciary would form a majority of the Court, and [if] either have a right to impeach, too much might depend on a combination of these departments. This objection would be still stronger, if the members of the Assembly were capable as proposed of holding offices, and were amenable in that capacity to the Court. 3: The H. of Delegates and either of those departments could appt. a majority of the Court. Here is another danger of combination, and the more to be apprehended as that branch of the Legisl: wd. also have the right to impeach, a right in their hands of itself sufficiently weighty; and as the power of the Court wd. extend to the head of the Ex. by whose independence the constituti'l. rights of that department are to be secured agst. Legislative usurpations. 4: The dangers in the two last cases would be still more formidable; as the power extends not only to deprivation; but to future incapacity of office.[27]

To Madison's thinking, Jefferson's plan would have encouraged all the corruption and collusion both men sought to avoid.

All these qualms about Jefferson's effort might have led another man to abandon impeachment altogether because no impartial trial court could be found. Madison was as much a perfectionist in his republicanism as Jefferson, but the practical and personal circumstances surrounding each man's contribution were different. Madison had repeatedly committed himself to support of impeachment in the state and federal governments. Indeed, he thought that impeachment was a necessary part of republicanism, whereas Jefferson, from the omission of impeachment in his first draft of a Virginia constitution through his own nasty near impeachment, had no such commitment. Madison wanted to make impeachment trial into a truly judicial process, not hobble it with restrictions. In 1785 he proposed to the Virginia House of Delegates that the procedure for impeachment trial conform to courtroom practice:

> Be it enacted by the General Assembly, that the process against any person impeached by resolution of the House of Delegates shall be summons, attachments and distress, bearing teste, the first of them the day of emanation, and the others the return-day of the process preceeding, and shall be issued and signed by the clerk of the said court. A copy of the articles of impeachment shall be delivered to the party accused, whensoever he shall require it, and the court shall from time to time make such rules for compelling him to answer and bringing the matter to issue speedily as to them shall seem reasonable; and every fact so put in issue shall be tried by a jury.[28]

The jury Madison mentioned would be empaneled by the supreme court at the trial of the impeachment, a last guarantee that defendants would have all the rights of anyone brought to trial in the regular courts.

It was thus with the best of intentions that Madison, avoiding Jefferson's mistakes, offered Brown another version of a court of impeachments:

> The 2 great desiderata in a Court of impeachts. are 1. impartiality 2. respectability—the first in order to a right—the second in order to a

satisfactory decision. These characteristics are arrived at in the following modification—Let the Senate be denied the right to impeach. Let 1/3 of the members be struck out, by alternate nominations of the prosecutors and party impeached; the remaining 2/3 to be the *Stamen* of the Court. When the H: of Del: impeach, let the Judges or a certain proportion of them—and the Council of State be associated in the trial. When the Govr. or Council impeaches, let the Judges only be associated. But if the party impeached by the H. of Dels. be a member of the Ex. or Judicy, let that of which he is a member not be associated. If the party impeached belong to one & be impeached by the other of these branches, let neither of them be associated, the decision being in this case left with the Senate alone or if that be thought exceptionable, a few members might be added by the H. of Ds. 2/3 of the Court should in all cases be necessary to a conviction, & the chief Magistrate *at least* should be exempt from a sentence of perpetual if not of temporary incapacity. It is extremely probable that a critical discussion of this outline may discover objections which do not occur. Some do occur; but appear not to be greater than are incident to any different modification of the Tribunal.[29]

Madison himself admitted that his own plan was far from perfect. Free of Jefferson's novel views on impeachment, Madison still could not evade the complexity of Jefferson's proposed court. Madison, wanting to please everyone with this court, changed arrangements in midsentence if anyone took "exception" to his arguments. Buried in the plan were the federal provisions of 1787—trial in the Senate and two-thirds margin for conviction—to which Madison had objected in Philadelphia, but added here for completeness. Faced with these tangled questions, he limited himself to a disinterested intellectual survey. One must remember that the year was 1788, and Madison did not wish to say anything that might slow ratification of the federal Constitution.

In Massachusetts, as in Virginia, the constitutional debates showed a commitment to impeachment coupled with genuine disagreement over the provision for trials. Massachusetts' draft constitution of 1778 provided for impeachment in the lower house, the "Grand Inquest" (Adams's term) of the commonwealth.[30] The republican stipulations for impeachment in the other states—limitation to officeholders for crimes done in office against public trust and official duties, with loss of and disqualification for office the only penalties—were reiterated in the 1778 draft. As Adams had planned, the court for trial was to be the governor and senate. A two-thirds vote was required for conviction.[31] This trial procedure was objected to by a number of the towns. Theophilus Parsons, writing for Newburyport, reported its resolve "that the 20th [impeachment trial] article is exceptionable because the supreme executive officer hath a voice, and must be present in that court."[32] The governor and the senate appointed state officials; it would be unrepublican for governor and senate to sit as a court for the removal of the same officials. From other towns came more general objections: impeachment permitted double jeopardy, denied the right of jury trial, and would become a political tool.[33] The revisers of the constitution answered Parsons' and others' rebukes simply by taking the appointment of state officials away from the senate and giving it to the governor, and then removing the governor from the trial court.[34] One suspects that the motive behind this solution extended beyond the question of conflict of interest in impeachment trials. Advocates of increased executive power in Massachusetts sought to give more responsibility and independence of action to the governors, including appointment of lesser officials. The reform of impeachment provisions was a fortuitous opportunity to promote their larger plan.[35]

The constitution adopted in 1780 defined impeachable offenses as misconduct and maladministration, eschewing mention of "crimes" or "misdemeanors."[36] A motion to extend impeachment to others than officeholders was defeated.[37] The two avenues by which the House of Commons approached unchecked jurisdiction in impeachment—the vast range of offenses which fell under its purview and the unrestricted pool from which it could draw suspects—were eliminated in the Massachusetts Constitution.

The formative period of adaptation of forms for impeachment and trial was drawing to a close. Impeachment increasingly wore republican garb. The draft New Hampshire Constitution of 1778 did not mention impeachment, but the version accepted in 1781 provided for trial of impeachments in the senate. All officers were impeachable for misconduct or maladministration.[38] Penalties were not to extend beyond loss of and disqualification for office. The words and timing of this draft owed themselves to the ratification of Massachusetts' Constitution the previous year. The New Hampshire lower house, like the Massachusetts assembly, styled itself "the Grand Inquest." Although the 1776 South Carolina Constitution made no provision for impeachment, the constitutional revision of 1778 included impeachment for all officers of the state suspected of "mal and corrupt conduct."[39] The senate would hear and determine charges pressed by the house.[40]

In the rush to adopt impeachment provisions, state constitutional framers stumbled momentarily over the contradiction between legislative trials and separation of powers. Jefferson and Madison in Virginia, Hamilton in New York, and Blount in North Carolina all argued that if no person should be a judge in his own cause, no legislature should hear cases against its own appointees. A partial solution was to remove from the senate the power to appoint officers, as Massachusetts did in 1780. Nevertheless, the stubborn problem of legislative judicature remained. Some way had to be found to legitimize the trial of impeachments. If impeachments could not be tried (the dilemma faced by the colony of Massachusetts in the Peter Oliver case), the effectiveness of impeachment—the threat of removal upon trial—would vanish. Trial in the upper house was the most common resolution of this dilemma, but such trials violated the doctrine of a strict separation of the functions of the legislative and judicial branches of government. This objection was answered though not overcome by the institution of trial court procedures at upper house impeachment hearings. Criminal process was introduced into the senate hearings to counter the charge of mixing legislative and judicial powers and to protect the rights of the accused. When state senates and councils sat to hear the trial of impeachments, they became, temporarily, courts of law. The speaker of the senate or the chief justice presided. The defendant had counsel as did the managers for the lower house, both of whom could subpoena witnesses and evidence to support their case. The senators or councillors swore to give judgment under the law, the same kind of oath that English and American judges took upon assuming their places on the bench. Madison's recommended revision of the Virginia Constitution spelled out these procedural rights; elsewhere they were adopted piecemeal.

Yet was it not true that the introduction of judicial proceedings into the regular business of an elected legislative body proved beyond any doubt that trial in the senate violated separation of powers? The fact that the upper house followed some regular court procedure could only intensify theoretical objections to trial of impeachments there. If there was no safe course around this obstacle, the passage of time revealed a practical reason for assigning trial to the senate or council. In states that provided for special impeachment courts combining superior court benches, upper houses, and executive officeholders, no cases were brought to trial; New York, Virginia, and North Carolina had none. Beyond the Confederation period, to the end of the eighteenth century, this relationship held: where special courts were created, no trials occurred. Those states with trial in the upper house saw many cases go to trial. From 1776 to 1805 New Jersey had nine trials, Vermont six, Massachusetts and Pennsylvania four apiece, South Carolina and Kentucky three each, Tennessee two (involving the same defendant), and Georgia one. Trial in the upper house was undoubtedly practical.

Experience with the new state laws tutored the Revolutionaries in the practical arts of bringing official misconduct to brook. The temptation to go beyond the letter of their own laws, to use impeachment and trial to harass opponents, was inevitable. Even without the distraction of partisan motives, each new case presented the lower houses with problems of interpretation and application of the law. The other side of the constitutional language thus was the case law, to which we must now turn.

5

IMPEACHMENT AND TRIAL
IN THE STATES

THE INCORPORATION OF IMPEACHMENT AND TRIAL PROVED IMMEDIATELY practical. Impeachment enabled new and unstable state governments to ferret out and punish fiscal misconduct, particularly mismanagement of public funds, bribery, fraud, extortion, and other forms of unethicality not covered by statute. Impeachment allowed state legislators to demonstrate publicly their commitment to honest government and their aversion to the corruption from which the Americans had rebelled. Such occasions were visible—sometimes overcrowded—proof of popular interest in seeing justice done.[1] Impeachment proceedings curbed officials who misused their power by bullying private citizens, disobeying their superiors, and encroaching upon the legal duties of other officers. Local incumbents who sponsored extralegal groups or led mobs, common activities in this era of revolution, and were immune to correction in local courts, were vulnerable to impeachment at the state capital. The threat of impeachment also hung above deliberately sloppy, incompetent, and inattentive officials. Finally, and perhaps most important, the availability of impeachment meant that the people did not have to take their complaints against officeholders into the streets. There was a well-tried, legal method for hearing, indictment, and trial of complaints against officials no matter how highly placed.

There was certainly potential for partisan misuse of impeachment—on occasion complaints were solicited by political opponents of the defendant; some investigations had a personal edge; the timing of some prosecutions was dictated by electoral considerations—but purely political impeachments did not succeed in this era. Membership in a minority party, nonviolent public opposition to the government, and unpopularity were not grounds for removal. Instead, conviction upon trial required that the impeachment managers establish the elements of *mens rea* (the guilty mind), actual causation of the offense, and damage of some kind to persons or the state itself. The offense need not be a crime, but the elements of evil intention, causation, and *actus reus* were drawn from the criminal law.[2]

Among these elements, the purpose of the official was thorniest. Did he seek some illegal or improper advantage, or to wrong another individual? Was malice the motive for irregular conduct? The formulas to answer these questions were drawn from cases in the regular courts involving justices of the peace and other officials. The central court judges had to draw some line between the authority and discretion a magistrate had to have and their misuse. As South Carolina Supreme Court Justice John F. Grimké (himself later impeached for overstepping this boundary) wrote in *Lining v. Bentham* (1796), if magistrates, "under color of office, should injure or oppress their fellow citizens, they were liable to be punished in a criminal court for their misconduct." Fining or jailing abusive litigants for contempt, determining bail, and taking other steps to keep the peace or keep order in a court, were privileged actions by justices. The state presumed they acted without wrongful intention unless proof of such a motive could be added to evidence of irregular conduct. In *Lining*, Charleston justice James Bentham acted "in his judicial capacity," and though he may have erred, he did not use his office to knowingly or purposely wrong a litigant.[3] In 1802 the South Carolina Supreme Court bench upheld the magistrates' privilege to fine or jail contemners, except where "corrupt or oppressive" motives were established. And if the conduct was correct on its face, there was never ground for any charge at all.[4] None of this prevented a litigant from bringing a civil suit against an official, for the official might wrong a citizen by negligence or recklessness without knowing or intending to violate the law or public trust. Such tortious misconduct was heard in superior courts but was not regarded by the assembly as sufficient grounds for impeachment.[5]

Bribery, extortion, and misuse of funds were the most common and easily proved impeachable offenses, for the Revolutionary War provided many opportunities for official corruption. In New Jersey, for example, the auction of Loyalists' holdings and the award of supply contracts for the army invited official corruption. A number of local judges dug their thumbs into the pie. On November 24, 1778, a committee of the New Jersey Assembly reported articles of impeachment against Thomas Denny, a justice of the peace for Glouster County. Denny had violated the price ceilings set by the assembly by overcharging his customers for scarce commodities, encouraged his friends to do likewise, and failed to prosecute others for this offense. Finally, he gave bail to a man who had taken the king's oath and freed two others accused of felony. The assembly voted the impeachment, and on December 4 of that year the council tried, convicted, and removed him from office.[6] In 1782 there were six more impeachments in New Jersey. Among the six, David Banks, Robert Wade, and John Peck, Essex magistrates, were accused of writing passes for illegal goods, illegally confiscating land, and failing to give the state treasury its portion of the revenues. The assembly found Banks impeachable upon the second offense and Wade upon the first. Peck was not prosecuted. The lower house then decided that, despite Banks's complicity, his case should be dropped as well. Wade was tried in the council for "malpractice" in office. He had condemned and sold goods from a captured ship, contrary to the 1782 New Jersey Admiralty Act, and then sold the goods under his own order for his own profit. The council found him guilty and dismissed him from office.[7]

Denny and Wade were the only New Jersey judges removed from office for corruption though a dozen were investigated for it. The lower house placed restrictions upon its own inquiries to ensure that impeachment for corruption followed republican precepts. Officials were liable to impeachments for extortion, bribery, misuse of funds, and partiality in fiscal judgments in their "official capacity" only.[8] What they did in their personal finances was the concern of the regular courts. The intention to defraud the state had to be established before the lower house would seek trial and removal from office. Many complaints were made by members of the legislature, private petitioners, and individual complainants, but the assembly impeached only for willful corruption.

In Vermont, another state to emerge from the Revolutionary War against Great Britain (though not a member of the Confederation), the state legislature also faced cases of officials' financial misconduct. On June 28, 1781, information reached the lower house that assemblyman John Abbot had exchanged state scrip for hard money at one-quarter of the statutory rate. Abbot confessed to speculating on the money market, naming fellow assemblyman Daniel Martin as his partner. Representative Matthew Lyon, himself later impeached for abuse of his office, drew up articles of impeachment which the assembly passed. The lower house then decided not to send its two errant members for trial in the council but admonished Abbot and expelled Martin. The two men then returned to the chamber and a chastened Martin made public recantation, "evidenced signs of sorrow and repentence." His colleagues voted to reseat him.[9] English parliamentary usage, made explicit in the Vermont Constitution, allowed the assembly to discipline its own members. Impeachments were also used to deal with erring state legislators.

The Vermont lower house was not finished with corrupt officeholders. In October 1783 its members impeached John Barret, a Windsor County justice of the peace. Four charges were brought against the county judge: he prejudicially and unjustly gave judgment for his friend Caleb Shaw in Shaw's suit against Ozemas Holmes; he harassed Asahel Powers in court when Powers had already signified his compliance with the court's orders; he delayed judgment on a suit by Richard Prouty for three years; and he "excited and encouraged many needless and vexacious Law suits to enhance [his] bill of

Costs to the oppression of the People." Pending trial, the assembly ordered him removed from office. Barret refused to step down before conviction, and on October 21, 1784, petitioned that he might be permitted to continue serving in office until his trial. Three days later a committee of the house reported that Barret had never been tried or even notified of the proceedings against him. Indeed, the affair had disarrayed the county court, where cases were heard for a year by a man who may or may not have been legally in office. The council ordered Barret reinstated as a justice; he had not yet been found guilty and was therefore not liable to punishment until convicted before the council. On June 18, 1785, the assembly finally prosecuted Barret in the council. After two separate hearings in the summer and fall of 1785, Barret was removed from office for six months.[10]

A more serious case of fiscal mismanagement arose in wartime Pennsylvania. Francis Hopkinson, a leader of the revolutionary party, chief judge of the admiralty court, and signer of the Declaration of Independence, was accused of receiving presents from litigants in prize cases. The war between American privateers and British cargo ships was as hotly contested in the admiralty courts as on the high seas, and judges like Hopkinson, according to his own collection of cases, had a great deal of latitude in determining the facts and applying the law.[11] Hopkinson, however, went too far, supposedly ordering the cargoes of prize ships sold before condemnation and then marketing the ships themselves without due notice. The impeachment inquiry began on November 22, 1780. James Wilson and Jared Ingersoll, Jr., influential members of the Philadelphia bar, defended Hopkinson. The managers for the lower house secured the assistance of attorney James Smith, another signer of the Declaration of Independence, and William Bradford, the attorney general. It was to be an all-star show.

Shown the charges and evidence, Hopkinson blamed Matthew Clarkson, state marshal, for ignoring orders from the admiralty court and fomenting disturbances in admiralty business. Clarkson, who in fact had brought the impeachment petition to the assembly, replied that Hopkinson's appetite for plunder was insatiable. More moderate witnesses agreed that Hopkinson and Clarkson did not get along and had disagreed on the distribution of patronage. Both were avid partisans. On December 8, 1780, the lower house, by a vote of 39 to 18, impeached Hopkinson for receiving a cask of wine in return for a favorable decision on the prize brig *Charlotte*. The assembly also found him guilty (47 to 10) for selling the *Charlotte* before it was legally condemned. Hopkinson was also charged, based on Clarkson's testimony, with reneging on a promise to appoint Blair McClenahan agent for the Charlotte sale. McClenahan, a close friend of Clarkson, supposedly lost Hopkinson's support because McClenahan failed to give the judge a new suit of clothes.

Shortly before the case went to the council for trial, Jonathan D. Sargent deposed that Hopkinson had charged double fees for each prize case in his court, a form of extortion. This became a fourth impeachment article.[12]

Hopkinson retorted that McClenahan was a rude and uncooperative man who was never promised anything in the admiralty court. The judge admitted that he had ordered the load of the *Charlotte* sold before the prize hearing, but only because its cargo of salt was needed in the city and would spoil if left on the ship. He was trying to do everyone a favor, particularly Robert Morris, whose privateer had captured the *Charlotte* at sea. Hopkinson admitted the error of selling the *Charlotte*'s cargo before condemnation. His intention, he pleaded, was not to help his friends or himself. Hopkinson last informed the councillors that it was the marshal's job to draw up bills of costs; if there was corruption it was Clarkson's. For his own part, he had mistakenly followed an outdated fee schedule. From his sickbed, Morris deposed that Hopkinson was an upright and honest man and that Clarkson sought Hopkinson's removal only because Hopkinson had already complained to the council about Clarkson's factiousness. The council rendered its decision on December 26. In a departure from the usual form of these judgments, the council handed down a legal opinion as well as its verdict. It found Hopkinson not guilty on the charge of accepting presents for cases because there was no evidence he solicited or expected a reward for his judgment. If there had been "any hint" of a bargain, "we would have been at no loss to have declared him guilty." On the second charge, without evidence of "wilfully wrong" conduct in selling the *Charlotte*, the council decided that there were no grounds on which to find him guilty. For overcharging litigants the statutory penalty was loss of office and prosecution "in a criminal way" in the regular courts of justice, but the council merely admonished Hopkinson, saying that he should have monitored the registrar of the court. Redress for excess fees could be obtained in the regular courts. Hopkinson was acquitted on all counts.[13]

The last portion of the council opinion in Hopkinson's case raised a question common to all prosecutions for corruption: why were they not taken up by the regular courts? Local judges might have been overawed by their superiors standing in the dock, and local juries may have been swayed by the influence of the accused in the county, but this potential always existed when men of substance stood accused of crimes. More to the point, some of these cases of extortion and corruption fell at the edge of illegality; they were not named in statute, or the participants' intention to commit a crime could not be established under the tests required in a regular criminal court. Finally, some judges were tried in the regular courts for corruption. In 1783 the Virginia Assembly decided not to impeach justice of the peace John Price Posey, whereupon he was prosecuted in the General Court for misappropriating funds that he administered for the estate of John Parke Curtis. When the governor turned down the request of the lower house to remove Posey, the council urged prosecution in the regular courts. There Posey was found guilty of "gross misdemeanors" and fined £200. In a separate proceeding he was removed from office a year and a half later.[14]

Cases of misuse of power by officials were also difficult for local courts to handle. The offense might not appear in the criminal codes. All the same, misuse of power undermined the legitimacy of state government and impeachment effectively redressed such misconduct. When officials played both sides of the revolutionary street—acting under commissions from revolutionary legislatures while bargaining with or aiding the king's forces—they were impeachable. One of the charges the New Jersey Assembly leveled against William Clayton was that he "favored persons disaffected to the present government."[15] On November 25, 1779, William Miller, a justice in Salem County, New Jersey, was unanimously impeached for speaking "seditious words, and telling people to lay down their arms."[16] Clayton's and Miller's impeachments were not merely political cases. A petition from William Shute and others informed the assembly that Miller was indicted at a December 1778 circuit court for "disaffection" to the revolutionary cause. Grand jurors in his own county did not trust him.[17] The revolutionary government of New Jersey could not survive if its officials openly supported the claims of the enemy. Clayton was convicted but the council found that his offense did not merit removal. Miller was removed from office.[18] Misuse of power might take a less dramatic course, for example, Jersey justice Peter Hopkins's browbeating of coroners and witnesses. Hopkins was impeached and removed.[19] The New Jersey Assembly also cautioned Knolton town constable Benjamin Fordenir to cease bullying his neighbors in the course of his duties.[20]

A more serious abuse of power occurred when an officer willfully disobeyed the legal commands of other branches of government. On October 15, 1785, the Vermont Council of Censors asked the lower house to impeach Matthew Lyon, clerk of the western part of the state and a powerful party leader, for refusing to give the censors documents on the confiscation of Loyalist property. Lyon had come to New England as a boy, served an apprenticeship to a merchant in Connecticut, and propelled himself into politics. He won friends among the Green Mountain boys. By the end of the war, he was Ira Allen's associate, a defender of the interests of small landholders against more conservative planters (and their ex-Loyalist friends). This placed him in the camp of the northwestern settlers: anti-lawyer, anti-Federalist, and later Republican in spirit. Unfortunately for Lyon, the eastern faction controlled the assembly, and Nathaniel Chipman, Isaac Tichenor, and Lewis R. Morris, the "aristos" Lyon challenged, held sway in the state. This did not stop Lyon and his allies, particularly Governor Thomas

Chittenden, from harassing Tichenor, which led, in turn, to Lyon's own impeachment. Lyon was a messy administrator, losing papers and failing to transcribe records, and his refusal to admit as much to the assembly gave his enemies in it leverage against him. Lyon thought little of their summons to him to account for missing paper work, but when he stepped from the assembly hall, his prosecutors were named, and an impeachment was voted. Trial followed, at which he was fined the cost of the prosecution and removed from office. The fine was a financial burden placed on the defendant in English and colonial criminal law even when he or she was found not guilty; it was not a punishment. Shortly after his conviction, Lyon reappeared and obtained a new trial, at which he turned over the books and the lower house dropped its charges. Perhaps Lyon convinced his prosecutors that the papers were too explosive to be produced as evidence. Or the affair may have been intended from the start as a censure of Lyon's high-handedness, excitability, and partisanship—traits he would soon bring to the national scene.[21]

An especially frightening misuse of power was officeholders' unauthorized leadership of extralegal associations. Justices of the peace who led mobs to remedy vague injustices or instructed vigilantes in midnight retribution were embracing the dark side of revolutionary methods. Such conduct dismayed republican leaders.[22] Impeachment upheld the central authority of state government against the momentary passions of localities without sacrificing the ideals of revolutionary liberty. When David Forman, a justice of the peace from the New Jersey county of Monmouth, abetted the "Associators'" illegal confiscation of private property, he was forced to answer for his conduct in the state lower house. Forman was also a militia officer (despite their complaints about English placemen's multiple officeholding, American revolutionary leaders wore many hats) and used his judicial office to further military ends. On October 7, 1777, he banished a number of women suspected of English sympathies across Loyalist lines—bringing appeals from husbands and fathers that Forman "be brought to answer for his actions before the legislature."[23] Undaunted and apparently unchecked, Forman rose to brigadier rank. Petitioners against his interference in county elections that fall finally forced the legislature to take heed and Governor William Livingston to report that "some misunderstanding with the Assembly" had induced Forman to resign his office.[24]

When Vermont assemblyman Jonathan Fassett was identified as one of the leaders of the Rutland County rioters, the assembly refused to reseat him and commenced impeachment proceedings.[25] The rioters had attempted to close the county court, forestalling the collection of debts. Fassett's version of Shays's Rebellion came to a quick end, and Fassett, with his cohorts, soon stood before the county bench. Meanwhile, at his trial on the impeachment, he was ordered by the council to pay £9.10.7, the cost of "the prosecution of his impeachment." Already denied his seat, he could not be removed from office but was barred from posts in the future. His was one of a very few cases which came before both the council and the regular courts but did not violate the double jeopardy clause of the constitution. The impeachment trial could only result in removal and disqualification and was thus a separate proceeding.[26] The final reckoning of accounts against the overzealous assemblyman went on for years. In January 1791 the assembly paid the last requisition for witnesses in the case. Fassett was still being sued in the regular courts for damages and begged the assembly to enact a bill freeing him from arrest warrants sworn out by his suitors. At the end of the month the assembly complied with his wishes, and he passed from the pages of their journal.[27]

Incompetence, inattention to duty, and excess partisanship in office were also grounds for impeachment when they endangered the state, but no one was impeached without evidence of intentional neglect or total incapacity to perform official duties. Well-meaning incompetence was forgiven, although the suspect often took the hint and resigned. In New Jersey, Enos Kelsey, the official clothier, and Edward Thomas, the quartermaster of the army, as well as Monmouth inspectors of confiscated lands Kenneth Hankinson and Samuel Foreman, all resigned when their inefficiency was disclosed by the assembly.[28] The threat of impeachment gave teeth to legislative supervision of appointed officers. When Vermont justice of the peace Abner Osgood incorrectly attached £15 from Nathaniel Goth when only £9.8.0 was asked in a suit, the assembly began impeachment proceedings against the justice. Osgood was found innocent of the charge, not because the facts were confuted, but because his error was not thought willful. He was nevertheless admonished.[29] The assembly reviewed the case on appeal from a lower court—not as a superior court to reverse judgment upon a point of law but to oversee the conduct of the lower judges.

The most publicized and far-reaching impeachment inquiry for incompetence was directed at Virginia Governor Thomas Jefferson. While no formal motion for impeachment was made against Jefferson, Edmund Randolph, a firsthand observer, termed the inquiry into Jefferson's gubernatorial conduct an "impeachment."[30] Jefferson's controversial handling of the Virginia militia, ineffective fiscal policy, and ineptitude in the administration of conscription law angered some and disappointed others in the revolutionary ranks. When the British invaded Virginia, in June 1781, Jefferson and the legislators fled the capital.[31] This was the last straw for George Nicholas, a young assembly delegate. Supported by Jefferson's old rivals Richard Henry Lee and Patrick Henry, Nicholas introduced a resolution "to inquire into the conduct of the executive of this state for the last two months."[32] Jefferson, already intending to retire, forbade friends even to place his name in nomination for a second term. The legislators, as provided in the constitution, selected General Thomas Nelson as governor. Jefferson, as an ex-governor, was now liable to an impeachment (according to the state constitution). Although the assembly dropped its inquiry into his conduct, Jefferson demanded a vote of confidence. He asked Nicholas for the specific charges against him and Nicholas cited unpreparedness during the invasion.[33] On November 26 the lower house reluctantly agreed to proceed with the investigation but, when a committee was created to receive evidence and formulate charges, no one came forward to testify[34]. Seeking to mollify Jefferson, the House of Assembly asked him to take James Blair's place in the state's congressional delegation.[35] He refused to accept the olive branch. On December 12 the committee conceded that hearsay had led to the June twelfth resolution: "Popular rumors, gaining some degree of credence, by more pointed accusations, rendered it necessary to make an inquiry . . . and delayed that retribution of public gratitude, so eminently merited" by Jefferson's conduct in office.[36] Edmund Pendleton, Jefferson's friend and mentor, reported Jefferson's vindication to Madison, and Madison returned his pleasure at the news.[37] John Harvie told Jefferson: "I have the Satisfaction to find that in the Opinions of all men I here converse with, that the Administration before the last [Jefferson's] is viewed as having been Honorable to the Chief Magistrate, and preservative of the Rights of the people, and the Constitution of the Land." Harvie attributed the incident to the "illiberality of the Invidious," but Jefferson had not been an able commander-in-chief.[38] His ineffectiveness, fortunately, was not deemed impeachable.

Jefferson's friends thought that the charges of incompetence were animated by envy, spite, and partisanship. Often this was true—but without proof of willful misuse of power (including failure to act when necessary), such charges fell to the ground. The only time that personal animosity carried weight in impeachments was when it could be coupled with evidence of misconduct—and willful misconduct at that. The defendant's purpose was a genuine issue. Moody Moriss, justice of the peace in Salem County, was the third New Hampshire justice to be investigated by the state lower house after the amended state constitution authorized impeachment and trial, and his misdeeds reeked of malice.[39] On August 30, 1787, examiners from a committee of the lower house took affidavits from Moriss and a number of complainants and witnesses. The line of volunteers to testify grew so long and Moody's trail of suspected wrongs so winding that the committee spent a week hearing the evidence. Moody denied fomenting strife in his community and produced eight petitions, averaging thirty signatures apiece, avowing "the benevolence, humanity, and uprightness" of his conduct. Unbeknownst to him, the assembly had on file a number of letters from signers of the various petitions swearing that their signatures were "obtained by undue influence."[40] To charges that he refused to draw complaints, permit appeals from his judgment to the county court, and otherwise violated his oath he replied, "I must have been a knave and a fool to think practices of this kind would go unpunished" and therefore "did not think to commit them." Those who called him partial and vicious he castigated as partisans, "slanderers," "envious litigants and designing men." Moriss was apologetic but upright: "I do not contend that I have in every instance conducted the office with perfect accuracy; and that I have never made a mistake." Against his mild words deponents cited Moriss's treatment of Mary Stickney. They alleged that he instigated John Cross to bring a suit against her, found for the plaintiff, refused to permit a number of the men present to pay the dollar necessary to register an appeal for the spinster, and summarily ordered her fined and whipped. To these men, witnesses swore, Moriss announced, "There is no appeal, for this is the end of the law."[41]

Moriss did not forget or forgive the men who offered to aid Stickney. After Nathaniel Woodman offered to pay for Stickney's appeal, Moriss ordered Woodman's house searched on a general warrant for stolen goods. No stolen goods were found. So too, the house of Thomas Dow, who had asked to act as Stickney's surety, was searched upon Moriss's general warrant—though these warrants were illegal. Not content, Morris then urged Elizabeth Cross, wife of the plaintiff in Stickney's case, to give information against Jonathan Spafford, a third would-be surety for Stickney, for "breach of the sabbath."[42] Cross refused. With all the evidence in its hands, the assembly found that the case against Moriss was compelling. His conduct, motivated by some private malice, was "disgraceful to government, contrary to law, and derogatory to the great trust and confidence this state had reposed in him." Moriss resigned in December before the assembly could formally vote the impeachment.[43]

Even without evidence of corruption, misuse of power, or incompetence, officeholders might imperil republican government by overstepping the bounds of their duty. These acts had to be intentional overextensions of official responsibility, for an illegal purpose, to be impeachable, but the line between zealous political activity and misuse of power could be very fine. The Founding Fathers agreed that ambition among men of affairs was inevitable. They were also aware that older republics had fallen when such men subverted government to their own ends. The system of separation of powers erected in the state governments took account of inherent human weaknesses. Checks by one branch upon another, bans upon multiple officeholding, and explicit delegation of functions to the different branches prevented any one man or faction within the government from controlling the whole. Impeachment was one legislative check upon executive and judicial officers.

The outstanding example of an impeachment intended to curb a branch of government in the period 1776–88 occurred in North Carolina. The judges of the superior court of the state, led by gnarled, cantankerous Chief Justice

Samuel Ashe, formerly speaker of the state senate, were engaged in continuous battle with a portion of the state bar. The bench itself was anti-federalist, far more democratically inclined than many of the lawyers.[44] Associate Justice John Williams owed his nomination to conservative counselor Archibald Maclaine, but Samuel Spencer, the other associate justice, took particular exception to Maclaine. A native Scot who had one of the state bar's most vituperative tongues, Maclaine did not avoid these confrontations. Spencer also wrangled with other Federalist lawyers, notably John Hay, Congressman William Hooper, and future Supreme Court Justice James Iredell, as well as with merchant Hugh Williamson and the Blount brothers, Thomas, John Gray, and William, later a United States senator from Tennessee. Spencer and Williams also quarreled with each other. The lawyers watched the judges' conduct with dismay.[45] As Maclaine wrote to Iredell: "At Superior Court we did business as usual—Tried about half-a-dozen jury causes; wrangled with the Judges, and they with each other; at least Spencer and Williams. The latter has sworn solemnly and openly, never to sit with the former again. The most shameful partiality disgraced the Bench."[46]

Caught in the middle of this unseemly wrangling were former Loyalist claimants seeking redress from state confiscation laws under the peace treaty of 1783. These litigants enlisted the services of Maclaine and Hooper, as well as other politically conservative members of the bar, to plead their cases. The justices were unsympathetic; they harassed Loyalist suitors while the attorneys fumed. Iredell, ordinarily a center of calm in his friends' turbulence, was not hopeful. He wrote to one client: "I formerly acquainted you, that there had been no laws passed here since the Peace in regard to *British Debts*, and that it was the opinion of many, and which had appeared to have the sanction of the Legislature, *that such Debts as were confiscated of Persons named . . .* stood upon the same footing as *other confiscated property.* . . . Should this be the case, you may imagine the state of your debts, and in the mean time your chance of receiving payment of any."[47] In 1785 the legislature passed a law prohibiting the superior court from hearing suits against the 1783 confiscation law; Iredell's fears were justified: the legislature had joined the courts in weakening the claims of ex-Loyalists. Maclaine, who had led the fight against the 1783 law, exploded: "The Assembly and the Judges have indeed found an easy way to evade the treaty. The former refuse to point out any method to ascertain what is confiscated, (for they know they cannot), and the Judges refuse to let any person, whose property may be taken by a rapacious Commissioner, maintain a suit; so that we seem to be at the mercy of a set of needy adventurers, whose interest it is to pillage us."[48]

From the point of view of the majority in the legislature these steps were necessary. North Carolina had committed itself to a policy of depreciation of certificates and scrip in order to retire its war debt.[49] A crucial part of this policy was the auction of confiscated land to holders of wartime bonds. The peace treaty of 1783 committed the states to return, at fair market value, goods and lands wrongfully taken during the war. The legislators instead encouraged the superior court to discount the claims of former Loyalists.

The conservatives could not convince the assembly to reverse itself on this policy (and by so doing condemn the judges' treatment of the Loyalists), but by impugning the judges' conduct in the court—accusing them of incompetence and partiality—Maclaine might curb them. The legislature had investigated and suspended a number of county justices already.[50] Though they were not optimistic about their chances, Maclaine and his comrades gradually convinced themselves to take some action.[51] As all of them were members of the assembly, they had the privilege of moving an impeachment against the judges. At the very least, this would embarrass the bench. On January 1, 1787, both houses of the state legislature met in a committee of the whole to hear Maclaine's charges against the judges.

Maclaine had drafted seven articles of impeachment. The first alleged that the justices refused to hear suits brought by Peter Mallett, a former Loyalist, despite a pardon from the governor. Second, at the December 1785 term, the judges directed the grand jury to bring misdemeanor indictments against Loyalists Francis Brice and Daniel McNeill for returning to North Carolina to recover confiscated property. The judges supposedly directed the prosecution against them, then found them guilty, and fined them. Brice was committed to jail until he paid his fine, and both men were ordered out of the state. Third, Spencer and Williams supposedly received money from forfeited recognizances and fines they themselves had imposed. Fourth, Williams, in the case of *John Hay and Co. v. Whithall*, went beyond the verdict of the jury to strike six years interest off a debt. Fifth, Judge Spencer, in September 1785, ordered the fine and imprisonment of a supposed defaulter when in fact the clerk had made an error. Maclaine and his investigatory committee found hasty and harsh conduct typical of the justices in cases of forfeit of bail and default of debt. Sixth, Ashe and Williams never attended the superior court when it sat for Morgan district. All the judges missed sessions. Even when they did all sit, "tedious" disputes between Spencer and Williams wasted the time of the court. Bickering, absenteeism, and arbitrariness extended the court docket and made delays "a matter of public notoriety." Finally, without legal cause or practical reason, the judges declined to rule on a series of confiscated land disputes brought in the May 1786 term.[52]

According to Attorney General Alfred Moore, the judges were free to come to plead their cases if they wished. Ashe declared that he had "clean hands, and a pure heart" and remained at home. Williams and Spencer testified before the assembly. Moore himself had been asked to attend though he did not know what his role would be.[53] He evidently was unaware that state attorneys general were often asked to join the prosecution. The two associate judges pleaded that they had not been willfully partial in their decisions but followed statute in determining suits before them. Were they guilty of the particular charges? Their personal animosities were well known, as was the vehemence with which their chief rendered his own judgments, but under the rules which had evolved during the period 1776–88, they could not be called guilty of impeachable offenses. This was the opinion of the committee of the whole—the lower house sitting without its speaker and its rules—when it voted upon Maclaine's petition. The committee of the whole failed to find sufficient evidence to ask the lower house to hear formal charges. The assembly, reconvened, formally voted to accept the guidance of its committee of the whole, 40 to 22. Blount voted with the minority, as did the members of Maclaine's investigating committee.[54]

Maclaine and his followers failed, for obvious reasons. They asked the legislative branch to curb lawmaking, as opposed to legitimate rendering of judgments, in the judicial branch. The associate justices replied that they were only instruments of legislative fiscal policy: in effect, the assembly itself had ordered the dismissal of Loyalists' claims. For their part, the prosecutors were known partisans. Representation of Loyalist clients exposed Maclaine and his friends to the charge of Toryism. Ashe grasped this weakness in Maclaine's case and exploited it. He wrote to the house: "I suppose, it is considered among the Tories as a mighty achievement, a matter of great exultation and triumph that their champion dare stand forth, and in the face of the legislature accuse the judicial powers of the State for presuming to molest those respectable personages."[55]

When the justices were exonerated by the legislature and given a vote of thanks for their long and faithful service, Maclaine composed and published a series of pamphlets attacking both the assembly and the judges. Instead of rehashing the January 2 vote, he accused the legislature and the court of conspiring against the most sacred principle of American jurisprudence: the right to a jury trial. Under the pseudonym "The Independent Citizen," he produced five pamphlets. As had Justice Ashe, Maclaine returned to the Revolution for arguments. The power of courts to take away property without due process of law, that is, without a jury, Maclaine believed anathema to revolutionary principles. Could the assembly, forgetting how Americans had risen up against parliament for the same offense, take from people their right to jury trial? "Did we not take up arms—did we not fight bloody battles—did we not endure hardship, poverty, and distress, in support of the constitutional rights of freemen? It was the voice of the people; it was the voice of our laws; and yet, have not the Assembly of this state, by this act of 1785, overturned the chartered rights of men?" The assembly had prefaced its act with a pledge that the speedy administration of justice would be served if the "great mischiefs" created by lawyers in confiscation suits were reduced. In reply to this slur Maclaine argued that the assembly gave untrammeled power to justices in suits under £20. "But the history of England (that land of liberty) points out no one instance, of even the property of the individual, in the smallest instance, being subject to the discretion of one man."[56]

The superior court itself was uneasy with the 1785 law. In *Bayard v. Singleton* (1787) they decided that the 1785 act violated the state constitutional guarantee of jury trials. Although the jury found for Singleton, the holder of a confiscated deed to the disputed property, Bayard was permitted to bring a suit. This instance of "judicial review" put the court on record in favor of Maclaine's position, while establishing the justices' independence from the assembly. Judicial review was as effective a judicial check upon the power of the legislative branch of government as impeachment was upon the judges.[57]

In the aftershock of the impeachment effort, Maclaine, Blount, Iredell, Hooper, and other advocates of impeachment continued to accuse the judges of malfeasance and the judges continued to defend themselves.[58] For refusing to come to the assembly, Ashe became the prime target of these attacks. Never a retiring man and well versed in the pamphlet wars of this partisan age, he retorted to the new impeachment rumblings with scorn. The inquiry was "a dark insidious proceeding." Blount's proposal for trial of impeachments in the county, with members of the bar joining the bench, Ashe decried as a plot against him. To Iredell, who had been Ashe's friend and co-worker, the chief justice expressed his sorrow and anger. How could Iredell have joined such a crew of pettifoggers, who flitted in and out of court "scouting and hunting after fees"? Maclaine found Ashe's letter to the assembly hotheaded and inflammatory. In October 1787 Maclaine published another pamphlet on the affair, claiming "a judge may be guilty of high crimes and misdemeanors, without receiving a bribe, or robbing the treasury. . . . [They] may openly violate the laws and constitution of their country." With his allies in the legislature, Maclaine insisted that Ashe come to testify about his conduct. At sessions of the court, the ground trembled with Ashe's fury and the lawyers' calumny. The legislature stepped into the widening breach with a reform bill, creating an additional judgeship, confining the remarks of the judges to matters of law, and providing for jury trials in appeals of cases over £20. The assembly sympathized with the high court bench but gave the final victory to the lawyers, many of whom sat in the house.[59]

So familiar were republican legislators with the concept that impeachment could maintain a balance of power among the branches that they reached for impeachment even when it was not mentioned in their state's constitution. Rhode Island, under its first constitution (derived from the colonial charter), did not provide for impeachment. Nevertheless, angered over the superior court's ruling in *Trevett v. Weeden* (1786), members of the general assembly did call for the impeachment of the judges. In the case, a cousin of *Bayard v. Singleton*, the judges ruled that a state law violated the right of jury trial guaranteed to individuals by the state constitution. After the judges refused to take jurisdiction in the case as provided under a law of the general court, the assembly called upon them to explain themselves. When they adopted the position that the judiciary was an independent branch and could not take jurisdiction or act in a manner contrary to the constitutional provisions for trying cases, the possibility of impeachment was actually raised—even though Rhode Island's constitution did not allow it. Perhaps the memory of Williams's attempted impeachment of an opponent in 1654 remained alive among his successors.[60]

Impeachment permitted private citizens to bring accusations of wrongdoing to the attention of state governments. Nearly all the twenty impeachment motions investigated in the New Jersey lower house arose from private citizens' petitions. If accusations of this type often ended with exoneration or a finding that there was insufficient evidence to impeach, every inquiry permitted an aggrieved individual to bring evidence to the legislature without necessitating special arrangements or stoppage of normal business. Petitioners alleged that they were denied jury trials, for example, when the law allowed them this privilege.[61] Many of these petitions today would take the form of an appeal to a higher court, for reversal and retrial, or a directed verdict, but in post-revolutionary America, the lower houses supervised judicial conduct. Even grand jurors took their grievances to the lower house. In a November 12, 1783, petition to the New Jersey Assembly, G. Bogart and eleven others of the Somerset County grand jury avowed that they had heard testimony against their own justice of the peace, and then had witnessed another justice concealing the offense. Justice Dubois was present at a fistfight between William Ganor and Abraham Stryker and encouraged Ganor to maul Stryker. When the beaten man complained to another justice, Henry van Middlesweart, Dubois intervened and asked van Middlesweart not to investigate; he, Dubois, would see that justice was done. Dubois then ignored Stryker's prosecution of Ganor for assault and battery. The lower house investigated the charges.[62] Impeachment inquiries of this type were a safety valve even if the lower house took no action, for they showed concern for the complaints of individuals and groups. If there were truth in the facts and malice in the suspect's conduct, a formal impeachment hearing would follow.

New Jersey was not alone in this view. The Connecticut Constitution first provided for impeachment in 1818, but so closely associated were private petitions for redress and impeachment in Americans' minds that in May 1785 the people of Simsbury sent petitions to both houses asking for the impeachment of Dudley Pettibone, tax collector and justice of the peace. James Strickland and Elizabeth Strong testified that Pettibone had tried to extort double taxes from them, then threatened them and destroyed their receipts. Strickland and Strong accused Pettibone of "malversions in office." Other complainants claimed that Pettibone, sitting as a justice, had ordered executions upon judgments already paid, added people to the tax lists and kept for himself the rates they paid, kept the town's school money for himself, extorted votes from town residents, and convinced others to instigate suits at law from which he profited.[63] The General Court appears to have referred these petitions to the regular courts. The judges, Pettibone's colleagues on the county bench, did not find sufficient evidence to warrant a trial and Pettibone retained his offices. Had Connecticut added an impeachment provision to its constitution before 1818, Pettibone might have faced judgment instead of escaping it.[64]

In states which did provide for impeachments, literally anyone could bring an impeachment by a report or complaint. On June 14, 1788, anti-Federalist printer Eleazer Oswald refused to come to court to answer a charge of libel brought against him by Federalist Andrew Brown. Oswald had printed newspaper pieces accusing Brown of being a "scribbling dunce" and "a pseudo-patriot." Though these pieces were signed "Peep" and "Obediah Forceps," Brown obtained a writ of *capias* from the supreme court to bring in Oswald and force him to reveal who had written the articles. Oswald ignored the writ, was arrested by the sheriff, and was brought to court on July 12, 1788, for contempt. The justices, Thomas McKean, William Atlee, and Jacob Rush, demanded that Oswald answer their questions on the libel, and after a day's delay to consider his reply, he refused. They ordered him to pay £10 (the costs of prosecution) and remain in the county jail for one month. Oswald's response was to petition the Pennsylvania Assembly for the impeachment of the justices.[65]

Brown v. Oswald was not the first occasion that the feisty partisan printer stood accused of libel and contempt before Chief Justice McKean. Robert Brunhouse has traced the earlier incident:

At the election of 1782 Colonel Thomas Procter of the Continental line took offense at inspector John Kling who was so "scrupulous" in demanding to see Procter's certificate of having taken the oath. The next day Procter met Kling and gave him a beating. Haled into court, Procter was fined eighty pounds. McKean then informed him that the army men held their heads too high and that he would teach them how to behave. Oswald published an account of the trial in which he complained of the high fine and of McKean's attitude toward army men. Then Oswald was called before the court on the charge of libel but that did not prevent him from printing an account of his experience before the irate McKean. When a grand jury repeatedly returned the Oswald bill *ignoramus*, the judge's wrath mounted. Even Attorney General Bradford could not browbeat the jury into submission.[66]

Both McKean's use of judicial power to cite Oswald for slandering the court and Oswald's perversity in regarding a minor incident as though it were a major threat to the liberties of the people were spiteful and excessively partisan. Nevertheless, beneath this seriocomic display of factional passion, there lay a very real conflict between the rights of a free press and the power of judges away from their courtrooms. Oswald had not slandered or condemned the chief justice in the course of any judicial proceeding and the printer had not resisted any legal orders from the bench. How far did the reach of the judges extend beyond their courtrooms into the normal course of politics? To what extent could the mere publication of a document or an eyewitness account be censured without endangering freedom of press? While the law of the new states on this question remained unclear, no printer and no judge could stand on safe ground.[67]

Oswald would not allow his second contempt judgment to go unanswered. On September 5, 1788, the speaker of the Pennsylvania House of Representatives read aloud Oswald's "address and memorial" praying the assembly examine information "of the most serious nature" against McKean, Atlee, and Rush. Oswald reported he had obeyed the *capias* issued against him and Supreme Court Justice Bryan had permitted him to go without bail. With Bryan absent on the last day of its session, the chief justice ordered Oswald to reappear and show cause why his property should not be attached for the £1,000 sum demanded by Brown for the libel. When he appeared, Oswald had to answer the justices' questions rather than having the opportunity to defend himself against Brown and Brown's witnesses. He refused, was fined, and was imprisoned for contempt of court. Despite the fact that the supreme executive council remitted Oswald's fine and his costs were paid by a friend, McKean refused to let the jailer free him. Perhaps this friend was Blair McClenahan, who had put up money for Oswald's recognizance to appear before the court. McClenahan may even have suggested the impeachment memorial, based upon his experience in the Hopkinson case. Finally, Oswald argued that commitment to gaol without jury trial was a violation of the constitution. Judges had no right to deviate from fundamental law. Oswald added that his constitutional rights to freedom of speech and press as well were violated by his imprisonment for contempt. The judges reached back into practices of the English Star Chamber courts to deny him his freedom.[68]

The accusation that the victorious Federalist party in the persons of Brown and McKean had engineered the imprisonment of an anti-Federalist printer and endangered the liberty of the press was serious business. On September 16, 1788, the lower house made itself into a grand inquest for the state, a committee of the whole to inquire into the truth of Oswald's charges. The speaker issued subpoenas for witnesses in the case. Oswald was allowed counsel to represent his views. On October 3 the committee of the whole found insufficient evidence to support Oswald's demand for impeachment. Nevertheless, the house admonished the court. The assembly reminded the judges that although they had the right to punish those contemning their authority, they ought not use that right to repress freedom of speech or press or to undermine the right of trial by jury. The lower house decreed that the fine and imprisonment of Oswald for statements he may have made against Brown or members of the court before a trial had established the facts of the case was an unwarrantable, "unconstitutional exercise of judicial power" and "sets an alarming precedent." They condemned such "constructive" definitions of contempt. The contempt had to be real and present, disrupting official duties of the court.[69]

The assemblymen also defined impeachable offenses for the first time. These were "bribery, corruption, or a willful and arbitrary infraction of the law," according to William Findley. McKean and his colleagues were not guilty of these misdemeanors, for no malicous intent could be proved in their treatment of Oswald. The assembly did not insist that impeachable acts be crimes, indictable in regular courts of law, as Judge Alexander Addison of Pennsylvania, at his impeachment trial, would interpret their comments. *Infraction of law* instead meant the deliberate, partisan mis-application of law (a position refined by its sponsor, Findley, when he later urged the impeachment of Justice Samuel Chase).[70]

If Oswald had not convinced the lower house to impeach the judges, he did find a forum for his grievances. His complaint was not dismissed out of hand. Receptivity proved that the new republican governments listened to their constituents; representative bodies were indeed representative. Whatever effect such near impeachments may have had in checking misuse of power by the judiciary, they displayed to all Americans who watched state government that impeachment was an appropriate instrument of republican rule.

6

IMPEACHMENT IN THE
FEDERAL CONSTITUTION

THE STATES' EXPERIENCE WITH IMPEACHMENT ENCOURAGED THE FRAMERS OF
the federal Constitution to adopt the procedure. The prime movers behind
incorporation of impeachment in the federal law, the only delegates who
spoke on impeachment, were intimately connected with state impeachment
law and cases. Among these delegates, Randolph, Madison, and Mason were
closely associated with the evolution of impeachment law in Virginia. Randolph, much influenced by Jefferson's case, told the convention that "the
propriety of impeachments was a favorite principle with him."[1] William
Paterson, attorney general of New Jersey, James Wilson, one of Hopkinson's
lawyers, and Hugh Williamson of North Carolina, just arrived from his part
in the unsuccessful attempt to impeach the superior court bench there, all
knew firsthand the effectiveness of impeachment. Elbridge Gerry and Rufus
King, drawing upon their political apprenticeship in revolutionary Massachusetts, Gouverneur Morris and Alexander Hamilton, well versed in the
constitutional debates in New York, and Charles Cotesworth Pinckney, one
of the authors of the revised South Carolina Constitution of 1778, all understood impeachment law. What is more, everyone who took part in debates
over impeachment during the convention was acquainted with it in its
American shape. From the first, all these delegates agreed to ground rules on
impeachment which mirrored state provisions—only officers could be impeached for crimes done in office, with removal and disqualification the only
punishments—rather than English precedent.

The English precedent had receded into a dim past. Despite the fact that
Parliament was engaged in a major impeachment throughout the time that
the convention met (the impeachment of Governor General Warren Hastings
of the East India Company), the case was mentioned only briefly during the
debates.[2] George Mason argued that under one definition of impeachable
offenses proposed by James Madison and the committee of eleven ("treason
and bribery"), Hastings could not have been impeached in America.[3] Madi-

son ignored the case, as did the other delegates, and Mason dropped it. There was no reference to the multitude of other English impeachments that occurred between Bacon's case in 1621 and Hastings's case.

References to English cases would have had disputable relevance; from the beginning of the convention, proposed federal impeachment law diverged from English precedent. Throughout the debates, the framers of the Constitution sought to define impeachable offenses precisely: from their first formula of "maladministrations and corruption in office" to their final compromise on "treason, bribery, or other high crimes and misdemeanors."[4] Parliament refused to limit its jurisdiction by defining impeachable offenses. Usage contained instances of impeachment to which the Commons or the Lords recurred for instruction, but precedent never ruled out a new charge. In addition, only officeholders could be impeached under the federal provisions; the framers never wavered on this point from May through September. In Britain, anyone, save the royal family, could be impeached. Next, in England, the House of Lords convicted upon a bare majority, but during the convention the delegates agreed that "no person shall be convicted without the concurrence of two thirds of the Members present."[5] One would look in vain for this two-thirds rule in Britain; it was a uniquely American formula with great significance in American conceptualization of trials upon impeachments. Finally, while the House of Lords could order any punishment upon conviction, the delegates brought to Philadelphia with them the idea that "judgment in cases of Impeachment shall not extend further than to removal from office, and disqualification to hold and enjoy any Office of honor, trust or profit under the United States," as in the state constitutions. Only regular federal courts could take life or limb for crimes, and a Federal official might face trial in these courts whatever the outcome of his impeachment. These great differences between American and English impeachment law originated in the colonies and fully matured in the Revolutionary states—a fact everywhere apparent in the convention debates.[6]

The first mention of impeachment in Philadelphia came from Randolph on May 29. He proposed the creation of a national judiciary, a final portion of his "Virginia Plan," which would hear and determine "impeachments of any national officers."[7] Assignment of impeachment trials to the regular courts followed the Virginia precedent, and Virginia leaders agreed that this manner of trial was best.[8] Randolph had consistently advocated the inclusion of impeachment in any national government.[9] The second reference to impeachment came in the debate on June 2 over the executive branch of government. Hugh Williamson proposed that the chief executive "be removable on impeachment and conviction of mal-practice or neglect of duty."[10] This was the law in North Carolina, Williamson's home. His definition of impeachable offenses duplicated the one used in his own state: offenses against the public interest which need not be indictable under the criminal law. Throughout June, Randolph and Madison urged that impeachment of national officers be triable in the national judiciary.

In the middle of the month, William Paterson of New Jersey brought to the floor a broad counterproposal to the Virginia Plan. The "New Jersey" Plan was radically different from Randolph's scheme, yet Paterson also gave a separate federal judiciary "the authority to hear and determine in the first instance on all impeachments of federal officers."[11] Paterson oddly neglected to provide for impeachment of officers by the lower house before they were tried. His proposed congress could only remove officers upon the application of a majority of the state governors but could not impeach. Three days later, James Wilson, as familiar as anyone else on the convention floor with impeachment, contrasted the Virginia and New Jersey provisions for removing officers.[12] He noted that the former stipulated removal of officers upon impeachment and conviction and, in error, gave only the application of a majority of governors as cause for removal in Paterson's plan.[13] Perhaps the damaging omission was oversight on Paterson's part, but another explanation is more consistent with the New Jersey experience. He forgot to specifically mention impeachment not because he blundered but, because after a decade of New Jersey cases, he simply assumed any congress must have that power.

The next speaker on impeachment also advocated placing trial in the judiciary. On June 18, Alexander Hamilton rose to make his longest, most formal, and last address to the delegates. In it he proposed that "The Governor, Senators and all officers of the United States were to be liable to impeachment for mal- and corrupt conduct; and upon conviction to be removed from office, and disqualified for holding any place of trust or profit—all impeachments to be tried by a Court to consist of the Chief or Judge of the Superior Court of Law of each State, provided such judge shall hold his place during good behavior, and have a permanent salary." Hamilton pressed the arrangements from the New York Constitution on the convention; his federal trial court was a modification of the New York court of impeachments and errors.[14]

The court for trials remained a sticky point, but men familiar with state cases eventually solved the problem. Late in July the committee of detail proposed trial "before the Senate and the judges of the federal judicial Court"[15] (although some on the committee, notably Madison, clung to trial before the supreme judiciary[16]). When all these revisions were presented to the entire convention, the delegates postponed discussion of trial; there was still no agreement.[17] Finally, on September 4, another committee of detail urged the convention to accept the clause "The Senate of the United States shall have power to try all impeachments; but no person shall be convicted without the concurrence of two-thirds of the Members present."[18]

The new section was part of a tangled debate over the manner of electing the president.[19] When the committee of detail decided to create a college of electors, the Senate, which had been slated to name the president, could now try him upon an impeachment without being compromised by having named him in the first place. Gouverneur Morris, who provided this explanation of the committee's thinking, was complimented by George Mason and Wilson for the committee's work.[20] Both men were convinced that the danger of cabals in the Senate was averted. Morris agreed that this had been one purpose of the creation of a college of electors, and the resulting availability of the Senate to hear trial upon impeachment of the president was a pleasant by-product.[21] After all was said, the Senate was considered the least of evils among the various trial courts. When the entire convention voted, only Pennsylvania and Virginia dissented from this arrangement.[22] Later, both James McHenry and Luther Martin of Maryland recalled that the Senate seemed to be the only body likely to view impeachments in a cool and dispassionate manner.[23]

Alexander Hamilton, who had left the convention for New York City long before this vote was taken, concurred with trial in the Senate in *Federalist No. 65*. He averred that the great danger of impeachment was that it would become a political tool. Inevitably, the suspected misconduct of public figures would rouse political passions. Insofar as impeachment had concerned misconduct and misuse of power rather than common law crimes, the danger of its misapplication was heightened. The lower house was not a place for the trial of these impeachments, for they were the accusers. The judges of the national courts were too few and too weak to carry out this assignment. What is more, they would hear any cases arising "in the ordinary course of law" from official wrongdoing before, during, or after the official was convicted upon the impeachment. In the *Federalist* Hamilton even put aside his own favored proposal for a special court of impeachment trials, though he had not given up hope that his plan for a special court of impeachment might be included in an amended federal Constitution.[24] He was nevertheless a practical man and a committed Federalist, who would not jeopardize the entire document for a pet proposal.[25] Under the pseudonym *Publius*, which he shared with Madison and Jay, he wrote, "It will not be easy to imagine any third mode materially different [from Senate trial or supreme court trial] which could rationally be proposed." Narrowing the choice further, Publius concluded, "Where else than in the Senate could have been found a tribunal sufficiently dignified, or sufficiently independent? What other body would be likely to feel confidence enough in its own situation to preserve, unawed and uninfluenced, the necessary impartiality between an individual accused and the representatives of the people, his accusers?"[26]

The Senate, Hamilton argued, was not taking away the powers of the regular courts by trying impeachments but acting as a check upon the "encroachments" of the courts and the executive. This manner of check limited power rather than giving too much of it to the Senate. Although the Senate would have confirmed some of the men whose impeachment trials it later heard, this was no reason to suppose the senators would forgive malfeasance. Trials in state senates had not proved this a real danger. Nor was there reason to assume that the Senate and the president, the makers and ratifiers of treaties, would have reason to overlook perfidy among diplomats. The guarantee of this was the requirement that two-thirds of the Senate concur in the making of treaties. If two-thirds of that body were corrupted, the entire republic might well be lost, but the Constitution had done all that was humanly possible to avert such a catastrophe.[27]

Madison could not reconcile himself to trials in the Senate and voted against this provision in Philadelphia. Thereafter he kept his own counsel, save in his private correspondence. The letter to Brown referred only to the Constitution of Virginia and the prospective constitution for Kentucky, so that Madison did not technically betray the Federalists' united front during the ratification struggle. He may have proposed something like his earlier plan to the committee of detail; with the complications of Madison's proposed court before them it is easy to see why Gouverneur Morris, reporting for the committee of eleven, said that all plans for tribunals other than the Senate seemed too complicated.[28]

While the delegates debated the court of trials, a second controversy flared over the impeachability of the president of the United States. The governors of states were liable to impeachment and the first drafts of the federal Constitution provided for impeachment of the president, but some delegates were disturbed by this check upon the executive branch.[29] On July 19 Gouverneur Morris voiced the central objection of this group; he feared that the prospect of impeachment would make the chief executive dependent upon the legislature.[30] Morris's doubts triggered a general debate the following day, when his views were echoed by Charles Cotesworth Pinckney of South Carolina. Mason, Wilson, Elbridge Gerry, and Benjamin Franklin argued in favor of impeachment of presidents, Franklin closing his case with the wry remark that impeachment was certainly preferable to assassination, the alternative means of removing an incumbent chief executive.[31] Randolph and Madison joined the debate with the argument underlying the impeachment of state governors: if a president could not be impeached while in office, who could stop his misuse of power? The only effective retort to this, as far as Rufus King and, later, Morris were concerned, was the difficulty of finding a place to try the president. Morris admitted that the debate had convinced him that impeachment of presidents was necessary. They could not be above the law. The compromise of September 4 solved the problem of where to try these impeachments.[32] In the end, only South Carolina (Pinckney, unlike Morris, had not been swayed) and Massachusetts voted against the impeachment of the chief officer.

A third controversy, over the definition of impeachable offenses, erupted late in the convention. Through the early debates, every speaker referred to mal- and corrupt administration, neglect of duty, and misconduct in office as the only impeachable offenses. Common-law crimes, such as treason, murder, and felony, were to be heard in regular courts of law. Officials of the new government did not have immunity from prosecution for these crimes. Following the examples in their own state constitutions and cases, Paterson, Randolph, Wilson, and Mason all saw impeachment lying against misuse of official power. As late as August 20, the committee of five reported that federal officials "shall be liable to impeachment and removal from office for neglect of duty, malversation, or corruption."[33] Five years later Wilson explained the thinking of the delegates: "Impeachments, and offenses and offenders impeachable, come not, in those descriptions, within the sphere of ordinary jurisprudence. They are founded on different principles; are governed by different maxims; and are directed to different objects: for this reason, the trial and punishment of an offence on an impeachment, is no bar to a trial and punishment of the same offence at common law."[34] Wilson did not mean to imply that these offenses were simply political acts obnoxious to the government's ruling faction. Impeachable offenses were "political," as Hamilton later wrote, but only because they constituted some palpable "abuse or violation of some public trust."[35] Nevertheless, on September 8, "bribery and other high crimes and misdemeanors" was substituted for the existing formula.[36] Mason objected. He found the new definition too limiting. The old terms could easily have subsumed treasons and briberies. He moved to reintroduce the term *maladministration* after bribery in order to permit impeachment upon less conventionally defined common-law offenses. Gerry seconded the motion; Oliver had not been guilty of either treason or bribery. Both Madison and Morris objected to the vagueness of the words used in the old definition—they were too political. Morris had asked for more "enumerated and defined" offenses two months before, during the July 20 debate. The officials would hold a place effectually "at pleasure" of the Senate and House, Madison warned. Mason then moved to add "high crimes and misdemeanors," a formula including, to his mind, maladministration. This passed, 8 to 3, and became the orthodox phraseology. Mason's original motion read "high crimes and misdemeanors against the state;" he was clearly trying to restate the old substantive rule that the offense must be primarily against the public weal rather than against a private citizen. Impeachable offenses thus remained very different from ordinary crimes.[37] The vote in favor of the compromise motion suggests that the delegates understood that the new terms included maladministration, corruption, and neglect of duty rather than excluding all but those offenses cognizable in regular courts of law. Thus Jefferson, in his Senate manual of 1797 (as in his draft constitution for Virginia) opined that high crimes were simply those committed by men in high places.[38] Treason and bribery were already among those offenses charged against officials in the new states. *Misdemeanor,* meaning lesser offenses, was by this time a catchall phrase in American criminal law, though it had once had more precise common-law meaning.[39] The addition of misdemeanors to the list of offenses meant that the House of Representatives was permitted to charge officials with minor breaches of ethical conduct, misuse of power, and neglect of duty, as well as more prolonged, egregious or financially rapacious misconduct.

With the communal effort to raise impeachments above partisanship to a higher plane of national interest, the debate over definitions of offenses closed. It would reopen with the very first federal case, by which time many state assemblies had shifted toward a very much more political view of the process. Hamilton's fears were justified, and there was nothing that the new definition of impeachable offenses could do to stop the politicization of impeachment and trial. Fearing this, the delegates placed a second obstacle in the path of purely partisan impeachments: the requirement of two-thirds vote of the Senate for conviction. This final stroke of constitutional planning gave federal impeachment law the shape it retains to this day.

The August 29 motion was not the first time the two-thirds formula was used in the convention. On June 6 Hugh Williamson had suggested that all congressional acts require a two-thirds vote.[40] The committee of detail shortly thereafter restricted Senate treaty ratification and confirmation of appointments to two-thirds divisions. The significance of the inclusion of impeachment conviction in this category cannot be overemphasized. The restriction of certain legislative issues to two-thirds votes was without parallel in pre-revolutionary constitutionalism. The two-thirds requirement does not appear in English parliamentary usage or constitutional theory save for quorum calls, a very different matter from substantive divisions of a house. The House of Lords carried all votes, including conviction upon impeachment, upon a simple majority. Furthermore, references to two-thirds votes cannot be found in American colonial legislative experience or theory, save in the Pennsylvania Charter of 1682. In the crib notes on confederations Madison intermittently prepared between 1784 and 1787, one finds a slender precedent. In the Achaean League, 10 of the 12 members had to consent to every common action. Beyond this single citation, Madison, along with Adams, Jefferson, Wilson, Hamilton, and the rest of the corps of revolutionary theorists, found precedent only for majoritarianism.[41] Two-thirds requirements emerged as part of the revolutionary republican compromise between representative assemblies and deliberative councils. The association of impeachment with the two-thirds rule signified a final Americanization and republicanization of the impeachment process.

Working backward from the federal constitutional debates one can uncover the trail of precedent for the two-thirds requirements leading to the original 1776 draft of the Articles of Confederation. Charles Cotesworth Pinckney's plan for a federal government, prepared before the convention met, provided for "The assent of Two-Thirds of both Houses, where the present [Articles of] Confederation has made the assent of Nine States necessary," and added "the Regulation of Trade, and Acts for levying an Impost and raising a Revenue."[42] In 1783 Jefferson had suggested that Virginia require a two-thirds vote to convict its officials on impeachments. Though his proposal led nowhere, a two-thirds majority was already required in the trial court under the Massachusetts Constitution of 1780 and the New York Constitution of 1777. The congressional committee created on June 12, 1776, to draft a confederation for the states reported to Congress on July 12, 1776, its proposed Articles of Confederation.[43] Article 18 (Article 9 in later versions), required 9 states out of the 13 in Congress, two-thirds of the total, to give assent to treaties and other important matters of business. Each state had, on all questions, a single vote. Congress was never to engage in a war, or grant letters of marque and reprisal in time of peace, or enter into any treaties or alliances, or coin money, or regulate its value, or ascertain the sums and expenses necessary for the defense and welfare of the United States, or appropriate money, or raise a navy, or determine the number of land or sea forces to be raised, or appoint a commander in chief of the army or the navy, unless 9 states agreed.[44]

The struggle to draft this article was fierce. Intense and opinionated men staffed this committee, and they admitted to correspondents that their discussions were heated.[45] John Dickinson, the penman of the document and the leader of the committee, trod carefully among its various factions. Some men, himself included, were slow to approve independence but wished to see a strong confederation.[46] Other nationalists, more eager for independence, wished to create a genuine national union, governed by a proportionally elected assembly. Franklin scribbled a critique of the articles along these lines but did not submit it to Congress.[47] Others, including a number of southerners, wished to reserve more power to the states, though they admitted the necessity of central direction of the war and foreign affairs. Still another faction in the committee welcomed independence but feared the position that an untested national government would take on the war with England. The two-thirds provision in Article 18 was a compromise. It delegated the power of treaty making, including the pressing questions of treaties with France and Spain and a peace treaty with England itself, to the new government. Given that one of the most important and obvious matters of everyday congressional business was foreign affairs, this was a necessary concession. To ensure that a few states could not dictate prolongation of the war or avert the ratification of treaties with allies, the committee did not specify a unanimous vote for treaties and other important business, as it did for amendments to the articles themselves. At the same time, nine states would, more or less, represent a majority of the population of the new nation. For those delegates to Congress like Franklin who opposed the articles because each state had only 1 vote in Congress, rather than votes proportional to its share of the nation's population, the 9-vote requirement virtually ensured that a majority of the people would have to approve any important piece of congressional legislation.

Dickinson left Congress before his handiwork was reported. Though opposed to independence himself, he remained silent at the July 2 vote in order to let his colony assent. After some buffeting, his political career would resume in Delaware.[48] Meanwhile, advocates of the articles struggled to retain the two-thirds provisions. In debates over revision of the articles covering many days in October 1777, Dickinson's original version survived an attack led by Samuel Adams, a member of the 1776 drafting committee, and the entire Virginia delegation, seeking to ensure that the nine states always represented a majority of the American people "excluding Negroes and Indians."[49] Their effort was defeated, further clarifying congressional understanding about the two-thirds rule. It was not merely a guarantee of majority rule but also forced the unicameral Congress to deliberate before deciding on important matters of state. By 1781, when the articles were finally adopted in Congress, the deliberative principle behind the two-thirds vote was integrated with the majoritarian practical outcome of it. Even outspoken majoritarians agreed that important matters ought to require a two-thirds majority.

This assumption passed into the conventional wisdom of constitutional writers, as illustrated in two episodes in Confederation government involving the treaty-making power of Congress. In the fall of 1783 the Paris peace treaty reached Congress, but only seven states were represented at the session. From Virginia, Jefferson, fearing that Congress would hastily ratify the treaty, prepared to send a resolution to the Virginia delegates: "Resolved that however earnestly and anxiously Congress wish to proceed to the ratification of the Definitive treaty, yet (Resolved that Congress) consisting at present of seven states only [;] they ought not to undertake (the) that ratification (of the Definitive treaty) without proper *explanations*" [our italics].[50] The two-thirds rule forced Congress to deliberate, to explain to reluctant delegates and the people at large the reasons for its conduct. Jefferson was a majoritarian, but the gravity of circumstances at the moment induced him to embrace the nonmajoritarian rationale for the two-thirds rule. Jefferson never sent his memorandum, but Madison informed him that the spirit of the two-thirds rule was followed in the peace treaty ratification debates.[51]

A second crucial test of the two-thirds rule gave Jefferson and Madison further reason to celebrate Dickinson's design. Both men opposed the Jay–Gardoqui Treaty, Secretary of State John Jay's agreement with Spanish envoy Don Diego de Gardoqui to exchange American rights to the navigation of the Mississippi for a treaty of commerce with Spain. In 1786 the draft was approved by 7 states, all in the Northeast, and opposed by 5, failing passage. Western and southern state representatives, including the Virginians, breathed a sigh of relief. The two-thirds rule had again proved its worth.[52]

Set alongside the absence of colonial and British precedent for two-thirds votes on impeachment or any other important matters, the pragmatic compromise that issued from Dickinson's committee seems an authentic display of American political genius. The compromise not only received the plaudits of Dickinson's fellow Revolutionaries, it also embodied a solution to the difficult problem of the dual nature of American legislative bodies. They were at the same time representative, the heirs of revolutionary theory and practice, and deliberative, the continuation of British tradition. The two-thirds rule would become orthodoxy in American upper houses. The Senate created at the Philadelphia convention adopted the two-thirds rule for treaties and appointments because the Senate was very clearly both a deliberative and a representative body.

To the credit of Dickinson's fellow federal constitutionalists in 1787, they saw that the rationale for two-thirds votes on treaties could also apply to Senate trials on impeachments. With the practicality they had already displayed in adopting constitutional ideas from other sources, they attached the two-thirds rule to impeachment trials. It is not clear who deserves the credit for this imaginative step. Dickinson's draft of Articles of Confederation was complete a year before the submission of a two-thirds conviction requirement in the New York State Constitution, and two years before similar requirements were promulgated in Massachusetts' draft constitution. Dickinson's own role in adding the two-thirds rule to impeachment trials at the federal convention is conjectural. During the early convention debates, Dickinson supported the removal of federal officials by application from the states, but he soon shifted his position and moved to add impeachment and removal provisions to the draft constitution.[53] The committee of eleven which reported the two-thirds provision included Dickinson, but he did not speak on its two-thirds proposal in the convention, perhaps because no one opposed it. It seems there was consensus on the point.

Behind consensus on the two-thirds requirement for conviction lay a shared appreciation of the deliberative role of legislatures rather than agreement about the functioning of courts. That is to say, the two-thirds rule was not meant as a compromise between the majority sufficient to convict in the

House of Lords and unanimity required of a trial jury. In defending this article of the federal law from those who decried deviations from majority rule, Hamilton did not discuss criminal court practices, but insisted that the deliberative function of an upper house was as important to republican government as the majoritarian representativeness of the lower house. The Senate sat to hear treaty ratification, executive appointments, and impeachment trials without the concurrence of the lower house for the same reason that all three types of business required two-thirds votes. These issues should not be "popular." The Constitution assigned this labor to the Senate because the delegates expected the upper house to rely upon its own wisdom, information, stability, and even temper. There was no occasion, Hamilton opined, upon which the Senate should be more deliberative and shielded from popular clamors than when it sat to hear impeachments. On the other hand, impeachment hearings were not trials in which the senators were jurors, despite the fact that they sat upon oath or affirmation, so much as deliberative sessions, when they decided whether an official had betrayed his public trust. The American impeachment trial, with its two-thirds requirement, was thus a hybrid of native origin, expressing truly republican compromises.[54]

The two-thirds requirement for conviction in the Senate was the capstone in the republicanization of impeachment and trial procedure. It ensured that the Senate would be as thoughtful and deliberate in its hearing and determining of cases as the House of Lords, without any of the aristocratic trappings of that English body. Indeed, this last piece to the puzzle of where to try impeachments in America was characteristic of constitutional thought in the new republic: a numerical formula was employed to reproduce the effects of usage and tradition in comparable English institutions.

PART III

IMPEACHMENT AND
PARTY GOVERNMENT,
1788–1805

INTRODUCTION

FROM PHILADELPHIA THE FEDERAL DRAFT CONSTITUTION WENT OUT TO THE states. In ratification conventions, delegates examined the provisions for impeachment and trial in the new document and found them persuasive. Old states revised their laws to conform to federal stipulations; new states adopted impeachment and trial under the guidelines laid out in Philadelphia. In effect, federal impeachment law was one of the first examples of a "model" code, not binding on the states, but soon adopted by them. As Hamilton warned in *The Federalist*, however, a much less circumscribed form of impeachment hovered in the shadows: impeachment by a numerically dominant party, to remove its partisan opponents from office.

At first glance, nothing would seem more antithetical in the universe of political forms than party government and impeachment, as the experience of eighteenth-century English politics amply proved. Between the cases of the discredited Tory advisors in 1715 and Warren Hastings's case in 1787, only Lord Chancellor Macclesfield, in 1725, was impeached and tried for malfeasance in office. In the mid-eighteenth-century Parliaments, impeachment was replaced by votes of censure. So rusty did the impeachment sword become by mid-century, that Robert Walpole had to remind the Commons it was their right. If the Commons disapproved of the ministers in the cabinet, it merely broke from their leadership. An opposition party stood ready to form its own government when the ruling ministry lost the confidence of the house.[1] Impeachment worked when a ruling clique was too entrenched to be receptive to party entreaty or threat, or when the party system was too weak to organize governments. Impeachment did not need parties; it was supposed to stand above party and faction. The lower house impeached as the "grand inquest" for the whole people, not just the portion of the people who elected the majority party. Indeed, party government might corrupt impeachment, turning it to partisan ends. To go a step further, one of the obvious targets of impeachment was the "party man" who put the advantage of a group above the public weal. When the framers of the Constitution provided for impeachment, they had no inkling that a standing two-party system would soon contest federal and state government, disputing elections and appointments to office. Party government and impeachment were alternative means of removal—at least in theory.

Proof of this antithesis emerges from the debates over ratification. Impeachment and party rule were divorced from one another; neither proponents nor attackers of the procedures for impeachment viewed it as a weapon of party. Instead, impeachment was defended and attacked on other grounds. Richard Henry Lee warned against the power concentrated in the Senate by commissioning it the trier of impeachments. Too much power in the hands of a few men would corrupt government, he told Edmund Randolph. Impeachment itself would not deter such men; it would be their tool.[2] James Wilson, facing objections to senatorial trial in Pennsylvania— "Cincinnatus" warned that the Senate would "screen from punishment" its own appointees—retorted that impeachment applied to senators as well. They and other federal officeholders could not escape the consequences of their iniquity. Even if impeachment failed or trial resulted in acquittal, senators and senatorial appointees could be tried for their offenses in the regular courts. Nothing was lost, and an important weapon against misuse of power was gained.[3] Neither Wilson nor "Cincinnatus" examined the connection between standing parties and trial verdicts. Thomas McKean added that Pennsylvania anti-Federalists (in many cases the same men who were responsible for the state's impeachment law) had more to fear from trial in the state executive council, which had little other business and less official responsibility. The Senate of the United States would be a more august and impartial body than any state council.[4] James Monroe, addressing the Virginia ratification convention the next year, still worried that the president could influence the Senate, "his own council," when it sat to hear an impeachment against him. "This subverts the principles of justice, as it secures him from punishment." He might use the army, or his diplomatic powers, to influence the Senate.[5] Madison answered this frightening hypothetical case: impeachment of the president was an added security against the misuse of power. If he could not corrupt the entire Senate, it might still convict and remove him. If he did, then nothing was lost by making the chief executive impeachable.[6] In North Carolina, Samuel Spencer and James Iredell, anti-Federalist and Federalist, respectively, followed the same lines of argument as Monroe and Madison.[7] The two Carolina lawyers were leaders of opposing factions in state government, and, as we have seen, opposed each other in the courts and the legislature. Yet neither man (nor any of the debaters), examined the effect of political parties upon impeachment; it did not seem relevant. Combinations and coalitions might bring an impeachment; shifting factions might rig a trial, but disciplined, standing, electoral and governing parties could not have a role in impeachment because they did not yet have a role in American republicanism.

Despite the Founding Fathers' genuine antipathy to parties, between 1788 and 1800 the introduction and legitimization of standing opposition parties profoundly transformed American politics.[8] Overturning established Anglo-American attitudes toward political contests, the new standing party system disciplined and organized competition for office. These new parties would direct the federal government through a second "revolution," a thoroughly peaceful rotation of men in power. National parties relied upon elections and patronage to remove offending incumbents; impeachment did not appear to fit their ideology or practice.

For the opposition party, self-justification demanded a wholesale over-turning of officeholders rather than selective removal for cause. The ideology of a standing opposition party drew elements from older English defenses of the "loyal opposition" and newer American notions of representative government. The former derived from the writings of "country party" men and stressed the constitutionality of a "responsible" opposition: men might organize in opposition to a ruling clique if they worked within the Constitution, were prepared to form a government of their own, and sought practical remedies for objectionable policies.[9] The English rationale was made more sweeping by Republicans here. In his 1792 "Candid State of Parties" admitting the organized efforts of the "Republican" opposition to Hamilton, Madison argued that an opposition party was legitimate because it represented the people. Members of both parties were elected, but Republicans adhered to the principles of the Revolution, whereas Federalists supposedly returned to the discredited politics of English imperial rule.[10] Jefferson concurred; parties were a necessity: "Free government," he thundered, "is founded in jealousy, and not in confidence; it is jealousy and not confidence which prescribes limited constitutions, to bind down those whom we are obliged to trust with power. . . ." In 1801, after his election to the presidency, Jefferson wrote to Elbridge Gerry: "We are the Whigs, they the Tories . . . the only difference from 1776 is that the leaders [of the Federalists] who remain behind are more numerous and bolder than the apostles of Toryism in '76."[11] Impeachment could not have answered the Republicans' ends; only over-whelming victory at the polls would do.

The Federalists' ideology had similarly little use for impeachment. Although they could undertake it (as the legislative majority), they had no need to remove the Federalists their majorities appointed to administrative and judicial posts. Nor would they use impeachment against their opponents, for, as Timothy Pickering asserted, his party was composed of men "of sense and experience, who gave the reins, not to . . . passions, but to reason." Fisher Ames agreed that among his colleagues, "reason" checked enthusiasm and built a stable federal government. "No sooner did the new government begin its auspicious course, than order seemed to arise out of confusion."[12] The Federalists had no need of impeachment; they merely had to maintain their electoral majority.

For all the rhetoric, impeachment had practical appeal to party men. It had already proved its utility in the states. And theory was no obstacle: during the Revolution, utility had overcome theoretical objections to adoption of impeachment. The same sequence of events—exigency leading ideology— opened the door in the 1790s to impeachments designed solely to remove the opposition from office. Justifications for this step came later, piecemeal. In large measure, managers of impeachments continued to claim that they acted under the strict constitutional rules, and most cases brought between 1788 and 1805 actually did fit this description. Nevertheless, the passions of party and the effectiveness of impeachment inclined politicians to prosecute their enemies through legislative means. The new impetus for impeachment and trial to remove, rather than find facts and establish guilt, did not replace the older, "constitutional" requirements. The limits of the procedure itself, allowing counsel and permitting the accused to prepare a case, and the controlling precedent of earlier impeachments—demanding proof of actual offenses, willful misdeeds violating the Constitution, known law, or accepted ethical standards—prevented an inundation of political impeachments. Against the growing tide of partisanship the old law did not collapse. Instead, it leaked. A trickle of cases appeared whose purpose was to remove an unpopular, out-of-step, or obnoxious official from his post when defeat at the polls was not possible.

The three chapters of this section trace the bifurcation of impeachment law. Under earlier state and federal guidelines, impeachments in the era 1788–95 might involve political issues as well as demonstrable misconduct in office but were never wholly partisan. We have termed these cases and their rule of law *constitutional* with a small *c*. They grew out of the state constitutional provisions and cases, which, in their turn, had been fashioned when the pervasive fear of far-reaching parliamentary impeachments was still vivid. The federal Constitution, as we have seen, derived its impeachment and trial provisions from state precedents, not from English law. Federal law thus embodied the states' doctrine of limited impeachments: culpability for willful misconduct, extortion, bribery, misuse of power, and criminal acts. The impeachments of William Greenleaf and William Hunt of Massachusetts, Alexander Moultrie and William Davis of South Carolina, Woodbury Langdon of New Hampshire, Henry Osbourne of Georgia, and John Nicholson of Pennsylvania among others in this era all involved accusations of either gross mismanagement of public funds or abusive and wanton misuse of power. As far as we can read the record these men were impeached and tried, prosecuted and judged under a strict construction of constitutional language, despite the fact that all these states were embroiled in partisan combat.

In the next half-decade, the Jay Treaty debates polarized Congress, and national parties entrenched themselves in local electoral districts, bringing

Republican–Federalist competition into impeachment law. While the great majority of state prosecutions remained "constitutional" in tone, a series of cases ending with the impeachment of William Blount played havoc with the intent of older American impeachment doctrine and politicized legislative jurisprudence.

The tension between the concurrent impeachment theories—the majority view ("constitutional") and the minority view (political)—sharpened the awareness of everyone connected with the process. The vast predominance of hearings "for cause," traced in chapter 9, did not relieve the strain upon managers of even the most solid cases to avert charges of partisanship. Some light upon this dilemma may be thrown from a parallel jurisdiction—that of parliamentary impeachment and trial in the 1780s and 1790s. As we have noted, impeachments were a rarity in England by this time, and Americans drew from their own tradition, not England's. Nevertheless, in the prosecution of Warren Hastings (1786–95), Edmund Burke faced a problem that was similar to the American party leaders' dilemma: how to use impeachment to further the establishment of party government without violating the older limitations on impeachable offenses. Hastings's offenses, if his prosecutors spoke the truth, were more intrigues than crimes, and Hastings had already resigned the governor generalship of the East India Company colony, but his case attracted the attention of Edmund Burke nonetheless. Burke had personal reasons to demand punishment of Hastings, but satisfaction of them was not the sole cause of his management of the impeachment and trial. He conceived that the prosecution of Hastings was a way to introduce and publicize a new conception of English government, a party government of the representative type.

Long before Hastings's case burst upon the scene, Burke had been agitating for political reform. Although not a radical Wilkesite, Burke condemned the mixture of interest and patronage that infused eighteenth-century Whig government in England. The cancer he diagnosed was "Influence," the rise of a royal governing faction, concentrating power in the hands of a few. A corrupt connection of men at court seeking all "honors, offices, and emoluments" ran the country. Against them were arrayed not a cabal, as they wrongfully declared, but representatives of the "people at large." Upon two secure foundations the will of the people might stand against Influence: "power arising from popularity; and power arising from connection." The first showed itself in the outpouring of support for an elder Pitt or a John Wilkes. The second grew from responsible opposition, organized and cohesive in its attack on corruption and self-interest among the ruling faction. Burke never embraced a delegate theory of representative government in which members of Parliament carried out the explicit wishes of the electorate, but he did defend electoral parties, "connections," and their role in government.[13] Unfortunately for Burke and his co-workers, if the enemy was corruption, party politics was no scourge. And corruption plagued government; Pitt's ministry was riddled with it. Visible above all others was Hastings, until January 1785 the governor general of the East India Company colony. Holding almost absolute power within the colony but unprotected in England when his powerful friends in the Pitt ministry deserted him, Hastings became to Burke the epitome of corrosive "Influence."[14] Hastings could do in the Far East what the king could not do in England: start wars, encourage uprisings, bribe and threaten princes, and destroy obstacles to the progress of the company and the profits of his friends. Though not alone in the effort—even Pitt condemned the conduct of the former governor—Burke became Hastings's nemesis.

During the course of Hastings's impeachment and trial, Burke labored to fit the older idea of impeachment, a grand inquest on behalf of all the people into wrongdoing by men in high places, to the idea of party government he espoused earlier in his career. A frank shift of the rationale for impeachable offenses was unthinkable; Burke had too much respect for precedent, and there was too much precedent to attempt this leap. Instead, Burke worked within the "usages of parliament" to gradually shift the boundary conditions of prosecution and defense. It would not be easy, he worried:

> Most of the facts, upon which we proceed, are confessed; some of them are boasted of. The labour will be on the criminality of the facts, where proof, as I apprehend, will not be contested. Guilt resides in the intention. But as we are before a tribunal, which having conceived a favourable opinion of Hastings (or what is of more moment, very favourable wishes for him) they will not judge of his intentions by the acts, but they will qualify his Acts by his presumed intentions. It is on this preposterous mode of judging that he has built all the Apologies for his conduct, which I have seen. Excuses, which in any criminal court would be considered with pity as the Straws, at which poor wretches drowning will catch, and which are such as no prosecutor thinks it worth his while to reply to, will be admitted in such a House of Commons as ours as a solid defence. . . .We know that we bring before a bribed tribunal a prejudged cause. In that situation all that we have to do is to make a case strong in proof and in importance, and to draw inferences from it justifiable in logick, policy and criminal justice. As to all the rest, it is vain and idle.[15]

Charging Hastings with the "general intention" of malfeasance and corruption, Burke could point to a body of precedent. The Lords had not insisted upon precise framing of charges in the 1690s and earlier 1700s. These cases, a fruitful source of citations, were political—as Burke undoubtedly understood. In fact, they were the product of an earlier party struggle between

Whigs and Tories, as he had argued years before. With these cases as precedent, Burke drove the case against Hastings into the Lords. As chief manager of the prosecution, he spoke at length at the trial. Were Hastings's failings evidence of corruption and avarice?: yes. Burke painted the governor as the perfect model of a tyrant: grasping, impatient, violent, and self-interested.[16] He knew that the usage of Parliament included many trials for official malfeasance far less fully documented than Hastings's, and was confident of victory.

The Lords acquitted the ex-governor, much to Burke's dismay. Never at a loss for words, Burke placed the blame for this verdict upon a faction in the upper house. Not willing to reveal, even at this stage of the game, the connection he had made between party and impeachment, Burke aimed his barbs at the illegitimate role played by the king's judges in the Lords' deliberations. Judges sitting with the Lords at earlier trials upheld the Commons' argument that impeachment tribunals were not precisely bounded by the same rules of pleading, evidence, and framing of charges that had evolved in the regular courts of law. At Hastings's trial, however, the judges attempted to narrow the great latitude the Lords had exercised in hearing impeachments. In these opinions, rendered to the upper house and, privately, to the defendant's counsel, the judges favored the defendant and abridged the rights of the lower house.[17] The acquittal of Hastings ended Burke's dream of truly responsible party government. That reform would ultimately come nearly a century later (by which time, ironically, Burke's name would be a synonym for conservatism).

American impeachment managers did not adopt Burke's tortured logic; they had no more than a general familiarity with the case, although it was mentioned at points in Blount's, Addison's, and Chase's trials.[18] Burke's thinking was nevertheless pregnant for America, for by accepting the utility of parties, he was forced to fit impeachment into a system of party government. True, he covered his tracks, silently adopting those impeachment precedents which most lent themselves to his ideal of party, but his passage from party defender to impeachment manager left a trail. In the 1790s American party leaders began to traverse the same course. As in Burke's journey, political opportunity in the New World made a shift or, more precisely, a splintering, in the rationale for impeachment necessary and inevitable. While Burke's impact upon American thought was often negative, he was read, and his work anticipated Americans' acceptance of a number of ideas.[19] His amalgamation of party and impeachment, while not directing American thought, illustrated a path that republican leaders would follow.

7

CONSTITUTIONAL IMPEACHMENT, 1788–1795

THE UTILITY AND LEGITIMACY OF IMPEACHMENT IN REPUBLICIAN CONSTITUTIONS were confirmed at the federal convention of 1787, but the future of impeachment remained uncertain. Its provisions (like much of the document) were couched in broad terms.[1] There was no federal case law yet. True, the states had fashioned an American precedent far more sharply hedged with limitations than the English experience, but would the federal government, whose provisions had drawn life from the states' experience, now operate within the confines of that experience, or would the higher stakes and grander passions of national government politicize and cripple impeachment as a constitutional tool? In part the answer depended upon the interpretation placed upon Article II, section 4, and within that, the nebulous yet encompassing formula of "high crimes and misdemeanors." The next seven years would reveal great wariness on the part of Congress to attempt impeachment but far less trepidation among the states. They continued to impeach malefactors according to the limited, narrow rules laid down after 1776. Curbed by these limitations, federal political leaders did not seize upon impeachment to harass their enemies until the seeds of conflict sown by the Jay Treaty blossomed into impeachments.

Hard as it had been to frame the federal law of impeachment, it proved still harder to give practical meaning to the federal definitions of impeachable offenses. In the Philadelphia convention the formula "treason, bribery, or other high crimes and misdemeanors" was taken to subsume corruption, maladministration, and neglect of duty. The addition of treason and bribery or, to be precise, the addition of "high crimes and misdemeanors" to "treason and bribery" in Article II, section 4, allowed charges upon innumerable offenses. In light of the diversity of opinion at the convention on the language of Article II, section 4, the task left to future legislators was perplexing at best and vexatious at worst. What were misdemeanors? Were they lesser crimes, as defined in criminal codes, or merely misconducts? Did every high crime or misdemeanor have to be a violation of written law, and, if so, did the law have to be federal statute, or would common law, state statutes, and earlier impeachment precedent be acceptable substitutes?

Federal legislators and state legislators would not be able to find answers to these questions in a federal criminal code, because there was none. While the Constitution defined treason explicitly, a deliberate effort to avoid the political treason trials prevalent during the English Civil War and Restoration, and while bribery had a common-law definition which no one had questioned, the omnibus *high crimes and misdemeanors* raised problems from the start. The Bill of Rights did not define types of crimes and gave no clue about the content of the formula for impeachable offenses. The Judiciary Act of 1789, creating the courts of original and appellate jurisdiction below the Supreme Court, did not include a federal criminal code. Federal district and circuit court judges were asked to follow procedures of the states in which they sat.[2]

The substance of federal criminal law would be filled out by congressional legislation over the 1790s, but large areas of jurisdiction of federal courts had no corresponding codes of substantive law. Congress might have allowed federal judges to adopt the English common law of crimes in those areas where the federal judiciary exercised jurisdiction, but this alternative was not chosen (with one short-lived and divisive exception, the alien and sedition laws of 1798). The Republican opposition rejected the prospect of wholesale incorporation of the common law. Jefferson and Madison railed against its "bloody maxims." Both men also feared that the common law gave uncontrolled discretion to judges.[3] Justice Samuel Chase, leading the Federalist attack on the Republicans from the high court bench, agreed with them on this point: in *United States v. Worrall* (1798) he denied that a federal grand jury could bring an indictment for a crime not specified in federal law. His dissent in *Worrall* would become the majority position in *U.S. v. Goodwin and Hudson* (1812), though at the time it remained a minority position. The common law of England, adopted in part by a number of the states after the Revolution, was never copied into federal law. When the Federalist Congress made seditious libel a crime, Chase did preside over the trials of Republicans for this offense.[4] There was thus no federal standard, except in a very few specific areas, for "high crimes and misdemeanors."

Scholars have assumed that the framers and their successors turned to English cases to fill this lacuna in impeachment law. The logic of this assumption is questionable. Without a common law of crimes, it is doubtful that English impeachment cases could be called precedent for American criminal proceedings. One cannot throw the common law out the front door and sneak it through a back window. If the common law had an impact on American understanding of "high crimes," it was not direct but lay in a manner of reasoning by precedent. The weight of precedent was paramount in the common law, and this mechanism prevailed as well in American legal thought in the 1780s and 1790.[5] The source and the substance of impeachment precedent was not England's but very much closer at hand. Interpreters of the new federal law could look upon a decade and a half of state law and cases. In other words, the influence of state experience with impeachment upon national law did not end with the framing of the Constitution of the United States. State cases reflected American understanding of the federal rules, offering a continuing flow of precedent and commentary upon the utility of impeachment in republics. This reciprocal effort on a "corresponding" power was evident in the state ratifying conventions and cases.

The ratification debates threw a little light on the framers' views of the offenses clause. In Virginia, Madison supposed that if a president "violated the interest of the nation" he would be impeachable—a far broader definition of offenses than bribery, treason, or crimes. Indeed, it seemed to apply the "good behavior" test for judicial tenure in Article III, section 1, of the Constitution to the president. Looking back to the state precedents, Madison merely confirmed his view that "high crimes and misdemeanors" did not exclude noncriminal acts. A close reading of his part in the debates on Article II, section 4, gives the same impression of his ideas. He did object to prosecution of inadvertent and ignorant errors in office. These were not impeachable.[6]

No framer wished to bring the English "bad advice" doctrine to American shores. As James Iredell told the North Carolina delegates: "God forbid that a man, in any country in the world, should be liable to be punished for want of judgment. This is not the case here. . . . Whatever mistake a man may make, he ought not to be punished for it, nor his posterity rendered infamous. But if a man be a villain, and wilfully abuse his trust, he is to be held up as a public offender, and ignominiously punished . . . nothing but real guilt can disgrace him." In the case of a president, receiving a bribe or acting "from some corrupt motive or other" would be enough. What was a "corrupt" motive? Did Iredell imply that only bribery, extortion, embezzlement, and fraud fell into this category? Or, more probably, did Iredell mean "self-interested" by "corrupt"? At any rate, simple political self-interest could not be sufficient ground for impeachment, or no officer would be left in his post.[7]

Madison's second phrase—"of the nation"—explored this question. The offense must present a real danger to the public or the government. Private offenses might be safely left to the regular courts. Excesses of political venom could be curbed at the polls. From the Virginia convention he carried his thoughts on impeachment to the first Congress. During an extended debate in the House of Representatives over the president's power to remove members of his cabinet, Madison took time to expound on impeachment. He was not afraid to give the chief executive the power to replace the cabinet because: "I know he is impeachable for any crime or misdemeanor, before the senate, at all times; and that at all events he is impeachable before the community at large every four years, and liable to be displaced if his conduct shall have given umbrage during the time he has been in office."[8] Madison's remarks proved that he had either shifted views since the convention in Philadelphia or had agreed in large measure with those he apparently opposed. In 1787 he had argued for a tightening of the definition of impeachable offenses. Two years later, in Congress, he argued that presidential removal of a man from appointive office whose merits required that he should be continued in it, was an abuse of power. The president who did this would be "impeachable by this house, before the senate, for such an act of maladministration; for I contend that the wanton removal of meritorious officers would subject him to impeachment and removal."[9] What can this position imply, coupled with Madison's restriction of impeachable offenses to "high crimes and misdemeanors" in the convention? There he explicitly rejected "maladministration" as too uncertain a charge; two years later he reintroduced the very word in characterizing a removable offense. Madison evidently believed (with Mason and others) that the latter could be subsumed by the former on appropriate occasions but was too vague by itself. In a second speech to the House on presidential removals, Madison noted that if the president was not impeached by the House for removing a man of "high merit" and "extensive influence," the chief executive would nevertheless be subject to "an impeachment before the community, who will have the power of punishment by refusing to re-elect him."[10] Were election defeats equivalent in his mind to removals upon trial in the Senate? In a purely party government, one might regard some impeachment trials as functional equivalents of elections—if the official in question were not an elected one. Republicans would explore this analogy a decade later, although Madison would then shy away from the experiment. This much is clear: he had not insisted upon evidence of criminality. Instead, he opted for the older state doctrine: there had to be some palpable wrongdoing, through self-interest or negligence, to impeach and try an incumbent. As he wrote to Edmund Pendleton after the debate, the overuse of impeachment to remove appointees would have made every office tenured on good behavior, the very antithesis of representative government.[11]

In the wave of state constitutional revision which followed ratification of the federal document, state legislators also grappled with the task of defining impeachable offenses. The effort brought forth a variety of answers. Jefferson's easy assurance that an assembly could precisely define all crimes meriting impeachment (in his 1776 draft of a constitution for Virginia) was naive. The 1789 constitution of Georgia merely provided that "the senate shall have

solely the power to try all impeachments" and the house "shall have solely
the power to impeach all persons who have been or may be in office."[12] In
1792, revision of the Delaware Constitution dropped the state's first definition of offenses and adopted the federal rule: "treason, bribery, or any other
high crime or misdemeanor"—to which the delegates later added the phrase
"or any crime or misdemeanor in office."[13] Whether this addendum broadened the range of offenses, following Madison's line of reasoning, or merely
reminded legislators to confine their impeachments to officials, is moot; the
Delaware lower house did not impeach anyone during this period. The
newly minted constitutions of Kentucky and Tennessee followed federal
guidelines, save that no attempt was made to delineate impeachable offenses
in the new states' laws—a change from the first states' provisions.[14] The
procedures were clearer because the federal model was clear. In 1784 Tennessee's founders' first attempt at constitution making copied the North Carolina example verbatim, and thus did not specify the place of trial, the limits of
liability, or the size of vote for conviction. The Tennessee Constitution of
1796 required trial in the senate, on a two-thirds vote, to result in loss of office,
along federal lines. The new constitution dropped the "maladministration,
and corruption" categories of offenses still valid in North Carolina, again,
presumably, under the influence of the federal document.[15] During the
debates in the Kentucky constitutional convention the delegates agreed to
remove legislators from office upon "conviction" for violation of oath, and
giving and taking bribes. Who was to find the verdict was not clear. Exclusion from officeholding was to be levied against men convicted of "bribery,
perjury, forgery, or other high crimes or misdemeanors" in the regular
courts.[16] This mixing and matching of legal formulas suggests that the
delegates wished to include all the older provisions in their own laws. The
fact that these provisions were of very different scope—some narrow and
requiring criminality, others broad and political—did not disturb the
Kentuckians.

Only in the Pennsylvania convention of 1789–90, called to revise the
constitution of 1776, did the subject of impeachable offenses receive careful,
extended attention. With Wilson and McKean leading them, the delegates
gave the power to "hear and determine" impeachments to the newly established senate, which replaced the weak council. The senate was to remove and
disqualify defendants upon a two-thirds vote only, though the defendant was
still liable to trial and punishment in the regular courts "according to law."
The influence of the federal Constitution was evident, but the Pennsylvania
delegates did not slavishly follow the federal example. The offenses were
"any misdemeanor in office," considerably less specific and broader language
than that of the federal rule. William Lewis joined McKean in an attempt to
confine prosecution to two years after the offense, but they failed. The

delegates limited offenses to those committed by officeholders, while in office. They had a clear conception that, although the offense might be "any misdemeanor," the victim must be the public or the state, as well as any individuals involved. Finally, at the very end of their deliberations, they voted that the governor could remove a judge on petition of two-thirds of both houses for grounds "not sufficient for impeachment." As in Madison's addresses to Congress on the removal power, an attempt by Wilson, McKean, and others to uphold the constitutional purity of impeachment ended with a concession to party politics. Pennsylvania was beset by fervent party struggles in the 1780s, climaxing in divisions over the state constitution. Judges were involved in these controversies; that is to say, party conflict politicized the bench. Impeachment and trial required proof of malicious violation of trust and law. Removal upon lesser grounds, even with two-thirds requirements, could be used to oust an unpopular judge guilty of no crime, whether misdemeanor or worse.[17]

A minority would cling to the notion that impeachable offenses had to be indictable in a court of criminal jurisdiction. In future years, Pennsylvania District Judge Alexander Addison, United States Supreme Court Justice Samuel Chase, and counselors Luther Martin and Robert Goodloe Harper of Maryland and a handful of others, defending themselves and their clients against impeachments for maladministration, pointed to the specific language of Article II, section 4. Treasons, bribery, and other high crimes and misdemeanors were grounds for criminal indictments in regular courts; impeachable offenses must therefore be indictable in regular courts—if they were to be punishable at all. The terms *maladministration* and *misconduct* had not survived the September 5, 1787, debate.

In practice this distinction worked in the regular courts but not in impeachments. Grand juries were enjoined to look into crimes by officials but not into maladministration. For example, in 1790, Chief Justice John Jay, who had been one of the authors of the New York State provisions for impeachment (which defined misconduct as impeachable), told a federal grand jury to direct their attention "to the conduct of the national officers, and let not any corruption, frauds, extortions, or criminal negligence with which you may find any of them justly chargeable pass unnoticed."[18] He did not instruct them to search out offenses against the public interest—misuse of power for private ends and mismanagement—which were covered in the states' constitutions by impeachment provisions. Jay must have assumed that Congress had similar powers under Article II, section 4, for if federal officials' misconduct in office were placed outside impeachment's reach following the federal Constitution, and was excluded from the reach of grand juries as well, then no branch of government could monitor and correct misuses of power, unethical conduct, influence peddling, favoritism, and other noncriminal malfeasance by officials. Chase and Addison might plead the independence of the judiciary in demurrer to the jurisdiction of Congress in these offenses, but the weight of state precedent in America was against them, and the framers took this precedent as their own. State governments did not agonize over the precise severity of offenses deemed impeachable or hold off impeachment when the offense was unindictable in a regular court of law.[19]

Some state assemblies did construct a floor of sorts for the severity of impeachable offenses when they summarily dismissed officials or addressed the governor to remove his own appointees. Only a few states built these alternatives to impeachment into their constitutions, but those states did not hesitate to use dismissal and address to oust misfeasant incumbents. The constitutional and statutory provisions for such procedures did not specify or limit offenses warranting removal, but a cursory review of precedent shows that the charges could be as minor as contempt of the lower house. North Carolina's Commons House of Assembly dismissed a justice of the peace accused of "sundry misdemeanors incompatible with the duty and dignity of his said office" when he did not appear before them to answer their complaints. The contempt he showed for their summons led to his dismissal. The New Jersey Assembly removed election commissioners and paymasters for incompetence. No malice, knowing violation of law, or even willful negligence was imputed to these men; they simply did not suitably perform their official duties. The Kentucky Assembly addressed the governor to remove a justice of the peace on similar grounds: through ignorance of the law, he had bullied litigants and given erroneous judgments.[20]

Erroneous judicial rulings were not quite grounds for an address for removal, as one notorious Kentucky case demonstrated. On December 20, 1794, the Kentucky senate "addressed" the lower house that appeals court judges Benjamin Sebastian and George Muter (two-thirds of the bench of that court) had given opinions in *Kenton v. McConnell* "contrary to the plain meaning and content of the law." The senate sought the lower house's concurrence in an address to the governor to remove the judges. Large-boned, amiable, and lazy, Sebastian, a "court" party aristocrat, land speculator, lawyer, and planter, was a Republican stalwart. Muter, a thin, small Scottish immigrant, was also a Republican but had been a Federalist and anti-Federalist by turns earlier in his career. The senate was narrowly Federalist, the house Republican, and the attack on the judges can be seen as politically motivated. On the other hand, their opinions in *Kenton v. McConnell* overturned land claims based upon the Virginia Land Company titles—an invitation to chaos. Despite political allegiances the lower house demanded Muter and Sebastian appear and, when they refused, voted their conduct "altogether destitute of that judgment, integrity, and firmness which are essential in every judge." The legislature was angry enough with the judges to condemn them but not enough to seek their formal removal. An unpopular, even incompetent judicial ruling was not nearly dangerous enough to warrant impeachment.[21]

By comparison with dismissal and address, impeachment required more serious misconduct than mere incompetence, neglect, or innocent error of judgment. Ashe, for example, was a bully in the Loyalist cases, and Jefferson was incompetent in his military command, but neither man was quite impeached. A line had been drawn in the first state cases, and, in the absence of any clarifying debate following the federal convention on the definition of impeachable offenses, that earlier line remained the guide. Despite the flurry of activity during the adoption of the federal procedures, the states' only guide in bringing cases was their past experience. Thus, the first state impeachments after the ratification of the federal Constitution resembled the state cases of the previous decade. They were not political—that is, their object was not solely to remove a politician from office. Gross, intentional, self-interested official misconduct, or some criminal act had to be alleged for the impeachment to go forward, as the first case in this era illustrated.

William Greenleaf of Worcester, Massachusetts, was a fixture in the power structure of the county. A Revolutionary War hero, he was by 1788 commander of the county militia and sheriff. On March 7 the inhabitants of Petersham petitioned the Massachusetts General Court that Greenleaf be ordered to suspend execution against alleged tax defaulters. The complaints did not aver that Greenleaf had pocketed the money, merely that he had failed to give credit for the payment.[22] Towns often petitioned the assembly for redress in abatement or adjustment of taxes, and this petition was routinely assigned to the committee on petitions. The committee ordered that Greenleaf receive a copy of the petition and summoned him to answer at the next session of the assembly. David Bigelow, representing Petersham, pushed the case in the June session of the legislature. The petitions committee gave way to a committee of the whole, and witnesses were summoned. Another petition had arrived from the town of Hardwick; Greenleaf was a brusk and hard man and had not taken kindly to questions about his authority. On June 12, after some procedural fumbling, the house voted, 157 to 10, that the complaints were "sufficient grounds for bringing forward articles of impeachment . . . for misconduct and maladministration in his office."[23]

The General Court, not having impeached anyone since Peter Oliver, regarded Greenleaf's case as precedent making and commented upon each step they undertook. A blue-ribbon committee to prepare articles was selected. Former governor Bowdoin was joined by Shearjashub Bourne, an old and a respected Barnstable lawyer and judge, Thomas Dawes, a leading Boston lawyer, John Phelps, a Westfield landowner, and John Choate, an Ipswich farmer. These men represented the spectrum of occupations that sat in the house. There was no particular party bias in the group; Greenleaf was not suspected of party excesses.[24] The lower house authorized Bowdoin and the others to bring witnesses and to subpoena evidence from Worcester. Witnesses and committeemen were paid out of the public treasury for their trouble.[25]

The final draft of the articles cited a long train of abuses, reaching back "for many years."[26] The articles charged both specific, that is, precisely named, offenses, and general ones. By including both categories, the assembly gave itself the power to go beyond the limitations of indictment in regular courts of law. In the latter, the "offense itself must also be set forth with clearness and certainty."[27] The Massachusetts representatives were almost the same body of men who debated the federal provisions for impeachment in the ratification convention. They knew that offenses need not be indictable in a criminal court. Closer to home, the same point was made in Massachusetts statutes. The Treason Act of February 1, 1777, gave the General Court power to hear and determine treason under strict procedural definitions drawn from regular courts of law. The statute then concluded: "such parts of this act as relate to the regulation of trials [in the General Court], shall not extend, or be construed to extend, to any impeachment or other proceeding in the general assembly of this state."[28] Although at that time there was no state constitution, and impeachment did not legally exist, the lawmakers understood that impeachment and trial in the legislature was not the same as indictment and trial in the regular courts. The explicit reference to "general" articles in Greenleaf's case was based on this understanding.

The six articles of impeachment brought against Greenleaf charged that he had "detained in his own hands" monies that should have gone to the public treasury, given false information to the treasury (both general accusations), and more specifically that he had improperly accounted for tax money from Petersham, obtained an execution against Petersham for this money illegally, returned this execution to the treasury marked unsatisfied, and finally, obtained a warrant to proceed against Petersham for the default. Dawes and Bourne were asked by the assembly to manage the case in the senate. They were joined by Fisher Ames, a young and able Federalist politician and lawyer, Theophilus Parsons, perhaps the leading jurist and legal educator in the state, and Martin Kingsly.[29]

The senate was as concerned about procedure as the lower house. William Heath, one of the assemblymen, recalled that "after opening the court, the trial was adjourned" and "the house walked from their own chamber to Faneuil Hall in procession, as was said by some to give importance to the occasion." The lower house was not about to fade from the picture; its members went en masse to the trial. The public also gathered. The sheriff of Suffolk County, responsible for keeping order, led the procession.[30] The county coroner for Worcester was ordered to bring affidavits and other evidence to the senate, and witnesses were subpoenaed.[31] Greenleaf chose as his counsel James Sullivan of Maine, one of the ablest young advocates in the state (though Sullivan was a popular party leader and would remain so). Joining Sullivan was John Sprague, a conservative lawyer and teacher. Sprague and Sullivan negotiated the right to object to the admissibility of evidence and to enter a special plea to the charges at any time they "shall see fit."[32]

Greenleaf's professional legal counsel sought for him the rights and privileges that any defendant would have in a criminal court under the Massachusetts bill of rights, among which was representation by legal counsel. Right to counsel itself was not automatic in impeachment law. Chief Justice Oliver was not represented by counsel in the pretrial stages of his own case. There is no evidence that Vetch and Borland had counsel. Counsel was permitted impeachment defendants before the bar of the House of Lords—but only to argue points of law. Sullivan and Sprague did more than argue points of law for Greenleaf; they conducted the defense, examined witnesses, and summed the case. This, along with other rights claimed and obtained for their client, originated in post-revolutionary criminal trial procedure, not in impeachment precedent.

The senate was scrupulous to protect Greenleaf's rights but did not attempt to determine whether the trial itself was a criminal procedure. The Massachusetts Constitution directed impeachment and trial for high crimes and misdemeanors but did not say that the senate was to be a criminal court. The state constitution had guaranteed jury trial of infamous crimes, but the senate cannot be equated with a jury from the vicinage of the crime. Although impeachment managers would wrestle over the next two decades with the question raised at the Greenleaf trial, his prosecutors, judges, and defense counsel arrived at a compromise. Strict adherence to criminal procedure would hamstring the jurisdiction of the upper house, for the senators were not jurors, and the offenses need not be crimes. Impeachment trial was to be distinguished from regular trials at law. This understanding was reiterated at the impeachment trials of ex-senator William Blount, federal judge John Pickering, and Supreme Court Justice Samuel Chase, though the extent of allowable deviation from criminal procedure was subject to controversy.[33] At the same time, the defendant was allowed many of the protections guaranteed in a criminal trial. Greenleaf's case established the senate as a unique jurisdiction, limited in the crimes it could hear and the defendants it could pursue.

Ames and Parsons, for the prosecution, and Sullivan, for the defense, battled vigorously. The prosecution found "unexpected evidence" and the defense was forced to seek refutation in additional witnesses. From November 5 to November 14 the senate devoted the better part of its afternoons to sitting as a court. On the fourteenth the verdict came down: 20 voted guilty, 3 voted not guilty. Elijah Dwight, Ebeneezer Bridge, and Charles Turner held out for acquittal. None of these men was a well-known partisan. The penalty for conviction followed: on the eighteenth the senate removed Greenleaf from his office. He was replaced as sheriff by Sprague—an ironic touch but not an unreasonable one given Sprague's influence and standing.[34]

Greenleaf's downfall lay not in a party combination against him but in the manners that had given him the sobriquet "high sheriff" of Worcester.[35] The general articles, alleging his high-handedness, were more telling than the single documented case of malfeasance in Petersham. The great concern for correct ceremony throughout the impeachment and trial suggests that the legislators regarded his as a test case. Massachusetts was learning what New Jersey, Vermont, and other states had already discovered: impeachment need not disrupt government or challenge authority. Trials could be conducted with dispatch and fairness. The next Massachusetts impeachment and trial would not take an entire year but little more than three weeks.

Massachusetts' neighbor, New Hampshire, had followed the Bay State's lead in adopting impeachment and had already begun a course of impeachments when the Massachusetts General Court heard *Greenleaf*. Impeachment in the White Mountain State after 1788 merely continued the precedent laid down before the federal Constitution. That is to say, there was no change in state procedure after its convention ratified the federal Constitution. Impeachable offenses still included misconducts as well as crimes. In a 1789 inquiry into the conduct of David Webster, sheriff of Grafton, Israel Morey, a petitioner, charged that Webster had not returned votes from the county for state offices, appointed crooked appraisers of land, illegally took bonds in criminal cases (only a justice could take bonds and give bail), colluded with a party in a lawsuit, packed a jury, refused to obey the orders of a Grafton justice, and made illegal exactions upon Israel Morey. The assembly voted a full-fledged inquiry and, after the committee reported, took a formal vote on the impeachment. The motion failed, 45 to 10. The charges were serious enough to warrant impeachment if proved, although much of what was alleged would not have been triable in a criminal court. If Webster was ultimately exonerated, the lower house evidently had regarded the allegations as serious business.[36]

Webster, like Moriss before him, was a minor official but impeachment also worked against those in high positions. As the charges against Webster were dismissed, the lower house began an investigation that would lead to impeachment of the highest state official yet: Supreme Court Justice Woodbury Langdon. Langdon came from a wealthy Portsmouth family, whose leader, his older brother John, was speaker of the house during the Revolution. Woodbury himself was a Son of Liberty and a councillor during the

Revolution, but once made a justice of the court (at his brother's request), he became far more erratic in his conduct. Twice he refused a seat on the highest court and, though named to Congress in 1779, he left that body and refused to serve again. United States Senator William Plumer, a political colleague, remembered Langdon's conduct on the state supreme court bench as abrupt and practical—perhaps even curt, Plumer ventured.[37]

Throughout 1788 the house and senate received regular complaints against Langdon for skipping court sessions. The justice provided a wealth of excuses—ill health, conflict of interest, bad weather—and continued to miss sessions.[38] The assembly's patience ebbed. Josiah Bartlett, one of Langdon's colleagues on the bench and later chief justice, told the house that without Langdon, the court could not sit, but Langdon still refused to appear. Bartlett, who knew why Langdon stayed home, let the recalcitrant judge speak for himself on that score.[39] Langdon expressed his own reasons to the house on December 23, 1789. First, he argued that the judges could adjourn sessions at will, and the lower house had no right to interpose itself between the judges and their duties. This was disingenuous of Langdon, for he was not even at the sessions to adjourn them. Second, judges often missed sessions and Langdon thought he was being singled out for blame. He insisted that the illness of Justice Livermore was really to blame—forcing cancellation of sessions when any one of the other judges could not attend. Most important to Langdon was the absence of a fixed and "honorable" salary. This was the basis of his discontent.[40]

Langdon had gone too far in his protests—even beyond the friendly shelter of his brother's influence. On June 16, 1790, the house began impeachment proceedings against the judge for neglect of duty. No office was to be "held as a sinecure." The resolution to impeach passed 35 to 29 the next day. One more day of consultation brought forth three articles, alleging three counts of "wilfull and corrupt ... misbehavior."[41] The *wilfull* in the articles implied as much as Langdon admitted, that his neglect was purposeful—intended to disrupt the court circuit. The *corrupt* presumably referred to his demand for a higher salary (since he did not barter his absence for remuneration from litigants). The *misbehavior* was the fact that he was absent from the bench. The articles the lower house prepared were read into the senate journal on June 19, 1790, and the senate ordered a trial for July 28.[42] When the trial opened, the managers were not ready, and a postponement was ordered until the next session, in January 1791.[43]

Plumer, then a member of the lower house (and later governor of the state), wrote to a friend that the impeachment was a chaotic business: a "long and fruitless tho' virulent attempt" to remove Langdon by an address of both houses to the governor had failed, and the impeachment resolution had only a shaky majority, though the "great stir" might still bring Langdon down.[44]

To Jeremiah Smith, an assemblyman who had voted against the impeachment but later agreed to manage it before the senate, Plumer's remarks were
more personal. Though Smith was now against Langdon, Plumer still
inveighed against the "duplicity" of the impeachment advocates. "The more
I know of Langdon," Plumer swore, "the more I admire his wit, penetration,
judgment and decision." Men "accustomed to think for themselves" found
the impeachment dishonorable. Plumer warned Smith and the senate against
trying Langdon when the lower house disbanded that summer. This
smacked of acting in the "character of a lawyer"—a weighty accusation![45] For
himself, Langdon dismissed the formal charges as he had the earlier inquiry:
he had already explained his conduct. He opined that all new accusations
were partial and put him in double jeopardy (though he had yet to come to
trial at all).[46]

At the first senate sessions of the new year Langdon's case was again called,
but the defendant did not come forth. The senate paid the witnesses' expenses
and tabled the house's renewed request for an address to the governor to
remove Langdon.[47] The cause of the senate's new course was simple: Langdon had resigned. Typically he sent along a defense, though none was now
needed. He had been too busy, he said, to run from court session to session; his
pay was inadequate; impeachment undermined the independence of the
judges; he had committed no crime; the charges were too loose and vague; no
one had suffered from his absence from court, and—his pièce de résistance—
the assemblymen were often absent from their sessions without penalty. He
was not willing to hold office at the mere will and pleasure of the senate and
happily let slip his burdens.[48] Late in 1790 he had accepted a post from the
federal government arranged by his brother as a commissioner of revolutionary accounts. The assembly, receiving word of his resignation from the
bench, had voted that Langdon, "being under impeachment of this house . . .
ought not to be permitted to resign the said office" before the senate heard the
case. The recommendation passed 32 to 25, but the senate could not compel
Langdon to resume his post in order that they remove him from it. The lower
house also voted that Langdon's letters to it on his inadequate salary were a
"contempt" and an "attempt to prejudice the minds" of the senators. When
Langdon refused to come to the next sessions of the trial court, the house
managers agreed to enter a nolle prosequi.[49] Langdon was out of the state and
out of his office; there was nothing to be done for it. The senate did inform the
house that "The Senate are of the Opinion . . . that the said Langdon's
conduct in his said office, on trial upon the merits of an impeachment, might
have been found extremely censurable" but his resignation ended the matter.
In any case, in his new job, he had an important task to perform for the state.[50]

Langdon, clear of the reach of the lower house, vented his relief and anger
to Plumer: "The attention you gave to [this] business lays me under very great

obligation. The very ridiculous, inconsistent as well as vile conduct of those persons who have brought the State into such contempt in that business must be held in the utmost detestation by every sensible honest man."[51] The ex-judge was not finished with political office in his native state. Twice he ran unsuccessfully for Congress, but he was returned to the state legislature. By then, the struggle between Langdon and the assembly had passed. He was a Federalist among Federalists, an elder statesman. In 1798, when the speaker and speaker pro-tem of the assembly were absent, Langdon was overwhelmingly chosen to assume the chair. Characteristically, he declined the honor. His anti-Federalist connections may have told against him in the late 1780s, and his unpopularity limited his prospects, but he had real talents and staunch friends.[52]

Langdon's insolent hauteur to one side, his quarrel with the lower house had justification of a sort: they were paying the associate justices only £150 a year for a strenuous circuit tour.[53] Twice in 1791, after Langdon resigned, the Grafton sessions were not attended by the justices. Three years after Langdon's tenure was a bad memory, the assembly passed a resolve to inquire why the superior court had not met in the counties of Hillsborough, Cheshire, and Grafton for the preceding terms.[54] The new chief justice, John Pickering, another Revolutionary War hero and lawyer of means, claimed to be so "fatigued" by the circuit that he could not preside at the court. Against this affront to their power, the lower house bridled. A petition to the governor and council to remove the chief justice failed in a tie vote.[55] Pickering's indisposition had the same pathology as Langdon's bouts of fatigue: inadequate funding by the assembly. When Pickering stepped down to accept a federal judgeship, the campaign for higher salaries was resumed by his successor, the infirm, aged John Dudley. In December 1796 the assembly addressed the governor and council that Dudley be removed for "not attending to the duties of his office" because he was too old. The senate, after some hesitation, concurred. The governor did not, though he agreed that something was wrong with the salaries.[56]

Langdon was not impeached for anti-Federalism, or unpopularity, or even for his arrogance. He was not the victim solely of "personal animosity." The articles against him cited "maladministration," and his absence from court for reasons of pique fit that characterization. Interruptions in the operation of the courts drove litigants to despair. Langdon may have thought that, if not above the laws, his position in society gave him the right to tinker with them. Had he come to court, his sharp voice and brusque manner may have offended some, but that could not be charged against him. By setting himself up outside the law, he violated the oath of his office. For this the appropriate response was impeachment.[57] As John Pickering would later discover, impeachment of a totally incompetent official could proceed even without evidence of willful or criminal intent. When removal was necessary on these grounds, criminality was not an issue.[58] Despite the furor surrounding Langdon's case, the assembly was not disrupted by it nor was the senate perturbed. A scramble for Langdon's post was the only vestige of his sudden departure. Impeachment in New Hampshire was a normal part of legislative business.[59]

At the same time that Langdon was dodging the bullet in New Hampshire, a congressional election in Georgia led to the impeachment and trial of superior court judge Henry Osborne. Osborne suffered for the rivalry between two Revolutionary giants, "Mad" Anthony Wayne and "Duelling" James Jackson. An Irish immigrant to Georgia, Osborne had risen from justice of peace of Camden County, in the southeast of the state, to become the first chief judge of the eastern division of the superior court. Though one of Camden's largest landholders, as well as a major holder in Glynn and Augusta, he was not satisfied with his lot.[60] In January 1788 he complained to the treasurer that the chief justice's office, which he held under the first state constitution, was too costly for him, and appealed to the "equity" of the assembly and governor to raise his salary.[61] In 1789 he was president of the constitutional convention that revised the state laws but a year later declined to take a seat in the newly established senate, "finding a torrent against those interests which I believe most dear to them (his constituents) and to my country."[62] He was not a reticent man, however, and soon his ardent political attachments brought him to grief.

The second protagonist in Osborne's impeachment was Anthony Wayne. The Revolutionary War general had spent time in Georgia as an Indian commissioner and sought to gain a seat in Congress from his adopted state. He settled briefly in Savannah and courted votes from Effingham, Camden, Glynn, and Chatham counties. All were filled with veterans, and they apparently raised their former leader to federal office in 1791. When the ballots were counted, Wayne had defeated the incumbent, James Jackson, by 21 votes.[63]

Jackson, a small, wiry, choleric politician, soldier, and speculator, was not easily trifled with. Though not from a gentle background—he emigrated from England at age 15—he had embraced the code duello with a vengeance, and used pistols, sword, and cane to batter his opponents.[64] While at first he seemed to take the defeat calmly (Wayne had, after all, endorsed Jackson's candidacy in 1789), he later averred that reports of managed elections and irregular pollings goaded him to public action. Many of these reports were traceable to his own agent's research. Throughout the summer of 1791 Jackson printed them in the Savannah *Gazette* and the Augusta *Chronicle*. On July 28, 1791, he informed the *Gazette* that "the Liberties and privileges of my fellow citizens have been grossly and wantonly trifled with" and produced affidavits from others who watched the judge keep the polls open and manufacture more votes for Wayne than there were voters.[65] Wayne's supporters fired back charges that Jackson's witnesses perjured themselves in order to curry favor with the powerful Georgian. John Burrows spat out that Jackson was "a brawling pygmy . . . of small mind" and his efforts to wrest the congressional seat from Wayne amounted to a "paper war."[66]

Jackson had by now isolated his target: Wayne's chief aid in the state—Osborne. The judge had evidently used his office to aid a friend, but Jackson would accept no quarter in the chastisement of his opponent. The "fighting creole" won election to the lower house and proceeded to ramrod an investigation through the lower house.[67] The last piece of evidence Jackson had gathered was presented: Alexander Speirs and Samuel Hammond deposed that Osborne had not brought the returns to the proper place but put them at Wayne's disposal instead. The investigating committee found "partial, arbitrary, illegal and manifest violation of the sacred engagement and trust reposed in [Osborne]. . . . ," for which he should be impeached. The "diverse high crimes and misdemeanors" alleged were "meddling" and "beguiling"—not offenses mentioned in the criminal laws of the state of Georgia[68]—but were very similar to those in New Jersey, New Hampshire, Massachusetts, and, later, in Kentucky, Tennessee, and Vermont cases: a breach of trust or a failure to carry out official duties because of partiality. The same definition would have no meaning applied to a private citizen, for private citizens did not assume these duties. The lower house agreed to impeach Osborne on November 23, and named managers. Jackson was among them—a show of his own strength in the state (for he could hardly be described as disinterested).

From Philadelphia, where his seat was already under attack from Jackson's attorneys using the Georgia affidavits, Wayne could send little reinforcement to his southern allies. He did what he could to support their position. He identified potential defense witnesses, confuted Jackson's attacks on the original poll takers, and paid part of the expense of the defense. Wayne was furious with "the conduct of the little man" but admitted that the effort to defend his seat in Congress had exhausted him. His letters conceded the force of Jackson's campaign against him.[69]

The senate was not so easily induced to condemn the judge. This was Georgia's first impeachment, and the upper house wished to establish its own precedents. Committees met and established rules: the senate would observe the procedures of criminal courts, save where impeachment generally required a broadening of these rules—a position comparable to the trial courts in *Greenleaf* and *Langdon*. Osborne was immediately granted the right to have counsel speak for him, that is, to conduct his case, examine witnesses, and summarize. Osborne was required to post bail, a step not required in earlier cases. Seabourn Jones, counsel for the defense, then moved for dismissal, on the grounds that the entire affair was political, not criminal, and should not be tried at all.[70]

To be sure, the Osborne case was a political impeachment in inception, conduct, and characters, but the offenses charged were a serious breach of ethics. True, the offense concerned an election, and the principals were contesting high political offices. Personal followings were deeply involved in the debate and voting, and insofar as these could be called parties, party affiliation played its role in the case. Osborne's offense was not his political activity, however. He had violated his official trust, misusing his power to manipulate an election. While, as Jones argued, the law may not have specifically condemned Osborne's acts, the Georgia Constitution did not name or limit the offenses for which an official might be removed from office—a silence that admitted the category of maladministration. If Osborne did what he was accused of doing, with the intention of adding to Wayne's totals and subtracting from Jackson's, the judge was guilty as charged of an impeachable offense. The articles alleged: first, that Osborne did not have the authority to tally the polls; second, that he added votes to Wayne's count at a second, unauthorized polling; third, that he violated the law regarding the place of the election; fourth, that he did not deliver the returns at the proper time or place; fifth, that he defended his misconduct by "debasing the dignity of his office," and, sixth, that he was guilty of "subversion of government." To these general charges (only the third referred to a violation of written law), Osborne answered "generally not guilty"—a response analogous to the "general denial" of the facts made in a criminal pleading.[71]

On December 3 Jones took a different tack: he demurred to the legality of the impeachment. He preferred to avoid any imputation of criminal purpose to his client and chose a course used in civil pleading instead. He averred, first, that inquiry into and definition of illegal practices in federal elections should be left to Congress, and only Congress could punish Osborne; second, that no crime was alleged in Osborne's official capacity—that is, as a judge of the superior court; third, if there were some aspersions upon his conduct as a magistrate, the county courts should hear the matter, as provided in Article III, section 4, of the Georgia Constitution; and, finally, that a judge could not be impeached for crimes (if the senate persisted in regarding Osborne's acts as criminal) without usurping the authority of the regular courts. Jones's argument confronted all possible interpretations of "crimes and misdemeanors" in the articles. If the senate read them to include maladministration in office, Jones denied that Osborne acted in his capacity as a judge; if the senate demanded proof of a crime, Jones insisted there was no crime, and if the senate disagreed with this, Jones demurred to the jurisdiction of the senate court of impeachments.[72]

The trial dragged through two more weeks of testimony, Jackson piling witness upon witness, and Osborne dodging each accusation as best he could.

The judge even insisted that he could no longer obtain a fair trial, given all the newspaper coverage Jackson had arranged for the impeachment hearing.[73] By the end of the trial, Osborne was confined to his house with a crippling headache. Jones continued to stress Osborne's fine record and long service, to which the managers replied by loading another impeachment article upon the stricken defendant. This charged that Osborne, acting as a judge, had issued an illegal warrant against William W. Gale. The matter was separate from Wayne's election and undermined Jones's argument on Osborne's good conduct in office.[74]

The weight of the evidence and the force of Jackson's prosecution told: Jones proposed that Wayne had, perhaps, been guilty of tampering, and that the weather conditions were actually responsible for the delay in delivering the ballots, but the senate convicted his client on the twenty-first of December.[75] The senators voted that Osborne was guilty of articles 1–3, 5, and 6. He was removed as a superior court judge and justice of the peace, disbarred from the practice of law, disqualified from office for thirty years, and ordered to pay $600 for court costs.[76] In a last comment the senate indicated that his gravest offense was physically doctoring the polls, an accusation made on the last day of the trial to which Osborne had made no defense. He had evidently erased the record and then changed it—in his own hand.[77] Two days later, the senate resolved to furnish Jackson with copies of the proceedings—to be used in Congress to remove Wayne.[78] Wayne later was expelled from his seat unanimously, but the House of Representatives, by one vote, refused to seat Jackson. Jackson later assisted in Osborne's restoration to full citizenship but never forgave Wayne.[79]

The end of 1791 brought a third state impeachment, this time in South Carolina. The case was not a momentous one and the perpetrator was not a leading officeholder, but it became a rehearsal for a second, far more momentous prosecution in the same court. On December 10, 1791, the house took up petitions from Winton County, alleging the misconduct of tax collector William Davis.[80] On the nineteenth, testimony from "respected persons in the county and from the state treasurer" established that Davis had misused or withheld tax returns for three years. The committee found his conduct "improper." In the house itself, witnesses were summoned, testimony was taken, and charges were drawn. A committee established for the purpose obtained the consent of the house to ask the governor to "suspend [Davis] from the execution of his office" until the affair was settled. The house resolved that day to impeach Davis for failing to keep tax books, seeking executions on payments already made, calculating rates arbitrarily, devising his own tax schedules, and converting taxes received to his own use. The first four were evidence of maladministration, the last an accusation of corruption. Henry DeSaussure, John Ward, and John Evans delivered the articles to the senate.[81]

The upper house, having already heard petitioners against Davis from his county, ordered the treasurer to investigate. The senate had never acted as a trial court and was unsure of its way. When the senators requested that the lower house merely seek the missing funds from Davis, the assembly demanded he be tried on the impeachment. December 10, 1792, was fixed as the day for trial.[82] The assembly had a hidden motive: throughout 1792 it had been investigating the financial manipulations of Attorney General Alexander Moultrie. Rumors of irregularities in collecting, discounting, and recording outstanding state debts, by law the responsibility of the attorney general, had reached the assembly, and Moultrie could not account for the shortfall. He was a man of prominence, with powerful connections, but procedures established in *Davis* could be used against him, and, compared to Moultrie's chicaneries, Davis's misconducts were minor. *Davis* might almost be regarded as a test case, though it was conducted with solemnity.

The senate proceeded carefully in Davis's case. The impeachment committee of DeSaussure, Edward Rutledge, Ward, John Edwards, Hunt, Marshall, and Robert Anderson was an imposing array of talent, and rehearsing their own deliberative impartiality, the senators swore their oath to "well and truly try" the case.[83] The articles were then read. Davis was not summoned to appear but the managers came and went en masse.[84] The senators issued writs for Davis and subpoenaed evidence. When Israel Barnwell from Winton moved that the impeachment be set aside, he was voted down.[85] Although Davis's case was not before them, for the defendant had not yet come to court, and Moultrie's impeachment was still eight months away, the senate heard its own special committee to make arrangements for trial: "Pres. of senate is chair placed at south window of the door—senate on chairs at his flanks, solicitors to sit opp him, and as points of law, managers for house sit at East side of the door, but speak uncovered, standing and facing senate. A.M. [Moultrie] and counsel to sit on west side ('with hats off')—to address the senate standing, when Pres. and senate reach judgment, they shall be covered [hats on]."[86] Meanwhile, Davis's case ended with a whimper: the managers reported to the senate that Davis had resigned. He had almost repaid all the missing assessments as well. The senate agreed to drop the prosecution. The speaker then ordered that "Mr. Moultrie be called in." The first South Carolina impeachment trial would not slip so quietly from the record as Davis's case had.[87]

Alexander Moultrie, Revolutionary War hero, lawyer, land speculator, planter, and former assemblyman, was one of the most powerful men in the state government.[88] As attorney general from 1776 to 1792, he directed not only the state's legal affairs but also collection of immense numbers of outstanding revolutionary certificates and land warrants. An investor himself, he walked the narrow line between legitimate personal investment and unethical use of public monies. When the western lands of Georgia were opened to settlement by the first Yazoo land companies, Moultrie plunged headlong into the scramble. What was more, he used notes from the state's creditors to speculate in land company shares. The Yazoo deal fell through, and in the spring of 1792 the attorney general found that he had to pay the piper.[89] His correspondence with the legislature and the treasurer's commission to settle public accounts humbled the once mighty official. He wrote a stream of apologies pleading "no motive of disrespect" and asking for copies of treasury records.[90] Fobbed off with excuses, the commission grew impatient. Moultrie's answers were "insufficient"—particularly regarding payments owed by the state to the original holders of notes. The commission sought the assembly's aid in compelling Moultrie to produce his accounts.[91]

Moultrie's willful mishandling of public funds was reported to the lower house. On December 18, 1792, the commission's report was read: Moultrie owed almost £65,000 to the treasury, of which £23,000 was indents lent by him and £42,000 was cash. Moultrie's request to settle the cash debt with specie at 5 to 1 discount could not disguise his "improper" conduct. The assembly voted the impeachment 76 to 9. DeSaussure, Edward Rutledge—prosecutors of Davis—and John Drayton were named managers and the senate was so informed. With this on their plate, they could not spend much time on Davis's case.[92] For his part, Moultrie remained on his plantation in the country, confined to bed with gout, private creditors howling at his door. Moultrie had speculated in state funds (he admitted as much) and his health and mental equanimity were collapsing "under the weight of calamity."[93] He had not lost his wits, however; he put off his private claimants with the excuse that his public debts came first.[94] The impeachment articles revealed the extent of his dilemma: he still owed £21,000 to the state, money he took in and then lent out to investors in the Yazoo Land Company. The notes he had from these speculators to secure the loans were not properly backed and he used his powers to pay off his own debts at a discount—"private arrangements made for his private benefit." If he were not an official, his conduct would not have been censurable but, done in office, it was "subversive of the trust reposed in him, contrary to the notion of his appointment," and "injurious to the interests of the people."[95]

Waiting outside the senate chamber as Davis's case came to its end, Moultrie knew that the senators had incontrovertible evidence of his deliberate use of public funds for personal gain. His contrition was riddled with rue: he had repaid much of the misappropriated money, and had the Yazoo speculation come to a better end, his conduct might well have gone unnoticed or uncensured.[96] He was trying to recover on the Yazoo notes from the estates of several of the speculators when he was called to account. In his hurry to return funds to the treasury, he discounted some of the debts—a course of action which aided the debtors but induced the house committee to accuse Moultrie of misconduct.[97]

On December 10, 1793, the senate convened as a trial court. The articles were read, and Moultrie answered for himself. He had trusted monies to "responsible gentlemen" without "fraudulent or unjust motives." The indents he had lent had little value at the time, and the recipients' security for the loans seemed ample. Only "sudden and unforeseen fluctuations" in market conditions created (in modern terminology) a cash flow problem. Moultrie could not repay the treasury, for the investors defaulted on him. Some of the loans, to a widow and a friend, were made "from benevolence of heart," grounds for Moultrie's plea for the "humanity and equity" of the senate.[98]

The impeachment managers were fully capable of replying to Moultrie. DeSaussure, the foremost legal authority in the lower house, aided by Drayton and Rutledge, able lawyers themselves, pressed home the charges.[99] Moultrie was unable to prevent the managers from introducing evidence on his past defaults, though he was permitted to establish his repayment of these debts in mitigation. The senate unanimously approved the articles on the eleventh of December and debated Moultrie's punishment. Motions to disqualify him for life, or for twenty-five years were rejected in favor of a seven-year disqualification.[100]

Despite the increasing polarization of South Carolina gentry into pro-Hamilton and pro-Jefferson factions, and Alexander Moultrie's pandering to citizen Gênet (seeking French succor for his insatiable land appetite), the impeachment, trial, and removal of 1791–93 were not political acts. If DeSaussure was a die-hard Federalist, Rutledge was not. Moultrie's actions as treasurer hurt all men of property and probity. In fact, his overtures to the visiting French ambassador came after the Carolinian's fall from power and shortly before the Frenchman made himself persona non grata with President Washington. Financial desperation drove Moultrie to radicalism, not the reverse.[101]

As Moultrie's case amply illustrated, there was a fine line between private employment and public duties in the eighteenth century. Public officials continued to practice law, invest in properties entailed in government litigation, seek public contracts for members of their families, and use their contacts in government to aid their private business ventures. There were no laws requiring revelation and divestment for conflict of interest. Moultrie had gone too far, that much was plain to the entire senate. But his colleagues knew that had his gamble paid off, he would not have been called to account. He was barred for only seven years, and no criminal or civil prosecution against him was even attempted by the state. His offenses were of the "general" rather than the "specific" sort, following *Greenleaf*.

In Pennsylvania, state comptroller general John Nicholson was playing a game similar to Moultrie's. If anything, Nicholson was far more active in promoting his own interest than Moultrie, for the Pennsylvanian brought into his web private banks, land companies, and other officials as well as speculating with funds placed under his care. Nicholson began his political career shoulder to shoulder with radical framers of the 1776 constitution. With some of them, he gambled heavily in state lands and war debt certificates. Using his office, he cemented economic alliances with politicians of all stripes, including the conservatives who ran the Bank of North America. Though Nicholson had great power under the constitution of 1776, he acquired powerful enemies with each passing election. In 1788 his office was divided and a register-general created. Nicholson's continued power, despite his anti-Federalism and the passage of a new state constitution by his opponents, was a tribute to his financial virtuosity. Only he knew the details of debits and credits in the state ledger books. The governor, Thomas Mifflin, was a friend and thwarted the attempts of the executive council to remove Nicholson for overpaying veteran pensioners. Eleazar Oswald published Nicholson's defense against these charges and brought down upon himself the anger meant for the collector. Another inquiry under the old assembly failed to find fault or malice though Nicholson had to adjust his payments. With his enemies nipping at his heels, Nicholson voluntarily relinquished part of his duties and salary in 1791.[102]

Unfortunately, the collector did not mend his ways. Constantly in debt to the state bank, Nicholson hedged and begged to cover his obligations. He admitted to Judge Jasper Yeates that he intended to seek redemption of wartime paper and debt certificates.[103] In 1792 the legislature foreclosed some of Nicholson's options by refusing to fund wartime certificates and New Loan certificates. Nicholson had amassed the latter despite the fact that laws passed in the 1791 and 1792 acts did not provide for redemption of New Loan notes.[104] Nevertheless, in the winter of 1792–93 Nicholson collected still more outstanding New Loan notes in his office, certified them redeemable by the treasury, purchased them himself, and then tried to exchange them for United States notes, under Hamilton's funding and assumption plans. Christian Febiger, the treasurer, blew the whistle on Nicholson, and his enemies in the lower house quickly raised hue and cry. Advisory opinions from Hamilton, state Attorney General Jared Ingersoll, Secretary of State Alexander James Dallas, and Register-General William Donaldson that New Loan notes were not assumable gave Albert Gallatin and his allies in the assembly ammunition to censure Nicholson's conduct.[105]

On April 3, 1793, the house committee on ways and means found Nicholson guilty of a "high misdemeanor" for certifying the New Loan notes without consulting the register-general or the treasurer, as required by law.

The House voted 53 to 4 to create a committee to write articles of impeachment and empowered the new committee to reexamine Nicholson's books.[106] Four months later, the committee reported its findings in the form of five articles of impeachment, to which the house would later add three of its own. It was a "fiery ordeal" for the besieged speculator-general. The committee found his books a shambles; entries were incomplete and unclear; funds were unaccounted for, resulting in a number of court suits for belated payment; receipts were missing; and the state was owed substantial sums for war certificates Nicholson had collected but not turned in to the treasury. They believed that Nicholson had also manipulated issues of notes and certificates, short changing creditors and the state, while speculating himself. In reply, Nicholson pleaded that he had almost no help with the bookkeeping in his office and had done his best. He promised to pay back whatever he had inadvertently failed to remit. The rest of the charges he termed "innuendo" spread by political enemies. Every transaction he performed to the best of his ability, within the prescribed limits of his discretion. The house was not convinced of his innocence. On December 20, managers were named, and the impeachment trial was scheduled for the next month.[107]

Nicholson appeared at his trial without any formal attachment; there was no warrant, summons, escort, or custody. He was not accused of any crime in the articles read later that day but of gross mismanagement of his office and putting personal profit ahead of public duty. With political support in the house he would never have been brought to the senate bar, but his trial was not merely political. While it is true that his opponents wanted to remove him and appoint their own man to his post, the impeachment did not go forward upon political grounds alone.

The overwhelming impeachment vote is evidence that the lower house thought Nicholson culpable of maladministration and corruption. The articles made these suspicions clear. First, "to promote his own emolument, under the color of his office," Nicholson had exchanged New Loan notes in his office after a 1789 law made them null and void. He certified them payable at the treasury contrary to law. This was contrary to the best interests of the state. Second, he violated the 1792 act by the same action. Third, he failed to consult with the register-general, as provided under the terms of another 1792 act. Fourth, he drew money on his own account from the treasury to pay off subscribers to the New Loan notes. Fifth, he bought the notes himself. The additional articles charged that he used the New Loan notes to purchase United States securities for himself, knowing the Pennsylvania paper was worthless, and that he exchanged the New Loan notes for other persons' United States securities.[108]

Nicholson pleaded not guilty and placed his defense in the hands of a very capable team: future supreme court justice and Attorney General William

Bradford, leading trial lawyer and Federalist William Lewis, Edward Tilghman, one of the wealthiest lawyers in the state, and junior councillors Nathaniel Higginson of Massachusetts and William Gibson. The managers, led by Benjamin Morgan, obtained the assistance of Attorney General Jared Ingersoll, Massachusetts Congressman Samuel Dexter, William Rawle, later a federal attorney for the state and a leading member of its bar, and Alexander Wilcocks.[109] The trial took six weeks, during which the prosecution insisted that Nicholson knowingly bilked the state of money due it to make a profit for himself, and the defense retorted that Nicholson believed that the New Loan notes could still circulate, despite the implications of the 1789, 1791, and 1792 laws. The "dangerous tendency" of Nicholson's actions, as Morgan told the senate at the start of the trial, was enough to threaten the credit of the state.[110] No officer ought to put his own financial gain above the interests of the people. Morgan did not develop the implications of a "dangerous tendency" doctrine or advocate it as a rule for determining impeachability of offenses (a road other Pennsylvania impeachment managers would follow seven years later). Morgan did insist that criminality was not necessary; a breach of trust was sufficient to impeach. Tilghman and Gibson replied that Nicholson's "construction" of the acts was reasonable—the laws never said that the New Loan notes were null and void, merely that payment of interest on them would no longer be made. Nicholson had protested the absence of provisions for payment of New Loan notes in the 1792 law to Gallatin while the bill was debated in the house; his counsel insisted that these protests established the comptroller's good intentions.[111]

During the trial, prosecution and defense counsel took turns, covering the same ground in grueling detail. Though the prosecution would have preferred to "probe the heart" of the defendant for "violations of confidence and trust" (Rawle's terms), Nicholson's counsel retorted that malicious intentions could not be proved. Instead, they tried to swamp the senate with the details of the revenue acts passed between 1786 and 1793. The harder Higginson and Gibson tried to untangle the legal stipulations of the acts, the better they established how easily anyone might misunderstand them. According to his counsel, Nicholson had objected to this confusion, for it harmed the lender and undermined the credit of the state. Even if Nicholson acted incorrectly (for failing to obtain advance approval from the governor and the treasurer, and dismissing advice from Gallatin and others), his mistakes were harmless. Only misconduct putting the state into "imminent danger" was impeachable, Higginson closed. As Morgan had done before him, Higginson had chanced upon a powerful doctrine to extend impeachment, but for obvious reasons he did not explore it. Higginson and Gibson had mapped out a strategy which effectively hamstrung the prosecution. If, as Samuel Dexter attempted, the managers followed the defense into the details of earlier

revenue acts, they provided further evidence of those laws' incomprehensibil-
ity. If, with Wilcocks, they tried to exonerate the state of Pennsylvania from
the charge of defaulting upon its debt, they shouldered the burden of proof
themselves rather than loading it onto the backs of the defense team.[112]

William Lewis, the wily, experienced old Federalist, closed for the defense,
knowing full well the obstacles that had been shoved in the path of the
managers. In a dazzling now-you-see-it, now-you-don't display of citations,
Lewis swept away English precedent. Only Pennsylvania cases counted:
Hopkinson was precedent, and the senate had acquitted the judge because he
was without evil intent. Nicholson's prosecutors, Lewis propounded, had
also failed to prove any wrongful intention in his client's activities. Moving
forward at a gallop, Lewis produced document after document to demonstrate the fiscal confusion surrounding the revolutionary debt laws.
Throughout all this, Nicholson defended the good name of Pennsylvania,
even against its legislators, and then fought for the honor and credit of the
new federal government. If any agent were at fault, it was the state, for
repudiating its lawful obligations. Left was a political vendetta against the
comptroller general by his personal enemies. [113]

Almost as important as these closely reasoned briefs was what the lawyers
left unsaid. Throughout the impeachment and trial, rampant speculation
among all political factions in the state came to light. Governor Mifflin,
Judge Alexander Addison, Bradford, and a number of banking houses were
all involved in Nicholson's own 1793 scam. Defaults on New Loan notes and
other revolutionary war debts, secured by land grants, funding plans, and
bank loans, had already toppled William Duer and imperiled Robert Morris,
James Wilson, and a host of other luminaries. The mania for speculation
broke many men and embarrassed others. Nicholson knew that if he fell
others would follow—including, perhaps, Governor Mifflin. The effect of so
many bankruptcies, involving such important and trusted men, might be
catastrophic. To get this message widely disseminated (no less than to repair
his reputation), Nicholson paid Edmund Hogan to take notes at the trial and
publish an account of the impeachment.[114]

The senate voted on the charges on April 5, 1794. None received a two-
thirds vote, though on articles 4 and 6 there were 10 votes to convict and only 7
to acquit. Only on article 3 was there a large majority in Nicholson's favor.[115]
He had warded off the thrust at his office but not the blow to his personal
credit. Shaken, he resigned on the eleventh, before the governor could respond to a resolution of the house calling for removal of the comptroller
general. Two months later, Attorney General Ingersoll instituted suit in the
state supreme court for monies due the treasury from its late comptroller
general.[116]

Although the object of the impeachment was to remove Nicholson, the
case was not merely partisan. He was defended by Federalists and attacked by

Republicans, his own political allies. Lewis had alleged that political malice motivated the lower house, but its 54 to 3 vote went beyond party feeling. Nicholson's greatest failing was his arrogance. Langdon, Lyon, Ashe, Hopkinson, and other victims of impeachment shared this characteristic, and it invariably undermined their pleas of innocence. Coupled with errors in judgment it was not enough to remove an incumbent, but when the errors were self-interested or were made with malice of forethought—that is, when they were deliberate breaches of trust or violations of law—they might lead to impeachment.

The smallest errors, swollen by arrogance and premeditation, were impeachable, no matter who committed them. No official, however lowly his position might be, was immune—for in this era the lower house was the watchdog of all officers, and to its chamber came petitions for relief from all manner of citizens for all types of injustices. Typical was the case of William Hunt, a justice of the peace for Middlesex. He was a Harvard graduate and M.A. who took over his father's law practice in Watertown and was elected in 1796 to the General Court. A conservative, he later joined other high Federalists in the state to attempt to save Massachusetts from the Jeffersonian heresy.[117] On January 20, 1794, Attorney General James Sullivan, no stranger to impeachment, passed on to the General Court charges brought to his office against Hunt. Sullivan informed the lower house that the grand jury of Watertown had indicted Hunt, and he supplied evidence which the managers would carry with them to the senate. In the lower house the committee report on the charges urged the lower house to impeach Hunt. Sullivan also transmitted complaints on Hunt's conduct as an attorney to the committee, but the articles excluded these matters. On February 12, 1794, by a 111 to 12 vote, Hunt was impeached for representing a litigant in a case before his own court and instituting suits for his own benefit.[118]

Hunt was a Federalist, and his chief accuser, Sullivan, was an ardent Jeffersonian, but the impeachment was not primarily political. If significant numbers of Federalists had not voted against the justice in the lower house, there would have been no impeachment. Hunt's remaining supporters were Middlesex Federalists; his defense team featured future Chief Justice Theophilus Parsons, an autocratic elitist, and Harrison Grey Otis, a brilliant leader of the young Federalists, but neither his friends nor his counsel could persuade rank and file Federalists of Hunt's innocence. The Republican minority in the two houses voted solidly against the justice, for his offenses were directly repugnant to their conception of republican government.[119]

At the trial, which opened in Faneuil Hall on February 20, Hunt replied to the charges. He denied that he had "corruptly, falsely, and wickedly" entered Stephen Hall as present in a suit before him. The case was hazy in his mind but he recalled that the parties did not contest the suit. If he made an error on the record, it was "formal" only, and not done with sinister intent. He could not wait for litigants who failed to attend court, particularly when they were bonded to do so. He did not force payment on their bonds after giving judgment against absent litigants, however, lest he "afford even a shadow for complaint to any man, of professional or official rigour." There was never any "bad intention" on his part to default litigants. He was a busy lawyer as well as a busy magistrate, and if there were "imperfect and deficient" entries in records and judgments on cases, he sincerely apologized.[120]

The senate was not mollified. For his misconduct and maladministration in office," Hunt was convicted on the 22d by a majority of 20 to 7 and sentenced to removal for one year.[121] The punishment was little more than a slap on the wrist, and it did not prevent Hunt from taking a seat in the General Court two years later. Nevertheless, one should not be quick to reproach the Federalist majority in the senate. Hunt's offense was not a crime but an example of willfulness. He had knowingly overstepped his authority and was warned by the suspension. Federalists had voted him guilty; even the Federalist *Massachusetts Centinel* thought the impeachment a "good thing." Both the *Centinel* and the *Mercury* viewed the events dispassionately and remarked on the dispatch of the impeachment and trial.[122] Substantial justice was done.

Efficiency of this sort was common in state impeachments but not universal. In New Jersey, where petitioners continued to bring complaints about officials to the lower house, delays sometimes occurred. One petitioner, Robert Walton of Cumberland, claimed to have been illegally imprisoned for debt by Justice William Mason, but his barrage of petitions to the general assembly and council took nine months to bring action. In November 1795 a committee finally sat to hear the charges. Mason supposedly had ignored the securities Walton put up as bond for a debt of 15 shillings, or so swore Walton's witnesses. After meeting for three days the committee found no "grounds for impeachment" in the justice's conduct and recommended the assembly dismiss the petition. Even though nothing came of it, Walton at least got his complaint heard.[123]

Corresponding understandings and precedent on impeachment in the states were not binding upon the federal government, but when impeachment was broached in Congress, the House of Representatives adhered to the state's unwritten, self-imposed restrictions. Two episodes illustrated this restraint. In April 1792 Supreme Court Justices John Jay and James Wilson, from their circuits, sent protests to the president against the Federal Pension Act of 1792. Jay rejected the law because it forced the Supreme Court to make preliminary judgments on pensions and then referred disputed cases to the secretary of war, followed by Congress. He found the new duties not suited to his court and refused to perform them. Wilson, writing three days later, adjourned his court rather than obey the law, and explained that a constitutional principle had been violated: the decisions of the highest court could not be subject to the executive branch or Congress. The outcry against the judges reversed party lines. Though Wilson and Jay were Federalists, Republicans, speaking through Freneau's *National Gazette,* applauded the court's resistance to the Federalist Congress, and Federalists, led by Fisher Ames and Elias Boudinot, thought the judges in violation of their sworn duties. The word *impeachment* appeared on the lips of the Federalists, according to both James Fenno's high Federalist *Gazette of the United States* and the arch-Republican Benjamin Franklin Bache's *Philadelphia Advertiser.* But no one made any formal impeachment motion. No investigation, save a call for the text of Wilson's letter, was demanded. The judges acted openly, under their best understanding of the law. The point was arguable, and the bench was united in its objections. Impeachment was clearly out of the question. [124]

The target of the second hint at impeachment was Secretary of the Treasury Alexander Hamilton. In the winter of 1792–93 Hamilton inflamed already burning political passions with a series of anonymous newspaper attacks on Jefferson. The Republican's reply, initiated by Jefferson's protégé in the House, William Branch Giles, was to seek congressional investigation of the manner of repayment of the national debt. To both Federalists and Republicans, an impeachment seemed in the offing.[125] At Hamilton's urging, two large loans had been floated in Europe, and the uses to which the monies had gone were obscure at best. In December and again in January, Giles induced the House to demand an accounting from the executive branch. The Giles Resolutions, passed on January 23, required the president to supply copies of the loan offers, names of recipients of payments, copies of balances and ledger books of the treasury, and a report, from Hamilton, of all deposits and unapplied monies.[126] Giles, perhaps prompted by Jefferson, and certainly speaking for a faction, alleged that the loan was being used to benefit the Bank of the United States rather than to retire the national debt. If Federalists were unconvinced of this accusation, Giles did tap the legislature's genuine confusion over Hamilton's fiscal methods.[127] The Federalist-dominated Senate passed similar resolutions, and Hamilton hurried to comply with both requests. His report concluded that there were very small discrepancies, which would go to pay numerous bills. The resolutions were based on incomplete information and "imperfect data," and Hamilton scolded his would-be censurers for "fallacy" and "misapprehension." Only his concern for the "weary ... patience" of the House prevented a more pointed reply to their accusations.[128]

Giles pressed for further congressional action on February 27, a week after Hamilton's reports were delivered. Using a text prepared in part by Jefferson, Giles read nine accusations to the lower house. These charged Hamilton with irregular discretionary use of funds, and violating statutory instructions, "the public interest," and the privileges of the house (by lecturing to it in his reports).[129] The debate on these charges carried into the night of March 7. In the division that followed, Republicans joined in an "overwhelming vote" against the resolutions. Twelve votes was the only support that Giles had for taking formal steps against Hamilton's purported maladministration.[130] Hamilton and his close friends regarded the affair as "a matter of party," a "dangerous effect . . . of the most active demogogues," by which he meant Jefferson.[131] He ignored the support Federalists gave to the January 23 resolutions, and Republican balloting on the March 7 vote. Hamilton's reports on the loans and debt revealed no wrongdoing, and he was exonerated. While party feeling was already bitter enough to harass him, it could not topple him without evidence of real misconduct or incompetence.

During the early 1790s, state legislatures and Congress routinely handled impeachment inquiries. Most of these involved minor officials accused of infractions of law or ethics. The assemblies processed these inquiries smoothly, often without a ripple in the surface of their other duties. The episodes were not milestones in the law—great men brought to brook for infamous offenses. For this very reason, these cases are significant. Their frequency is overwhelming evidence that the ordinary citizens of the states came to the lower house when troubled by apparent official misconduct. The people trusted their assemblies—a critical bond in the young states. The assemblies repaid this trust; petitions and informations received attention. An official decision was made on them, no matter how minute the charge or inferior the suspect's office. In an age before the vast bureaucratic machinery of executive investigation, regulation, and oversight, the assembly served as a clearinghouse of complaint and criticism. Public opinion played an increasingly visible role in government in that era, and through impeachment hearings, the opinion of angry private citizens made its weight felt upon nonelective officials.[132] The dispatch with which the assembly handled the cases did not preclude careful investigation of each. Petitions and affidavits were given to committees, hearings were held, and evidence was solicited or subpoenaed. At the same time, efficiency did not prevent thoroughness. The inquiries were also fair. The accused was offered a chance to reply to the charges, assisted by counsel if he chose. He, too, could compel witnesses to come and evidence to be brought. All this took place before any vote on impeachment and hence before the upper house prepared for trial. An impeachment hearing in the lower house was more accessible to the accused than a grand jury deliberation would have been. Private complainants appear to have respected the assemblies for their conduct, and defendants submitted to the lower house's decisions. The republicanization of impeachment ventured in the preceding decade was a success.

The outcomes of the impeachments between 1788 and 1795 are also instructive. Greenleaf, Osborne, and Moultrie were impeached by large majorities and convicted by two-third votes. Davis resigned before his trial was complete, satisfying his prosecutors. Langdon refused to appear at his trial and subsequently resigned, satisfying neither house but ending his career as a judge. Nicholson survived his trial by a narrow margin but retired when it was over. Hunt was convicted by a lopsided vote. All the trials were brief affairs, except Nicholson's—due to the complexity of his financial manipulations. Votes for and against impeachment and for and against conviction at trial crossed party lines. Seen at a distance of two hundred years, the charges against all these men were substantial, though in all cases except Moultrie's and Osborne's, no grounds existed for regular court proceedings against them. Under the category of *general* offenses, that is, acts dangerous to the public weal or violating the public trust, managers and triers classed mismanagement of funds, arbitrariness on the bench, and incompetence in office. As the penalty for conviction was nothing more than removal and disqualification, the impeachment and trial of these men fit the republican prescription (or rather, limitation) of impeachment enunciated in the revolutionary era. Just as important, none of the charges involved mere political behavior, that is, excesses of partisanship, electoral conduct, or party organizing. Political activity was not impeachable—unless it involved some other offense against the public interest.

8

THE POLITICIZATION
OF IMPEACHMENT, 1795–1800

BY 1795, IMPEACHMENT HAD PROVED ITSELF AN EFFECTIVE AND A FAIR TOOL OF republican government. In case after case from 1776 through 1795 it had enabled lower houses to respond to popular claims of wrongdoing while protecting the rights of the accused and the public. Yet the worm was already in the bud, for its very effectiveness entangled impeachment in the struggle between the Federalists and Republicans. The debate over the Jay Treaty spawned impeachment threats and thrusts of a new type: prosecutions designed solely to remove partisan or unpopular incumbents on grounds of their partiality and politically unacceptable views. Advocates of these impeachments did not seek to replace the older constitutional view of impeachment but to supplement it, leaving two classes of impeachment cases. The first would pursue obnoxious minority political figures. The second would be limited to willful, knowing, self-interested wrongdoing and crime. The coexistence of the two gave impeachment law and practice in this era its dramatic and uncertain character.

The bifurcation of American impeachment in mid-decade was not marked by a landmark case or a formal ruling but by a cumulative series of incidents: demands for impeachments and formal inquiries brought without evidence of actual offenses. Behind the new type of case was a heightening of party activity. In theory, political parties had no need of impeachment, and impeachment had no need of parties. A majority party using patronage, the dispensing power of the executive and legislative branches, and the ballot should have been able to remove all officers not to its liking. Impeachment should not, under its older American precedent, have been employed to alter policies of government or to chastise unpopular officials, but the very utility and frequency of impeachment in its limited role made it increasingly attractive to party leaders as the party wars intensified. In the midst of national debate over American ties with England and France, the Federalists, seeking to allay criticism of English treatment of Americans, dispatched

John Jay to London. Republicans watched his negotiations with the British with growing dismay.[1] When the Republicans learned the terms of his treaty, they were outraged with the ambassador and his party. In 1795 Republican legislatures in Virginia and Kentucky asked Congress to initiate revisions in the federal impeachment law aimed at Jay—or even Washington himself. The Senate, Virginia insisted, could not be the court for hearing impeachment so long as its members pandered to a single party. Fisher Ames interpreted this as a first step toward the impeachment of President Washington for supporting the Jay Treaty. In the House, Edward Livingston and other Republicans called for the confidential minutes of the negotiations, another alarming step to Ames's mind.[2] Perhaps Washington also feared an impeachment—of Jay rather than himself. He refused to surrender the papers, unless Congress demanded them as part of an impeachment proceeding.[3] Hamilton, a private citizen whose business remained the affairs of state, promptly (if anonymously) defended his party and the treaty against the power of the lower house to impeach.[4] He shared Ames's fears, as did South Carolina's Robert Goodloe Harper, a Federalist leader in the House.[5]

Jay and Washington were not the only Federalists threatened with impeachment because of the treaty with Britain. Kentucky senator Humphrey Marshall, a bullish Federalist in a Republican state, courted the ire of his constituents for his support of the treaty. Marshall, a land speculator, war hero, and lawyer whose conservatism and proconstitutional sympathies marked him as a Federalist from the beginning of his political career in Kentucky, went from the state assembly to the United States Senate by a very narrow margin. No sooner was he seated in Philadelphia than the Federalists were called upon to support the treaty. A man of giant proportions and passions, Marshall showed unstinting commitment.[6] From Kentucky came a wail of protest, led by Republicans in the Senate and the lower house who were incensed at Marshall's apparent disregard for his state's interests. At public dinners and on the courthouse steps Jeffersonian politicians called for the removal of Marshall. A motion to revise the United States Constitution to permit recall of senators and shorten their terms fizzled, but Marshall's opponents were not finished with him.[7]

Marshall was engaged in a newspaper war with two of the judges in the state, George Muter and Benjamin Sebastian, both Republicans. The object of the dispute was a suit Marshall was litigating in the state supreme court, in the course of which one litigant alleged that Marshall had perjured himself. The judges' ruling went against the senator, and he turned to the press to demand that they produce proof of the perjury or apologize. On November 21, 1795, the Kentucky House of Representatives decided to petition the United States Senate to examine the case. By December 10 the document was ready:

Our duty under these circumstances strongly and unequivocally requires that we should request your serious attention to the considerations which this case suggests—important indeed it is to society, that
those intrusted with the exercise of the powers of government should be
men of unshaken virtue and integrity. . . . But it is further to be observed
that they should not only be virtuous, but free even from the imputations
of crime; more especially of those infamous crimes, the perpetration of
which destroys the bonds of society, prostrates the obligations of truth,
morality and religion, and violates the human criterion of truth and
falsehood—the sole support of well-grounded confidence. . . .
In these reflections we feel our own situation implicated: the character of
the Senator may involve the reputation of the State which he represents;
nor does the situation of Humphrey Marshall, charged as he is, with an
infamous crime, affect only himself and the State from which he is
deputed; it is highly interesting to the honor, dignity and consideration
of the highly intrusted body of which he is a member.[8]

The United States Senate debated and rejected the call for an investigation by
a strict party vote and referred the matter to a jury in Kentucky.[9]

The Federalists were not opposed to political impeachment, for they too
had recognized its effectiveness. When Elbridge Gerry remained in Paris after
the disastrous mission of the ministers plenipotentiary in 1798, Federalists
were delighted to place the impeachment shoe upon the other party's foot.
Secretary of State Timothy Pickering suggested to John Adams that Gerry be
impeached. Adams, then pressing for the impeachment of Senator William
Blount, an apostate Federalist, demurred; Gerry was an old friend.[10] Harper
led the impeachment against Blount and managed the case in the Senate.[11] If
Federalists had less to do with impeachment, it was because, in the main, they
could remove their enemies by other means. For example, Edmund Randolph, the Virginia Republican who replaced Jefferson as secretary of state,
was a thorn in the Federalists' side. Washington, a surrogate father to
Randolph, trusted the younger man's counsel—until Timothy Pickering
proved to Washington that Randolph leaked state secrets to French ambassador Joseph Fauchet. Washington then demanded Randolph's resignation. No
action by Congress was necessary.[12] Similarly, the president had the power to
recall American diplomats, which Pickering urged Washington to do in
James Monroe's case. Monroe, another Virginia Republican, was too
friendly to the French for the high Federalists' taste. They did not need a vote
of impeachment to remove him; President Washington did it for them.

In these brandishments of impeachment it was the end result that mattered.
Instead of focusing upon gathering evidence, proving intent, and establishing a case—in fine all the paraphernalia of prosecution at trial—the would-

be impeachers sought political advantage. Resignation of the defendant or a change in his policies ended the matter. There was no attempt to pursue the charges into the regular courts, for no crimes were alleged. The difference between the threatened impeachments of 1795–96 and limited, "constitutional" ones, which continued alongside the former, was not the mere influence of party. The novelty lay in growing interest in discrediting opposing politicians. This shift in the definition of the goal of some impeachments was not possible in America until the state constitutions limited punishment by the upper house to removal and disqualification. Once that was done, the way lay open to change the purpose of the prosecution from conviction and punishment to the objective of forcing an opponent out of office. Without "constitutional" impeachment there could have been no political impeachments. The irony notwithstanding, impeachment law now faced its most uncertain years.

A typical episode of experiment with new definitions of impeachable offenses in this era involving James Jackson of Georgia illustrates the political utility of mere threats of prosecution. Jackson had already led a successful effort to oust Georgia Supreme Court Judge William Osborne in 1791. In 1796 Jackson led a drive in the assembly to impeach Philip Clayton, state treasurer, and Thomas Rabun and James Gunn, state senators, for bribing other assemblymen to vote for the Yazoo Land Company bill.

Though a land speculator, Jackson had been excluded from the inner circle in the Yazoo scramble and vociferously had opposed it. The November 1795 elections had brought the anti-Yazoo faction into power, led by Jackson, and they wasted no time censuring the previous administration. Jackson headed a house committee decrying the "fraud, corruption, and collusion" in which "the public good was placed entirely out of view, and private interest alone consulted." The house agreed: an "offer of any money or other advantage to any member of this house in order to influence his vote . . . is one of the highest crimes which can be committed against the rights of a free people." Acceptance of a bribe would be grounds for removal and disqualification.[13] Jackson had the culprits in mind, and his committee brought charges of fraud against ex-representative Thomas Rabun for accepting a bribe and state senator Thomas Wylley for offering one. Neither of these men was punished, though a rescinding act of February 15 wiped the Yazoo sales off the books. Holders of certificates were to be paid within sixty days, current balance in the treasury permitting. While the Yazoo land certificates were collected and burned, Jackson was gathering evidence against other rivals. In March 1796 he initiated a house investigation of state senator James Gunn. Gunn stood accused of bribing a representative to vote for the Yazoo bill. When the lower house voted that Gunn had lost the confidence of the people, Gunn retorted that Jackson, a personal as well as political enemy, fabricated the evidence. Gunn demanded access to the affidavits held by Congressman Abraham Baldwin, and after Baldwin refused, Gunn challenged him to a duel. The assembly finally compromised by dropping the investigation with the parting shot that Gunn had abused its privileges.[14] Jackson, convinced that the "daily attacks on his reputation" were the work of the Yazoo survivors, pushed on with his personal inquiries.[15] His next target was state treasurer Philip Clayton.

Clayton was a political placeman who could hardly have escaped some taint of the Yazoo scandal, even had his intentions been pure. His career suggested otherwise. As Richmond County tobacco inspector and court clerk, he collected fees on all records and papers and weighed and certified the tobacco for the county. These lucrative posts were not enough; in 1794 he solicited and received appointment as state treasurer from Governor Matthews.[16] In his short stay in the office he left the books a muddle, for unlike his predecessor and his successor, he did not head each page of his ledgers or keep subtotals for different categories of expenditures. He entered expenses and receipts for payment willy-nilly, leaving plenty of room in his books for illegal payments to assemblymen who supported the Yazoo bill.[17]

On February 17, 1796, the assembly committee examined Clayton on the matter of bribery during the Yazoo land bill voting. The senate required him to put up a bond of £400,000 for any missing funds, during his handling of the treasury, but the house demurred.[18] Led by Jackson, it was considering impeachment. Jackson went so far as to write, and perhaps circulate, articles of impeachment:

> Whereas it appears to this House from the Information on Oath of John Shepherd esquire a Member of the last Legislature that Philip Clayton esquire Treasurer of this State did during the sitting of the said last Legislature and pending the Usurped Act for the sale of Western lands attempt to bribe the said John Shepherd to go home by an offer of seventy pounds from the Publick Treasury in lieu of his pay as a Member which the said Clayton calculated at twenty eight pounds. . . .
>
> And whereas attempts of this nature are not only culpable and highly imm[oral] . . .when made by a publick Servant entrusted with the purse of the State become barefaced attacks on the Freedom of the Legislature and the rights of the People and which if permitted to pass with impunity would found a precedent dangerous to publick liberty and this House has viewed with regret the success of corrupt practices in the said last Legislature during the passage of the said usurped Act.[19]

Jackson's case was based upon hearsay and rumor, but Clayton's impeachment was a near certainty; he had too many political enemies in the anti-Yazoo majority of the Assembly. Although his ledgers did not show any special payments to Shepherd, other than for expenses, and these on the warrant of the speaker of the house, and although Shepherd did not stay home in any case, Clayton immediately resigned. Jackson simply wanted Clayton out, and the threatened impeachment drove the treasurer from office.[20]

The impeachment of Senator William Blount, North Carolina Federalist turned Tennessee Republican, was also a matter of party politics but again— as in Clayton—not an avowedly political case. The house managers, with James Bayard and Robert Goodloe Harper in the lead, prosecuted a Federalist turncoat, at the height of Federalist power in Congress, but the charges did not stem from Blount's anti-English voting record. Instead, they alleged that Blount had conspired with others to maneuver the British into invasion of the Spanish Southwest, leaving Spain's possessions at the mercy of Blount and other speculators. His grandiose plotting, encompassing a cabal of adventurers, a small private army, two Indian tribes, Spain, and Great Britain, was so distasteful to his fellow senators that they expelled him after a mere two days' debate. Partisan animosity, coupled with Blount's relative isolation within his new party, hastened his departure from the government, but this impeachment's implications went far beyond the defendant's loss of office.

Federalist leaders in the lower house were not content with Blount's expulsion from the Senate. Samuel Sitgreaves, an eastern Pennsylvania Federalist, joined by Harper, the "champion" of Southern Federalism, and James Bayard, a Delaware Federalist—all of them lawyers—pressed for Blount's impeachment after the Tennessean had been ousted from the upper house. If removal was all Sitgreaves could expect after a trial and Blount was already out of office, what could be the point of impeachment? Disqualification was the obvious answer, but one discerns in the determination and passion of the managers a covert political motive broader than the chastisement of disqualification. Blount's scheme came to nothing; his plotting was exposed, and, exposed, appeared ludicrous. Yet if Blount, an elective officeholder, could be impeached and disqualified, then all the Republicans in Congress might be threatened as long as Federalists controlled both houses. Impeachment and trial of Blount, in this context, anticipated the Alien and Sedition Acts passed in 1798. Impeachment of legislators for misconducts (not for crimes, for the articles, as we shall see, did not allege crimes but betrayal of public trust) undercut the electoral support that brought Republicans to office. What is more, if they could be disqualified, they could not obtain office, no matter how popular they were. Impeachment and trial would reduce their numbers and ward off potential candidates. Blount's case was an opening gambit in this strategy and would have politicized impeachment to its core. Blount's excesses gave a slight tactical advantage to Congressman Bayard and his allies, but the Senate's preemptive action forced the prosecutors to seek sweeping arguments for their continued assault upon Blount.

At first, Blount seemed a perfect target for this larger objective. He was an unscrupulous, self-interested, and (the worse for him) chronically overextended landjobber. His peculations encumbered his own family, old North Carolina political allies, part of the Tennessee elite, and a web of speculators reaching from the Albemarle to Philadelphia. There was nothing illegal or unethical in this, though it did land other men of means in trouble with their creditors. Blount's speculation had drawn to his side powerful politicians in his adopted state and elsewhere in the new West. Together these men pored over surveys, made and remade deals, and constantly sought new sources of funding. It was a craft in which Blount was a master. Even as his debtors closed in on him, he wheeled and dealt his way across the land.[21] In 1796 Blount began to discuss, through intermediaries, British intervention against Spain in the Southwest. Plans included an invasion from the western states.[22] While the ideas made the rounds of diplomatic London, Blount took stock of his allies. A letter to Indian interpreter James Carey, hinting at the extent of Blount's agitation and mentioning a cast of unholy troublemakers, was sent by the recipient to Indian agent David Henley, Blount's enemy, and thence found its way to Secretary of State Timothy Pickering. Pickering, who preferred caution because of Britain's involvement and begged the British to deny their complicity, gave the letter to President Adams. Adams would not allow the matter to die. Immersed in delicate diplomatic negotiations and appalled by Blount's attempt to direct foreign policy, the president demanded an investigation by the Senate. The debate on the facts behind the mysterious missive took place in July and led directly to a motion for impeachment in the lower house. Blount, vulnerable to the onslaught by the Federalists because he had sided with their enemies, was to be accused of unethical dealings with the Federalists' own friend, Great Britain.[23] The irony was not lost on Blount, as he watched his political friends shrink from him. Even leading Republicans seized upon his indiscretions to lambaste the British.[24]

Blount actually strolled into the Senate chamber just as Adams's request for an investigation was read. The senator heard his importunings to Carey broadcast to the Senate.[25] Its members took little time to expel him for unethical conduct—the Constitution conferring upon both houses of Congress the power to "punish its members for disorderly behavior, and, with the concurrence of two thirds, expel a member."[26] Nowhere in the Constitution were limitations placed upon the expulsion power. Criminal activity might or might not lead to expulsion; Congress was to decide each case on its own merits. On July 8, 1797, the Senate voted, 25 to 1, to expel Blount for "a high misdemeanor, entirely inconsistent with his public trust and duty as a

Senator."[27] The term *high misdemeanor* does not appear to have been a crime, for Blount was not accused of any recognized crime or any violation of the law. His *misdemeanor* was to mis-demean himself; to misuse his office for his own speculative ends.

The Federalist majority in the lower house was not content with the Senate's investigation. On July 3 the House of Representatives formed a committee to reply to the president's message. Though Republicans sat on the committee, its leaders, Sitgreaves of Pennsylvania and Samuel W. Dana of Connecticut, were Federalist lawyers. They went on to form, with Bayard of Delaware (replacing Dana) and Harper, also lawyers, the core of the prosecutorial team. The committee wasted no time informing the Senate that articles of impeachment were forthcoming. The committee then ordered that Blount's personal belongings be searched and his papers be seized to obtain evidence for the framing of articles. This fishing expedition was justified on grounds that Blount's "conspiracy" threatened the nation. The committee then obtained leave to sit in the recess of Congress to finish its business. Blount, furious and frightened, bolted for Tennessee just as his adversaries formally impeached him.[28]

In the four months between the recess of Congress and its reassembly in November, Sitgreaves had amassed a bundle of embarrassing letters and depositions. Blount had tried to remain in the shadows of the plot, but he did tell Nicholas Romayne, one of his New York allies, "I persevere in my determination respecting a certain business, as expressed to you at New York."[29] The most damning piece of evidence was Blount's letter to Carey, dated April 27, 1797. In it Blount obliquely mentioned "the plan" that Chisholm, the chief adventurer, Romayne, the confidential agent, British ambassador Robert Liston, the patron, and Blount, the mastermind, together concocted.[30] Romayne filled in the details in a deposition: Blount knew everything, engaged willingly in the intrigue, and hoped to gain personally from its success.[31] Other deponents supplied equally devastating testimony. The Spanish minister, D'Yrujo, was particularly eager to assist. His target was Pickering, the pro-English secretary of state. By the following January, Sitgreaves was ready to exhibit the articles to the lower house. The representatives agreed, on the twenty-ninth, to send five articles to the Senate.[32] The first accused Blount of intending to bring the United States into war against Spain, despite American neutrality. The "military, hostile expedition" Blount supposedly organized would begin its career on American soil. The second article charged him with fomenting a Creek and Cherokee attack upon the Spanish borderlands, in violation of the 1795 Pinckney Treaty with Spain. Blount's "criminal designs" had led him, according to the third article, to undermine the influence of the Indian agent, Benjamin Hawkins. Fourth, Blount was accused of tampering with the allegiance of Indian interpreter James Carey. Finally, Blount had contrived "to diminish and impair" Cherokee faith in the federal government.[33] Sitgreaves and his committee had gathered data, subpoenaed witnesses, and met continuously. One admires the determination with which they stretched Blount's desperate, harebrained scheme into a genuine peril. There was no act of any sort, save the correspondence of conspiracy itself. This would be enough for culpability under a common-law charge of treason, but the United States Constitution required an overt act. The Republicans scoffed, hammered at the British connection, but did not, at first, object. Blount had to be chastised.[34]

Did intended, or even attempted, filibustering (to use a later term) amount to an impeachable offense? The charges were reminiscent of those lodged against English ministers, primarily councillors of King William and Queen Anne during the long wars against France. A succession of secretaries of state and privy councillors were impeached by the Commons for misusing their offices, upon evidence of advising unpopular foreign policy. In the last episode of this type the Tory ministry of Robert Harley and Henry St. John collapsed in 1713. One or both its principals had corresponded with the Pretender, Charles Stuart, with a view to return him to England when Anne, childless, died. Both men were impeached, in part for the correspondence, though there was no overt act in furtherance of it. Conspiracy to bring back the Stuarts might have been regarded as a constructive treason, for English law did not require an overt act against the state or the person of the king. When Bayard later pressed the Senate to accept the English cases as precedent for the trial of Blount, he verged on this analogy but never explicitly made it.

However flimsy one might regard the grounds against Harley and St. John, their offenses were official acts. Blount had no official diplomatic duties to perform, save to advise and consent upon treaties and appointments under consideration by the Senate. His dalliance with Liston was not a breach of his official duties, his correspondence with Chisolm and Romayne not in any way official. Sitgreaves's committee recognized this difficulty in their case and accused Blount of misusing his office and abusing the public trust. In fact, neither Blount's mania for land nor his meddling in foreign affairs was uncommon or indictable in a regular court. Americans often engaged in personal diplomacy, whether they held other offices or were private citizens. For example, Elbridge Gerry stayed on in France as a private citizen after the other ministers plenipotentiary left, much to the dismay of the Federalists. Pickering's attempt to impeach Gerry fizzled.

Officials acting in a private capacity could certainly be charged with ordinary crimes, but the regular criminal courts had jurisdiction of these cases. Article II, section 4, did include one crime, treason, which could result in either the Senate or a superior court taking jurisdiction. Indeed, Article I, section 3, part 7, explicitly stated that conviction on an impeachment did not bar indictment, trial, and conviction for the same offense in a regular court of law. The overlapping jurisdiction of the court of the Senate and the regular criminal courts was rationalized at the Constitutional Convention: the former could only remove and disqualify, while the latter could take life and limb. The one offense clearly in this category was treason. A felony committed in private life might not fit the adjective *high* in *high crimes and misdemeanors.* There was no state precedent to guide the Senate.

The prosecution put both these considerations aside by viewing Blount's conduct as an offense cognizable in the lower house. In the court of the Senate defense counsel would build new obstacles: Blount no longer held office; could he be tried upon an impeachment if he were no longer an officer? Second, was he ever a "civil officer?" That is, were legislators subject to impeachment and trial? Finally, did trial in the Senate violate the Sixth Amendment guarantee to a jury trial in the vicinage of the offense? Blount's counsel, Alexander James Dallas and Jared Ingersoll, would demur to the impeachment on these grounds. Should any one of them stand, Blount would be safe. To Harper and Bayard, what first appeared to be an open and shut case of one man's reckless cupidity was now a highly technical case with broad repercussions. Political "vacillations" were put aside, if only for a moment, to hear a refresher course on the meaning of the constitutional provisions at a pretrial hearing in the Senate.[35]

Blount did not attend this hearing. From December 17, 1798, through the final arguments on January 11, the ex-senator remained in Tennessee, occupied in a different role with another impeachment. Dallas and Ingersoll entered his response to the articles on December 24. They argued that Blount, a private citizen, could be tried only by a regular court of law, that he was never a "civil officer," and that he had committed no crime.[36] The managers agreed with the defense counsel that prosecution arguments should go first. Bayard rose to his feet immediately.

Despite their partisan advantage in Congress, the managers knew that conviction would be difficult. The frank revelations of Blount's conspiracy were now eighteen months old, and the investigation had stalled. Although the Federalists controlled the upper house and could have mustered a two-thirds majority, the managers could not rely on political allegiances. Here was the rub: the upper house could be expected to act as a brake upon the lower house—demanding sound grounds for conviction. Over and over again, impeachment cases proved that upper houses took their quasi-judicial jobs seriously. If *Blount* was a political case in the lower house, the Senate could still be expected to demand doctrinal arguments before it condemned one of its own. This was the final obstacle: Blount had been a senator, and Bayard had to convince the senators that they were liable to impeachment by their rivals for power in the lower house. The Lords were liable to impeachment in England, but then, in England, anyone could be impeached. Practically, peers were impeached only when they erred as councillors, ministers, and judges, not merely because they committed a private offense. In the latter case the Lords tried their own without impeachment.

Bayard struck first at the weakest portion of the defense: if impeachments, under the Sixth Amendment, had to be tried before local juries, the judicial duties of the Senate disappeared, for the impeachment trial provisions would be superfluous. The upper house would have no way to remove wrongdoers anywhere in the government. The Sixth Amendment would take away from the Senate what the framers, three years before, had expressly given. This made little sense; trial by jury was guaranteed officials indicted in regular courts, and trial in the Senate was limited to "political capacity."[37] Bayard was right: impeachment touched only officials and threatened only their official status; it was "designed to secure the state."[38] To this day, Bayard's simple refutation of the jury trial clause stands, buttressed by Wilson's lectures on impeachment and Mason's original definition of impeachable offenses in Philadelphia (reaching back to his impeachment provisions for the 1776 Virginia Constitution). Unfortunately for Bayard, the argument undercut the prosecution's later contention that impeachment lay against any citizen. If the process was aimed at malefactors in their "political capacity," how could it apply to private citizens? Only, of course, if the English precedent was readmitted. Dallas and Ingersoll had cleverly left this knot for Bayard to untie: if he pulled at the thread of jury trial, he loosened the grip of universal liability.

Bayard had next to dismantle Dallas's claim that senators were not "civil officers." One of his contentions was labored but relevant: senators were civil officers "in common parlance," by function, by precedent in the records of the Continental Congress, and by their prohibition (Article I, section 9, first clause) from accepting titles and emoluments from kings.[39] His other argument, introduced first, was broader but shakier. Bayard opined that, as the framers adopted impeachment from England, and "mould[ed] it into a suitable shape," they did not explicitly exclude impeachment of others than "civil officers." When in doubt about the meaning of a constitutional provision, one recurred to English precedent: "It remains as at common law."[40] And in English law, anyone might be impeached. It was therefore irrelevant whether Blount was a civil officer. This is a common adversarial technique: to argue in stages against a proposition. For Bayard, it backfired—he pressed for a reading of impeachment law even more extreme than that desired by his party. The arch-Federalists did not want to impeach anyone except obnoxious Republican legislators. Worst of all, he had opened his case with this deformity. Recognizing his error, and the extent to which it jeopardized his ultimate aim—not just by revealing the extent to which the Federalists were willing to politicize impeachment law, but by giving the defense a target to fire upon far removed from Blount's execrable behavior—Bayard apologized to the Senate. "I am sensible of some embarrassment in opening the argument . . . I have nothing to direct me, but . . . the objections which appear on the face of the plea [by Blount's counsel]."[41] Bayard could not leave his ground entirely, for Blount was no longer a federal officer of any kind. He therefore fumbled on: "It is also alleged in the plea, that the party impeached is not now a Senator. It is enough that he was a Senator at the time the articles were preferred. If the impeachment were regular and maintainable when preferred, I apprehend no subsequent event, grounded on the wilful act, or caused by the delinquency of the party, can vitiate or obstruct the proceeding." Without impeachment, Blount derived "a benefit from his own wrong."[42] Bayard was staggering under the burden of his sweeping argument; expulsion from the Senate hardly could be beneficial to Blount.

He closed with refutation of the defense's demurrer that Blount's conduct did not "regard" his office: "there is not a syllable in the Constitution which confines impeachment to official acts, and because it is against the plain dictates of common sense, that such restraint should be imposed on it." Bayard was technically correct; high crimes and misdemeanors might be committed away from or in disregard of official duties. His hypothetical case of a judge who failed to use "his authority, in case of an insurrection, to quell the insurgents" but aided "them in their violence" was an example of an impeachable offense, similar to those in a number of state cases, which told against Blount's defense.[43]

Despite his recovery on the final issue, Bayard left the defense case intact. All they needed was one of their three objections to the impeachment, and Bayard could not overturn the limitation of liability to current officeholders. When he introduced the notion that anyone was impeachable by the federal government, he annexed more power to Congress than any of the framers (Hamilton, possibly, excepted) desired. He substituted common law for fundamental law, reversing one of the triumphs of Revolutionary republicanism. He created for no gain a specter more frightening than all Blount's plots and invited the defense to shift the debate from Blount to the common law's inferiority to the federal Constitution.

Bayard's technically able exposition of the "civil" office issue was lost in the debris.[44] Joseph Story and later commentators simply took their text from the final Senate ruling against the impeachment of a senator. In recent years Raoul Berger has resuscitated the framers' assumption that impeachment would lie against members of the upper house. Wilson, Hamilton, Mason, and others had objected to making the Senate a trial court of impeachments for precisely this reason, and away from Philadelphia others reached the same conclusion. At the ratification conventions this assumption continued to prevail. All commentators exempted legislative acts from impeachment, but corruption of individual senators was to be grounds for their trial and removal by their peers.[45] Although Berger is correct on this point, Bayard himself did more than anyone else to obscure it by setting up the common-law precedent of universal impeachment. As Bayard's audience, particularly Dallas, well knew, the first states had fashioned a very different set of impeachment rules, rules which informed the federal Constitution. By wheeling in English history, Bayard attempted to overturn almost a quarter of a century of American experience—and failed.

Why? Bayard might have introduced the common-law inclusive definition of who might be impeached in order to make his real argument—that legislators were liable to impeachment—appear more reasonable. This ploy also overcame the objection that Blount was no longer in office. It was a calculated risk, for the Senate had taken the wind out of the House Federalists' sails by rushing to expel Blount before the impeachment was fairly begun. There is little evidence of coordination between the House leadership and their opposite numbers in the Senate, assuming that both groups wanted to threaten Republican congressmen with impeachment. Federalists at the Senate session of January–March 1798 did try to assist the managers over this obstacle on one occasion. Jacob Read, a Federalist senator from South Carolina and an English-trained lawyer, proposed that no senator be impeachable but that any private citizen might be impeached and tried. Thus the Federalists, as long as they held a majority in both houses, were safe from impeachment, but any would-be Republican, in his private station, was open to it.[46] Vice-President Jefferson, presiding at the session, was aghast; he raged that impeachment would become a gag upon the opposition. Even Federalists were unsure of the consequences of this extension of impeachment. Constitutional scruples aside, it made any person liable. Jefferson fretted: the "universality of the impeaching power" could still become a reality if the upper house followed Read's lead, and the lower house concurred.[47] Jefferson was confused; neither he nor Theodore Sedgwick, the arch-Federalist from Massachusetts, nor Read, could quite decide if senators were immune or not, for if they could be impeached as private citizens, their rank in the government was not relevant. Madison, watching developments from outside the chamber, predicted that the "extravagant novelty" of universal impeachment would not stand the test of public scrutiny.[48] He was right; the measure never came to a vote. With that failure, the only batture upon which Bayard could lean impeachment of the departed Blount was swept away. Bayard then hauled up the common-law argument for universality, hoping to be able to fall back upon the impeachment of legislators as a sound and reasonable position. In this light, the continued prosecution of Blount was meant as a blind, a way of introducing and obtaining approval for a new doctrine, not a particular verdict in a particular case. Unfortunately, Bayard and the managers miscalculated the resistance to the common-law universality argument, and the effect that resistance would have upon their actual purpose.

Although Bayard was not the strongest of the advocates and apologized for parts of his performance, he was the first to speak, covered all the points in the defense plea, and advanced a broad, novel thesis. His arguments thus became the focus of the pretrial hearings. Dallas, a far more experienced trial lawyer, though a more ponderous and labored orator, retorted that the doctrine of universal impeachability violated the division of powers between state and federal government. Universal impeachment would replace restrictive constitutional prosecutions (designed to limit the reach of Congress) with the broad and undefined powers of Parliament under common law—and this in the face of a federal constitution that refused to incorporate the common law. Good sense underlay the present American law: common-law impeachments were excessive and partisan, contradicted American policy, and were unwelcome.[49]

Dallas's next task was to exclude senators from impeachment, though it was not a vital point for his client—Blount was no longer a senator. He opened with the proposition that impeachment and removal checked judicial and executive power, for prosecution in a regular court might fail when the defendant was a judge or was appointed by the same organ (the executive) which appointed the judges. None was needed in the case of an erring legislator, for he had no special protection against the ordinary course of criminal law. Of course, if universal impeachment were the rule, fine distinctions about misuse of power in the different branches would be irrelevant, but universal impeachment was not the rule. A nice twist, this, using the weakness of Bayard's universality thesis against his much stronger argument that senators were liable to impeachment. To cope with the absence of any explicit constitutional exclusion of legislators, the many examples of Parliamentary impeachment of peers, and the consensus, ten years before, that members of the upper house would be impeachable, Dallas assembled an army of cavils. He marshaled the fact that nothing in the Constitution named congressmen as civil officers, or mandated their impeachment, and pounced on the detail that the president, under sections 2 and 3 of Article II of the Constitution, appointed officers, but he did not appoint senators. He labored the technicality that the description of those persons liable to impeachment appeared in the executive article of the Constitution, not the first article, on Congress. For the next few hours Dallas marched on, attacking portions of the Constitution, enfilading its language, sallying out against the meaning of phrases. His ammunition and time nearly exhausted, he maintained that his distinctions were not mere skirmishes, for the very nature of "free government" required that legislators not be "civil officers." They were representatives of the people, not appointees. Though Congress and the other branches did interact, they were of different substance. For this reason, the Senate could expel a member, and although it could not destroy his political capacity by disqualifying him, it could protect the republic amply with the powers it had. To do more, by adding impeachment to expulsion, would upset the delicate equilibrium created by checks and balances. His mock combat done, Dallas gave way to Jared Ingersoll.[50]

On January 5, Ingersoll completed argument for the pretrial motions of the defense seeking dismissal of the impeachment. Ingersoll had the advantage of following Dallas; the former could ramble about in byways of English precedent because the latter had demolished the universality argument. Ingersoll was free to explore an extremity of the defense case (a freedom Dallas had not sought): the argument that trial by jury must not be abridged by impeachment when the defendant was already out of office. In effect, he was free to toy with the obverse implications of the universality argument, and he did. If anyone could be impeached, impeachment violated the guarantee of trial by jury. The only reason the two did not clash in the Constitution was that impeachment had a "salutary limitation" to those in office and could result only in removal from office. It was a clever point developed in leisurely fashion by a formidable advocate. Indeed, Ingersoll may have been too casual in his argument and too clever on this point, for a number of his listeners mistakenly believed he meant to abolish impeachment altogether.[51]

Ingersoll next meandered through the Constitution to support Dallas's contention that senators were not civil officers. Again he was at liberty to follow strands of logic which Dallas elected not to trace. Ingersoll raised questions which had bothered a number of anti-Federalists in the ratification convention. How could the Senate sit in judgment upon one of its own? Would not impeachment merely duplicate the power of expulsion set out in the first article? He skirted the logic behind impeachment of those already removed from office: what could its motive be? He even hinted at the ulterior plot of the managers, but he was a Federalist himself, a friend of the managers, and would not embarrass them on this point. He considered both matters—the universality of impeachment and the liability of senators— already refuted. Still, he could not resist twitting the managers. Did they want to impeach Blount before the Senate knowing that he could not be tried? Had not the Senate itself refused to approve the doctrine a year before?[52]

However well Dallas and Ingersoll appreciated the true aim of the Federalists, their defense did not rest upon exposing the underlying, general thrust at Republican legislators. Instead, they tried to move the debate as far away from Blount's conduct as possible. With the exception of Ingersoll's brief rejoinder that Blount had been merely indecorous, the defense counsel ignored their client and struck at their adversaries' views of impeachment. The managers had exposed themselves to this tactic by advancing the universality thesis rather than simply demanding that a dangerous man never regain office. As they moved away from Blount, his counsel were only too happy to follow.

Harper tried to make up as much ground as he could in the final address for the prosecution. He recast the universality theme by praising the value of common law and assured the Senate he only meant to apply it to a very limited subject. The framers did not confine the persons liable to be impeached to the president, vice-president, and civil officers. Why impeach those who are out of office—of course "to punish and thereby prevent offenses which are of such a nature as to endanger the safety, or injure the interests of the United States."[53] These sorts of offenses might be committed by persons who did not hold office, "yet it may often be extremely important to prevent such offenders from getting into office, as well as to remove them when they are in."[54] Harper had to let the cat out of the bag. A recognized leader of the Federalists' attempts to muzzle the opposition, Harper was appealing to the Federalist majority of 22 to 10 in the upper house to assist in this task. One must remember that the seditious libel law was now in effect, prohibiting malicious and untruthful attacks upon the government (leaving questions of fact to Federalist grand juries, trial juries, and attorneys general, not to mention trial judges).

After expounding the text of the new doctrine, Harper applied it. Senators were liable to the same chastisement through disqualification as any other officer or ex-officer of the government. Equally important, the offense need not be a crime. The only persons excluded by the *civil* in civil officers were military officers. But as Harper shouldered past the defense's delicate distinctions between common-law officers and constitutional ones, he tripped and brought down the first part of his case. He insisted that inclusion of the phrase *and no other persons* after *civil officers* in Article II, section 4, would have been ungainly and ludicrous. Plainly, congressmen were officers. Yet, by this reasoning, the framers must have meant to exclude private citizens. Harper insisted that it would have been unnecessary to have written in that exclusion. One can almost hear the defense counsel murmuring surprised assent. Harper was rushed, but such a lapse was inexcusable. He evidently did not notice the second interpretation to which his aside on constitutional writing style could be put, and he spent the closing hours of the day proving that senators were officers. His mistake, while inadvertent, was all but inescapable: however right the prosecutors were about the liability of seated senators, Blount was now a private citizen.[55]

After three days of debate behind closed doors, the Senate Federalists rejected Harper's appeal. They voted, 14 to 11, to refuse jurisdiction in the case. Among the naysayers were a near majority of Federalists, including Read, who feared that senators would become targets of political reprisal, John Langdon of New Hampshire, James Hillhouse, a Connecticut lawyer, and Humphrey Marshall, whose own taste of impeachment could not have been pleasant. The finding of the court of the Senate was read into the record on the eleventh of January and delivered to counsel for the lower house and the defendant on the fourteenth.[56]

Blount's case was an object lesson to both Federalists and Republicans: there was no hope for a sweeping politicization of impeachment law without a suitable revision or extension of the doctrine of impeachment. The new doctrine had to be consonant with the language of the Constitution; common-law fillers would not do. More important, any new doctrine must fit the general lines of development of republicanism. Impeachment law could be extended (it was done in 1776 and 1787) but only and always in accord with larger developments in republican thinking. To reach the goal of impeachment of Republicans in Congress, Bayard and Harper harkened back to the common law of universal impeachment. Narrower grounds— pressing the liability of senators—would have worked better but would not have been appropriate for Blount, who no longer belonged to that body. In the end, *Blount*, the vehicle for a larger campaign, caused its abrupt demise but did not end the search for a broader doctrine. In three years the Republicans would try their hand at fashioning a new rationale for political impeachment.

In cases like *Marshall, Clayton*, and *Blount*, Republicans and Federalists probed the politicization of impeachment. Their efforts failed because the bulk of American impeachment precedent prevented them from using impeachment to censure and remove politically malodorous officials. It remained limited to provable offenses against incumbents. Had the Federalists been able to use it against Blount, his career might have been shattered by disqualification. No defector to the Republican side would then have been safe, in or out of office. *Marshall* and similar cases were a political lesson of another sort; had the senator been impeached, political mavericks within their own states would have been cautioned to avoid insulting the majority party there. Clayton escaped formal prosecution but Jackson's intent was plain: the new majority party would have its way with its former enemies. None of these impeachment taunts and threats led to conviction upon trial, but one of the three defendants fled before the prospect of impeachment, and another was expelled from office by his colleagues. Their fates demonstrated the growing willingness of lower houses to pursue officials for partisanship.

The motive for such prosecutions waxed larger with each passing day, as party combat on the national and state levels reached fever pitch. The near war with France drove Federalism toward suppression of Republican opposition and stirred the Republicans to recrimination and renewed electoral activity against the ruling Federalists. In control of Congress, the courts, the executive branch of the federal government, and a majority of state offices, especially the judiciary, the Federalists had little need of impeachment. For them the Blount case was an aberration. Instead of legislative removal, they curbed their opponents with judicial tools. In state and federal courts, Federalist judges enforced seditious libel laws. Using common-law standards and later, under the Seditious Libel Act of 1798, Federalists muzzled the opposition press. The Federalists thus could belittle the Republican's flirtation with impeachment in states with Republican legislative majorities, attributing it to their amateurish misunderstanding of impeachment law (the same ignorance of legal principles which supposedly caused them to attack wise judges). An unnamed pundit in the *Gazette of the United States* compared the Republicans' dilemma to Hamlet's: "to impeach or not to impeach, that is the question . . . the cankered envy and the thousand pangs, we democrats are heir to . . . to Impeach, harangue . . . perchance to fail; aye, there's the rub. . . ."[57]

Spectacular failures like *Blount* would have dissipated all the respectability impeachment owned, had it not been for a countervailing force: the continuing limitation of almost all the state cases to palpable misconduct and willful misuse of power. As the states had framed, tested, and proved impeachment before 1787, so they kept it a viable constitutional instrument in the face of party government. This was the other half of the bifurcated stream of impeachment law after 1795.

9

IMPEACHMENT FOR CAUSE, 1796–1805

WHILE THE EMERGING TWO-PARTY SYSTEM EXERTED A MAGNETIC ATTRACTION upon impeachment in state legislatures and Congress, attracting political prosecutions against opponents, the restricted, "constitutional" cases did not disappear. Quite the contrary: impeachment for cause remained by far the more common of the two sorts of cases. The law has an inertia, particularly in a case-law system. Precedent piled upon precedent in the years before and after the federal convention legitimized and made uniform earlier state provisions, compacting a mass of impeachments for willful, self-interested violation of law, misuse of power, corruption, and prejudicial conduct, if not criminality. Before 1795 all of this exerted a drag upon politicians' desire to use impeachment to remove obnoxious incumbents. Insofar as the entire experience of post-revolutionary impeachment had proved the wisdom of limiting impeachment to republican goals, so that same experience militated against wholesale politicization of impeachment after 1795. Instead of altering the course of impeachment, the galvanic pull of party deflected only a part of the whole.

The practical utility of "constitutional" impeachment—controlling the misconduct of lesser judicial and executive officials—was, if anything, more apparent after 1795 than before. The vituperative, self-interested competition of national parties added one more occasion and incentive for local officials to bend their offices to corrupt ends. Federalists decried this in Republican officials, in the few states whose legislatures had Republican majorities capable of appointing justices, tax collectors, and magistrates. Republicans were even louder in protesting the supposedly illegal activities of Federalist appointees. Even discounting some of the protests, there were real grievances on both sides. Political appointees could not help being influenced by party; and some—weak or vicious—went too far in their loyalty to party. In all, standing political parties simultaneously heightened the sensitivity of everyone in government to real misconduct while providing a new motive for such misconduct. The old problem of corruption in a republic, so prominent in the first stages of state making, raised its head. Would party allegiance so corrupt officials that the republic would fall? Impeachment once again provided a check by the representatives of the people upon gross misuses of authority.

What is more, the lower house remained the institution responsible for receiving petitions of redress, complaints, informations, and even grand jury presentments of officials (when local courts could not or did not take action) regarding official malfeasance. Although the volume of state legislative business was growing and sessions were getting longer, the lower houses jealously guarded their powers of inquiry into official behavior. It is not surprising that the great bulk of the cases between 1796 and 1805 fall into the category of limited impeachment, for cause. In case after case, legislators put aside party to act as the "Grand Inquest" of the people.

When Vermont became one of the United States, in 1793, it restated its intention to impeach officials for "maladministration." Its new constitution added that, as in federal cases, impeachment and trial in the General Assembly was no bar to prosecution in the regular courts.[1] Although no one was impeached in Vermont between Fassett, in 1787, and the end of the era considered in this book, four men were placed in jeopardy for suspected misconduct in office. On October 21, 1799, the Council of Censors, still at work in this state, found that William Cooley, Bennington County's sheriff, had "wittingly and willfully" taken excessive expenses for summoning grand jurors to the superior court sessions that February. The council ordered that Cooley "be impeached before the governor and [legislative] council," for the "maladministration" of his office.[2] The assembly did investigate, but Cooley testified that he had to visit some of the towns twice in order to fill out the jury panel. The treasurer's report and Cooley's accounts showed that the sheriff's explanation was plausible, and the case was dropped.[3] The following year, the censors ordered that John Chipman, sheriff of Addison County, be impeached for charging excessive fees. To this they added a second call for impeachment, of Prince B. Hall, sheriff of Franklin County.[4] The censors were evidently poring over the treasurer's books. On October 14, 1800, the assembly recommended the naming of managers to prosecute Chipman. The vote was close (85 to 84), and a motion to reconsider passed 90 to 78. Instead of rushing to select managers, the house decided to create a special committee to investigate the charges.[5] On October 21, the committee reported that Chipman also had to return to a number of towns to gather potential grand jurors, and, at the time, the superior court approved his accounts.[6] The lower house resolved that the censors, "not being informed of special facts, or of the Superior Court's allowance," had erred in bringing charges against Chipman, and no further action was taken.[7] Hall convinced the house that he, too, had filled returns marked "non est" on writs for jurors from a number of towns, proof that he had to return to these towns to find jurors for the superior court. The assembly bought his story and dropped the charges.[8] Finally, on February 1, 1804, assemblyman Lewis Morris moved an inquiry into the official conduct of Charles Leavens, justice of the peace for Windsor County. After agreeing to Morris's motion, the lower house plunged into the source of Leavens's alleged malfeasance: *Willard v. Hall*. The judge found for the plaintiff $15 damage and $4.95 court costs. Within two hours, according to Morris, the defendant asked to appeal to the county court and offered a surety to prosecute the appeal. Morris continued: "The said Justice knowing the premises and intending to oppress the defendant, in violation of his duty as a justice of the peace, and of the laws of this state, did wholly refuse to grant the said appeal." The defendant, wishing to petition the assembly, asked Leavens for a copy of the record, but the justice "to secure himself from an impeachment, for his malconduct [this was Morris's surmise] falsely rewrote the record to show that an appeal had been granted."[9] Falsifying records, for whatever reason, was a serious breach of ethics, and the assembly appointed a committee to investigate further. Two days later the committee accepted Hall's version of the facts but arrived at a different reading of Leavens's motives: "Said judge, finding he had done wrong in refusing said bail [actually a surety for performance] applied to both plaintiff and defendant, who each expressed his consent that the said bail should be taken." Then and only then did Leavens change the record. The committee concluded that the justice "in his official capacity conducted [himself] ignorantly and impudently but not corruptly" and advised no further action be taken. The assembly concurred.[10] The Council of Censors and the lower house acted the role of watchdogs. Fee inflation and botched local court procedure were common and vexing problems, for which impeachment was one solution.[11] While the state's Republicans were harried by its Federalist majority, and in 1799–1800 were ravaged by prosecutions of Republican Matthew Lyon and his supporters for seditious libel, its impeachments remained above its politics.[12]

This pattern was repeated in other states. Throughout the decade 1795–1805, New Jersey was torn by partisan competition, erupting at election time into battles between mobs. There was plenty of motive for the majority in the legislature to use impeachment for its own ends, or for the minority to demand impeachment of officials appointed by the majority. When the Federalists controlled the legislature, and with it the appointment of justices of the peace, county judges, and court clerks, Republicans claimed that the judges were "incorporated with the Government" for political purposes.[13] When, after 1801, the shoe was on the other foot, outraged Federalists insisted that the Republican majority named illiterate men as justices of the peace.

The lower house was highly politicized, and judicial appointments were clearly political matters—but in case after case the entire lower house agreed on impeachment votes, one way or the other—even against their own party's appointments. When the Republicans took power, they did not try to impeach Federalists in the judiciary simply to remove them. They appointed Republicans when they could, and when they could not, in the case of the appellate and supreme court judges, they did not manufacture causes for impeachment.[14]

The New Jersey legislature impeached and tried officials when there was evidence of willful misconduct or criminality, and dismissed complaints when they failed this test. The first serious case in this era involved Elijah Godfrey, a Cape May County justice of the peace. On November 4, 1799, the assembly heard a petition from Eleazer Hand, complaining of Godfrey's misconduct. Three days later the committee to which the petition was committed reported that Godfrey's conduct justified an impeachment. The articles alleged that Godfrey had rendered judgment against Hand, another justice of the peace for Cape May, in a civil proceeding. This was hardly a misconduct in itself, but Godfrey had taken upon himself to give judgment when the jury in the case could not agree. The articles also imputed "improper or corrupt motives"—Godfrey, the assembly believed, overstepped his authority out of personal malice (rather than innocent error) against his judicial counterpart. On the nineteenth the impeachment for "malpractice" was passed, 30 to 7. Abijah Smith, the only representative from Cape May, voted against the impeachment, but the legislative council heard the case a year later and unanimously voted to convict. Godfrey was removed.[15] Godfrey's malconduct was a malicious abuse of power, but not a crime. It did not involve financial gain for him but did bend the judicial system to his personal ends. For its part, the assembly case against him could not prove criminality but did establish misuse of official power. There is no evidence that this was a political case, and, as in the Vermont investigation of justices for overcharging the superior court, everyone involved, including the defendant, agreed that impeachment for an offense not criminal was proper, if willful misconduct could be proved. The upper house in New Jersey gave a unanimous seal of approval to the assembly definition of misconduct as an impeachable offense.

Equally important, the Vermont house and senate, and the New Jersey house and council appear to have regarded most impeachments as matters of no great moment. It was not reserved for great offenses or great crimes—a modern misreading of the term *high crimes*. One measure of this view of impeachment in the states is the dispatch with which they were heard. While fairness was not abandoned—witnesses were obtained from Cape May in Godfrey's impeachment and again at his trial—the normal business of the assembly went smoothly on through these hearings. Time was set aside for them, but no storm broke upon the legislators when they voted to remove someone from office.

The New Jersey assembly fit a number of prospective impeachment cases into its ordinary business in 1799. The November session had barely begun when John Lacey, a justice of the peace for Burlington, was accused of prejudicial proceedings in the court of common pleas for the county.[16] Lacey was a controversial and an outspoken Federalist, but the eight draft articles of impeachment rested upon his arrogance and inattention to duty, not his party affiliation. Despite confession by a defendant, he had ordered a constable not to execute a judgment, then issued a stay of execution to obtain a payment of a debt due himself from the plaintiff. On another occasion, he found against a defendant in one suit and dismissed a second for nonappearance of the plaintiff, when both were scheduled for hearing before another justice. He had also given blank precepts to the constables, pleaded to juries in cases before his own court, and "uttered certain opprobrious expressions, respecting the present legislature." The assembly found that he had illegally issued the *supercedas*, reopened a case judged in default by another justice, and given blank precepts to his officers but otherwise did no wrong. His comments on the legislature respected "the legislature only, and is not a charge against him, as a justice of the peace." The legislature wanted no imputations of partisanship. Lacey was censured for violating his duties, and the assembly voted 18 to 17 to record a "high disapprobation of the official conduct of John Lacey."[17] He resigned, informing the lower house that he had accepted judicial office from the lower house "with great reluctance." He intended to leave it before the charges were made against him, as the voters of Burlington had sent him to the assembly, and had waited only to see if a defense was necessary. The vote of disapproval thus came from his new colleagues—and, to judge from his letter to them—gave him great pain.[18] His Federalism undoubtedly played a part in the close vote of censure, but the Republicans did not try to impeach him—despite his opposition to them.

The flow of petitions of complaint to the New Jersey lower house continued. Most complaints, as in the charges against George Brockover, a Morris County justice of the peace, were dismissed as "trivial" or, after an inquiry, as in the cases of James Steelman and Jeremiah Smith, justices from Glouster, and later, against Garret van Hauten, were found to be unsupported.[19] Often, no one came to testify against the defendants. When charges came to a vote, for example in the matter of Clement Acton, clerk of the Salem County court, the vote was lopsided: no 34, yes 3.[20] When, obversely, there were grounds for suspicion, as in complaints against Robert Wilson, a justice for Middlesex, a full and extensive hearing, committee reports, and votes were taken. The litigants in *Fried v. Tice* reported that Wilson failed to give a proper reading of the law in the case. The committee of inquiry refused to make a recommendation, but on November 11, 1805, the assembly agreed to draw up articles by a 22 to 17 vote. The articles alleged that Wilson had "fraudulently, oppressively, and in violation of the duties of his office, failed to give a rule of reference," causing Tice to forfeit a surety. The assembly agreed that Wilson had "corrupt motives" for his "misdemeanor," though it was no crime, but a misconduct. After two postponements upon the absence of the state's witnesses, Wilson's trial proceeded on February 18, 1806. On the nineteenth, the senate voted, 9 to 1, to acquit the justice.[21] He had acted in error but not willfully. The upper house again read the law of impeachment to permit it to remove a defendant for less than a crime, but refused to convict if the suspect did not act maliciously.

Massachusetts' General Court disposed of cases following the same un-written limitations as Vermont and New Jersey. In the first case removal was all but automatic; in the second the petition for impeachment was heard, discussed, and brushed aside. Criminality was proved in the first; partiality was alleged but not established in the second. On the last Friday of August 1799, justice of the peace John Vinal faced trial in the supreme judicial court of the state for taking money from tavern keepers in return for liquor licenses. He pleaded not guilty but the jury gave a different verdict. He was fined $200 and required by the court to post a bond of $100 for his good behavior over the next year.[22] On February 24, 1800, six months after the trial, state Attorney General James Sullivan sent a copy of Vinal's conviction to the speaker of the house. The speaker committed the papers to a special committee, which, a day later, voted to write articles. The next day, the entire house agreed to articles and sent them to the senate. The special committee had told the lower house that the supreme court had convicted Vinal of extortion, and believed it "the duty of the house of representatives to prepare impeachment articles" for misconduct.[23] The offense was obviously a criminal one, but lower house action was the only proper way to remove a convicted official. The represen-tatives could have joined with the senate to ask the governor to remove Vinal, but did not.

The senate told the house it would try Vinal, and then debated where everyone would sit, the rights that Vinal and the managers would have to make written statements and call witnesses, and the admissibility of evidence. Once again, the upper house was asserting its powers to make legal rulings, as any court of law might. The senate issued warrants for witnesses and principals, writs for evidence, paid expenses and even determined the lengths of the tables to be occupied by counsel. The trial itself took three successive afternoons, March 1–3, 1800. Vinal was found guilty by a unanimous vote, removed from office, and disqualified from holding any future office. The senate agreed with the house that impeachment was the proper way to remove an official.[24]

The second Massachusetts impeachment inquiry in this period grew out of the contest for land on the coast of Maine. A province of Massachusetts, Maine was growing in population and wealth throughout the Federal period. Paul Dudley Sargent was a leader in this enterprise. Born in Salem, a war hero during the Revolution, Sargent became a merchant after the war. By 1787 he had established himself in Sullivan, Maine, and was shortly thereafter named chief justice of the court of common pleas for Hancock County. He was commissioned by the governor of Massachusetts, John Hancock, as first judge of probate and justice of the peace for the county at the same time as he was made the first judge of the county court.[25] The county lay along Maine's rugged coast, poorly developed, short of roads, filled with debtors, and without a gaol when Sargent took charge of its court. Appeals to the general court in Boston were of little avail; by force of character, their status in the county, and periodic displays of authority, the local judges brought order of a sort.[26] By the end of the decade, property along the Penobscot and other rivers leading to the interior was appreciating, and county court dockets grew apace, as merchants, vendors, and farmers battled for choice lots. Sargent, one of these, sued in court (stepping down for a time himself) for debts owed him.[27]

The Hancock County court records for the sessions of May–December 1798 included a complicated suit of ejectment among two groups of investors. The losers in the suit, led by Jeremiah Wardwell, sought to appeal the case to the supreme judicial court when it met for the Northern Maine counties on its normal circuit. The bench, led by Sargent, prevented the appeal.[28] Frustrated in their own courts, the litigants petitioned the Massachusetts General Court to inquire into the conduct of Sargent, William Vinall, Oliver Parker, and F. L. B. Goodwin, the judges of the court of common pleas. On June 1, 1801, the investigation began. The petition to "remove" the judges was given to a committee, which held public hearings on the twelfth. Sargent and his colleagues were represented by counsel; the petitioners came and spoke for themselves. The next day the house overwhelmingly voted not to impeach or to address the governor to remove the judges. The committee resolution anticipated that the uproar "should subside." The assembly paid the witnesses, and they returned without having done more than harass the judges. High-handedness, without partiality or self-interested corruption, was not impeachable.[29]

Sargent's case is noteworthy in another respect. His brush with impeachment differed from investigations upon "the grand inquest" in the House of Commons in that he was permitted counsel during the lower house proceeding. An English defendant could obtain counsel only during the trial (though he might be advised by counsel, without doors, at any time). Sargent was "represented by counsel" at the assembly hearings. This step is not common; early American state legislatures did not permit counsel in the initial stages of investigation. In 1794 Hunt was not represented by counsel during the impeachment, although he watched the debate with great care and chose his counsel from the General Court after hearing its deliberations. The Massachusetts bill of rights did not guarantee impeachment suspects the right to counsel, for impeachments were not trials. In the United States Congress, Blount, Pickering, and Chase were not represented by counsel at all in the impeachment proceedings. Sargent may have claimed an exception because he could not leave his duties in Maine and reach Boston as easily as Hunt or Greenleaf. In a later Massachusetts case, the impeachment of James Prescott in 1821, counsel was again permitted to conduct the defense in the lower house. Sargent's case had set a precedent.[30]

In Kentucky a sense of necessity, stimulated by manifest wrongdoing, rather than mere political chicanery, motivated the lower house to a series of impeachments. Reform of the Kentucky Court of Appeals in 1794 did not reach down to the local "quarter sessions courts," staffed by poorly trained judges and swamped with business. During the general movement for constitutional reform, resulting in the new constitution of 1799, Felix Grundy argued for sweeping reform of the lower courts. Though Grundy lost on this issue, the political biases and lack of training of the local judges remained nettlesome matters of public record. Conservative John Breckinridge and his allies lost a motion to bar impeachment without a prior grand jury indictment of a judge, the opposition led by the legal reformers whose proposals Breckinridge had scuttled. Correction of judicial misbehavior was not given to the judiciary; the assembly remained the watchdog of the courts.[31]

The demand for reform of the courts could not be stilled: a bill for circuit courts passed in November 1802, and the assembly continued to keep a sharp eye out for misuse of power in the courts.[32] The lawyers in the lower house appear to have taken their scrutiny of the courts seriously. Intracounty politics and lack of preparation of judges made the lawyers' work more taxing, and feuds among local officials tied up the courts. Even those justices who held assembly seats were provoked into action against their brethren by these situations. From 1792 to 1820 every session had one investigative hearing, on average, and some of them led to votes for removal.[33]

On December 14, 1801, the lower house reported to the senate articles of impeachment against Elijah Craig, a justice of the peace for Gallatin County. Craig had left the bench when a litigant made a motion that the judge did not want to hear, and he was otherwise "tyrannical and overbearing" in his conduct toward the other judges. He had used abusive language to the clerk.

For his own benefit he connived with his uncle, Benjamin Craig, to prevent the formation of a new town despite an assembly directive to the contrary. He changed warrants, encouraged quarreling in court, misappropriated the goods of convicted criminals, and extorted costs of court from litigants. Many of these offenses could have resulted from Craig's ignorance of criminal and civil procedure. The assembly suggested as much when, instead of pressing for a trial, it asked the senate to join it in a petition to the governor to remove Craig. The senate took no action.[34]

In 1803 the senate heard the house prosecute its first formal impeachment, against Thomas Jones, surveyor of Bourbon County. Jones had overcharged the state for his work, failed to perform his duties, and surveyed the wrong tracts. There were twenty-one specific charges, and a twenty-second article, alleging that Jones attempted to corrupt an election for a clerkship. Jones, who had come without counsel, now asked permission to use one and pleaded not guilty to all charges. The senate then asked the sheriff of the county to summon a jury into the chamber, and the jury found Jones guilty. The upper house did not act as judge and jury despite its constitutional impeachment power. Jones resigned during the trial, but the senate decided that his resignation did not end their jurisdiction over the case. They permitted the house's managers to renew the prosecution and again summoned a jury of citizens to decide whether Jones had, in fact, overcharged the county. When this second jury voted that the surveyor was guilty, the senate pronounced Jones guilty of five of the articles and ordered him perpetually disqualified from office. He was to pay the costs of the prosecution, including that of the jury. The senate acted as a court, but not, as in other state impeachment trials, the part of the jury as well. This is the only state case in which such a jury was summoned.[35]

Two years later, the house and senate again explored procedural novelties to investigate official wrongdoing. On November 25, 1805, Reuben Humphrey, a justice for Henry County, was charged by the lower house with taking bribes, fighting with litigants, and generally "destroying public confidence" in his office. One can see how a brawling judge might have this effect upon litigants. The lower house then asked the senate to join it in a special joint committee of inquiry. The senate did not accept the invitation but did deliberate on Humphrey's case. The justice by now had admitted to taking the bribe and humbled himself before them. Two-thirds of the senate concurred in a vote of censure. This conclusion they asked the lower house to accept, to no avail. The assembly wanted Humphrey removed by the senate. A conference of both houses finally agreed to petition the governor to remove the erring justice. In all three of these cases, politics, other than the ever-present wrangle between upper and lower houses over their respective prerogatives, did not create impeachments. If the procedure became entangled, the cases themselves were straightforward and well within the older constitutional limitations.[36]

South Carolina continued to impeach suspected malfeasors under the established constitutional guidelines. On December 10, 1803, the house of assembly informed the senate of the impeachment of James Bentham, a notary and justice of the quorum for Charleston. Bentham, an old Revolutionary War hero, did not care for the neutrality policy of Jefferson's first administration.[37] He sold certificates to two sailors to prove that they were born in America, when he knew that they were British citizens (the object not being greed but defiance of British attempts to prevent desertion from their fleet). The assembly voted that Bentham "endangered the good understanding that subsists between the said kingdom and the said United States." Managers were named, but Bentham's request for a delay in the trial postponed the event until the next session, in the fall of 1804.[38] A committee to manage the charges was again named on December 10, 1804. On the fourteenth the senate sat as a court, administered the oath to its members, heard the articles, and let John Richardson, counsel for the defendant, speak for the absent defendant. The managers arrived and received a copy of the reply, at which point the trial court adjourned until the next session.[39] The record notes that vital documents in the hands of one of the managers were not available because he was ill. A year later, on November 25, 1805, the senate again sat as a court. Bentham asked to be excused from attendance when the senate ordered him to appear. The vote to continue the hearing, 14 to 11, was close enough to suggest that the trial was becoming too long for many of the senators. The assembly now asked a delay, for one of the managers had died. The senate, in exasperation, questioned whether the house would ever be ready to prosecute the case. The house did not send managers to the senate and on December 19, 1805, withdrew the articles. Bentham had evidently mended his ways.[40] South Carolina's legislative majority had shifted from Federalist to Republican, but Bentham's party affiliation was not at issue. His anti-English zeal violated his oath of office as much as American neutrality policy. The South Carolina lower house was not protecting the county from the aged magistrate so much as restating that justices of the peace were commissioned to obey the law.

The line between political impeachments, designed to remove or hamstring an opponent, and impeachment for cause, upon evidence of palpable misconduct, cannot be drawn precisely. While these categories are justifiable and did in fact coexist, assignment of certain cases to one or the other involves disentanglement of intricate political arrangements and assessment of highly confusing accusations. Two impeachments for cause in Tennessee, involving the very same defendant, illustrate the continuing tension among the principals over this question.

In the December 1798 session of the Tennessee lower house, Supreme Court Justice David Campbell was impeached for giving an illegal writ to quash the slander suit of William Blount against Elisha Hall, "leaving Blount without remedy." Campbell had also issued a precept freeing Hall from liability in the case, without hearing it in court. A second draft article alleged that Campbell deliberately missed a session of the high court. A third article accused Campbell of pronouncing an inflammatory antigovernment charge to a Nashville grand jury the previous spring. Behind these charges was a mixture of personal animosity, political ambition, and genuine official high-handedness.[41]

When Blount spurred away from Philadelphia in the late spring of 1797, he knew that his political fortune and his speculative empire depended upon reestablishing his base of support in Tennessee. Though he was nominally a Republican, his politics were personal, not ideological. He had to convince Governor John Sevier and other old allies that he was not finished as a local politician. Although Senator William Cocke's defection in the expulsion vote hurt, Blount's credibility was not destroyed by the action of Congress. Part of his appeal in the new state, and one of the reasons that he had left the Federalist fold, was the cold reception Congress gave to Tennessee's application for statehood. Blount worked diligently upon his return, gaining election to the next session of the state senate and ascending to its presidency in the spring of 1798. He believed that Sevier would shortly step down as governor and allow his own election to that position.[42]

One of Blount's problems was to straighten out the Western Tennessee land situation, muddled since North Carolina speculators (himself included) went about surveying, buying, and selling land whose true ownership remained in question. Sevier's answer to this, during the short-lived existence of the state of Franklin, was to write his own boundary treaty with the Indians. By the end of 1797 the federal government and the state of Tennessee were renegotiating land rights with the Cherokees. Both governments had sent delegations to the tribe, the federal commissioners led by Elisha Hall and the state delegation by Sevier himself, aided by Lachlan MacIntosh. As the Indians watched, land speculators in the two delegations jockeyed for advantage. The two sides soon publicly accused the other of fraud, with Hall and Blount at each others' throats. Blount took umbrage at Hall's remarks and brought a slander suit. Campbell, allied by personal and pecuniary ties to the Hall faction, wrote an anonymous newspaper article accusing Sevier of incompetence and meddling in the treaty negotiations. The governor discovered the author's identity and brought his own suit for libel.[43]

While it is tempting to regard this contretemps as a mere name-calling contest, it led directly to Campbell's impeachment. Sevier, who had been Campbell's patron (appointing him chief justice of the short-lived state of Franklin), now withdrew his support. Blount, who had aided Campbell's career, saw the judge in league with Hall against Sevier, whose favor the desperate ex-senator needed. The charges certainly fail to impress the reader with the severity of Campbell's misdeeds. Missing the occasional session of court was not a disciplinary matter if the judge could prove that he was ill, and at his impeachment, Campbell produced affidavits to that effect. Depositions from Hugh Lawson White, a lawyer (and later United States senator) who followed the circuit of the high court, Campbell's physician, and other witnesses verified the judge's indisposition. Only Blount asserted that Campbell boasted of walking out of court because he did not want to hear a particular suit.[44] On the second charge: Campbell averred that judges often inserted political comments in their grand jury charges. The practice was common in the revolutionary era and widely used by patriot judges to advance the quarrel with England.[45] Finally, if Campbell quashed Blount's suit in error, misreading the law or a technical matter of procedure, it would not be the first time that Tennessee judges had shown such ignorance. While the courts in the old and new states used the same texts and books of forms, the level of pleading and ruling on pleas on the frontier was a cut below that in the courts of the seaboard states.[46]

Campbell and later observers regarded the impeachment as a political ploy. They were wrong. Campbell, not his opponents, had politicized the courts, using his power as a judge to harass—albeit in a petty way—Blount and Sevier. Campbell's offenses were not excusable, honorable mistakes but deliberate and voluntary slaps at men who had offended him. Throughout his career Campbell had refused to bow to authority. In 1798, he was elected the highest judicial official, an experienced (if not expert) judge and one of the first settlers—not a man to be treated lightly.[47] Yet on the evening of February 3, 1798, federal troops commanded by Colonel Thomas Butler detained the judge for a day at the edge of the Indian grants. He brayed his outrage to Sevier, Senator Andrew Jackson, and President John Adams. Though witnesses said his arrest was polite and his treatment gracious, Campbell thought it a grave insult to his personal and official dignity.[48] After the fact, Jackson officially protested to John Adams: "To you Sir, as the Guardian of the Constitution, and the Supporter of the Laws, we appeal for redress—and trust, that you will take Such measures, as will not only hereafter, protect the Citizens of our State, from Such wanton Violence; but will cause, the most ample attonement to be made; for the indignity offered to the State—Which we conceive, can only be done, by removing from his Command, the author of Such Military Tyranny."[49] Campbell, unmollified, refused to forgive either Sevier, for his incompetence, or Blount, the gray eminence behind the governor in the reshuffling of Indian titles.

Two months later, at the close of the Mero district session of the supreme court, White heard Campbell accuse the governor of not doing his duty. The "executive," by which White believed the judge meant Sevier, had allowed federal troops to forcibly remove settlers. What was worse, Campbell continued, the governor had interfered in the function of the courts, a not-so-veiled reference to Sevier's suit against Campbell. Campbell also attacked the federal government for its strong-arm tactics.[50] The shot had found its mark among the grand jurors, for at least a few of them promised to take notice of the judge's instructions in their presentment.[51] Blount was not mentioned; but he was not forgotten. Before the November session of the supreme court, Campbell issued the notorious "precept mandatorial" to the Knox District sheriff "outcharging," that is, discharging, Hall of all liability in Blount's suit. When Campbell finished, Blount's innings began.[52]

To the December 1798 meeting of the legislature, Blount directed a flood of complaints against the judge. James Jackson could not have done better. Depositions from witnesses at the two court sessions, and an affidavit from the new speaker of the state senate (Blount himself) attested to the judge's misconduct. Blount stage-managed the impeachment from the upper house, correctly reminding the assemblymen that by state law all writs had to be certified (whether returned or unreturned) by the court clerk, in court. He reminded the lower house that Campbell discharged Hall without bothering to come to court, against the explicit instructions of the Constitution and in an arbitrary manner. The judge contemned the law, his office, and his oath.

Campbell remained unrepentant. He "demanded"—a word he repeatedly used—a right to be heard in the impeachment and appointed counsel for the purpose. He also claimed compulsory process to obtain testimony on oath from the other supreme court justices, the Knox District sheriff, and witnesses to his grand jury charge, as well as all copies of evidence used against him. He made it plain that he would open all the wounds received and given during the negotiation of the recent treaty. In his formal "memorial" to the assembly, Campbell declaimed on "the nature of our government": the state constitution was the supreme law, and the constitution, "by implication" allowed judges to issue writs of mandamus, upon a litigant's petition, in or out of court. Campbell could not recall a case in which the executive or the legislature had blocked a judge from doing his duty, including the issuance of writs. The issuance of such a writ was not a "misdemeanor." It did not proceed from "corrupt motives, or notorious and plain venality." In *Blount*, it was a writ of right, and Hall had correctly applied for it. Not to respond would be to set a "ruinous precedent." So much for *Blount v. Hall*; Campbell plunged next into the Indian treaty negotiations. Sevier had proved that the executive had no respect for separation of powers by "appointing agents to attend the Cherokee treaty, which was certainly a legislative act." "The same man," Sevier, told the assembly that he could and would have suspended Campbell, had the lower house not been ready to hear the case. The judge lectured the assemblymen: "I should have paid a little respect to his illegal mandate, as I do to his and Mr. Blount's persecuting charge."[53]

The house withdrew the first two articles and voted an impeachment upon the *Blount v. Hall* matter alone. This, after all, was the bone of contention with Blount. Between the assembly vote on the fourteenth and the trial on the twenty-fourth, the senate reviewed procedure. Lachlan MacIntosh, Sevier's aid in the Indian treaty negotiations (and a notorious speculator), was hired as counsel for the state. The senate decreed that the judge would answer to "contempts and misdemeanors."[54] He was summoned to Knoxville—a summons duly signed by the speaker, Blount.[55] If there was conflict of interest in Blount's participation, the procedure committee did not press the point. When the senate met as a court, witnesses were heard and a vote was taken within the space of one day. The judge was found guilty, 6 to 5, but the vote failed the two-thirds requirement, and Campbell was discharged. Still, Blount had made his point.[56]

Campbell would remain on the bench until 1807, surviving a second impeachment, this time for corruption. (He allegedly took a bribe of a horse to give a favorable decision in an 1801 case.)[57] Blount died a bare year and three months after the 1798 trial ended. Sevier remained governor and went on to quarrel violently with Andrew Jackson (a quarrel in which Campbell was again a scapegoat of sorts). No one mended his ways. Although the trial vote upon Campbell's second impeachment was guilty 3, not guilty 9, the evidence at least was substantial enough (the gift of the horse was not denied) to warrant investigation.[58] The judge, the governor, and the late speaker all regarded office as a personal possession and did not hesitate to use office as a fulcrum for personal ends. Impeachment curbed some, if hardly all, of these abuses.

The impeachments for cause between 1795 and 1805 differed from the pre-1795 impeachments because the former coexisted with wholly political cases. After 1795, lower houses had to draw a line between impeachment aimed at removal, and that directed at palpable misconduct. The task was not easy, for prosecutors in the latter cast their allegations in terms of misconducts and misuses of public trust. The two types of impeachment thus intersected on doctrinal but not on practical grounds. Impeachments intended to remove an incumbent in order to silence him, or give his place to another, had to establish real misconduct. As long as the requirement of willful misconduct ruled in both types of cases, managers of both would have to frame articles alleging voluntary, intentional wrongdoing. Only a new doctrine could free the prosecution from these restraints. Morgan and Higginson inadvertently broke ground for such a doctrine in *Nicholson*, but because they had no reason to seek a new doctrine, they did not pursue their own lines of inquiry. Bayard, in *Blount*, went further but was repulsed. Now it was the Republicans' turn. After 1800 they formulated the necessary legal tests and put them into practice.

PART IV

REPUBLICAN
IMPEACHMENT DOCTRINES:
"DANGEROUS TENDENCY"
AND "POPULAR WILL,"
1801–1805

INTRODUCTION

AGAINST A RULING PARTY COMMITTED TO THEIR DESTRUCTION, THE REPUBLICANS
entered the election of 1800 with desperate energy. Their immediate aim was
conquest of the Congress and the presidency, but their victory would not be
safe until the Federalist judiciary was curbed as well. Federalist judges, the
triers of seditious libel and treason indictments, held their offices "for good
behavior." Only impeachment and trial could remove them.

Electoral victory in 1800 brought Republicans the legislative majorities
needed for impeachment. The Federalists watched in fury as the campaign,
spearheaded by Jefferson's lieutenants in Congress, gathered strength. There
remained two obstacles in its path. The first was the new president himself.
Jefferson did not trust the impeachment power; he still shivered from his
brush with it. During Blount's trial in the Senate (over which then Vice-
President Jefferson presided), he had written: "I see nothing in the mode of
proceeding by impeachment but the most formidable weapon for the purposes of a dominant faction that ever was contrived."[1] In a draft of his first
inaugural address Jefferson dilated upon the "essential principles of our
government," central to which was his faith in "free and frequent elections by
the people in person, and the more frequent within the limits of their
convenience, and the more extensive the right of suffrage," which would
bring America "the more perfectly within the definition of a genuine republic."[2] Though Jefferson deleted these phrases from his final draft, they
implied that he remained in 1800, as in 1776, wedded to alternative procedures for removal other than impeachment. The omitted lines suggested that
all offices ought to be filled by frequent popular elections, permitting the
electorate rather than a legislature to express their will. The subtlest connotation of the word *frequent* was that presidents (chosen by a process which
had almost brought Jefferson to grief in 1800) and judges, who held tenure for
good behavior, ought also to be directly elected by the people.

In office, Jefferson gravitated toward a second method of removal. A
certain number of federal officials held their posts at the pleasure of the
president. Jefferson summarily relieved Federalist marshals, attorneys, and
appointees to office named after December 12, 1800, and was pushed by local
Republican leaders to replace other Federalists with the party faithful. He
refused to be rushed into wholesale removals, however.[3] To William Branch

Giles he insisted that "good men, to whom there is no objection but a difference of political principle, practised on only as far as the right of a private citizen will justify, are not proper subjects of removal."[4] On other occasions during his first year of office, he promised that only provable malconduct by an officeholder would force his dismissal.[5] Nevertheless, about one-third of all federal officeholders were turned over (counting the president's cabinet and their upper-echelon staff) in his first term, and all the positions went to Republicans. In his effort to give the victorious party a proportionate share of posts in the federal government, Jefferson increasingly made removal a matter of party loyalty.

Jefferson's victory was a triumph of party, and his dual program for removal of officials belonging to the other party by electoral and administrative methods bespoke his commitment to party government. Impeachment had never been a favorite principle with him, and he found alternatives to it. Why then, by 1804, had he become the nominal leader of the most sweeping impeachment movement in American history? Admirers of Henry Adams's *Administrations of Jefferson and Madison* may see cause to rejoice in this additional evidence of Jefferson's duplicity, but the president's temporary flirtation with impeachment was merely part of a more general, albeit experimental integration of party government and legislative removal. Jefferson was a committed party leader, intervening in congressional voting, state party affairs, and electoral campaigns. Everywhere he saw his party triumphant, but the voice of Federalist judges could not be stilled. In a series of thrusts and lunges, Jefferson attacked these bastions of unregenerate Federalism, but no weapon short of impeachment sufficed. If party government was to work, impeachment seemed increasingly necessary.

The second obstacle to this impeachment campaign was doctrinal—the old conundrum of finding a constitutional rationale for quasi-political prosecutions. Impeachment to remove political enemies had little precedent in earlier American cases, and new impeachments had to be framed under the constitutional formula of "high crimes and misdemeanors" (including, from the precedent in the states, misconduct, maladministration, misuse of power, wanton neglect, and palpable incapacity). Without a more congenial doctrine, proponents of impeachment had to struggle along, case by case, trying to stretch political excess by the defendant into palpable misconduct. The Republicans did not need a comprehensive revision of impeachment law but merely a crack into which they might insert a wedge, an additional interpretation of the law suitable for impeaching the most vituperative and biased of their enemies.

Necessity spurred invention. The Republicans adopted the "bad tendency" test used by Federalists to prosecute Republicans for constructive treason and seditious libel. The bad tendency test made the potential ill effects of criticism of the government into grounds for a prosecution. It was natural for the Federalists to absorb bad tendency from the English law of constructive treason and seditious libel—despite the limitations posed upon the common-law handling of treasons and libels by Article III, section 3, and the First Amendment—because the Federalists were a party of Anglophiles. The Republicans attacked the common law but transformed bad tendency into a "dangerous tendency" test in impeachment—a perverse but brilliant achievement. In technical terms, the Republicans expanded the bad consequences test for libel and constructive treasons into a doctrine of the impeachability of any political act having a dangerous tendency to undermine republican institutions. The tie between the English legal test and the Republican impeachment doctrine thus lay in a shared legal heritage but, like impeachment itself, was given a uniquely American form.

The doctrine of bad tendency, the prototype of dangerous tendency, originated in English treason and seditious libel cases. In common-law prosecutions bad tendency tests checked opposition to the crown and, later, to Parliament. The treason statute of 25 Edward III, contained a *salvo*, or rider, that permitted Parliament to prohibit all those actions which were constructive of the seven types of treason specified in the act itself.[6] In other "pleas of the crown" the prosecution had to prove that the conduct amounted to a crime, that is, it specifically fit the provisions of criminal law. In a murder indictment, for example, intent, *actus reus*, and efficient cause had to be established. The federal Constitution defined treason in Article III, section 3, according to the latter rule. Overt acts of war-making or giving aid and comfort to the enemy in time of war were required to establish criminal conduct. The English law of treason remained aloof from this requirement of other crimes, in that a constructive treason could consist in mere words, or listening to words, that had the distant implication of harming the king. In *Messenger's Case*, the court of King's Bench constructed treason out of mob destruction of bawdy houses in London.[7] Bad tendency, as a later commentator wrote, "made treasons, where the letter of the law has not done it."[8] The construction of treason saw riots and civil disorder as attempts to compass the death of the king or levy war against him.

Opposition to the party in power was not treasonous in the United States, whatever suspicions high Federalists might have of the motives of Jefferson and his allies, but in the 1790s Federalist judges and attorneys general suppressed Jeffersonian popular demonstrations against the government using, as in England, charges of treason. Mobbing a federal official was treason in the Pennsylvania Whiskey Rebellion of 1794. William Paterson, presiding at the trial of Philip Vigol, a minor character in the uprising, instructed the trial jury to find Vigol guilty of treason if the intent to levy war was joined with some act of violence against federal authority. Vigol and

John Mitchell were convicted under this ruling. Paterson followed English precedent in equating levying war with the use of force against the operation of a statute or the person of officers of the government in the course of their duties. He insisted that the actions of all the insurgents were levying war, not riot, again citing English cases to support his opinion. President Washington, moved by appeals to humanity and the almost trivial part the defendants played in the rebellion, pardoned the convicts.[9] Nevertheless, Republicans could not be certain how far the Federalists would press this doctrine.

The Fries trials did not reassure them. The facts in this case were not disputed so hotly, or with such pregnant implications, as the law. John Fries was a German American who led a mob of inebriated farmers to Bethlehem, Pennsylvania, to free another group of men imprisoned for not paying a dwelling tax. Opposed entry to the gaol by the militia and the sheriff, Fries authorized his motley troop to return violence with violence. Calmer heads soon prevailed and Fries surrendered himself. He might have been charged with riot, or the misdemeanor of sedition, but John Adams's proclamation ordering Fries's little army to disband termed their operations "treason." Fries faced trial in a federal court in 1799, Supreme Court Justice James Iredell and Judge Richard Peters presiding. The bench ruled that armed resistance against an act of Congress was treason—drawing upon Paterson's opinion in *Vigol*. William Rawle, federal attorney for Pennsylvania, and both judges reminded the jurors that Fries intended to levy war upon the government, and had acted under this intention, upon which the jurors returned a verdict of guilty. Defense arguments that Fries acted without intent to overturn the government, but merely to redress a bad law, were ineffective. The implication of the judges' opinion was ominous: if a riot against Federalist tax policy was treason, was any organized opposition to such laws safe? At what point would vigorous protest against Federalist policies constitute constructive treason of the type that Rawle, Paterson, Iredell, and their political allies—all staunch Federalists—decried? *Fries* brought home the potential for treason charges against Republicans.[10]

Republicans rallied to Fries's defense while Federalists cheered on the prosecution—both parties recognizing that the case had more than local interest. William Duane's Philadelphia *Aurora* warned that the Federalists planned to use these tactics to disrupt the opposition.[11] Dallas was already on record accusing Federalist attorneys general of political prosecutions. His seven-hour closing speech at Fries's trial did not renew this accusation, but Dallas agreed out-of-doors that Fries's trial was a bad omen.[12] Federalists also watched the trial of the "Northampton insurgents" with keen interest. Justice Samuel Chase wanted wholesale indictments but the case was out of his jurisdiction—or so it seemed. But after the verdict was pronounced, Fries's counsel managed to convince the court that one of the jurors was biased, and the case was reheard before Peters and Chase at the next session of the district court. Chase's conduct toward Fries's counsel would become the first of the impeachment articles levied against him in 1804, but at the trial his strictures on the law of treason were more frightening than Iredell's had been. In court he announced that there was no legal brief that would convince him Iredell (and Paterson) were wrong. Out of court he swore to repress any resistance to the laws of Congress, no matter how small a disturbance they entailed.[13]

All of this took place on the very eve of impeachment of Alexander Addison in Pennsylvania. Dallas, counsel for Fries, prosecuted Addison, a Federalist state judge. Fries's German-American allies in the lower house, led by Michael Leib, were leaders of the impeachment effort. Members of the state legislature were eager spectators at the federal district court; there was no way the managers could have missed the potency of the law of constructive treason and its crucial doctrine of bad tendency. As we shall see, Addison was impeached and tried for offenses that amounted to bad, or dangerous, tendency.[14]

The potential association between dangerous tendency and impeachment was even stronger in a second area of law which the Federalists themselves raised to national prominence: seditious libel. In 1798 the Federalists, riding the crest of popular animosity against France, passed three "Alien and Sedition" laws. One of these, the Seditious Libel Act, made false and malicious criticism of the president and Congress into felonies.[15] Although the new law officially dropped the common-law test of bad tendency (in which the court decided if the publication had bad consequences), and authorized the jury to decide if the piece was a libel, the burden of proof of good intention and truth still fell upon defendants. In case after case, all directed at Republican editors, Federalist presiding judges insisted that the defendant have evidence at hand of the truth of their publications. When the Republicans printed their opinions, which, by nature, had neither demonstrable truth nor falsity, prosecutors and judges instructed jurors that the defendant ought to be found guilty. This the jurors did. In effect, the old common-law presumption of bad tendency was revived.[16]

The Federalists, like the English judges and crown attorneys from whom they derived their arguments, believed that seditious words, even if they were mere opinions, could topple a government. In the balance between the language of their own statute and the common-law precedent, Federalists found the latter a weightier consideration. Disaffection and rebellion always followed seditious words and the offense still rested upon the tendency of the document, though the allied considerations of its truth and its author's intent were made defenses under the congressional act of 1798. In *Tuchin's Case* (1704) Lord Chief Justice Holt regarded it settled that "if people should not be called to account for possessing the people with an ill opinion of the

government, no government can subsist."[17] In England and its colonies, the
king's courts, Parliament, and colonial assemblies all punished seditious
libels. Holt's view, the common-law position on seditious libel, was used to
oust John Wilkes from his seat in the Commons after he was discovered to be
the author of the *North Briton No. 45.* The House of Commons resolved that
the magazine contained insults toward the king "most manifestly tending to
alienate the affections of the people from his Majesty."[18] In *Woodfall's Case*
(1770) a newspaper editor was tried and convicted by the House of Commons
for a seditious libel after a common-law court jury found him guilty of the
"printing and publishing" only, not of a "libel." Woodfall had reprinted,
with supportive comments, letters on the Zenger trial—some thirty-five years
over and done. Parliament stepped in when a jury at the common-law court
failed to follow the law instructions of the judge, that the tendency of the
publication made its dissemination a seditious libel.[19]

Bad tendency greatly eased the burden of the prosecution. In English
seditious libel law, as in constructive treasons, malicious intent was not a
separate fact to be proved by the prosecution. The consequences of the act
itself made it unlawful. Since criticism of the government tended to undermine public confidence in the government no matter what the intentions of
the author were, the seditious libel was proved whenever the authorship was
proved. Of course, in constructive treasons and seditious libels, the prosecution stipulated the consequences and assumed that they would harm the
government, for that was the basis of the charge. In reply to this, the defendant had to prove—it was his burden to prove, according to Mansfield in
Woodfall—that no harm would ensue.[20]

Every Federalist prosecution of a Republican editor for seditious libel—a
multitude of cases reaching into the heart of the opposition party by 1800—
bore aloft in triumph the doctrine of bad tendency. In *Duane's Case* this
doctrine was explicitly proclaimed by the Federalists. At first, the scene was
not the federal courts (in which bad tendency ruled by implication only), but
the Federalist-dominated United States Senate, which could, following Parliament in *Wilkes* and *Woodfall*, base its objection to Duane's libel upon
dangerous tendency. On February 19, 1800, Duane published a bill that had
been proposed to the Senate by Pennsylvanian James Ross, revising the
electoral college. Not only did Duane print the bill without permission of its
author or the Senate, but he editorialized that the measure would "destroy
popular authority and engross every power" which the people rightly possessed.[21] Uriah Tracy of Connecticut, Ross, and other Federalists were familiar with the diatribes of Duane and decided to silence him. Tracy proposed
that the Senate proceed against the editor for a contempt of its privileges. The
language of the resolution was the mirror of their thinking: Duane's editorial

had a "bad tendency."[22] The Federalist majority in the Senate could not determine if they had been libeled, for the defendant, after a heated confrontation, could not be found to testify to the truth or maliciousness of his charges. When Duane refused to cooperate with the upper house, the Senate supported Rawle's attempt to obtain a grand jury indictment against Duane for seditious libel.[23] Duane eventually would be indicted and arraigned on the charges, but, again, the Senate's reference to bad tendency could not be missed by Pennsylvania's Republican state legislators, since the Senate still sat in Philadelphia.

Even after the Republicans gained control of the federal legislature and the presidency in 1800, Federalist judges clung to bad tendency tests. Judges like Samuel Chase pressed home the old English doctrine of bad consequences. At Thomas Cooper's trial for seditious libel in April 1801, Chase instructed the jury: "If you destroy the confidence of the people in their supreme magistrate and the legislature, you effectually sap and undermine the government." Apart from the immediate effect upon the radicals' search for a doctrine to use against Addison, Chase's words were pregnant for his own career. They would form the basis of another one of the articles of impeachment against him passed in 1804.[24]

There is one more piece to fit in the puzzle: the connection between bad tendency in seditious libel law and impeachment was pointedly made in Sacheverell's case. In 1709 the Whig junto had the choice of prosecuting this high Tory clergyman in the regular courts for a seditious libel—his sermons having the tendency of disaffecting the people from the settlement of 1689— or bringing an impeachment against him for the same offense. They elected the latter, fearing, perhaps, that a jury of the reverend doctor's peers might not be convinced that his pamphlets had the terrible consequences ascribed to them. The Lords would not scruple at these charges, particularly because the liberal bishops among them had worked out the tolerationist settlement which Sacheverell condemned. The case, as we have already noted, was widely publicized and ended with rioting in the streets in London. Though not cited by Republican impeachers, it did link bad tendency in seditious libel law with impeachment and might have been suggested to the radical Republicans by the prosecution of Duane in 1800.

The trial of Alexander Addison under the doctrine of dangerous tendency offered to Republicans a chance to legally revenge themselves upon the very Federalist judges who had harassed them the most in the past two years, and yet remained immune to electoral pressure. Even with the new doctrine Republicans were constrained by the existence of the tradition of impeachment for cause. They could not pursue any judge but had to seize upon palpable mistakes or expressions of prejudice and expand them, using dangerous tendency, into impeachable offenses. In the process, they wiped away the English-tainted origins of dangerous tendency, Americanizing it as they had impeachment itself.

Dangerous tendency was an opportunistic adaptation of common law. The second Republican doctrine of impeachable offenses combined partisanship and political theory. Although Jefferson himself might be hesitant to bring impeachments on purely political grounds, certain of his lieutenants itched to remove the opposition. As early as March 1801 Monroe reminded Jefferson: "The [Federalist] party had retired into the judiciary, in a strong body where it lives on the treasury, and therefore cannot be starved out. While in possession of that ground it can check the popular current which runs against them." Monroe and others urged Jefferson to purge all traces of Federalism. Jeffersonians gave the highest priority to repeal of the Judiciary Act of 1801. Giles in the House and Breckinridge in the Senate called it an inexcusable politicization of the judicial branch, observing that all the "midnight judges" the act commissioned were Federalists. Republican majorities in both houses swept away the law in March 1802.[25]

Though Jefferson still wavered and moderates in his circle, especially Speaker of the House Nathaniel Macon and Madison, urged caution, others of his party were avid for further cleansing of the judiciary. Giles had already urged Jefferson to begin "a pretty general purgation of office . . . although an indiscriminate privation of office, merely for a difference in political sentiments might not be expected; yet is expected that obnoxious men will be ousted." Giles was not constrained by eighteenth-century notions of tenure in office (the judges regarded it as a species of personal property), and he was unhappy with Jefferson's progress in the first year of the new administration. He was an early supporter of repeal of the Judiciary Act of 1801 and led the fight in Congress against the vested right of the new judges to their offices. Judges were the delegates of the people no less than legislators and ought to be removable at the desire of the people. Illness prevented Giles from going to Congress from 1801 to 1804, but his ideas circulated and he reentered the Senate in time for the session of 1804.[26]

John Randolph's role in promoting the Republican campaign against Federalist judges is better known than Giles's. The Southside Virginia politician and party theoretician was elected to Congress in 1799. Arriving at the high tide of Federalism, he nevertheless treated the House to a taste of his ardent dislike of England, strong national government, and Federalist economic policy. After the Republican victories of 1800 he was rewarded with chairmanship of the House Ways and Means Committee. His strident, if not always popular, voice was thereafter heard in the party's inner councils. With Giles, he led the effort to repeal the Judiciary Act of 1801. His fear of central government and loose construction of the Constitution would soon estrange him from Jefferson, particularly over the Louisiana and Yazoo questions, but until 1805 he was a force to be reckoned with in Congress. To Plumer and others, Randolph seemed the originator of the thesis that impeachment was merely a question of popular feeling. His conversations with Giles on the question, held in front of Federalists in the Senate antechamber and in streets of the capital (Randolph never rowed with muffled oars; he paddle-wheeled his way to his objectives), were frightening to Plumer and John Quincy Adams. Among the party rank-and-file, Randolph popularized the idea that the lower house could define impeachable offenses as it wished. Under such an arrangement, immense power was conferred upon the House—a development pleasing to Randolph, whose gifts lay in persuading the representatives to follow him. With this in mind, he argued that the judges' tenure during "good behavior" protected them from the executive only; it did not limit Congress's power to remove judges.[27]

Giles and Randolph concluded that the will of the people defined "high crimes and misdemeanors," for, as the Addison case proved, impeachment and trial were not criminal but political processes. They would leave the upper house to debate fine points of law at the trial. While much can be said about the political ambitions of these men, there is some ground in republican theory for their view of impeachment. America in 1803 was not a democracy; furthermore the majority of the Republican party did not foresee the changes that would, in the next three decades, begin to make America into a democracy. Part of the structure was already there: public dissent and electoral opposition to those in office were legitimate. Missing still was a broad franchise and grassroots control of party operation. With the absence of these vital links between public opinion and government operation, many a misuser of power could remain in office. Using impeachment to remove such officials, without alleging or proving criminal misdeeds, was one way in which the rights of the commonest people might be protected—before these people could join in the political process.

Three cases conjoined and tested the dangerous tendency and popular will doctrines after the Addison verdict. In the first, federal district judge John Pickering was impeached and tried for incompetence and partisanship. In the second, three of the four judges of the Supreme Court of Pennsylvania— Edward Shippen Jr., Thomas Smith, and Jasper Yeates (Hugh Brackenridge was not impeached)—were brought to trial for fining and imprisoning a litigant, Thomas Passmore, for contempt of court. These two cases, tried between January 1804 and January 1805, served as dress rehearsals for the most ambitious and legally significant of the Republicans' impeachments, that of Supreme Court Justice Samuel Chase. Chase was charged with misusing his powers to aid his party and was lambasted as a veritable American Jeffries. With his trial, both dangerous tendency and removal for popular will received thorough tests and were found wanting.

The attempted exploitation of dangerous tendency and popular will doctrines of impeachment represented the flood tide of "Republican impeachment." Both new doctrines had grown out of and depended upon the Republicans' oft-repeated allegiance to truly representative government. As we will see, the two doctrines were not just glosses upon a crude hankering for office, or shields in patronage fights. There was a higher tone to much of what the Republicans argued in defense of these briefs, for they truly feared the tyranny and antipathy of Federalist judges, safe from the electorate, and there was no other form of removal save impeachment and trial. The period 1803–05 contained the four trials which tested the extension of these Republican views of impeachment law.

Failure to remove Chase demonstrated not only the limits of "Republican" impeachment law but also the impracticality of impeachment without stronger evidence of willful misconduct. After Chase was excused from the bar of the Senate to resume, with shaken health, his place upon the high court bench, the Republicans could still have brought other impeachments in the House of Representatives. Supreme Court Justices William Paterson and James Iredell had made partisan statements from the bench in trials of Republicans for seditious libel. Chief Justice Marshall was also vulnerable. Other Federalists had compromised their official impartiality with criticism of Jefferson and congressional policy. Why did the Republicans stop with Chase? Nothing in the law could bar them from trying to impeach and convict other Federalist judges, should Republican prosecutors choose to distinguish *Chase* from other cases. This puzzle we unravel in our epilogue.

10

A REPUBLICAN SCRIPT FOR IMPEACHMENT:
ADDISON, 1801–1803

IN 1801 THE PENNSYLVANIA ASSEMBLY PROVIDED REPUBLICANISM WITH A DOC-
trine that could be used to scourge the Federalist judicial phalanx. Pennsylvania had already played a major role in the fashioning of American impeachment law, and the state's lower house was as familiar with impeachment as any in the country. Before 1800, Hopkinson, McKean, and
Nicholson had all come before it upon charges of misconduct. The swirl of
partisanship and party conflict within the state had at last resolved itself into
Republican domination of the lower house, permitting the latter to bring
impeachments. Members of the majority were witness to the party conflict in
Congress, still sitting in Philadelphia. Republican editors in the city had
already faced the wrath of federal courts. At the same time, there raged a
vigorous controversy over judicial reform within the state—throwing an
additional spotlight upon the conduct of Federalists in judicial office. Finally, the Pennsylvania bar was studded with brilliant and able advocates,
men who could and would lift the debates over impeachment to a higher level
of generality than would a less able bar.

The state's intense political contests were the strongest incentives to a
Republican impeachment campaign. Pennsylvania was never a Federalist
stronghold, but its Federalists were able, educated, and prominent.[1] Judge
Richard Peters, Jared Ingersoll, Jr., William Lewis, and William Rawle, all
prominent lawyers, led in the East, their power concentrated in the mercantile and professional elite in the city and in the counties surrounding Philadelphia. The proximity of the Federalist-dominated national government
aided their cause. United States Senator James Ross, long popular among the
common people, stood for the governorship under the banner of the state
Federalist party in 1799, confident of victory, as a younger generation of
Federalists set out to do battle with the "Jacobins."[2] For its part, the Republican party ran the gamut from radicals like editor William Duane and
Congressman Michael Lieb, both of the city, and William Maclay, in the

United States Senate, to conservative Republicans like Chief Justice and later Governor Thomas McKean and Dallas, his secretary of state.

Opposition to the Hamiltonians had held the wings of the state's Republican party together and had enabled it to make increasing inroads upon the Federalist minority. In the West, the Republican party was building strength in farming communities from Harrisburg to Pittsburgh and beyond. Sparked by periodic uprisings against Federalist national policy and spurred by able organizers like Swiss-born Albert Gallatin and Judge Hugh Henry Brackenridge of Pittsburgh, and state assemblymen (later congressional representatives) William Findley and John Smilie—all radicals—the Republicans gained ascendency over the Federalists by the end of the 1790s.[3]

At first, the Republican party asserted its control of state offices without recourse to impeachment. McKean was no sooner elected governor in 1799 than he began wholesale removal of Federalists from posts within his patronage. Republican party workers were rewarded for their efforts with the vacancies. The lower house, controlled by Republicans, moved to break up Federalist domination of vast Allegheny County by parceling its outskirts into new counties—diluting Federalist strength in Pittsburgh and shifting assembly seats from Federalist control. The new counties' officials were then appointed by the Republicans. As Republicans organized to solidify these gains in the 1802 electoral campaign, one stumbling block remained. Federalist judges could not be removed by patronage or the electoral process. They held office during good behavior. What was more, despite the decline of their party's fortunes at the polls, they refused to be silent on political issues. The judges continued to lash McKean and Jefferson while working actively for Federalist electoral victories.[4]

The Republican majority in the state house might have overlooked the Federalist judges but for a division in Republican ranks. Their party was an amalgam of radicals and moderates. A rift between the factions grew wider when the radicals insisted on pressing a reform platform dear to their own and their constituents' interests: democratization of the judicial process. This divisive issue, troubling four successive sessions of the legislature, continually forced both wings of the party to face the apparent invulnerability of the Federalist judiciary. The radicals, led by Nathanial Boileau, wanted a complete recasting of the laws, removing all Latin and technical terms. They proposed arbitration of small claims and expansion of the jurisdiction of justices of the peace, both programs involving extension of the role of lay persons in the legal process. They championed a bill which would permit justices of the peace, a corps of nonlawyers, to hear and determine all causes under $100. The moderates, led by lawyers McKean and Dallas, wanted far less drastic changes. They were trained professionals and feared the invasion of their domain by amateurs. The underlying issue was who was competent to revise the laws, as much as what the laws should be.[5]

Federalist judges in the state recognized the debate over reform as a threat to their independence. Judge Alexander Addison led the attack on reform in his charges to grand juries. The incursion of legislative fiat into the courtroom would undermine the republic, he warned. The question was not one of amateurs replacing professionals, but a wholly different and a more dangerous threat of courts being reduced to rubber stamps of legislative majorities. Addison had political reason to fear the reforms, but his larger arguments were echoed by the Federalist party and press. In Philadelphia and Washington, D.C., Federalists agreed that the Republicans, under color of judicial reform, plotted to dismantle the courts and drive off Federalist judges.[6]

Even if, as Federalists feared, the real aim of radical judicial reform was the removal of Federalist judges, the reformers had legitimate suspicions of incumbent judicial officers. Many were vocal advocates of Federalist policies, including those pieces of legislation which brought Republicans to trial in their own courts. The partisanship of the Federalist bench underlined the power which seated judges had in America, and added to radicals' fears of an unfettered judiciary in a republican system. The immense powers and independence of superior court judges in the United States was something of an anomaly. The control which a judge had over conduct in his courtroom, his power to declare the meaning of the law—and the force that these rulings had as precedent in later cases—was drawn from the common law and common-law courts, despite the repudiation of English authority over the colonies a scant quarter-century before. How were such men, with such powers, to be monitored and curbed? Though there was some precedent for higher court judges controlling the behavior of lower court magistrates, there was no system for supervision in many states or in the federal government. The superior court judges served during good behavior, and there were no precise definitions of bad behavior in the new states' statutes. In 1773 John Adams and General William Brattle spent the winter futilely disputing whether English judges were removable at pleasure or only for breach of official duties.[7] This controversy continues among modern scholars.[8] The surest guide to early national understandings remains the state precedent, in which impeachable misdemeanors included abuse of power, neglect, and indifference to duty. Although Berger argues that misbehavior warranting removal was not to be confused with "high crimes and misdemeanors" justifying impeachment, the voluminous state precedent in which minor officials of the courts and petty court judges were impeached, tried, and removed for very small offenses—though never inadvertent error—contradicts his impression.[9] Whatever other forms of removal may have existed, impeachment for petty offenses could reach down to the lowest rung of the judicial ladder and up to the highest.

Despite Federalist warnings of disaster and cries of foul play, the radicals in Pennsylvania could point to similar efforts to rein judicial power in the other states and in the federal government. In Massachusetts, Judge Francis Dana of the Supreme Judicial Court, accused of blatant partisanship, was forced to defend himself in the newspapers. His radical attackers replied, "There is a question, whether you, sir, have a right to go around the state, and thus impeach the legislative and executive branches of the government."[10] Thomas Bradbury, Dana's senile colleague, was driven from the high court bench by reformers; even Federalists agreed to petition the governor to retire the old judge.[11] The Federalists were worried. From New York, Hamilton ("Lucius Crassus" this time) satirically warned:

> Much trouble would have been avoided by saying: "The Legislature will have a complete controul over the Judges, by the discretionary power of reducing the number of those of the Supreme Court, and of abolishing the existing Judges of the Inferior Courts, by the abolition of the Courts themselves." But this pretension is a novelty reserved for the crooked ingenuity of after discoveries.[12]

Hamilton's *Examination* of Jefferson's first annual message had dismissed the president's call for judicial reform as a partisan ploy, designed to harass or oust Federalist judges. But before Hamilton finished his review of the Republicans' first year in the presidency, Congress repealed the Judiciary Act of 1801. With the debris of his party's last-ditch effort to secure the judiciary flying about his head, Hamilton penned additional numbers of the *Examination*. Driven by his fears of a wholesale purge, he claimed for himself the mantle of authority of a Framer of the Constitution, and under its protection lectured his readers on the dangers of "INNOVATION" by a power-hungry legislature. In *Federalist No. 78* (which he wrote) the judiciary had been portrayed as the defender of liberty. He reiterated the theme in 1802: the courts must protect the people against the overweening ambition of legislative majorities and demagogues in the executive branch. The only safe republic was one with checks and balances, and these could be preserved only by an independent judiciary. The abolition of the circuit courts created by the Federalist Judiciary Act of 1801 was a storm warning: soon no judge would be safe from his political enemies; nor would any provision of the Constitution be safe from its democratic besiegers.[13]

In a number of states, reform of the judiciary included joint legislative petitions to the governor to remove incompetent seated judges. The Pennsylvania Constitution contained such a procedure, but the radicals' attention in the Keystone State was drawn to impeachment rather than petition in large part because Pennsylvania experience with impeachment had been satisfying to the lower house, while appeals to the governor had no noteworthy success. Perhaps more important was a basic rivalry among the branches. In its previous six impeachment movements, the lower house had regarded itself as the foremost organ of government. The debate leading to the creation of a unicameral legislature in 1776 had underlined this presumption, and despite the limitations placed upon the assembly by the revised constitution of 1790, nothing in the debate at that convention contravened the primacy of the lower house. As Brackenridge, a Republican supreme court justice, wrote with some asperity in 1804: "There are two sprigs to the legislative branch. Which is strongest? That of the *house of representatives.* . . . the great sprig of the house of representatives is 'the rod of Aaron that will swallow up the other rods.'"[14] The exercise of legislative power to remove judges with impeachment and trial flowed from this conception of representative government: the commons house was the protector of the rights of all the people. The assembly's conception of its own importance, and the role of impeachment as a conduit for the voice of the common people, reinforced each other in a rationale for removal of misbehaving Federalist judges.

Finally, and equally significant, Pennsylvania developed the new doctrine because it possessed the finest bar in the land. James Wilson's law lectures, delivered in Philadelphia, inaugurated a tradition of legal excellence. Dallas, Rawle, Lewis, Ingersoll, and their comrades played important roles in the management of public affairs, the improvement of legal education, and the maintenance of high standards at the bar. They represented defendants and counseled the prosecution in impeachment cases, and the cases were, in turn, showplaces for their acumen. This mutually beneficial arrangement gave far greater intellectual depth to impeachment trials, placing the law of impeachment in the center of the stage.[15]

The most obvious target, and therefore the test case, for the Republicans was Alexander Addison, president of the fifth district court of Pennsylvania. He was the very model of a high-handed Federalist partisan, at least according to his many Republican detractors. Addison was a tall, burly Scot who migrated to Washington County in 1785, studied law, and was admitted to the bar. He assumed judicial office in 1791 and immediately began a career of harassing anti-Federalist politicians.[16] An ardent supporter of the Alien and Sedition Acts, he lectured grand juries upon the evils of licentious speech (though cases under the acts were heard in the federal district courts) and warned against sinister conspiracies among the French, the Irish, and the "society of illuminati." In his grand jury charges he incorporated common-law dicta on seditious libel, a move certain to raise the hackles of radicals in the assembly. He then condemned the Virginia resolutions against the Alien and Sedition Acts as "a declaration of war against the government of the United States." Not content with harpooning Jeffersonian Republicanism in Virginia, he stabbed at the Pennsylvania lower house's concern with judicial reform: "Judicial power is vested not in the state legislatures, but in *courts.*"[17] His views were published and disseminated among Federalists all over the country—George Washington, John Marshall, Supreme Court Justice Oliver Ellsworth, and Secretary of State Timothy Pickering all took note of the judge's opinions.[18]

Addison's alleged victim was not a litigant, but a fellow judge. John B. C. Lucas, a naturalized French immigrant, was added to Addison's tribunal in 1799, the first Jeffersonian on the panel. A western Pennsylvania partisan, Lucas was not a trained lawyer and he heard Addison's 1799 and 1800 grand jury charges with horror. When the newly appointed Lucas rose to make his own remarks to the grand jury at the 1800 December sessions of the common pleas, Addison silenced him. Republican papers in the West called for Addison's removal, while Lucas consulted his mentor and co-worker, newly appointed state Supreme Court Justice Hugh Brackenridge. Brackenridge knew all about Addison's politics, for the Republican lawyer and author had practiced in Addison's court for more than a decade, but since his brush with disaster in the Whiskey Rebellion, Brackenridge had become cautious.[19] Instead of intervening directly in the quarrel, he stood off to one side and advised Lucas. The justice urged the county judge to swear out an affidavit to the state attorney general, Joseph McKean, bringing the case before the supreme court. At its March 1801 session, the high court agreed that Addison's conduct was censurable but concluded that it could find no remedy for Lucas.[20] When the supreme court would not act, Brackenridge unleashed the newspaper he controlled. The Pittsburgh *Tree of Liberty* found grounds in the court's opinion to sustain an impeachment against Addison. Brackenridge, who had disqualified himself when Addison's case was called before the supreme court, privately advised Lucas to press for his rights at the next session of the common pleas. The supreme court had informed Lucas that associate judges had every right possessed by the presiding judge. Specifically, Brackenridge instructed Lucas to come to the June session of Addison's court with a grand jury address of his own and to insist upon reading it. Lucas was to carry the banner of the "friends of liberty" in a formal reply to Addison's charge.[21] On June 21, 1801, in a courtroom packed with partisans jostling for seats, Addison again squelched Lucas. Lucas now turned to the legislature, both of whose houses the Republicans controlled.

On January 11, 1802, Representative John McMaster, newly chosen to represent Allegheny County in the Pennsylvania Assembly, presented a petition from 384 of his constituents. Those inhabitants of "the western country" excoriated Addison as "oppressive, tyrannical, and partial" in conduct. They then instructed the lower house in its constitutional duties: "the right of impeachment or demanding the removal of judicial officers."[22] The petitioners regarded impeachment and trial merely as a form of removal. A second petition from Allegheny, Beaver, and Butler counties gave specific charges of irregularity: on December 22, 1800, and June 22, 1801, Addison had interrupted and silenced Associate Judge Lucas, "newly appointed to the court." This was a violation of the right of the people to the services of all the judges, an engrossment of power by the chief justice and a dangerously unconstitutional precedent, even if no substantive harm was done to litigants and no violation of state law was committed.[23] On February 19 the additional petitioners warned the assembly that "the constitutional independence of the associate judges of the courts of common pleas within the said circuit will be annihilated," that is to say, that Addison's misconduct was an act conducive to destruction of the constitution.[24]

On February 23 the assembly adopted a report to frame articles of impeachment against Addison—two of which were passed and engrossed on March 19. Appointed to manage were Nathanial Boileau, Jeff Moore, F. Smith, David Mitchell, and R. Porter. On the same day Addison wrote to Speaker Isaac Weaver that "every man who accepts an office does it at the risk of being ruined, when any malicious man chooses to make oath against him." He admitted no "misdemeanor" and demanded to know the names of all the petitioners against him, as well as the particulars of the articles.[25] The house refused to do any of this but did agree to ask the senate to postpone the trial until December 1802 to give Addison time to prepare a defense.

Two weeks before the senate was to meet as a trial court, the house debated the difference between the grounds for impeachment and an alternative constitutional method of removal—two-thirds of both houses petitioning the governor for the dismissal of Addison. Offenses meriting impeachment were "misdemeanor in office," while the latter required "any reasonable cause."[26] The distinction was not easy to make—it certainly was not spelled out in the constitution. The committee had raised a complicated point, and the lower house had to stop and ponder the question. The Pennsylvania Constitution of 1790 enabled the governor to remove a judge upon a petition of two-thirds of both houses of the state legislature. Because this power extended to offices held for good behavior, an address to the governor presumably had to allege improprieties in office. Addresses of this sort did not necessitate a hearing, much less a trial, however. The implication was clear that removal by address ought not to extend to serious offenses.

Pennsylvania's legislators were unsure of the distinction between offenses demanding impeachment and trial and those warranting only a joint address to the governor, a confusion shared by other states' legislators. While the lower house made no reference to other states' precedents, the timing of its debate on this point is suggestive. In 1803 both houses of the General Court had asked Massachusetts Governor Caleb Strong to remove Supreme Court Justice Bradbury. Before that, the New Hampshire legislature repeatedly had asked the governor to remove judges. There were common understandings among the states regarding ranges of definitions of offenses. The Pennsylvania lower house decided to impeach Addison rather than address the governor, a decision in accord with other state assemblies' actions. Addison's malfeasance went beyond that of Justices Muter and Sebastian in Tennessee. They may have acted in error once. He acted repeatedly, and willfully, even after the state supreme court had censured him. Addison had gone beyond the misconduct alleged against Pickering and Bradbury in New England in one clear respect. Whereas the other judges had simply demonstrated their incapacity to perform their duties, he had struck at the very foundation of republican government. Addison had strong-armed a colleague on the bench. This act may have been innocent, as he claimed, or, as he asserted later, misunderstood, but however motivated, it was different in its implications from simple incompetence. He had tried to muzzle another official in the regular performance of that official's duties. Left unchecked, this could lead to dire consequences. Seen from another, related perspective, Addison's offense was an excess of partisan zeal. Partisanship was not censurable—even use of the grand jury charge and the public press to push one's beliefs was not impeachable—but using one's official power to advance one's partisan views was sufficient grounds to bring down the wrath of the legislature.[27]

The old bugbear remained, however: how could Addison's acts be shoehorned into the confines of "high crimes and misdemeanors"? The difficulty materialized the first day of his trial. Republican moderates in the lower house had balked at impeachment because of this dilemma, but the senate concurred with the recommendation of the full house, and Addison was put on trial on January 17, 1803. The two articles were read. The first, that on March 28, 1801, he interrupted Lucas's address to a trial jury in a pending case, sneering that Lucas's words had nothing to do with the case and ought to be disregarded. In effect, this alleged an obstruction of justice. Second, on June 22, 1801, Addison prevented Lucas from speaking to the grand jury of the court of common pleas. These things Addison did "unjustly, illegally, and unconstitutionally." There was no attribution of criminal intent, for Addison "acted under pretense" of "discharging and performing his said official duties."[28] If the acts were regarded as misconduct, the lower house would have grounds for impeachment under the state constitutions—the Pennsylvania Constitution of 1776 did not define impeachable offenses—but the 1790 document adopted the federal formula, "high crimes and misdemeanors." An alternative reading of the law, to permit the lower house to decide, de novo, which acts were "misdemeanors" was not yet broached by anyone in the house.

To overcome these inconsistencies the managers pleaded that Addison acted in a way that undermined the constitution—that is to say, the consequences of his acts were the real misdemeanor. Acts like his, left without correction, would deny equal justice to litigants, cost the courts the confidence of the people, and bring government to a halt. Attorney General Joseph McKean opened for the prosecution with this very premise: "An attempt to subvert the fundamental laws of a court of justice is a fit subject of impeachment."[29] When Addison brought Lucas's authority into dispute at the June 22, 1801, session, he shook the foundations of public trust in government. Robert Whitehill, a revolutionary wheel horse and Republican leader, pushed forward with this premise: "The subject of our enquiry is not whether the charge of one judge was relevant and that of the other irrelevant, but whether one judge did not assume over the other an authority not allowed by the constitution or laws."[30] Addison's acts tended to the disruption of republican institutions and thus constituted impeachable offenses. This doctrine did not supplant the common understanding of "high crimes and misdemeanors" (including blatant incapacity, neglect, or indifference to duty). "Dangerous tendency" merely added another category of impeachable offense, one that dispensed with the willful malice that the prosecution had to establish in most crimes, while substituting another, far plainer issue. Neither specific intent nor violation of law need be present, for the consequence of the judges' acts, rather than their purposefulness or their relationship to positive law, was the measure of their dangerous tendency. The crucial test was: would they, left unchecked, undermine the people's confidence in their rulers? Would they erode the rights and liberties of the people? Would they foster tyranny? At the trial, the prosecution merely had to uncover a pattern of conduct which, in the eyes of the court (for Addison, the politically hostile senate), appeared to undermine the foundations of the state constitution or the republic it protected. The tests for this included disaffecting the people from their government and other partisan acts.

The Federalists, who had adopted bad tendency from English treason and seditious libel laws, were now about to receive a large dose of their own medicine. Addison himself subscribed to the doctrine that there was a federal common law of crimes, derived from the English common law, which incorporated bad tendency. This he drew from Blackstone and applied to seditious libels and treasons charged against Republicans. Federalists did not anticipate that the doctrine they wielded to bloody their opponents would be turned upon them with such telling effect.[31]

At the same time, there was something ingenuous at best, and cynical at worst, in the way the Republicans seized the dangerous tendency doctrine to hoist Addison. To be sure, it was his own—but it derived from the common law of libels and treason, the same "bloody" maxims that so enraged Madison and Jefferson. Republicans in Virginia, Pennsylvania, and elsewhere were campaigning for excision of these portions of common law from state codes even as the Pennsylvania lower house found in common law the instrument to extend impeachment to obnoxious Federalists. Politics has always made strange bedfellows in the United States, and never more so than in the hands of radical judicial reformers, like Boileau, adopting the common law of bad tendency to pry Addison from office.[32]

Opening for his own defense, Addison stressed the innocence of his acts. They violated no law. They were not meant to abridge Lucas's rights. Not yet recognizing the thrust of the prosecution, he insisted that impeachment only lay for crimes: violations of known law or acts malicious in themselves. He had not spoken abusively about Lucas to the jury but merely gave his opinion on the law, which, it happened, was contrary to Lucas's view. Addison admitted stopping Lucas twice in June and, in the interim, trying to dissuade him from charging the grand jury, but only because it was customary for the chief justice alone to address the grand jury in that court. Addison stressed that no construction of his acts could make them "high crimes or misdemeanors."[33]

At first, Addison did not recognize the novelty of the prosecution case. Dangerous tendency was mentioned in *Nicholson* but not explored. Addison himself had used it to explain the Federalists' seditious libel law but did not immediately grasp its application to his own behavior. Midway in his opening remarks, he realized his predicament. If he relied upon a reply to traditional charges, he left his flank open to dangerous tendency. There were two ways to combat the new doctrine, and Addison, proving that he was an able and intelligent jurist, tried both in turn. First he denied that his actions had caused whatever evil consequences the confrontation with Lucas might entail. To give substance to this argument, Addison had to claim a station high above politics while casting Lucas as the mincing partisan, the mouthpiece of Justice Brackenridge. Addison also turned his guns upon the absent justice—a figure hovering over the proceedings like Banquo's ghost at Macbeth's court. The speaker of the senate had to remind Addison that Brackenridge was not on trial.[34]

Unfortunately for the defense, this imposture was easily confuted. Called to the stand by the prosecution, Lucas testified that Addison was a partisan bully, with jurors and witnesses as well as colleagues on the bench. "I had heard Mr. Addison denounce from the bench a description of men, in a manner likely to render those who are within it, objects of persecution."[35] Thus Addison branded Jacobins, radicals, and other opponents of the Adams administration. Even after the state supreme court told both judges that Lucas had the right to address the grand jury, Addison used his power to compel Lucas's silence.[36] Other witnesses deposed that the chief judge had made political charges to the grand jurors.[37] Dallas made great capital of the judge's sally that he was not political, for Addison's reputation had preceded him into the senate chamber. No one doubted the politicization of the western county courts (Lucas's appointment was patently political) but

Dallas insisted that Addison had gone too far by using his office to muzzle another judge, in the course of the latter's duty.

Assaulting his adversary's weakened front against dangerous tendency, Dallas inadvertently left a gap in the prosecution line, through which the defendant bolted. To demonstrate the extent of Addison's partisanship, Dallas quoted Attorney General Joseph McKean's remarks at the trial: Addison's acts were more than "misbehavior in office." They were an indictable offense, the attorney general and the prosecution counsel agreed, because they were specifically designed to violate the constitution. That is to say, there was an intention to violate the laws, as well as actual violations. Tactically, this line of argument was a mistake, for the high court did not find that Addison had committed any indictable offense. Chief Justice Edward Shippen sided with Addison on this point: "It would seem to be a mistake of right. Unless a crime is stated in the information or complaint the Supreme Court cannot take cognizance."[38] Seeing the opening between Dallas's traditional approach and the dangerous tendency line, Addison counterattacked. He aimed his argument at the stronger of his foes—dangerous tendency—for he knew he had committed no crime. Using Shippen's opinion as a springboard, Addison contended that his acts had no dangerous tendency. Quite the contrary was true: they were common and healthy expressions of a vigorous judiciary. Judges who cared about their work always had disputes among themselves, and his argument with Lucas was nothing more than a failure to communicate. Addison acted from "his sense of duty." In this, he was supported by "the court" (by which the defendant again meant the other Federalist judge—Irish-born John McDowell of Washington County) sitting with Lucas and the chief.[39] There was no malice in Addison's acts; at best, there was a difference of opinion in which Addison, as the senior judge, insisted upon his customary prerogatives. McDowell, called to testify, corroborated Addison's position: the parts of charges which Lucas saw as political were not so. Warning a grand jury against potential civil dissidents and rioters was a judge's duty.[40] Addison again pleaded that his acts were not heinous or unusual. Even his charges to the grand juries (for which he was not under accusation but which Dallas brought up over and over to prove Addison's factious state of mind) were a feature of American courts from the revolutionary years. That much was true; William Henry Drayton, John Jay, and other patriots had inflamed revolutionary passions with charges to grand juries.[41]

Dallas, an experienced trial lawyer, immediately moved to repair the damage to his case, not by extending or reinforcing dangerous tendency, the object of Addison's attack, but by extending the traditional terminology of impeachable offenses: "Permit me now to procede to show," he asked, "that in depriving Mr. Lucas of the right, which he claimed, Mr. Addison has been guilty of a misdemeanor in office."[42] Lawyers are not bound by Aristotle's rules of logical exclusion. Dallas wanted to have his cake and eat it. First, he implied that Addison had committed the crimes of disorderly conduct and obstruction of justice, serious misdemeanors. He prevented another judge from doing his duty for reasons of "personal hostility." Criminal purpose was implied in his "words" if not in his "manner of speaking."[43] He had used art and cunning to get McDowell's approval to stall and embarrass Lucas. He must have known how contrary to the state constitution were his acts; at any rate Dallas decried them as a species of "public malice."[44]

The judge's biases notwithstanding, Dallas had to admit that Addison had not broken any positive law. Dallas therefore introduced a second, noncriminal definition of misdemeanor. Misdemeanor, he proposed, comprehended the entire "scale of delinquency and it embraces, equally, those cases of official misconduct which may also be prosecuted by indictment or information and those cases which are only cognizable in a course of impeachment."[45] For example, "arbitrary deportment and oppressive conduct" may not be indictable, but they were misconduct and therefore impeachable. To prove this, he called to his side the shades of Lord Chancellor Francis Bacon, impeached for taking bribes, and Chief Justice William Scroggs, impeached for bullying grand juries and harassing litigants.[46] Dallas did not show any particular interest in the details of the English cases; they merely gave depth and color to his argument. His audience did not need to be told that Nicholson and Hopkinson were impeached for misusing their authority.

Dallas did not return to the dangerous tendency argument. It had already done its work: demolishing Addison's first line of defense and forcing the judge to fight a two-front war. At the same time, Dallas seemed to have had a personal aversion to it. Unlike Boileau, Findley, Leib, and Smilie in the assembly, and later, Caesar Rodney, Joseph Nicholson, and others in Congress, and supporters of Jefferson all over the country, Dallas decided to do without the novelty of a new impeachment doctrine. One may surmise multiple sources for his distaste for dangerous tendency in *Addison*. Perhaps he feared to add unnecessary complexities to a case already won. He was McKean's right-hand man—the state secretary; he could count votes in the senate and knew that Addison was finished. Why add complications? Lawyers abhor novelty and Dallas was a lawyer's lawyer (he was already the collector of Pennsylvania court precedents and soon would perform the task for the United States Supreme Court). We may surmise that his conservative legal training dampened his ardor for a line of argument that had never been openly advocated in an American impeachment trial. Perhaps, he did not agree with the other members of the prosecution team. They were the house's managers; he was hired counsel. They advocated the paramount importance of the lower house; he ordinarily spoke for the executive branch. Apparently he sensed that they had gone too far with this new impeachment doctrine of dangerous tendency—a doctrine that could (and soon would) threaten his own patron, Governor McKean. Dallas would enroll himself later that year as the counsel for Shippen and the other Pennsylvania justices, defending them against charges brought under the dangerous tendency doctrine. Although his later choice of clients does not prove a prior aversion to the doctrine, at Shippen's trial he demonstrated his ability to punch holes in a prosecution based solely on dangerous tendency.[47]

In his own closing remarks, Addison wandered over the prosecution case, protesting his good will and blustering at the thought that he would undermine the laws. He returned to his first defense that he had committed no crime—knowing that it was the soundest in law and unwilling to admit, or concede, that dangerous tendency made it irrelevant. He persisted: "There is no difference in a trial by indictment and impeachment: they are both modes of trying criminal offenses."[48] His acts and motivation, whatever construction the senate put upon them, were not crimes. He knew that the old law was still on his side, but he must have realized that the senate was packed with votes against him. They would naturally find both the dangerous-tendency charges and Dallas's two-sided logic on "misdemeanor" convincing. As did Ann Hutchinson before the puritan magistrates at her trial, he lost control on this last day. With sarcastic thanks to the court for listening to his side, he challenged the managers' and witnesses' credibility. The senate was treated to a display of the same bullish self-regard that induced him to muzzle Lucas even after the supreme court had censured him for it. He protested that his long service on the court, without adequate compensation, was not given due weight, and reminded the senators that he had never been overruled by the supreme court. No bill of exceptions or writ of error was ever filed from his judgment. This, and not Dallas's fabrication, was the true pattern of his service. And even if his conduct toward Lucas was incorrect, it was not a violation of known law.[49] Released by the knowledge that his case was hopeless, he lectured the senate on the independence of the judiciary. If judges could be impeached for any offense, their objectivity would be destroyed. Removal for mere adherence to a party would make judges the pawns of party rather than freeing them from it.[50]

To prove himself above party, he tried to introduce affidavits from his former companions on the bench. To this Dallas objected that a summation was not a proper moment to introduce new evidence. Addison persisted—the impeachment court "are not bound down to the strict rules of evidence, which govern a common court of justice."[51] It was an able rejoinder (if inconsistent with Addison's earlier contention that no offense was impeachable unless it were also indictable in a regular court of law). The court of the senate ruled that the depositions could not be read. Addison then tried another variant of the independence of the judiciary argument. All judges made errors of judgment, technical mistakes, and poor rulings. These were not impeachable. The Pennsylvania Assembly, Addison noted, had chided Chief Justice McKean for misusing his powers in Oswald's libel suit, but the representatives did not demand an impeachment.[52] By recalling this precedent, Addison simultaneously attacked McKean and bolstered his own defense. Oswald's petition had induced western radicals to charge Chief Justice McKean with overusing his powers on the bench, and some of these were the very men who, in 1801, were McKean's uneasy allies in the Republican party and joined him to urge Addison's removal. The point was obvious: despite McKean's "bullying" of Oswald, the lower house did not impeach him. Why then was Addison impeached for doing (in his own mind) a less obnoxious act? Politics was the answer! The moderate Republicans—McKean, Dallas, and their friends—had joined the radicals to drive all Federalists from office. As Addison's arguments fell without effect, he grew increasingly bitter. His final words abused the petitioners to the lower house a year before: they were "the very dregs of the society . . . picked up on the highway, or in taverns, strangers, boys, and silly men."[53] What then for the assemblymen who presented these documents—those who would weigh this evidence against him? Less a desperate gamble than a despairing swipe, Addison's closing words augured his fate.

On the twenty-sixth of January, the senate voted 20 to 4 to convict.[54] Only Federalists dissented. The senate, in a series of amended bills, at last took his long service into account. Following Dallas's suggestion, they only disqualified him from holding judicial office.[55] This final penalty, although a compromise between a brief term of disqualification and disqualification from all future offices and positions, gave heart to the Republicans in the West. Federalist law enforcement and tax collection in that part of the state had already led to two civil insurrections, the Republican instigators of which Federalist judges had vigorously prosecuted. The disqualification of Addison was a concession to strong popular feeling as well as a warning to other judges on the bench.

The legal significance of *Addison* is far more complex. Despite Dallas's unwillingness to adopt the dangerous tendency argument, Addison's impeachment was widely seen as a vindication of that doctrine. Duane and other Republican publicists hailed the precedent.[56] Smilie and Findley carried it to the United States Congress.[57] Out of the tangled cloth of personality and politics that wrapped Addison's case emerged the thread of a new doctrine of impeachment law. Dangerous tendency fit the Republicans' needs perfectly, for it extended the older rules of impeachment to a class of essentially political offenses. Overzealous practices of political partisans—today called "dirty tricks"—may not be criminal but they are unethical and they do misuse power. Judges like Addison practiced politics in their offices; the new impeachment doctrine caught them when they went too far. But how far was this? Despite the notoriety of Addison's case, the bulk of impeachment precedent was far more restrictive in definition of impeachable offenses. It is not uncommon for competing, or at least varying, legal doctrines to coexist (one thinks of the rival tests for free speech and pornography today), but the coexistence is rarely a peaceful one. In 1803 the United States was still a new nation, and impeachments were important forms of prosecution. The door was opened a crack by dangerous tendency to a much larger exercise of legislative jurisprudence.

Even if lower houses would push their shoulders to the door to widen the opening, no one could say for certain what lay beyond the entrance way. If bullying a colleague was an impeachable offense, was bullying a defendant or plaintiff? Was harassing and belittling counsel? What degree of overt political partisanship must be displayed before the conduct could be regarded as willful misuse of power? Judges in America, following English and colonial models, had great power and discretion in their courtrooms. Could the new doctrine be used to punish this customary behavior, or did an element of partisan purpose, supported by overt acts against a political enemy done in the guise of one's duty, have to be established? The Republicans had drawn the sword of "dangerous tendency" from the forge; it remained to be seen whether the blade would cut thicker necks than Addison's. A federal judge, three of the four members of the supreme court bench of Pennsylvania, and a United States Supreme Court justice would shortly find themselves on the block.

11

DRESS REHEARSALS: *PICKERING* AND *SHIPPEN ET AL.*, 1803–1805

the Republicans. Riding a high tide of popular support, leading to a second term for Thomas Jefferson, they had achieved the goal of all opposition parties: victory at the polls in national and state elections. The demolition of the Federalist party seemed at hand. The widely reported result of the Addison trial was welcome news to the Republicans and Jefferson praised the result. For their part, the Federalists trembled. Plumer and John Quincy Adams found it waiting for them when they returned to Congress in 1803. To Federalists the doctrine broached in Addison's case seemed ominous. No longer were crimes required for impeachment and conviction, they brooded. Any act might be constructed into an impeachable offense by a partisan lower house, a cover for political opportunism of the most cynical type.[1]

For their part, leading Republicans still did not agree upon a campaign of wholesale impeachment. They were divided in their counsels—though all who discussed the matter recognized that impeachment presented an opportunity to root out entrenched Federalist judges. By 1803 Jefferson, hitherto indecisive on this point, was no longer averse to testing impeachment. He was well aware of Federalist strength in the judiciary, offices which might become a power base for a Federalist counterattack on the presidency and Congress in future elections. Using their judicial posts, some Federalists still harassed Republican supporters. Thus, in the year before the election of 1804, the largest number of Republicans did not share Giles's and Randolph's appetite for impeachment but viewed the cases piecemeal. They were intrigued by the dangerous tendency doctrine but adopted a wait-and-see posture. Dangerous tendency, although its origins lay in the seditious libel law so hated by Republicans, had become "Republican." There were acts dangerous to a republic when done by officeholders which were not dangerous when done by private citizens. These acts had to be curbed because they undermined people's trust in government or, left unpunished, they would undermine government itself. It was to be left to the people's elected representatives to uncover and frame impeachment articles based upon dangerous tendency.[2] The doctrine of judicial independence did not protect American judges from removal when they crossed this line, whether they meant to subvert the republic or not. The consequences (as in Addison's case) constituted the crime, not the intention to do wrong, or the act itself.

The dilemma lay now not in the doctrine, which stood ready, but in finding the right case to which to apply the doctrine. *Addison* was perfect, but it was a state case. The Republican leadership in Congress could only proceed upon a report of judicial misdeeds on the federal level.[3] There were candidates aplenty from the late 1790s, and many Federalists suspected that Jefferson had taken aim at John Marshall. Marshall himself was antsy but need not have worried. The two cases that did present themselves as rehearsals of dangerous tendency turned out unsuited to that doctrine. The first concerned an inebriated and half-mad federal judge, whose misconduct was longstanding but not criminal: John Pickering of the New Hampshire federal court district. The second case involved the supreme court bench of Pennsylvania. The charges were drafted in accordance with the new doctrine, but the offense itself was hardly consequential: fine and imprisonment for contempt against a civil suit litigant. In the end, the rehearsals for wider use of dangerous tendency disappointed their Republican backers.

John Pickering had studied for the ministry at Harvard but a change of heart led him to the law. In colonial Portsmouth, New Hampshire, he gravitated to the Revolutionary party but never consorted with its radical wing. Though elected to the Continental Congress, he refused to go—a youthful aversion to travel over water had become a phobia of crossing water on a boat. His career in New Hampshire was distinguished, however, by service as a state assemblyman and as attorney general. Strict, conservative, and intelligent, he led the ratification movement for the federal Constitution and became chief justice of the state in 1790.[4]

Pickering's mental imbalance became evident during his term as chief justice. Plumer, a good friend, remarked on Pickering's eccentric behavior: "his timidity, his dread of crossing rivers, his tendency to seek seclusion at periodic intervals" showed "a somewhat abnormal mentality."[5] Erratic behavior, featuring frequent and prolonged absences from court, led to serious complaints by the citizenry of New Hampshire and legislative censure in 1794.[6] A bill to remove Pickering was voted on by the lower house and sent to the senate, where it received a similar reception. Jointly the two houses transmitted the bill to the governor, who allowed it to languish. Meanwhile, for loyal service to the Federalist party, Justice Pickering was elevated to the federal bench. His conduct in New Hampshire was either ignored or unknown (a less likely prospect) by his friends in Philadelphia.

Pickering's "condition" deteriorated after 1794. By 1803 his bizarre behavior affected his judicial duties sufficiently to bring about another legislative inquiry—this time by the United States House of Representatives. Secretary of the Treasury Albert Gallatin had been collecting evidence that Pickering was not following correct procedures in enforcement of the customs laws. Gallatin passed the word to Jefferson, who mentioned the matter to Congress in his annual message.[7] The lower house, to whose "cognizance" Jefferson directed the "complaints" against Pickering, named Nicholson, Bayard, Randolph, Samuel Tenney from New Hampshire, and New York's Lucas Elmendorf to a committee of inquiry. Randolph and Nicholson dominated the committee and pushed for impeachment of the judge. Nicholson, in the president's confidence, knew that Jefferson had hinted that the judge had to go. Bayard, parent of the Federalists' universal impeachability doctrine in *Blount*, had retreated from that position. He dragged his feet, knowing that he was a lame-duck member of the lower house and hoping that delay would aid his party. Adjournment of the Seventh Congress temporarily stopped the inquiry, but when the new Congress met in October 1803, a motion for delay by the Federalists was swept aside and the judge was impeached by a vote of 45 to 8. All the nays were Federalists, including Tenney from the committee.[8] The House selected Nicholson, Randolph, and Peter Early, Republicans, and Bayard's replacement as Federalist leader, Roger Griswold of Connecticut, as well as Samuel Thatcher, a Republican from Massachusetts, to prepare articles. On the floor, Tenney balked at their passage; the judge had "arisen" from his madness, Tenney reported. Nicholson, ready with the documents supplied from the executive department and the committee's own researches, replied that Pickering was still a drunkard. On January 2 and 3, 1804, the articles were passed and managers were named: Nicholson, Early, and Randolph were reappointed. Griswold, for obvious reasons, declined to serve.[9]

The impeachment articles grew out of one confiscation case, *U.S. v. the Brig Eliza* (1802). The precise terminology of the charges was significant: madness (or incapacity caused by madness) was not the offense. Instead, it was Pickering's violation of a congressional statute, "contrary to his trust and duty," causing "manifest injury" to the country. What is more, the judge supposedly acted "wickedly, meaning and intending to injure the revenues of the United States, and thereby to impair public credit." What had he done? Pickering summarily dismissed a federal suit, brought under the Customs Duty Act of 1789, against a shipmaster, William Ladd. Despite the information of the harbor surveyor and over the protests of the federal attorney, "the said John Pickering, judge of the said district court of the said district of New Hampshire, the said act of Congress not regarding, but with intent to evade the same, did order the said ship called the Eliza, with her furniture, tackle, and apparel, and the said two cables, to be delivered to a certain Eliphalet Ladd." When John S. Sherburne, attorney for the United States, tried to prosecute the case and produced witnesses to prove the facts charged by the United States, "yet the said John Pickering, with intent to defeat the just claims of the United States did refuse to hear the testimony of the said witnesses so as aforesaid . . . and without hearing the said testimony . . . did order and decree the said ship Eliza, with her furniture, tackle, and apparel, to be restored to the said Eliphalet Ladd, the claimant." In reply to Sherburne's appeal from the decree of the district court to the next circuit court (as allowed under the statute), Pickering, "disregarding the authority of the law . . . did absolutely and positively refuse to allow the said appeal." The final article speaks for itself:

> ART. 4. That whereas for the due, faithful, and impartial administra-
> tion of justice, temperance and sobriety are essential qualities in the
> character of a judge; and the said John Pickering, being a man of loose
> morals and intemperate habits, on the 11th and 12th days of November,
> in the year 1802, being then judge of the district court, in and for the
> district of New Hampshire, did appear on the bench of the said court, for
> the administration of justice, in a state of total intoxication, produced by
> the free and intemperate use of intoxicating liquors; and did then and
> there frequently, in a most profane and indecent manner, invoke the
> name of the Supreme Being, to the evil example of all the good citizens of
> the United States; and was then and there guilty of other high misde-
> meanors, disgraceful to his own character as a judge, and degrading to
> the honor of the United States.[10]

While the division in the lower house was highly partisan and both sides were (by reflex, if not by explicit reference) thinking in terms of party, the case was not merely a political one. Pickering was incapacitated and there seemed no other way to remove him. Giles was at home sick, and Randolph's views on impeachment-as-removal were suspected but not heard so loudly as they would be after the *Pickering* verdict. Macon had come around to this posi-tion, already occupied by Nicholson, chairman of the managers, and others in the House. Bloc alignments in the pretrial and trial debates, followed by the vote in the Senate, would make the case political, and by so doing, misrepresent the legal issues involved. Only the failure of the Chase im-peachment effort would restore the *Pickering* precedent to its proper place.[11]

Senators followed the Pickering impeachment as it unfolded in the lower house. Two months before the managers presented themselves at the door of the Senate chamber, members of the upper house informally debated the procedure for bringing the judge to trial. Knowing his reputation, no one could be certain he would appear if summoned. Impeachment debates and votes had taken place in the state legislatures without the presence (or even representation) of the accused, but trials in upper houses had the trappings, if not all the guarantees, of a jury trial in a regular court. Defendants pleaded in person or by counsel to charges. A special committee was appointed, with Uriah Tracy at its head, to sift through precedent and report to the Senate. Tracy saw no way to dodge the problems that Pickering's mental condition posed. By early December the managers were waiting for the Senate to constitute itself as a court, pressing, as the lower house was wont to do in impeachments, to make law as well as to prosecute. Tracy, for the committee, urged the Senate to arrive at its own ruling on Pickering's fitness to stand trial.[12]

The tenor of these sessions did not resemble the cut and thrust of a trial, for even when the actual trial began, neither the defendant nor his counsel was present. There was no cross-examination of witnesses, no testimony from the judge himself, no one to speak for him—except members of the upper house itself, and their arguments, interjections, and rebuttals could not be openly adversarial. Though all his leading defenders were lawyers, none of them formally represented him. Their points, the responses of the managers, and the comments of other senators had a plotted, deliberate quality, reminiscent of players at a game of chess.

The intricate maneuvers of the Federalists, building a defense against the headlong rush to trial of the impeachers, was a coordinated effort. Tracy, John Quincy Adams, and William Plumer delayed the trial, while they worked to split the overwhelming Republican majority in the upper house. Tracy had blunted the opening moves of the managers by insisting upon Senate control of procedure. If he could slow the Senate inquiry and shunt it into a maze of technical legal questions, he might be able to avert a trial until Pickering resigned or regained his senses. If the Federalists prevented the impeachment from ending in removal, they might bring the entire Republican impeachment movement to a halt.

Tennessee's William Cocke, a strong supporter of Jefferson and an advocate of a speedy trial, recognized this tactic and pushed another prosecution game-piece forward. He seized upon the wording of the oath to insist that the trial was not a criminal proceeding. He suggested amending the oath—"I . . . solemnly swear (or affirm as the case may be) that in all things appertaining to the trial of the impeachment of John Pickering, Judge of the district court of the District of New Hampshire, I will do impartial justice, *according to law*"—to read "I will do impartial justice, to the United States, and John Pickering." His rationale introduced the central contention of the Republicans: "If the Senators take the Oath proposed, it will then be incumbent on the House of Representatives to prove that John Pickering has committed an offense against *law*, and that perhaps they cannot prove—for I understand the Judge is deranged—and I *know of no law that makes derangement criminal.*" Instead, the issues for him were: first, what offenses were definable as "high crimes and misdemeanors"? second, was impeachment and trial a criminal process? third, if the defendant in the proceedings was insane, could he be held responsible or "tried" for his actions? fourth, how were incompetent and publicly dangerous judges to be removed from office? and fifth, could someone be tried "in absentia"? Cocke's motion raised these issues perhaps prematurely—none of the other senators wished to face such sensitive procedural problems, and "the motion was lost no man voting in favor of it except the mover." Cocke's motion was stillborn, but it put positional pressure on the pawn Tracy advanced and supported the managers' other pieces.[13]

John Quincy Adams responded for the defense. He tried the same ploy that Addison ventured before his trial. Adams proposed that senators who had voted in the House on the original impeachment should be disqualified from sitting and voting at the trial in the Senate. His objection referred to three new members of the Senate—Theodorus Bailey of New York, John Condit of New Jersey, and Samuel Smith of Maryland—all of whom had voted for Pickering's impeachment. Kentucky Senator John Breckinridge opposed Adams's motion, arguing that "those gentlemen as members of the House of Representatives are now dead, they live and act in a different capacity as senators." Also in opposition, but on more practical grounds, was Georgia's James Jackson. He worried about the precedent such a rule would establish— "that may on some future occasion exclude so many of the senators, as the two-thirds of those who may be present and sit in judgement cannot be induced to *convict* the accused." Finally, Jackson's colleague Abraham Baldwin extended his fellow Georgian's point to the absurd extreme: if, for instance, "the trial should last as long as Hastings's [seven years] it may happen that nearly all the senators may be in the situation of those gentlemen." Adams, exasperated by his colleagues, protested that such a situation was unlikely and pleaded in "the cause of justice & humanity" that "those who voted the accusation should not decide it." To bolster his position Adams pointed out that "it is improper and very indelicate that judges who have given an opinion in a particular cause [as these members had by voting for the original impeachment] should afterwards sit in judgement in that cause." He continued that, after all, "jurors may be challenged—but judges cannot." This last was a response to one of Senator Baldwin's points that "impeachments are not like indictments—[n]or is the House and Senate to be compared to Grand and petit jurors." Baldwin felt that the liberty of judges was unlimited, that "it is no challenge to a judge that he has formed an opinion and even promulgated that opinion" (a view neither side saw fit to expand or explore further, though it would form the basis of the first article against Chase). Adams's motion, like Cocke's the day before, prematurely raised questions which the Senate preferred to postpone. Immediately after the vote to table the issue, all the senators, including the three in question, were duly sworn.[14]

The managers were admitted to the Senate chamber, the court was formally convened, and the articles were read. As senators drifted into town from their brief vacations, they took the oath and sat down to watch the game of wits between Tracy, Adams, and their allies, and the Republican leadership. Federalist protests notwithstanding, the senators agreed to begin their formal hearings on March 2. Pickering was summoned and money and subpoenas were set aside to bring evidence from New Hampshire.[15] Out of doors, the Federalists fretted. Plumer dined with President Jefferson and privately admitted to the president that he "had no doubt that the judge was *insane*" but queried Jefferson as to "whether insanity was good cause for impeachment and removal from office." Jefferson, ignoring the legal implications of an insanity defense, replied: "If the facts of his denying an appeal and of his intoxication, as stated in the impeachment are proven, that will be sufficient cause of removal without further enquiry." Conversation turned to the House inquiry on an impeachment of Supreme Court Justice Chase then being debated. Jefferson again supported removal of the erring Federalist judge but concluded: "This business of removing Judges by impeachment is a *bungling way*." Jefferson may have been prodding Plumer to press for Pickering's resignation. Plumer either did not understand or refused to take the hint.[16]

One reason why Plumer dug in his heels was the growing evidence of a sweeping Republican attack on Federalist judges. He took note of the inquiry into Chase's behavior, and expressed disappointment that an amendment to table the resolution so that members would have time "to examine precedents" had failed. With obvious disgust he watched as a House committee was formed to dredge up any grounds for articles. Plumer concluded that this procedure "is similar to the French *denouncing* a victim and like them his condemnation will follow of course." Plumer's sincerity notwithstanding, the specter of a reign of terror by the Jeffersonians was an obvious exaggeration of the situation since American impeachments could not and never did result in such dire personal consequences to those impeached. It might be argued, in fact, that impeachment, even in its most partisan incarnation, acted as a safety valve, inhibiting the excesses so disastrous for the first French republic.[17]

Federal marshals returned the subpoenas but the most important participant refused to obey. Pickering's response was predictable: the old judge received the summons in high dudgeon, demanded "trial by battle," and challenged Jefferson to a duel. His health crumbled even as he girded for this combat, and witnesses concluded he was mad.[18] There was no question of his coming to Washington, and without counsel to speak for him, he could not conduct a defense. If he were insane, could he be tried at all? The question remained unanswered.

On Wednesday, March 2, 1804, the Senate again met in closed session, as a court of impeachment of John Pickering. The players returned to the chess board. Adams renewed his motion against allowing previous members of the House when the articles of impeachment were passed to vote against Pickering in the Senate. When Adams originally made his motion, three members were affected: Bailey, Condit, and Samuel Smith of Maryland. In the meantime Bailey resigned and was replaced by John Armstrong. New York also sent up John Smith to replace De Witt Clinton. Armstrong, unlike Bailey, was not a prior member of the House, but Smith was—so the New York delegation still included one former member of the House. Condit and John Smith, on Adams's insistence, voluntarily withdrew from participation in the trial. Samuel Smith vigorously opposed the suggestion that he could not remain impartial and insisted on his right to judge Pickering. The final vote on Adams's motion was 20 to 8 against.[19] The opening moves were complete.

The court immediately turned to the trial itself. The sergeant-at-arms reported that Pickering's summons had been delivered. Pickering was publicly called three times and did not appear. President of the Senate Aaron Burr then informed the court that he had received a letter from Robert Goodloe Harper which included a petition from Pickering's son, Jacob.[20] The middle game began with a Federalist gambit: playing upon the doubts of some Republicans about the propriety of trying an insane man and the desire of other Republicans to conduct a model trial. Harper's allies within the Senate begged permission for him to read Jacob Pickering's affidavit and then speak to the issues it raised. Despite some Republicans' wishful thinking that Harper would finally consent to act for the judge, the Maryland lawyer never assumed this responsibility. Instead, he intended to prove that Pickering was currently unfit to stand trial, and, this failing to prevent a trial, that the judge was incapable of criminal intent in *Eliza* by reason of insanity, without ever entering a plea for the judge. Beginning on the third of March and running through the entirety of the pretrial hearings, a furious debate raged over the noncounsel's introduction of the son's nonevidence. The Federalists won the first skirmish. Harper was permitted to read Jacob Pickering's piteous plea for his father. Common fame had preceded its revelations; there was no doubt that Pickering was unfit for his office. The heart of the Federalist gambit was to use the evidence of his incapacity as a bar in law to his trial.[21] The Federalists tactics galled some Republicans. Jackson demanded that Jacob Pickering bring his father to court or persuade the judge to resign. The Federalists' plan was working: Jackson found himself arguing with others in his own camp over the technicality of noting Harper's appearance in the record. Wright, indulging in fantasy, wished Harper named counsel for the judge, but John Smith of Ohio—his ally—balked; why not force Pickering to attend, he counseled. Adams and Tracy cleverly fed the dissension within the Republicans' ranks, supporting Harper's contention that there could be no trial.[22]

Jacob Pickering's petition evinced the belief that the impeachment proceedings were tantamount to a criminal trial, a confusion later shared by several senators. It was perfectly clear, from the son's own words, that the elder Pickering was totally incapable of performing his judicial office. There had already been considerable delay, and further delay offered no assurance that the situation would improve. He claimed that at the time when the "crimes wherewith [his father was] charged, are supposed to have been committed, [he] was, and for more than two years before and ever since has been, and now is, insane, his mind wholly deranged." By Jacob Pickering's reasoning the judge was "altogether incapable of transacting any kind of business which requires the exercise of judgment, or the faculties of reason; and, therefore, . . . John Pickering is incapable of corruption of judgement, no subject of impeachment, or amenable to any tribunal for his actions." Indeed, he was incapable of defending himself or of appointing counsel to appear for him. His physical state of health was so precarious that a trip to Washington to exhibit his imbalance to the impeachment court was impossible. The younger Pickering concluded by requesting an indefinite delay of Senate proceedings until his father could be well enough to appear.[23]

In the delicate positional play of the middle game, the Federalists were holding their own. They did not accuse the Republicans of railroading Pickering, a questioning of motives which might have unified their opponents. Instead, they owned themselves ready to try the impeachment, but only under proper procedural rules. Over and over, Burr was forced to close the doors of the Senate chamber to allow the members to debate Harper's case. Georgia's Jackson, George Logan, a Republican whose pro-French activities in the late 1790s led to the Logan Act, and Robert Wright, a Maryland Republican lawyer, all pressed for an immediate hearing. Wright thought the issue a "civil" one; there was no need for criminal procedure. John Smith of Ohio adduced that Pickering's nonappearance ought to be viewed as a default. Breckinridge chimed in that the Senate could not compel attendance, for its jurisdiction was limited. This was ingenuous and incorrect, but he was generous to Harper. Unlike Cocke and Wright, Breckinridge consented to hear evidence of insanity at the trial. The division of the Republicans over Harper's right to speak and present evidence was music to the Federalists' ears, not only because they wished Pickering fairly tried but also because divisions of this kind stalled the momentum of removal by impeachment.[24]

The Federalists had built a defensive position which the Republicans were hard pressed to penetrate. Pickering's incompetence derived from his insanity, and the insane were not culpable for crimes (if the managers insisted, following the letter of the articles, on categorizing his conduct in *Eliza* as criminal). What is more, no man could be made to stand trial for a crime without the capacity of defending himself. Pickering had no counsel to speak for him and his son had piled up depositions to prove that Pickering's insanity was real. But if he was insane, he could not perform his duties. The Judiciary Act of 1801 provided for a shifting of cases from temporarily incapacitated judges, but the Republicans had repealed that act. Now it seemed that they would have to wait for Pickering to regain his sanity.

The managers, followed by the Republican Senate leadership, tried to breach the defensive wall, while the Federalists marshaled their forces to guard it. Caesar Rodney reasoned that Harper could be heard only if the Senate sat as a court upon the impeachment. Then he might appear as counsel for Pickering, and for no other purpose. Burr prevented Harper from replying, for he was not counsel for the defense, and again asked the Senate for direction.[25] The Republicans disagreed among themselves. Israel Smith of Vermont, siding with Federalists Timothy Pickering, John Quincy Adams, and James Hillhouse, fellow New Englanders, worried that guilt could not be pronounced when the defendant was not a "moral agent"; "insanity does away guilt." The Federalists won, 18 to 12; Harper could make his case without formally representing Pickering.[26]

Harper's tactics paralleled those of the Senate Federalists: he established the fact that Pickering did not act from malicious purpose, but madness. The *Eliza* orders were "deranged" and "incoherent." The judge had no idea of what was happening. Pickering drank, but only as a consequence of his madness. Harper then concluded in a statement, not a plea, that "the mildness and humanity of our laws exempt the insane from prosecution and punishment."[27]

Nicholson, spokesman for the managers, had directed a losing effort to bar Harper's participation. Now Nicholson elected a bold course. He declared that Harper's role was "irregular" and led the managers out of the chamber until the Senate began a real trial. The struggle between lower houses and upper houses for control of impeachment law is as old as impeachment, but Nicholson's pique did rouse the Senate's Republican majority to determine the law in its court. On the next day, March 7, 1804, the Senate asked the managers to return, and on the eighth, Peter Early of Georgia was allowed to open the prosecution. The middle game was over. Trial would proceed without the judge.[28]

The end game now began, for the trial was a pursuit of the judge without any of his supporting pieces. After reading the first article (the first time an impeachment article had been formally presented to the Senate), Early entered the *Eliza* minutes into the record. Ladd had come into Pickering's court to contest the seizure of his ship. Joseph Whipple, collector of the port, had testified that no duties were paid, but Edward Livermore, counsel for Ladd, had replied that the cables were not part of the cargo; they belonged to the ship. Pickering then had ruled for the defendant. When federal attorney Sherburne tried to present witnesses to deny this fact, Pickering summarily gave judgment on the entire ship and cargo to Ladd. The judge would hear no objection from the prosecution and needed no motion from the defense. Sherburne testified to the Senate that the judge had "declared . . . he could finish the business in four minutes," and then, in "profane language," had refused to allow the appeal. A "scene of confusion" ensued, after which the judge, drunk and loud, ordered court adjourned, and decamped. Other witnesses subpoenaed from New Hampshire recalled the judge's frequent bouts of inebriation. Drunkenness was not insanity, that is, not a plea in bar of culpability. On the ninth, Pickering's defenders in the Senate had themselves sworn, to establish the causal sequence between the judge's intoxication and his madness. Pickering's drinking was a symptom of his derangement, William Plumer testified, although often the former camouflaged the latter.[29]

The next day, Samuel White, a Federalist senator from Delaware, made the formal motion toward which his party had been working throughout the deliberations. Hoping to capitalize on the divisions he heard among the Republicans over the insanity question, White moved to postpone the trial until Pickering was sane enough to come or to name counsel. When Wilson Cary Nicholas, a Republican replacement for Virginia's Tazewell, objected, Burr shut the doors of the chamber and allowed both sides to thrash out the issue. Adams insisted that White's motion was in order; White taunted Nicholas that the proceeding was "a mock trial." As the two men hurled insults, Plumer rushed to cool the debate; obviously, the Senate was not ready to proceed in a judicious manner. Logan persisted: Pickering had to be removed because he was unfit. White's motion was defeated, 19 to 9.[30]

Adams went home with a cold and spent his vitriol in letters to Timothy Pickering. Adams proposed that the Federalists walk out of the Senate chamber when the verdict was given, using the rationale that Pickering was mad when he heard *Eliza* and so not responsible for his actions. What was more, the judge was still insane that March and unable to assist in his defense. Impeachment was a "criminal prosecution" and must wait upon representation of the defendant's interests; yet the Senate proceeded without defense examination of witnesses or challenge of admissibility of evidence (particularly hearsay on Pickering's long-term inebriation).[31]

With Jesse Franklin of North Carolina presiding in Burr's absence, the Senate rendered its verdict on the twelfth of March. The game was almost over. White and Joseph Anderson, a Tennessee Republican, clashed over the language of the charge to the Senate; White urged that the vote declare Pickering innocent or guilty of "high crimes and misdemeanors" upon each article. Anderson preferred "guilty as charged." White lost 18 to 10, then Anderson's choice won 18 to 9. Every positive vote on White's motion was cast by a Federalist; every negative vote by a Republican. Stephen Bradley of Vermont, John Brown of Kentucky, David Stone of North Carolina, John Armstrong of New York, and John Condit of New Jersey, all Republicans, did not vote; they left the hall. This was the rift in Republican ranks the Federalists had expected—but, in the end, could not exploit. The end result was that a two-thirds majority of the Senate stood ready to regard Pickering's conduct as culpable, whether or not it met some strict standard (undefined by either side, though presumably equivalent to criminal acts) of "high crimes and misdemeanors." Now the Federalists knew their cause was lost.[32]

Adams recorded the confusion of the upper house, still sputtering as the final votes were taken, while the entire lower house demanded entry, the speaker at its head. Franklin ordered the record of the proceedings read, but James Jackson, impatient to be done with the business, called for the reading of the articles and the vote upon them. White refused to be rushed by anyone. The defense was not yet checkmated. He confessed now that he believed the judge had acted irregularly but was not capable of a crime because he was insane. He would not stay in his chair to hear the basic principles of criminal law twisted. Nicholas evidently groaned during White's review of the previous week's nastiness, for John Dayton, a Federalist from New Jersey, rubbed salt in Nicholson's wounds: the manager would just have to accustom himself to hearing the trial called a mock proceeding. The Senate, Dayton continued, misused its power to remove when it did not require real crimes. White then demanded to know whether the Senate would vote on "guilt" without evidence of crime. When Franklin said that the Anderson formula stood, White and Dayton pushed their way out of the crowded hall, having, for the past hour, put their objections on record. They did not join the seven remaining Federalists who voted not guilty on the articles. The judge had been found guilty on all counts, 19 to 7, and removed by a 20 to 6 vote, when Delaware's William Wells shifted his ground. After the vote, Adams took the Delaware Federalist aside and after some conversation, Wells admitted that "he had not fully reflected on the subject."[33]

The Federalists were frightened by the vote. Plumer wrote that the future was now revealed to all: the independence of the judiciary was gone. He noticed that the "star" witnesses against Pickering were later elevated to higher posts.[34] Adams concluded that no judge could measure up to the new standard and that any "trivial error" could become grounds for impeachment.[35] He watched with apprehension the arrival of Randolph and Early at the bar of the Senate to announce the impeachment of Chase. The irony of the

Federalists' fears is that they drew the wrong conclusion from the *Pickering* verdict. The voluntary absence of the five Republican senators, combined with the feeling of other Republicans that something had to be done with Pickering because he was simply incapable of carrying on, indicated that the judge's politics were not an issue of prime importance. Pickering was removed because there was no other way to replace him. While some Republicans had plans for other, more political, prosecutions, Pickering's was not a partisan case. He was not accused of misusing his office for political ends or of hectoring his political enemies in his court (though he was a Federalist and very forthright about it). It was the Federalists in the Senate who used questions of law as a shield for one of their own, and voted as a bloc. They politicized Pickering's case, creating a specter which would haunt them until Chase was found innocent. Of course, they had help from Nicholson and Randolph, Giles and Jackson, but not from a massed phalanx of Republicans bent on removing Federalist judges any more so than Bayard and Harper were able to mobilize the Federalists in the Senate in *Blount*.

Before one condemns the Federalists as prisoners of their own political propaganda (or too gullible consumers of the most extreme Republican antijudicial sales pitches), one must concede one sound reason for increased Federalist anxiety after *Pickering*. In the main, the Federalists had supported the doctrine of judicial tenure during good behavior. Without this, they argued, there could be no judicial independence. More important, the demise of judicial independence would remove an insulation between the democracy—the rank and file voters—and the one branch of government which stood safe from periodic elections. With the exception of a number of their youngest spokesmen, the Federalists had not reconciled themselves to mass political participation or to the dominant voice of the "common man" in national politics. They were elitists, and nowhere more so than in their insistence that the judiciary remain above politics. Seen in the context of the highly political comments of Federalist judges in seditious libel trials and their charges to the grand juries, this revulsion to politicization of the courts may seem hypocritical (it did to the Republicans), but such an assessment of Federalist views is not fair. By calling for a judicial branch above politics, they meant to put the courts above the clamor of crowds, the vagaries of frequent elections, and the will of popular demagogues. The various states and the federal government protected judges with good-behavior tenure, but impeachment, under the new Republican doctrine of dangerous tendency, exposed, albeit indirectly, the judges to the popular passions the Federalists feared.

The removal of Pickering did not help the Republican cause so much as the Federalists feared, or particularly harm their own. In general the Republicans were not seeking to oust incompetents who failed to attend sessions of the court, but to curb Federalist judges whose presence and bias so dominated the courts that Republicans could not obtain justice in them. The Federalists who had turned the Pickering case into a straight party issue misunderstood the significance of the verdict. Out of the confusion over the liability of Pickering's conduct—whether a person incapable of crime (and incompetent to stand trial) could be impeached, tried, and removed—came the clear rule that incompetence was an impeachable offense. This rule had nothing to do with the doctrines of popular will or dangerous tendency, the real threats to Federalists in these cases. In the trial of Pickering, Federalists had voted as a bloc for they regarded the case as the opening wedge of a Republican assault. The Federalists had underestimated the doctrinal difficulties which still slowed the Republican impeachment effort. Moderate Republicans, particularly those with legal training, were not ready to remove judges without strong cause. Five Republicans left rather than vote against the insane judge. By resisting the trial and voting to acquit *en banc*, the Federalists informed the Republicans that *no removals* of Federalists would be tolerated if they could help it. This attitude made impeachment into a test of party will—not at all what the Federalists desired.

While Pickering was not convicted under the dangerous tendency rule (or the still-to-be-revealed doctrine of popular will), his verdict nevertheless appeared to support those doctrines. Both the Republicans, who had removed him on a strictly party vote, and the Federalists knew that the victors were considering prosecution of other judges. This concomitance of events brought *Pickering*'s outcome and the doctrine introduced in *Addison* together. More to the point, Pickering was not accused of any crime. Evil intent was irrelevant to his prosecutors. Although his decisions were highly partisan, no one argued that they were rationally malign. He was convicted and removed for misconduct, not "high crimes and misdemeanors" in the sense of crimes or violations of known laws. While his offense did fall wholly under dangerous tendency, it did fit some of the requirements of the new doctrine. Dangerous tendency did not require a crime (though it could be conjoined or asserted in charges of criminal activity—to magnify the significance of the crime). Strictly speaking, although its advocates in *Addison* hedged their bets on the point, dangerous tendency did not require evidence of *mens rea*. Coming so close to the Addison case, pressed by the same men who trumpeted *Addison*'s outcome, and linked to a larger program of impeachment, *Pickering* seemed at the time to give strength to the dangerous tendency interpretation of Article II, section 4.

There was one procedural precedent in *Pickering* which made it appear to anticipate *Chase*. Pickering was tried *in absentia*. This could not be done in a criminal trial unless the suspect was represented by counsel. Then his defense was, by his choice, in their hands. Even incompetence to stand trial is determined after representations by defense counsel at pretrial hearings. Though absent himself, Blount was represented by counsel at his pretrial hearing. He was never actually tried for the offense, that is, called to the bar to defend himself. *Pickering* did set precedent for a trial without counsel, plea, right of cross-examination, and all the other procedural guarantees of the Fourth, Fifth, Sixth, and Eighth amendments. Chase could not claim that his trial was a criminal trial—*Pickering* would queer that line of argument for him.

The second case to test dangerous tendency after *Addison* erupted in Pennsylvania—the crucible of Republican impeachment. Addison's removal there had spurred the radicals' demand for thorough revision of the laws. Part of his defense rested on the crucial area of dispute between radicals and moderates (with their Federalist bedfellows): the lingering influence of common-law judicial procedure. Though the radicals decried the common law, many Republican lawyers upheld its value. Hugh Henry Brackenridge, from the high court bench, echoed these sentiments: the common law brought the right to trial by jury, the right to representation. Ingersoll and Dallas, from opposite sides of the party fence, found much to praise in the older English conceptions of judicial discretion. Some judges might use their discretion as an excuse for partisan forays, but the discretion itself was necessary. Brackenridge agreed: it was not so easy to make a judge; it would be folly to hobble him in his own court when so much time and travail went into teaching him how to run proceedings. Without judicial independence, guaranteed in the common law (at least the English judges from Holt's time had conferred it on themselves), a judge "would be under the temptation to be looking about, and turning in his mind, the probability of being turned out in consequence of the judgment he was then about to give." The law would not guide the judge, political considerations would—the very calamity that everyone claimed they wished to avoid.[36]

The radicals in the Pennsylvania house were not mollified by these mild sentiments. They continued to demand that British precedent not be read in any Pennsylvania court opinion. Facing the opposition of lawyers to their reforms, they attacked the lawyers as well. Duane and his cohorts opened up a drumfire of criticism upon the "overgrown power of the bar": in league with the judges, some of whom grasped their commissions only "as they bring them fees," the lawyers preyed upon the common people. The radicals' demand for arbitration of petty causes and an extension of the powers of the local justices drawn from the ranks of nonlawyers, at the expense of the jurisdiction of county court judges, gained momentum from the removal of Addison but could not overcome conservative opposition in the state senate.[37]

Into this boiling controversy dropped the matter of Thomas Passmore. Passmore was one of a group of obstreperous, indefatigable Philadelphia businessmen whose careers kept them in the public eye. Like Oswald, he was quick to resent an insult and to publicize his choler. On February 23, 1803, Passmore presented a memorial to the assembly condemning the barbarity of the supreme court bench (less Brackenridge). Passmore himself was the victim. The firm of Bayard and Pettit had insured a ship Passmore owned and, through a convoluted process, had managed to delay payment of the premium when the ship was lost at sea. Passmore went to court, won a jury verdict, and then watched as Bayard and Pettit maneuvered in the courts to avoid execution of the judgment. It seemed to the shipowner a clear case of legal hijinks—lawyers standing in the way of justice. He put up a broadside in a tavern saying just that. Bayard went to the supreme court and brought a suit for libel. The court ordered Passmore to appear and, when he did, asked him why he ought not to be regarded as standing in contempt of court. He replied that there was no case pending when he posted the broadside. The court then asked him to apologize to Bayard, which Passmore refused to do. He had called Bayard and Pettit "quibbling underwriters" and named Bayard a "liar, rascal, and coward." For refusing to retract his words, the court ordered him fined $50 and confined to gaol for 30 days. Passmore demurred to the right of the judges to fine and imprison him without a jury trial, but to no avail—to gaol he went.[38]

Passmore's petition was committed and a report presented to the lower house on the ninth of March. The committee of inquiry agreed that the "'summary mode' of punishing contempts was not agreeable to the genius of the constitutions and laws of the commonwealth of Pennsylvania." There was nothing in the laws that forbade such summary proceedings. The judges had silently used powers derived from the common law. The report came at the end of a session, but the next gathering of the assembly found the radicals willing to continue the case. In this they had the support of Republicans elsewhere. Monroe, for example, agreed with Kentucky's John Breckinridge that "application of the principles of the English common-law to our constitution" was "good cause of impeachment." On January 17, 1804, a second committee reported: "Your committee find that the judges have exercised a stretch of power in this case, not warranted by the constitution and laws of our country." The behavior of the judges was "unprecedented," both in the severity of punishment and the definition of the scope of contempt. By a 57 to 24 vote, the lower house decided to write these findings into articles of impeachment. The articles alleged that the fine and imprisonment of Passmore was "arbitary, unconstitutional, and a high misdemeanor."[39]

Not by accident, the three judges accused—Edward Shippen, Thomas Smith, and Jasper Yeates—were all Federalists. Shippen had even been a Loyalist, "intimate with the British" during their wartime occupation of Philadelphia.[40] Duane goaded the radicals forward in January: "A very indignant sensation has been excited here by the conduct of the judges of the supreme court . . . a further evidence of the dangers to which the liberties of the people are subjected by the high-handed measures of the court of law. The affair of Passmore's arbitrary and wanton imprisonment," Duane believed, ought to "lead to an article of impeachment."[41] The *Aurora* directed criticism at the judges' tenure and adherence to common-law procedure as the greatest stumbling blocks to reform of the law. To Federalists in and out of the state, the affair wore an equally somber garb, for a different reason. Jonathan Mason, a Boston Federalist lawyer passing through the city, noted in November:

> The Federalists are beaten and out of date and conversation. . . . Next month the four [*sic*] judges of the Supreme Court—men of respectability, integrity and talent, grey in the service of their country—are to be tried upon an impeachment for having acted oppressively in punishing a Republican for contempt of court. This state under the control of ignorance and Jacobinism.[42]

Shippen, Smith, and Yeates were confident of vindication. Friends in the lower house confided that they were "husbanding their influence."[43] Conservative Republican members of the bar refused to serve as prosecutors, and McKean's son, Joseph, the attorney general, joined the governor in opposing the impeachment. Dallas agreed to defend the judges, joining Ingersoll.[44] Even before the impeachment was voted, Shippen wrote Yeates suggesting the judges adhere to the defense they made to the impeachment: they were not partial in their order to Passmore or in their handling of the matter; the case was still alive when Passmore libeled the court, and the judges leaned over backward to be generous to Passmore in merely seeking an apology from him.[45] Shippen urged that Yeates, a man known for his short temper, keep himself in check. Thomas Smith had already recommended to Yeates a "clear and cool head." He warned that the prosecutors were "demagogues" and would stop at nothing to tear down justice in the state. Smith could not forbear one "I-told-you-so": "You have often laughed me to scorn as a croaker, to use your own word, on my uniformly declaring that not withstanding the firm ground on which we stand were Law and Reason to prevail, yet I was convinced they were determined to oust us."[46] Yeates himself was convinced that all would be well; "our spirits are good," he beamed.[47]

Though Brackenridge was not impeached because he was away from the bench when Passmore was called to account, he supported his brethren. Into the April 1804 numbers of his *Modern Chivalry*, he inserted a satire on the impeachment:

It was carried that there should be new judges.

But having disposed of the old, it became a question whom they should elect for new. The bog-trotter [the picaresque Irish hero of *Modern Chivalry*] was proposed for one, having had his name up before in the matter of the newspaper.

What, my waiter, said the Captain? Yes, your waiter, said a wag, or a fool, I do not know which.

You astonish me; said the Captain. My waiter a judge of the courts. He will make sad work on a bench of justice. He will put down all law. He will silence all lawyers. He will have no law: no books; no cases; all plain sailing with him. Every man his own lawyer, state his own cases, and speak for himself. No Hooks and Crooks reports; no Hawkins; no Bacons; or Blackstones; or Whitestones; no Strange cases, no law of evidence. Every man sworn and tell what he knows, whether he has seen it, or heard it, at second, or at first hand: interest or no interest; all the same; let the jury believe what they think proper; and the judge state law from his thumbs ends without books.[48]

He was, of course, intimately connected with the removal of Addison, and in a soberer vein recast his position:

There is such a thing as tyranny in judges; and I am no enemy to the investigation of official conduct. But let . . . people take care that they exercise not tyranny themselves; or give way to passion, which even in a body politic, is possible. Let the sovereign, like that of all the earth, do justice; and consider that the possession of power is upheld by justice.[49]

Brackenridge was convinced that the bench acted properly in *Passmore*. Passmore's contempt may not have been related to his presence before the court, but there was also a solid body of law on "consequential contempt"—a disrespect "of the law."[50] Any interference with a case *sub judice* was such a contempt, according to Blackstone. Judges had the power and the duty to protect the rights of litigants in cases before them from the harassment of outsiders or other litigants. This power did not extend to general expressions (or it would abridge the freedom of speech amendment in the federal and Pennsylvania constitutions), but it did apply to speech and writing on the facts of any case still in court. If judges could not, under their contempt powers, suppress interference with their handling of cases, there could be no impartial justice. And if judges were to be prey to impeachment every time they used this power, there would be no judge safe from continual impeachment threats. Moreover, even if the contempt power was used excessively, or in error, it was not a misdemeanor but an excusable mistake of judgment. Finally, to insist that all summary causes required a jury trial would endlessly tie up minor matters in complicated proceedings, so that little business transpired. It was well-established practice and good sense that judges disposed of contempts summarily. Brackenridge turned to the authority of the common law, in full knowledge that it was under attack by the radicals. In this recourse he knew he had the support of the bench and bar, Federalist and Republican, for the language of the common law was their preserve and their profession. They would not surrender it without a struggle.[51]

Trial began on the first of the new year, 1805. Despite the speaker's appeal for "impartial justice," all the major participants were interested parties. Boileau and the other managers were the leaders of the radical party; Ingersoll and Dallas, counsel for the accused, had been counsel for Bayard in Passmore's original suit. Boileau claimed, in his recitation of the charges, to speak for jury trial and the "rights of man" against arbitrary power, but all present knew that reform of the judiciary was his hidden agenda. The first witness called, Passmore testified that he did not attack the court and thought the lawsuit settled when judgment was awarded. The judges replied that Passmore was abusive to them on the bench, as well as in his tavern broadside. Expert witnesses called by both sides disputed the meaning of minor words and gestures at Passmore's hearing. Building on these bits, Dallas insisted that Passmore had insulted the law, not just the person of the judges. Custom decreed that such contempts be punished summarily. If the penalty was excessive, it was an honest error. Because he worked closely with the lower house on other occasions, he took time to praise their honesty as well: "They have shown that the poorest man [a reference to Passmore's bankruptcy] in the community will be as patiently heard and receive the same justice as the most opulent and dignified."[52]

Dallas did not hesitate to recur to the common law on contempts. If the state senate intended to convict the judges for obeying common law, knowing that every court followed it, then there was no hope for the judges, Dallas persisted. James Wilson, in his law lectures a decade before, had approved the common law; it was received in all Pennsylvania courts; it "belongs to society"; even Jefferson urged its use when necessary. Indeed, the Pennsylvania Constitution allowed the use of the common law. True, trial by jury was required under the 1790 state constitution, but only in cases of indictment. Surely a false step in this gray area could not be equated with the "criminal violation of the constitution" alleged in the articles of impeachment.[53]

Boileau spoke for the prosecution. Yeates found him energetic but ineffectual, but the judge was not impartial to the assemblyman's argument. Boileau all but ignored the judges, to take aim at the common law and its aristocratic defenders. In this category he included the defendants and Brackenridge, a "creature of the governor" and his clique. Under the thumb of these wealthy, privileged men, the poor and oppressed had no hope of redress—for the ever presence of the common law gave a monopoly of knowledge and power to its few, highly placed minions. Instead, Boileau thumped, "The judges ought to follow the spirit of the laws of this state and the spirit of our constitution, and not of a [British] constitution hostile to our government, our manners and our customs." For Boileau, the impeachment trial was another occasion to push for revision of language and codification of titles of the law.[54]

Boileau saw his campaign to remove the encrustations of common law, along with prosecution of judges who clung to common law, as the work of the people. He acted in their behalf, at their behest. Since only a procedural error was charged, whatever its larger implication might be, Boileau was literally asking the senate to remove the judges because they had thwarted the popular will. The people wanted an end to attachment for contempt, which amounted to arbitrary imprisonment at the judges' pleasure. Boileau did not say that the judges themselves were unpopular, or that their removal catered to the whim of the voters. While this might have fit his and other radicals' emerging view of truly democratic politics, it was hardly the time or place to introduce a comprehensive theory of political reform. With the senate left to its own devices to determine the true will of the people, Boileau offered counsel. He tried to read into the record published materials on judicial reform, in effect introducing public opinion into the trial. Dallas objected: "Let him read all the system of Utopia," he could not read extraneous opinions. Boileau replied that even without these items, there was plenty of precedent for punishment of misconduct against the people and cited Dallas's own arguments in *Addison* as proof.[55]

Caesar Rodney followed Boileau to the floor. A Wilmington lawyer, congressman, and one of the Republican managers in *Pickering*, Rodney was hired as prosecution counsel for his experience and political views. He was not personally involved in the case although he did practice law in Pennsylvania on occasion and had trained in Philadelphia. He declared that Shippen was a venerable and good man; no party animus sparked his brief for the prosecution against the judges. He impeached the contempt procedure rather than its wielders. No other courts in the country used attachment on a contempt in a civil suit. Only the common law supported such a step, and as Dallas had noted in defense of Blount, much of the common law was not received in America. What was more, there was no suit before the court when Passmore scribbled his attack on Bayard. Had Bayard wished to obtain damages, he could have brought a libel suit in the proper manner.[56]

While Rodney did not support impeachment and removal for errors of opinion, the use of attachment—with the injury done to Passmore—was an offense. Without curb, there was no end to this "exercise of power. Where will it end?" No one could guess "to what cases . . . it will be made to stretch."

Rodney did not allege criminal intent or even the violation of the constitution that Boileau found. Instead, it was the dangerous consequences of the judges' license which made the offense impeachable. Thus the other novel Republican doctrine of impeachability entered the trial record.[57]

Ingersoll closed for the defense. His message was brief: destroy the separation of powers between the legislative and the judicial branches and one destroys respect for law. He pointed to evil omens already in the air: Brackenridge, though not charged with any offense, was attacked in public for giving an opinion on the case. Ingersoll also took pains to dismiss Rodney's reference to *Blount*—in which he was co-counsel with Dallas. They did not mean to sweep away the common law where it was sanctioned by usage in America. The common law, among other things, was the source of impeachment. Ingersoll ended quietly: attachment was necessary for the courts to function. He was sorry that, given Passmore's impudence, he was not more provident.[58]

On January 26, 1805, the court of the senate voted, 13 to 11, to find the judges guilty, the vote falling 3 shy of the required two-thirds.[59] Among the yeas was Whitehill, now the speaker of the senate and one of the formulators of dangerous tendency. The judges' ordeal was over, but public reaction to the acquittal continued.

As the trial progressed, partisans on both sides had expressed their opinion on the case publicly. Forgetting or ignoring the power of a court to compel silence on a case before it—the very power that brought Passmore low—Duane pressed for conviction in the *Aurora*. "It is a prodigious monster in a free government to see a class of men set apart, not simply to administer the law, but [to] exert a direct legislative and even an executive power . . . under the color of the unwritten, undefined, contrary, heterogeneous, and in numberless instances barbarous and cruel maxims of common law!"[60] Dallas, in the midst of the defense, took time to report to Governor McKean: "The conduct of some of my old friends is extravagant and unexpected. However, I know the strength of your mind, and I am not afraid of the result of the session."[61] Dallas was right; the impeachment registered a near miss. Unshaken, Duane predicted "dangers and afflictions not inferior in consequences to those which produced the revolution of 1776."[62] Beneath this bit of hyperbole was the dangerous tendency argument, dramatized for the lay public.

In the days after the acquittal the *Aurora* served as a forum for proposed constitutional amendments. The thrust of these accorded with the impeachment doctrine pressed by Boileau. The will of the people was thwarted by the judges, and their removal by impeachment failing, the state constitution must alter the tenure of the judges from good behavior to periodic election.[63] On the defense side, letters poured in to Dallas and Ingersoll congratulating them on their victory: "Republicanism won over factions, and conscience . . .

over party spirit, intrigues, and denunciation."[64] William Barton, another lawyer, confided to Ingersoll that "common sense and common honesty have triumphed over Anarchy, Folly, and Rascality. . . . The arch-fiend, Duane, is down. . . . Rodney and his squad are effectively disgraced."[65] Federalists were relieved and effusive in their expressions of victory. Dallas, closer to the Republican side, was more cautious. The impeachers had overstepped their case. With a phalanx of lawyers against them, and no proof of malice or even bias, they could not get the two-thirds vote.[66] But they came very close indeed. The *Shippen* precedent could be read as an encouragement to obtain conviction on either dangerous tendency or popular will tests against less respected defendants, for more serious offenses than Shippen and his brethren committed.

The impeachment and trial of Shippen and his colleagues formed a natural sequel to the removal of Addison. It was not specifically undertaken to lay a groundwork for impeachment and trial of federal judges, but the power to impeach was one having a corresponding place in federal and state government. Both governments were free to borrow from each other, though precedent from one was not binding upon the other. Shippen's trial preceded Chase's because the Senate postponed the latter at the request of the defendant. This gave the Republican radicals in Pennsylvania a chance to test and refine the popular will and dangerous tendency tests. These radicals were the same men who had brought the original charges against Addison. Their allies were now in Congress and had argued for Chase's impeachment. Duane recognized the relationship between the two cases and feared, in the acquittal of Shippen, that the entire case against Chase would fall.[67] This was unnecessarily pessimistic. The misapplied momentum of the *Pickering* verdict still outweighed *Shippen*. The prosecution of Chase could easily prove that Passmore had not suffered so much as Chase's many victims—including counsel, witnesses, and defendants. Even the lawyers, opposed to impeachment of Shippen, divided on Chase's guilt. Popular will and dangerous tendency were not rejected in the Shippen case but restrained. The final act was yet to be played.

12

POWER AND PRECEDENT: THE IMPEACHMENT AND TRIAL OF SAMUEL CHASE, 1804-1805

IN ADDISON AND SHIPPEN ET AL. REPUBLICAN MANAGERS HAD EXPLORED THE doctrine of impeachment and removal for acts dangerous in their tendency. The results were mixed. Dangerous tendency was an effective rationale in lower houses but did not uniformly convince upper houses, sitting as trial courts, to convict defendants. The second novel Republican doctrine of impeachable offenses, that they might be anything a lower house constructed into a "high crime and misdemeanor," waited in the wings. Briefly tested by Boileau, nurtured by Giles and Randolph, both politicos, popular will weighted the scales of trial verdicts in favor of legislative descretion. By advocating popular will, Randolph did not hope to advance the cause of democracy but the power of the legislative branch over officers of the other branches of government. Nevertheless, it could not practically be used against any but the most unpopular Federalists; too many Republicans had proved their loyalty to a more moderate course in impeachments. The target Randolph chose was acceptable to the majority of these moderates: virulently partisan, arrogant, and imposing Supreme Court Justice Samuel Chase.

At the hightide of Federalism, Justice Chase reminded a federal grand jury of its duties under the Seditious Libel Act:

> There can be no government without subordination, which implies submission; and submission implies that the minority surrender up their judgement and will to the Decision of a Majority. . . . It cannot be credited that Congress will intentionally violate the Federal Constitution contrary to their sacred trust; or wilfully impose unreasonable and unjust burthens in which they must participate. . . . You have no right to decide on the justice or the validity of the law; and if you should exercise the power . . . you would thereby usurp the authority entrusted by the Federal Constitution to the Legislature.[1]

The message was characteristic of the man's politics—so long as his party wrote the laws.

· In the late 1790s and early 1800s, Chase's career on the federal bench was marked not only by political controversy, for his virulent Federalism was well known, but by a series of tumultuous circuit sessions. Even the Federalist district judges who sat with him found him short-tempered, harsh, and mercurial—traits Chase exhibited throughout his career. His personal fortunes were still subject to the vagaries that made his earlier forays in Maryland politics a maze of shifting alliances. His commitment to prosecution of political opposition was far distant from his revolutionary dissents of the 1770s; his championship of federal judicial power confuted his earlier anti-Federalism. His espousal of the adoption of parts of the common law of seditious libel in the statute of 1798 repudiated his own dissent in *U.S. v. Worrall* (1798). Convinced that war with France was inevitable, he pursued Republicans with special vigor in the late 1790s. In charges to grand juries along the federal court circuit and at trials for treason and seditious libel he showed Republican defendants, counsel, and witnesses no mercy.[2]

To Republicans, it appeared that the tall, broad-shouldered Federalist was looking for chances to scourge their supporters. The second trial of Fries gave Chase this opportunity. When Fries's riot was first reported, Chase had lobbied for treason charges—a prophecy that his conduct of Fries's trial might not be above criticism. When the first trial of the Pennsylvania German rioter ended in a court order for retrial signed by Iredell and Peters, Chase was not on circuit, but he recovered his health in time to preside at the second trial. Before the prisoner and his counsel approached the bar to plead, Chase prepared a brief ruling on the charges, essentially repeating what Paterson had written in *Vigol*. As formal proceedings commenced he passed this opinion across the bench to Fries's counsel William Lewis. Lewis read far enough in the three-page document to realize that he and Dallas would not be able to argue against the Paterson opinion, adopted by Iredell at the first trial. Dallas had prepared a number of new points to convince the jury that riot and unlawful assembly did not amount to treason. Lewis, though a Federalist, was furious with the timing of Chase's opinion and with the judge's refusal to let counsel argue the law. The lawyer threw the paper down, announced he would not be a party to such high-handedness, and left the chamber. The next day, Dallas too withdrew from the case. Peters had warned Chase that this would happen, and prevailed upon the justice to back off. The clerk hurriedly gathered up all copies of the opinion, but Dallas and Lewis still refused to represent Fries before a judge who had already reached an opinion on a key point of law. Of course, both counselors knew Chase's view of the case before the incident at the bench, and their refusal to remain Fries's counsel might have been a ploy to gain him an eventual pardon. In any case, they convinced him to put himself upon the court for counsel. Chase assured the defendant that the bench would guard his rights, but no one could expect the bench to carry on a defense for him. While there was precedent for this in English jurisprudence—in fact, until 1692 only the judge protected the rights of accused traitors (counsel was allowed to speak to points of law only)—in America all suspected felons had the positive right to hire counsel to speak for them, examine witnesses, and address the jury on matters of fact as well as law. Fries was convicted and sentenced to death, but Adams, moved by the plight of the defendant (part of which was the absence of counsel) pardoned him. Washington had done no less for the Whiskey Rebellion defendants.[3]

Chase was not finished with the Republicans, however. In Annapolis, before his carriage ride down to Richmond for the next stop on the circuit, he received a package from Luther Martin. Enclosed was James Callender's scurrilous pamphlet, *The Prospect Before Us*. Using language even more insulting than was customary in that day, Callender, a Virginia propagandist, accused Adams of playing the aristocrat and leading the country toward despotism. Chase spent the rest of the trip and his stay in a Richmond boardinghouse planning to make Callender pay for the libel. Chase brought Callender to court upon a warrant usually reserved for felons, and proceeded to try him without the delay customary in Virginia—all of which was fought by Callender's counsel. The best and brightest Republicans of the Virginia bar had offered to defend Callender, not because he was respected or even because they agreed with his words, but because he had become the symbol of freedom of the press for them. Philip Nicholas, the state attorney general, George Hay, a later occupant of that office, and William Wirt, soon to be United States attorney general, tried to prove the truth of Callender's statements, for truth was a defense under the 1798 act. Chase cut them short. He bullied Hay and argued with the others. What was worse in their eyes, he did not permit a key witness, John Taylor of Caroline, to testify, because, as far as he could determine, the testimony would go to only one of the counts against Callender. On top of this, he refused to excuse one prospective juror who admitted to prejudging the case against the defendant. The conviction, inevitable given Chase's rulings during the trial, infuriated Republicans in the state and personally insulted Callender's counsel.[4]

From Richmond, Chase traveled to Newcastle, Delaware. There, upon his own information, he instructed a federal grand jury to seek out evidence against a Republican newspaper editor. Over the protestations of the federal district judge, Gunning Bedford, Chase sought a repetition of the Callender affair. As it happened, neither the district attorney nor the grand jury found any objectionable matter in the newspaper, and the issue was dropped.[5]

Unlike a number of his Federalist brethren, Chase did not trim his sails after the Republican victories of 1800 and 1802. He vociferously opposed the repeal of the Judiciary Act of 1801 and even urged making the Supreme Court into a fulcrum for resistance to the new president's policy. Marshall, to whom Chase directed his proposal, was far more circumspect in maintaining the independence of the court from the other branches, and resisted Chase's call for direct confrontation.[6] While charging a Baltimore grand jury in 1803, Chase publicly condemned the administration from the bench. To this he added a call for repudiation of electoral reforms then pending in the state legislature. John Montgomery, a Maryland lawyer, state legislator, and Republican leader, was present at the session, took note of the charge, and publicized it. Jefferson reported his distaste for the speech to Joseph Nicholson. While Nicholson considered the matter, in the fall of 1803, John Randolph seized the chance to move against Chase.[7]

The manner in which the impeachment arose, not directly from *Fries* or *Callender*, but two years later, from a partisan charge to a grand jury passing through Jefferson's hand to Nicholson, and then to the desk of Randolph, a rabid party man, confirmed the Federalists' anxiety about the politicization of impeachment. Chase's prosecution seemed to Fisher Ames to be the next step in a political war. Whereas Ames was an alarmist, other Federalists coolly weighed the Republicans' purposes and strength. Bayard, temporarily retired from Congress by his constituents (though the Delaware Assembly would shortly return him to the Senate), worried that "the prosecution is on political grounds." Bayard declined to serve as Chase's counsel precisely because the prosecution was partisan; the Delaware lawyer said he did not want to weaken Chase's chances by reappearing at his side so soon after losing an election. Plumer knew that Chase was high-handed, but he objected to the form of the accusations. "[They] are not confined to any *specific charge*," he noted in his journal, but rested upon general accusations. Plumer might have recalled that Woodbury Langdon and other defendants in state cases were routinely impeached for general offenses, but the senator did not wish Republicans to have that opportunity on a national scale. John Quincy Adams, campaigning at home in the fall of 1804, informed Massachusetts voters that a season of judge-hunting was upon them, and only an outpouring of Federalist ballots could stop the Republicans' crusade.[8]

Although he did not admit or could not see it, Chase himself was a prisoner of that same psychology—the same self-righteous, partisan bias. Perhaps the federal seditious libel law had given too much power to the judges and thus put too much temptation in their path. To Chase and his colleagues' habitual bruskness on the bench the act added the statutory power to suppress public opposition. To his credit, he did not seek an indictment of the Newcastle editor who was villifying him, but this was a pause in a tourn of relentless partisanship. In effect, Adams, Plumer, and their Federalist allies were demanding that impeachment be above the very politics which their judges practiced at the federal courts for so long. The irony in *Pickering*—

that they themselves contributed to the politicization of impeachment by their bloc vote for the district judge—was one they would never grasp.

Without another mechanism to curb Chase's abuse of power on the bench, Republicans of all ideological persuasions agreed to impeach him. Caesar Rodney denounced Chase for taunting Congress "with impunity." Macon, always cautious, nevertheless feared Chase's attempts to "lull the people" to the dangers of Federalist policy. Chase was intemperate and even brutal to witnesses, defendants, and counsel—this much Peters and Bedford admitted. Even Marshall was to agree with this estimate of Chase's performance. Modern legal scholars have disagreed on the extent of this misconduct, but in the eyes of some of its victims it must have seemed harsh indeed.[9]

Beneath the issue of legitimate discretion lay another, sensed but not probed by the contenders on either side. Common-law judges of Chase's era claimed that they found the law rather than made it. Chase had cited this dictum in *U.S. v. Worrall* (1798), explicitly denying his power to create common-law crimes. A more realistic view is that laws and courts are institutions, and institutions respond to change or they die. Even the language of the law changes—old words get new meanings, new words and phrases are coined—to facilitate these changes. Chase's era itself was a time of reform in criminal law and procedure. Following the example of Chase's antagonist, Jefferson, lawyers and politicians had begun the codification of criminal law, elimination of capital penalties for all but a few crimes, and introduction of "bills of rights" to safeguard procedural privileges. There was great movement in the criminal law toward protection of the defendant in the court. To this entire process Chase remained a virtual stranger. His manners on the bench were reminiscent of English jurists of a century before. He acted as though virtually everyone brought before him upon a criminal charge was guilty. He did not truly accept the adversarial process in criminal trials mandated in federal courts by the Sixth Amendment. He was impatient with defense counsel not just because they represented radicals and democrats, but because he had not accommodated himself to the idea of defense counsel conducting the defendants' cases. He was a throwback—making law by moving backward instead of forward. Although he used his powers in the courtroom no more often than Paterson or Iredell, he used them to reestablish a rule of law left behind in 1776. Marshall said as much to him in 1804, when Chase sought assistance from the chief justice in preparation for his impeachment trial. Marshall implied that Chase preferred "ancient" to "modern" ways of handling procedural error. At his trial Chase's prosecutors groped toward the same conclusion with references to the tyrannous ways of pre-Revolutionary judges, and they identified Chase's views with those of the Tories.[10]

On this issue, the conflict between Chase and his prosecutors went far beyond party politics. Both sides were sincere. Though the Jeffersonians had the future in their camp, Chases's ways were familiar to every lawyer in his enemies' array. Chase, in part because he did not recognize how out of step he was, failed to come to grips with this charge. If anachronism on the bench was impeachable, he had no defense. In his opening statement he grappled with a forepaw of the beast: if he erred, it was through ignorance, not malice. To some extent, the scholar will sympathize. Within the context of his genuinely sincere Federalism and his old-fashioned social views, Chase was not acting with bias. He did not intend to penalize counsel and defendant for their views but for their insolence to his office. His understanding of the law—of the necessary and proper conduct of government—merely required that disorder in the courtroom be suppressed, counsel be curbed, and the disrupters of government be penalized.

The opening rounds of the Chase impeachment occupied the members of the House in January 1804. Neither *Pickering* nor *Shippen* had been resolved, although both impeachments were already complete. On the fifth, Randolph asked for a formal inquiry into a report made the previous session by Republican John Smilie of Pennsylvania. Smilie questioned Chase's conduct at Fries's trial. James Elliott, a young Federalist lawyer from Vermont, objected. The New Englander could see where this inquiry would lead. Smilie had asked for permission merely to recite the facts, but Elliot retorted that the lower house could not censor a judge for questionable conduct, and there was no evidence of "flagrant misconduct." Any vote to inquire without evidence amounted to a prima facie censure. Smilie persisted: without the facts, how could the House proceed? Matthew Clay, a seasoned Virginia Republican, joined the call for an inquiry, for "judicial independence" left unexamined could "become dangerous to the liberties of the country." Clay had opened the door and the dangerous tendency test bounded into the chamber. Clay claimed to be unbiased, a necessary assertion when raising the question of dangerous tendency, for party bias could masquerade as disinterested concern for the republic. Roger Griswold, the veteran Federalist leader, was not comforted by Clay's disclaimer and immediately began construction of a groundwork for Chases's defense against an impeachment. The judge may have erred in interpreting a point of law to Fries's counsel, but it was an error of judgment, not of party malice. It was not grounds for impeachment. What evidence was there, Griswold (himself a practicing attorney) entreated to prove a malicious irregularity? He too denied any partisan interest in the matter, necessary if he was to be objective in judging malicious motives. Elliott jumped into the debate to agree with Griswold and to call for delay of the inquiry, but the two lacked the necessary votes.[11]

Randolph forged ahead. For reasons of his own, he was taking over the lead from Nicholson. His persistence was already making Jefferson think twice about his own role in the affair. Jefferson and Randolph had split over the purchase of Louisiana, and the president saw Randolph as a man capable of dividing the party. Randolph, for his part, tried to maintain cordial relations with the White House but knew he had lost the confidence of its occupant. The tension which his leadership of the impeachment inquiry brought to party unity was felt from the first debates and undoubtedly played some part in their still distant outcome. Over the course of the year-long preparations, Randolph was brought to the brink of serious illness by his pursuit of Chase, but the Virginia Republican harried the judge unceasingly.[12]

Though Randolph had read law, he rarely practiced in the courts, and throughout his prosecution of Chase, he argued along the most general lines. A common sense approach worked well in the House. On the matter of Fries's trial, Randolph argued: "What does it amount to? A person under a criminal prosecution, having a Constitutional right to the aid of counsel in his defence, has, by the arbitrary and vexatious conduct of the court, been denied this right. Such is the nature of the charge."[13] Republican members of the bar must have shivered when Randolph tossed away the "crutches of precedent" in favor of common sense. The common law nevertheless offered too many examples of the sort of discretion Chase exhibited. Far better to deny the relevance of all English precedent (even though it contained the roots of dangerous tendency), than to allow the Federalists to cite the claims that English jurists made for discretion on the bench. The adoption of this strategy made strange bedfellows among the impeachment forces, joining radicals like Smilie to conservatives like Randolph. The lawyers among this corps did not have to sweep away all precedent, for they had ample American precedent on both the proper conduct of judges and the character of impeachable offenses to keep them happy. Thus, midway in the House inquiry, the Jeffersonians hit their stride—combining common sense and American impeachment precedent in condemnation of Chase.

When the Federalists tried to sidetrack the inquiry with complex procedural questions, the Republicans refused to slow their pace. The Pennsylvania delegation took the lead, for among its number were the leaders of the state legal reform movement. Though Smilie's report was only an information without supporting affidavits or formal evidence against the judge, Smilie insisted that English precedents "are not necessary." When Michael Leib, the radical German Republican from Philadelphia, wanted to inquire into the conduct of Richard Peters, the district court judge at the trial of Fries, Nicholson agreed, as did William Findley, that to do this, "there is no need to be entangled in precedents." Findley's attacks on the common law were meant for the Pennsylvania lower house, reconsidering the impeachment of Shippen at that very moment, as much as for Congress. Whatever his motive, Findley insisted on the appropriateness of the impeachment. "In the Federal Government there is no method provided for removing [judges] for the most scandalous indiscretions or incapacity, as even when they may unfortunately be under mental derangement, except by impeachment, which is inapplicable to official crimes, and conducted with tedious forms. The power of impeaching being the only shield provided by the Government for the protection of the citizens from judicial oppression, and this House being the only Constitutional organ for obtaining information of official excesses, and bringing forward articles of impeachment, ought not to bind up their own hands from doing their duty, and this they will do if they reject the resolution now on the table."[14]

The Federalists threw themselves in front of the Republican hard chargers, hoping, perhaps, to split the majority. If the Republicans plunged ahead without copious reference to authorities, the Federalists would fill the record with it; if the Republicans eschewed English precedent, the Federalists would supply it for them.[15] The issue they seized was the absence of a formal motion to impeach the judge. Griswold plucked materials from Hastings's case to show that Burke had not hesitated to bring a motion for impeachment. Why, then, did the Republicans not move an impeachment? Griswold regarded the current inquiry as a fishing expedition, a search for evidence. Bolingbroke was immediately impeached by the Commons, Griswold continued, because they had evidence; Randolph had none. A committee of inquiry was a de facto censure, besmirching Chase's reputation without proving anything. Griswold's citations were not extensive (or exactly correct), but this is understandable, for he did not presume that the English precedent applied here. Instead, he was playing for time. If the Republicans agreed to drop the inquiry and wait for sufficient evidence to move impeachment, their momentum might be slowed.[16]

Undaunted by Griswold's cries of "inquisition," the Republicans pressed ahead (though Nicholson stopped long enough to note that Burke did not immediately demand Hastings's impeachment; an inquiry had preceded the motion). After the inquiry was officially approved, 61 to 43, Randolph put a few more of his cards on the table. He told the members that the lower house need not consider itself a court of law. Chase would not be present and he would not be represented by counsel. Neither an inquiry nor an impeachment was a trial. Next, he informed the House that the investigation need not be limited to the Fries trial; the committee would hear all charges against Chase. Following Nicholson, he paid brief obeisance to English cases of impeachment. He did not explore them; they were window dressing. No one was going to accuse him of ignorance of the law, including Samuel Dana, a Connecticut Federalist and member of the bar, whose remarks briefly interrupted Randolph's recitation. Dana was ready to read the "English constitution" to the House, but was forestalled by Nicholson. Together, Randolph and Nicholson reviewed English impeachment cases in order to dispose of them, and deny Federalists like Dana and Griswold any toehold in the debate.[17]

The beleagured Federalists did not have long to wait for the next blow to fall. Randolph and his comrades had followed *Callender* as it developed. They did not charge Callender's case to Chase's account themselves but allowed William Eustis, a Boston surgeon and leading Republican from that Federalist state, to add Callender's trial to the inquiry. Eustis thought the judge's behavior "tyrannical and indecent," an outrage against common sense. Many of the senators in his party were not lawyers (roughly half followed other professions), and he was eventually chosen to join the impeachment managers to appeal to these senators.[18]

The House next created a committee to study charges against Chase. Dominated by Randolph and Nicholson, the committee also included Joseph Clay, Peter Early, a Republican lawyer from Georgia, and John Boyle, a Republican member of the bar in Kentucky. The committee had two members from the minority: Griswold and Benjamin Huger, a South Carolina planter. Both Griswold and Huger dissented from the committee report. The other committee members would become impeachment managers. On March 12 the committee reported to the House its recommendation that Chase be impeached. Judge Peters was not, in their opinion, culpable of any offense.[19]

The committee recommendation to impeach the judge was adopted, 73 to 32. On March 26, 1804, Randolph presented seven articles of impeachment to the house. The first charged Chase with three counts of misconduct in *Fries*: "In a manner highly arbitrary, oppressive, and unjust" driven by partiality, Chase tried to prejudice the minds of the jurors against Fries. By refusing to allow Lewis and Dallas to argue the law of treason, Chase denied Fries a defense in law. The second article accused Chase of "irregular conduct" in depriving Fries of the right to counsel, under the Eighth Amendment to the Constitution. The third article found that Chase, "prompted by a similar spirit of persecution and injustice . . . with intent to oppress and procure the conviction" of James Callender, refused to excuse a juror for prejudice. The panel member, John Basset, admitted that he had made up his mind that the Callender pamphlet was a libel, but Chase insisted that Basset be sworn, and he served. A fourth article charged Chase with suppressing the evidence of John Taylor for insufficient reasons. The fifth article gathered the remaining misfeasances of Chase during Callender's trial. Chase was accused of exhibiting "manifest injustice, partiality and intemperance" for refusing to postpone the trial, using rude language to the defense team, interrupting counsel for the defendant, and generally informing everyone of his own opinion of the offense and the offender. The article concluded that such "solicitude" for conviction was "unbecoming even a public prosecutor, but highly disgraceful to the character of a judge, as it was subversive of justice." The sixth article raised the impropriety of Chase's behavior at the Newcastle grand jury session of June 1800. Chase was again charged with disregarding his duties and stooping "to the level of an informer" to spread rumors about "a most seditious printer, unrestrained by any principle of virtue." When no presentment came forward, Chase instructed the district attorney to investigate, that some case might be made against the printer. The final article was the most important, for not only had it brought Chase to grief, it was the only evidence that Chase aimed at the destruction of government. His "political harangue," disguised as an address to the Baltimore grand jury in 1803, had the "intent to excite the fears and resentment of the said grand jury, and of the good people of Maryland, against their state government and constitution."[20] The last article combined dangerous tendency and popular will tests. The language of criminality, to which the Republicans had adhered as late as *Pickering*, was all but ignored in *Chase*. The House adjourned until the fall without voting on the articles, but Chase's fate was assured.

Chase was impeached at the start of a crucial electoral year for Republicans and Federalists. If Jefferson's presidential victory in 1801 was a fluke, the Federalists might regain control of the executive. This they ardently wished and campaigned vigorously to achieve. The Republicans were just as committed to retain their new supremacy. Although no further action was taken against Chase until the next session of Congress in December, Federalists could not put it out of their minds. In canvassing for Federalist presidential electors, campaigners stressed the danger a Jeffersonian victory presented to Federalists in the judiciary. At the same time, worried about their own political future, many Federalists shunned contact with the all but condemned justice. Chase's brethren on the bench and party comrades offered sympathy, but such experienced battlers as Timothy Pickering and Fisher Ames thought the justice doomed to removal. Chase himself had expected the blow to fall: "You cannot retire," he had told a friend in 1803, "therefore expect disappointment, deceit, and disgrace as far as party can give it."[21]

The electoral results stiffened the resolve of the prosecution. Giles returned to Congress, Nicholson forgot his caution, and Jefferson set aside his gnawing doubts. The articles were accepted at the start of the next session, on November 30, 1804, and sent to the Senate on December 7. One new charge, numbered article 5, had been added, based upon a closer reading of the Judiciary Act of 1789. According to the act, Callender was to have the procedural rights of a defendant in a Virginia criminal case, including the right to be summoned to court, rather than be brought in under arrest. Chase, either not knowing the Virginia rule (passed in 1792), wishing to ensure that Callender did not flee, as Duane had, or simply to embarrass the virulent propagandist, bade the marshal arrest Callender. The House had also framed Chase's refusal to allow Callender the delay permitted by Virginia law into a separate article.[22]

Chase had used the recess of Congress to assemble a defense team and

gather evidence. Bayard and Hamilton refused to serve, but Harper volun-
teered and Luther Martin rushed to the aid of his longtime Maryland patron.
Martin was not the brilliant speaker that Harper was and his appearance did
not inspire confidence, but he knew the law and his passion was worn on his
sleeve. Adams and Plumer would find him the most impressive of Chase's
defenders. Harper may have directed the defense, for Chase left the chamber
soon after the trial convened, but Martin was its soul. Charles Lee and Joseph
Hopkinson joined the effort, the former a Virginia lawyer of national reputation and later attorney general of the United States, and the latter a rising star
of the Philadelphia bar. Philip Barton Key, a London-trained Maryland
lawyer, rounded out the defense side. Lee and Key were briefly federal judges
whose careers on the bench the Republicans had aborted in 1802.[23]

On January 4, 1805, Chase responded to the charges at the bar of the Senate
but was interrupted so often by Aaron Burr that the judge seemed to sink in
weakness and despair. His plea for a three-month delay to obtain further
evidence and gather witnesses was reduced to one month. Plumer accused
Burr of harassing the judge, but Duane detected the same old "shuffling and
prevarication." While Chase hurried to comply, out of doors—in the lobbies
of boardinghouses and before glowing fireplaces in the capitol building—
Republican congressmen and senators discussed the case. Randolph, leading
the managers, and Giles, again in the Senate, conferred continuously. Giles
conveyed the substance of these conversations to the upper house. Judges
whose behavior endangered the "public good" ought to be removed, and
any act dangerous to the rights of the people was impeachable. Blatant
partiality, associated with irregular conduct, provided motive and *actus reus*.
John Quincy Adams and William Plumer shivered at these remarks. When
the Senate took up Giles's views, both New Englanders would object
strenuously.[24]

On February 4, 1805, defendant, counsel, and House managers again
trouped into the Senate chamber. The rest of the representatives took their
seats en masse. The galleries overflowed and the trial began. Chase, with help
from Harper and Hopkinson, read his opening speech, his voice weakened by
illness but easily heard by his judges.[25] In Fries's case, he insisted that his
opinion on the law was sound and based upon earlier rulings by Iredell and
Paterson. He had considered the law on treason as settled and was bound to
communicate this to Fries's counsel and the jury. If he had made a mistake, it
was not deliberate and hardly amounted to a crime. He did not reply to the
thrust of the article (which found deliberation and malice in the timing and
manner of his ruling on the law), but fell back upon Addison's and Shippen's
defense. Chase saw that impeachment law was at issue and did not dispute the
essential facts of the charges (though he did cast doubt upon the veracity and
motives of his accusers). He simply maintained that "only for treason,

bribery, and corruption, or other high crime or misdemeanor, consisting in some act done or omitted, in violation of some law forbidding or commanding it; on conviction of which act they *must* be removed from office . . . and may, after conviction, be indicted and punished therefore, according to law. Hence it clearly results, that no civil officer of the United States can be impeached, except for some offense for which he may be indicted at law; and that no evidence can be received on an impeachment, except such as on an indictment at law, for the same offense would be admissible." Chase narrowly interpreted Article II, section 4. Under his reading there was no grounds for removing Pickering. The strict confines of the language—that is, its denotation for a reader who did not know about the debates in Philadelphia, the state cases, or *Pickering*—seemed to require a crime cognizable in a regular court of law. Chase must have known that this reading flew in the face of precedent. For him to abandon *stare decisis* in state and federal impeachments while upholding it as the highest principle of law in his discussion of Fries's case is contradictory at best. He pressed on to a third point in his favor: "Through error of judgment merely, without corrupt motives, however manifest the error may be," a justice was not liable to conviction and removal. In this, Chase finally found solid ground. For errors in judgment, manifest though they were, Hopkinson and McKean were not removed. The errors were not corrupt, although the behavior was found censurable by the legislature. Addison had gone too far in hindering the liberty of a fellow judge, but Chase was not accused of this. Of course, Chase's argument could not stop the Senate from removing him for his partisanship. He could and did say, in effect, that his removal must be for political reasons since, under his view of the law of impeachment, his acts did not show the criminality necessary for conviction.[26]

Whether in conceding errors and mistakes Chase had second thoughts about his conduct at these trials and in his grand jury charges, or he wanted to elicit the sympathy which some Republicans had already shown for his age and previous service, one cannot know. He had written to private correspondents that he feared his actions would be misunderstood, and admitted as much to Marshall in 1802. Even then he felt the cold breath of Republican animosity. He would not "hesitate one moment between the performance of my duty and the loss of office" but he knew that Congress was launching a massive assault upon the independence of the judiciary. What was a single judge to do? Between 1801 and 1803 Chase attacked and withdrew, denounced politics and then gave political advice to grand juries. His defense in the Senate displayed the same ambivalence. He flouted his contempt for Callender in his statement, then denied that he was at all biased in Callender's case. He was free from all intentional impropriety. Was this a cynical posturing, or a genuine conviction that a judge could do and say what he pleased and not influence a jury? Was Chase defying the Senate or appealing to its better nature? He continued: he only did his duty in Newcastle. He could not remember if he had used derogatory terms to describe the Wilmington *Mirror*'s publisher to the Newcastle grand jury. It was his responsibility to report to them what he had heard (though surely the reverse was the standard procedure).[27]

He did remember saying to the grand jury in Baltimore that changing the state constitution to permit universal male suffrage would "in my judgment take away all security from property and personal liberty." This was the phrase which John Montgomery reported in the newspapers and which led to the impeachment of Chase. Chase knew that this was the last straw for his opponents. His address occurred long after the Jeffersonian victory at the polls and the beginning of the movement to impeach Federalist judges. Addison's conviction was a warning that blatant political bias in grand jury charges would not be overlooked by a judge's enemies, but Chase went ahead anyway. Never known for his patience or good temper, he might have simply blurted out his fear of "democracy" to the jury. He did have in hand the rough draft of his charge to the jurors. It was his habit to prepare notes in longhand a day or so before he was to read them, so his Baltimore tirade was not spontaneous. To the senators he avowed that he had meant to libel no one—correctly anticipating prosecution analogies between his intemperate words about Jefferson and Jeffersonian democracy and Callender's animadversions upon Adams's love of aristocracy. He merely expressed his own "opinions, perhaps ill-founded, but not criminal." If he were to be prosecuted for sharing his thoughts, "error in political opinion, however honestly entertained, might be a crime." It was a valid point, and one Republicans had pleaded when they were under the heel of the seditious libel law (though a point receiving little sympathy from Chase at the time). The shoe, now on the other foot, must have pinched, for Chase insisted that Callender's "writing and publishing as facts malicious falsehoods, with intent to defame," differed from his own opinions concerning the tendency of public measures. All told, his performance was uninspired, but fortunately for him, Chase's defense did not depend upon his own efforts.[28]

Randolph replied for the managers. At this stage of the proceedings, it still did not harm the prosecution to give the simple sense of the justice's misconduct. Chase supposedly had not allowed counsel to be heard; prejudged cases; tried to influence juries on factual matters; ruled testimony inadmissible to keep it out of the record rather than because it was irrelevant; bullied and harassed everyone in the courtroom; and used the bench to preach politics. Taken together, the judge's misfeasances added up to gross misuse of power, for which the people had no remedy save impeachment, trial, and removal. Randolph made no brief for the criminality of Chase's conduct. The danger lay in unrestricted use of office for private or party ends. Read in one way,

Randolph's address recalled his earlier remarks about Pickering: the House could impeach for any cause which in its view reflected the will of the people, but he did not say this. There was a stronger and safer ground upon which to lay the case against the judge. The prosecution knew that dangerous tendency was available, and so did Chase's defense team. Because Randolph did not yet name the demon, Chase's counsel did not attempt to slay it. But variants of the dangerous tendency test appeared over and over throughout the examination of witnesses and the presentation of evidence.[29]

After the opening statements, opposing counsel spent two weeks battling over the facts at issue. Unspoken but understood was the question: how dangerous and unprecedented was Chase's conduct? Had counselor Lewis read and rejected Chase's ruling on constitutional grounds or torn it up in a fit of pique? Had Chase ordered or asked counselor Hay to sit down at Callender's trial? The points made were confusing; too many cooks were stirring the broth. For example, was Chase's conduct at Callender's trial unusual? John Marshall joined witnesses from the Republican party to say it was, but some Republicans, including eyewitness Edmund Randolph, reported that they did not see anything amiss. The judge's lawyers were unable to shake the testimony of witnesses to the fact that he was brusque, facetious, curt, and hard on counsel. In mitigation was his reputation for being hard on everyone. Even John Randolph conceded this. In general, the crucial issues in all the articles were not factual, but legal. Had he exceeded his powers by ruling on the law of treason before counsel presented briefs, by refusing to let Taylor testify, by silencing Hay, by arraigning Callender without regard to Virginia's criminal practices, by urging a prosecution upon a Delaware grand jury, and by denouncing a proposed constitutional amendment to a Maryland grand jury? What were the limits of discretion on the bench? Some of his high-handedness in *Callender* was designed to poke fun at counsel, although John Taylor, who finally got his chance to speak at Chase's trial, recalled that "the audience laughed, but the counsel never laughed at all" at Chase's remarks.[30]

Randolph put his own interpretation upon the facts. He concluded that Chase went to Philadelphia prepared to find Fries guilty, and to Richmond to convict Callender. He had read *The Prospect Before Us* on the coach ride down and could hardly be called fair-minded. His conduct merely betrayed his thoughts. One witness on the judge's state of mind during the trial (a fellow boarder at the inn) told the Senate: "Before he left Richmond, he [said he] would teach the people to distinguish between liberty and licentiousness of the press." Another witness to a meeting of the judge and the federal marshal reported that Chase urged the marshal to strike from the jury list all "creatures called democrats." To Randolph and the other managers, testimony on all the articles proved that an evil state of mind motivated the partisanship in behavior.[31]

Chase's counsel read the evidence differently. As had Jefferson when he urged Nicholson to bring the impeachment, they concentrated upon the last article. They feared that Chase's remarks were pointed enough against the president to constitute a seditious libel—a wrong that was no longer tried in federal courts but was still a censurable act by a judge. Whereas his conduct toward witnesses, jurors, counsel, and defendants might be protected by the custom of courts, his attack on Jefferson during the performance of an official duty was a misconduct. Harper in particular labored to mitigate the severity of Chase's oratory, and later admited that Chase's language at Baltimore was misleading. His client only meant to belabor the misguided policy of the Republicans. Free expression of political opinions was permitted under the Republican defense of the First Amendment, Harper would insist.[32]

Throughout the cross-examination the force of both sides' arguments passed each other like armies in the night. The defense would not credit the dangerous tendency test but insisted that Chase had committed no crime. Errors were not impeachable, whatever thesis Randolph and Giles bandied about in corridors and streets. The prosecution would not concede that impeachable offenses had to be crimes, much less indictable in a regular court of law. Even while fumbling over this point, both sides began to close on a real issue: the motive for Chase's conduct. Were Chase's irregularities mere excesses of honest zeal or malicious and purposeful thrusts at a political opposition?

On February 20 the managers began the summation for their side. Peter Early, Virginia born, Philadelphia trained in the law, now representing Georgia in the lower house, spoke first for the prosecution. He had managed *Pickering* and fully understood the force of dangerous tendency, though it was ultimately not needed so much in that case as in *Chase*. The managers did not discuss the articles in seriatim but under broad headings, and following the lines of Randolph's opening argument, Early enumerated the dangerous consequences of Chase's conduct. The judge threatened trial by jury, right to counsel, and the very idea of judicial independence by prejudging cases. He usurped the role of the jury, the prosecutor, and in Fries's case, even that of the defense counsel. The danger was written on the face of his conduct: how could justice survive in a republic whose judges were so avid for power?[33]

Early hedged the prosecution's bets on dangerous tendency or rather wove the former doctrine and the notion of malicious intent into a single strand. He could not prove that Chase committed a crime but he could not concede to the defense the issue of motivation by his silence. Indeed, Chase's antipathy to Republicanism was the most easily proved fact of all. Instead of relying only on dangerous tendency, in which intent to undermine the republic was not a necessary condition, Early danced back and forth between evil consequences and evil mind.

George Campbell joined Early in this groping attempt to buttress dangerous tendency with the very different doctrine of *mens rea*. To the Tennessee
lawyer, the two were related. Campbell began with a stirring repetition of the
dangerous consequences of partisan misuse of power: "This is the corrupt
origin from which have issued all the evils complained of; this has for ages
been the scourge of society; and it is all important, that in our country, which
is yet in its infancy, when this poisonous germ cannot have taken deep root, it
should be crushed in its embryo, and not permitted to gather strength by the
sanction of high and superior authority." But how did the prosecution know
that Chase's conduct proceeded from evil purposes? Was it not possible that
the judge thought he was merely obeying the law? Campbell chided the
senators that no intelligent person needed evidence of prior design, calcula-
tion, or intent; these were written on the face of the acts themselves.[34]

At the Fries and Callender trials, Chase's "conduct was such a flagrant
violation of his duty, as could only spring from corrupt motives, and a
disposition to oppress those who became the objects of his resentment."
Chase's answer to this charge (as Addison's and Shippen's before him) had
been denial of the intention to mistreat—indeed, he believed that he acted in
the defendants' best interests. The motive-in-the-act argument (used in common law prosecutions for treason and seditious libel) did away with the
presumption of innocence by shifting the burden of proof to the defendant.
Only one possible interpretation of motive was allowed when the act itself
was flagrant, unless the defendant could prove otherwise. Campbell pressed
hard on this issue, for (unlike much of the prosecution case) it did confront an
issue raised in defense of Chase: "I lay it down as a settled rule of decision, that
when a man violates a law, or commits a manifest breach of his duty, an evil
intent, or corrupt motive must be presumed, to have actuated his conduct; as
every man is presumed to know the law, and every officer or judge to
understand his duty; and if the party will undertake to excuse himself, for
misconduct, on the score of pure motives, and unintentional error, it is
incumbent on him to make the same appear by satisfactory and incontestible
evidence." In presenting the thesis that the facts spoke for themselves, Campbell effectively shifted the burden of proving Chase's innocent motives onto
the defense's shoulders. They must show why he diverged from Iredell's
willingness to let Lewis and Dallas argue the law, and from the practices of
the Virginia courts in Callender's case:

Why did he not consider himself equally bound by the practice they
adopted in criminal cases? They gave the utmost latitude to counsel in
making their defence to the jury, both on the law and the fact, did not
restrict them as to the authorities they should cite, and delivered no
opinion until the cause was heard. Judge Chase reversed the whole of
this mode of proceeding. What good reason can be given for his adhering

to their opinion in the one instance, and totally departing from their practice and example in the other? No excuse can be formed for this conduct. This is the strongest possible evidence of corrupt motives, of partiality, and a determined design to overleap all former rules of proceeding, to oppress the unfortunate defendant, that was arraigned at his bar for trial. The whole course of the judge's conduct in this transaction goes to establish the same spirit of oppression.[35]

In spite of Early's long-windedness and Campbell's ill-health, the first two managers had provided the court of the Senate with two ways to find Chase guilty. If the senators accepted dangerous tendency, they could find that the justice had persisted in subordinating justice, or at least decorum and procedural impartiality, to political malice, party advantage, and personal vengeance. Left unchecked, his conduct undermined the people's faith in government and denied those who faced him their rights. What was more, he was the very worst model for other judges to follow. For those senators who preferred the more restricted constitutional guidelines (which included willful, malicious misconducts) Chase could be viewed as a "mis-demeanor." His offense did not have to violate positive law but did have to exhibit malign intent. Campbell provided evidence of this from the pattern of the acts. For a judge to have partisan opinions was no crime, nor was keeping order in a court, but when the virulence in the former could be linked to partiality in the latter, there was grounds to suspect misuse of power.

For all their efforts, the two managers could not join the dangerous tendency test and the classic elements of criminal culpability; it remained an odd coupling. Nevertheless, by giving the impression that the two doctrines fit together, Early and Campbell tried to conceal a central weakness in their case. The problem originated in their own party's recent, partisan successes. As Jeffersonians proved in 1800 and 1804, partisanship was hardly a crime. The longer the party system was around and the increasingly democratic elections became, the less Republican leaders could deny the legitimacy of partisanship. What was more, a reputation for party favoritism could hardly be censurable when Federalists and Republicans knew that hewing to the Republican party line was becoming a prerequisite to gaining and holding appointive office. Federalists complained that this requirement was reaching into the judiciary, hitherto (in their view) a preserve of impartiality. With the independence of judges under Republican attack, a proposition both sides were used to hearing, how could Early and Campbell argue that Chase's party bias was an offense?

At the same time, and equally vexing to the prosecution, the republic was filled with judges who bullied and blustered in their courtrooms. Kentucky was in the throes of a rebellion against the powers of its local court judges; Pennsylvania reformers were forcing reduction of the jurisdiction of professional judges; the demand for codification of the laws to reduce the power of judges to apply common law (among other aims) was heard throughout the land. Chase's humbling of counsel and others was persistent but not unique. *Shippen* was precedent for absolving judges of punishment for using their power to keep order, so long as they meant to keep order. By bringing dangerous tendency together with malicious motives, the managers hoped to prevent the defense from separating Chase's opinions from his acts, and exculpating him for each in turn.

Facing a Republican majority in the Senate disposed by long years of harassment to dislike and distrust Chase's motives, his defenders showed the mettle of first-rate trial counsel. As a body, they were more experienced and more highly regarded in legal circles than the managers. They recognized that Chase's case was not cut and dried, for the offenses which had most often led to conviction in impeachment trials—corruption, extortion, peculation, and criminal activities—could not be alleged against Chase. In private conversation and public address they treated the case as a political persecution. Unfortunately for them, the Senate was not a regular court of law, wherein rules of reasonable doubt might apply. It was a political body which rarely sat as a court. Though lawyers made up a majority of its number, many of them were Republicans and openly regarded noncriminal acts as impeachable. Before a trial jury in a criminal case, the task of the defense might be satisfied with punching holes in the prosecution's facts, as Chase's defenders had tried to do during its examination and cross-examination of witnesses. Nothing that any of Chase's counsel did or said could counter the impression that their client was a man of ill-tempered and arrogant ways, however. Any one of the articles, if there were no question about their sufficiency in law, might convict the justice. The main thrust of the defense was therefore to dispute the prosecution's view of impeachment law. Parceling out the articles among themselves, the defense team crafted an often moving, occasionally profound, and always able plea for their client.

Hopkinson, chosen to open for the defense, was straightforward. He tried everything once, beginning with an appeal to the sympathy of the jury. The prosecution hounded a patriot, gray and infirm in his country's service. His offenses were "frivolous occurences," not the grave breaches of public trust that Randolph, Early, and Campbell portrayed. Had they been so serious, Chase might have been—ought to have been—indicted in the regular courts. A nice touch this, which Hopkinson supported with reference to English manuals—comparing Chase's conduct to graver irregularities. The Senate was treated to a genuine trial lawyer at work, who watched his jury and measured its reaction to his sallies.[36]

Hopkinson next conceded that Article II, section 1, of the Constitution did not place limits upon the lower house's right to impeach, but Article II, section 4, did restrict the nature of offenses. Chase's acts were neither crimes nor "high misdemeanors." He had neither broken the law nor failed to enforce any law then on the books. Ignoring dangerous tendency for a moment, Hopkinson struck at the weaker Giles–Randolph doctrine of popular will impeachment. Taking Randolph to task by name, Hopkinson warned that removal upon popular disapproval for petty misconducts (he mentioned drinking, a slur upon the prosecutors of Pickering) would fatally undermine the republic by breaking down the separation of powers. The lower house was not to "create the offense, and make any act criminal and impeachable at their will and pleasure." If it did this, the judiciary and the executive would find themselves "at the foot of this omnipotent House of Representatives." Here was a reverse reading of dangerous tendency: evidence that Hopkinson understood all along that dangerous tendency was the more potent of the two Republican impeachment doctrines. He borrowed its logic to warn that were removal upon the whim of the majority of the House made into a rule, no one would be safe from factions and demagogues.[37]

Hopkinson finished his summation with a detailed refutation of impeachment articles 1, 2, and 3. At its core was a new interpretation of Chase's motives: the judge acted as he did to save time and money. Under known and accepted rules he tried to speed trials along. He had no desire to rob defendants of their rights but merely wanted to expedite the execution of justice. Chase, too, in his opening address had mentioned the backlog of civil cases created by the *Fries* logjam. Hopkinson evidently did not know which, if any, of his arguments had struck home; if a few of them hit the mark, he might save his client from conviction. That, after all, was a defense counsel's primary task.[38]

Philip Barton Key followed Hopkinson for the defense. Key would later serve as a Federalist member of the House, but when he joined the defense he was a well-established lawyer in Annapolis and a leading Federalist in the state legislature. Where Hopkinson bristled and darted, Key gently trod. He conceded that Chase might have made mistakes but urged that they be considered errors of judgment. Key then reminded the upper house that the English practice was well established (among judges at least) that one can never infer corruption from the judgment itself. He had found the answer to the *res ipso* argument that Early and Campbell championed. Judges' rulings were not to be compared to the acts of suspected traitors and libelers. The judges' intent could be inferred only from their stated opinions. If Chase did not say he acted from malice, then no one could assume it of him. Key did not dwell on the point that judges, unlike other officials in a republic, could not be charged with excess partisanship without their consent.[39]

Key's particular task was to defend Chase's conduct at Callender's trial. As had Hopkinson, Key had a ready explanation for the entire business: Callender's attorneys were inept and partisan. Though they were reputed to be among the finest in the state, they bungled and prolonged the case. Deliberately, they dallied, made repeated and frivolous motions, and refused to accept the judge's rulings. Chase alone had the right to determine the admissibility and relevance of evidence and rightfully prevented them from interfering. Hopkinson, albeit briefly, had questioned the motives of Lewis and Dallas in leaving Fries without counsel. Key extended this line of attack. He pictured a stern judge badgered by a legion of unruly, hectoring, partisan lawyers. The Senate had now been treated to antilawyer slurs by both prosecution and defense counsel—all of whom were lawyers.[40]

Charles Lee then rose to close the defense on the fifth article, the *capias* Chase issued against Callender, when Virginia procedure provided for a summons. Lee was the Virginia Federalist who had argued *Marbury v. Madison* (1803) so forcefully before the Supreme Court. Plumer and Adams expected Lee to demolish article 5, and he did. He placed the blame on Virginia, whose procedure differed from the federal process (U.S. Code, 1793, sections 14 and 33), resulting in a "heterogenous and unequal mode of administering justice." Not finished, he reminded the senators that the offense Callender committed was not against Virginia but against the United States (an irrelevancy under the Judiciary Act of 1789 governing *federal* procedure, but a few votes might make the difference on any of the articles). Finally, he argued that the text of section 34 of the 1789 act applied to trials only. Pretrial procedure was to be determined by the federal judges. Lee had some justification for this reading of the federal and Virginia statutes. The United States statute was confusing, and federal judges had no body of procedure of their own to follow. State rules conflicted on a multitude of small items, and a federal judge might innocently misapply one state's rules in a different state. What was more, counsel for Callender did not raise the point at the time by asking the judge to amend his order. Hopkinson, arguing earlier on a parallel point, conceded the irregularity but denied the allegation of malicious intent. Lee took another tack: "It was therefore perfectly correct in the court to bestow no attention upon the laws of Virginia concerning the process to be awarded against Callender." Lee carried his aggressive posture into his defense of Chase on the sixth article. Virginia law permitted a suspect of misdemeanor the right to appear at the next session of the court, although he could waive the right by coming to the current session and pleading. In "petty misdemeanors" delay was common, Lee recalled from his own experience in the state's courts, but in serious misdemeanors, particularly libels, it was not. Federal precedent required a speedy trial; the practice was similar in Virginia. Lee's familiarity with his own state's judicial experience governed his assignment to refute these articles for the defense. Counsel for Callender, on the other hand, "slighted" Chase's office by objecting on petty procedural grounds. Lee's thrust at Callender's defense team, following Key, shifted attention from Chase's procedural mistakes. The best defense was an attack upon the opposition—if not aimed at the other litigant, then at the conduct of his case by his counsel. In effect, Lee impeached Callender's counsel.[41]

Luther Martin now rose for the defense. Long a friend and client of Chase, deeply committed to the Federalist party, well versed in political controversy, and long immersed in the cut and parry of courts, Martin was an obvious choice for the defense. Observers noted the ravages of drink upon his features and posture, but no one could deny that he had been present at the creation of the Constitution and could speak with authority upon the intentions of some of the framers. Friendship, ideology, and long practice as an advocate combined to make his the most striking performance at the bar of the Senate. He held back nothing in his sweeping preparatory remarks. He did not respect Jefferson and his party and regarded the impeachment as a political act. High crimes and misdemeanors, in contrast, had to be violations of the law. Even offenses by officials away from their duties should be dealt with in the regular courts or not at all. Lesser offenses, harmless errors, even those violations of statutes resulting in grand jury presentments for drunkenness and swearing, ought to be punished in the normal way and not by impeachment. If any minor breach could lead to impeachment and removal, party animosities would hamstring and topple republican government. People were not perfect, and officials must go about their duties without the continual threat of impeachment and removal by their enemies.[42]

Martin was aware that the dangerous tendency argument did not rest upon the sort of offenses he excluded (harmless errors and idiosyncrasies) and he tried to dismiss the Pennsylvania precedent so important to the managers: "I have not here the proceedings against Judge Addison and therefore it is possible that the Senate of Pennsylvania erected themselves into a court of honor to punish what they might consider breaches of politeness." This was a thorough misreading of *Addison*, reducing it to a case of contempt against the legislature. In fact, the offense was not a breach of privilege of the Senate but against another judge. Martin's next point was to distinguish the precedent entirely for a difference of jurisdiction. "Doth this honorable court sit here to take precedents from the state of Pennsylvania or any other state, however respectable?" Martin bearded the dragon in its den: state precedent in Addison's case was against Chase, and such precedent could not therefore be admitted without endangering his client.[43]

The rest of Martin's closing speech rehabilitated Chase's demeanor on the bench. The counsel consulted his own experience to prove that the judge acted as all judges act. Martin rehearsed Key's and Lee's lament: the Republican bar of Virginia drove the judge to use his power to keep order. Chase was stern, but the crowd of political roughnecks and howlers at the trials required a stern hand. For the better part of three days the rheumy Maryland counselor heaped coals upon the heads of Lewis, Hay, and others who did not treat Chase with respect. Out of this furnace came a defense that would stand against dangerous tendency should the latter test be accepted by the Senate. Chase's actions were not dangerous at all; instead, they rescued his court from anarchy. Without judges of this caliber and character, courts in the republic would flounder and law be flouted.[44]

Robert Goodloe Harper concluded the defense. Though no great friend of Chase, he had settled after 1800 in Maryland and practiced law there. His reputation and steady politics would gain him a Senate seat from Maryland after the War of 1812. There was no sense to this eminently sensible man in denying Chase's bullishness. Martin was Chase's friend and comrade; Harper was hired counsel. He was also one of the most politically astute men in the chamber. He asked the senators to put aside any party animosities they might have (and that Martin may have enflamed). He knew that more than two-thirds of the Senate was Republican, and he beseeched them to lean in the judge's favor "wherever there remains a doubt of guilt." He begged sympathy for "an aged patriot and statesman," reducing Martin's magisterial giant to a doddering veteran "bearing on his head the frost of 70 winters, bowed by infirmities" whose steps were now "hunted from place to place to find indiscretions." Martin's defense had been out of line with the team—his own attachments carrying him away. Harper sounded a more moderate note.[45]

Harper recognized that neither praise nor pity made headway against dangerous tendency. He too must confront it, and conceding as he did Chase's indiscretions meant that he could not defend the judge by denying all errors. How then to limit the damage? Harper's method was to equate dangerous tendency with its weaker cousin, removal upon public will. The attack on Chase became an example of "party spirit," a matter of expediency. There had to be some manifest wrongdoing—but there was none in Chase's case. Differing again with Martin's tactics on the Addison case (for he knew as well as his opponents that state precedent did have an impact upon federal law), Harper found that the Pennsylvania Senate removed Addison for "usurpation of power," a serious offense. With Lloyd's report of the trial in his hand (far more effective than Martin's admission of not reading it), Harper assured the senators that if Addison was guilty in fact, the offense merited removal. There can be no better or more telling evidence of the impact of Addison's case upon Chase's prosecution than this. Harper abandoned the English law, for the senators surrounding him did not regard it as having any weight in impeachment, and turned to the language of American provisions and cases. Had Chase done what Addison purportedly did, there would be no question about conviction, but he was innocent of such imputations.[46]

Harper finished his brief with the specifics of the final two articles. Chase's search for seditious libel in Newcastle was not motivated by a "vindictive spirit of oppression." He had authorized Harper to report that in Baltimore he had meant no offense to "the present administration." Warnings of "tendencies" which Chase admitted he had pronounced did not amount to the kind of vicious slander in which Callender reveled. Chase also conceded to Harper that he tried to persuade Maryland voters to resist the constitutional amendment for universal suffrage. His concern was natural— Maryland politics was his life. Harper noted that the account presented by Nicholson to the Senate did not square with Montgomery's testimony—an inconsistency that Harper seized with avidity. This was a crucial moment for the defense because Chase's words might be regarded as untoward and slanderous. His accusation against universal suffrage was coupled with criticism of the repeal of the 1801 judiciary act. Both, he told the grand jurors, "take away all security for property, and personal liberty." At the time, Chase also warned of "mobocracy" raging in the streets like some rabid animal. Harper's defense here paralleled Addison's: judges had used the grand jury charge to warn of political calamity in the Revolutionary crisis and regularly thereafter. And, Harper observed, Addison's intemperance in address to Pennsylvania grand juries was not one of the offenses for which he was impeached. If an overzealous partisanship in grand jury charges was dangerous, it had brought no bad consequences yet. It was a sound point, and Harper rested on it.[47]

Nicholson resumed the summation for the prosecution on the morning of February 26, 1805. He immediately restated the doctrine of dangerous tendency, for by now the charges against Chase rested upon it. Chase was impeached to "preserve this unity of safety, to avert this common danger" to the impartial administration of justice. Chase's example led to an "invasion" of the courts by "party feeling." Against the "lawyers' insistence" that a crime must be alleged (the prosecution's turn to attack the "lawyers," now identified with Chase's defenders) Nicholson had to be bold. He knew that *misdemeanor* had a specific meaning in the common law and that he had to cut the ground away from this defense. He threw his first shovelful upon those who would "resort to foreign precedents," for there was abundant evidence in America that dangerous acts were impeachable. Violations of the good behavior clause of the Constitution might not be indictable, but they were impeachable. Misdemeanor in Article II, section 4, simply meant misconduct—consonant with Article III, section 1, of the federal Constitution. "When I speak of a misdemeanor, I mean an act of official misconduct," he declared, citing Pickering's conviction. If misdemeanor had its common-law meaning, it would be all but undefinable in a federal impeachment, for there was no federal law of misdemeanor! State codes diverged so widely on misdemeanors as to be unusable as guides. If there were no uniformity, how could anyone know what was impeachable and what not? Was Pickering to be safe in New Hampshire for conduct that was a misdemeanor in South Carolina?[48]

Nicholson gave way to Caesar Rodney, fresh from his prosecution of Shippen. Rodney, a member of Congress from Delaware, was a natural addition to the managers. He was a Republican lawyer from a family whose political services went back to the pre-Revolutionary era. Like Martin, he gave no quarter. He was not sympathetic to Harper's call for humanity and brushed aside Hopkinson's objection to the delay of the impeachment. Chase continued his offensive behavior through 1803, a living refutation of the myth of judicial independence. For Chase, the "inviolability of judges" was an invitation to libel and tyranny, just as it was for a monarch. Indeed, even in England a judge could be removed more easily than his American counterpart. Chase and his defenders crippled the doctrine of popular rule, teaching one more lesson that "the people should watch with a jealous eye over those whom they have entrusted with authority."[49]

For the Delaware advocate, both popular will and dangerous tendency were sufficient technical grounds for an impeachment. The criminal law need not be consulted. First, Rodney raised the popular will theory lampooned by Martin. The lower house of Congress alone could impeach, for it was the "grand jury" of the nation. This gave a new connotation to the word *indictable*, wholly within the scope of legislative jurisprudence. The legislative power to indict was governed only by the Constitution, not by common-law procedure. In impeachments the indictment of Congress "supercedes all other modes." To balance the scope of Congress's original jurisdiction in impeachment, it was limited to officials, whose conviction could bring no more than loss of office and disqualification. The "misdemeanor" named in Article II, section 4, incorporated misconduct. This interpretation also tailored impeachment to fit the provisions in Article IV, section 1, confining judicial tenure to "good behavior." Misbehavior was synonymous with misdemeanor, and impeachment was a proper remedy (and some argued, though Rodney did not, the sole remedy) for aberrant judicial actions. "It makes the constitution consistent with itself, and preserves uniformity throughout all the parts." These were the strongest arguments ever given for popular will removals, but Rodney knew they were not strong enough by themselves.[50]

Rodney still had to demonstrate that Chase's actions amounted to misdemeanors. Using similar reasoning to Nicholson's, Rodney held that there were misdemeanors requiring impeachment that would not be indictable in a regular court. Pickering had committed many, though his defenders argued that madness and resulting inebriation, not criminal intent, motivated the

New Hampshire judge. Rodney found a perfect test in *Addison*. Here was a "stronger" precedent than the political trials of English judges, for it occurred in a republican state. Rodney then read, line and verse, Addison's impeachment articles to the Senate. The judge violated not positive law but "common sense and common manners." Rodney interjected that *Shippen* could be ignored, for Dallas, Shippen's counsel, did not argue that impeachment required an indictable offense. Shippen's offense lay in applying the common law, an error the state senate had found excusable because it was not malicious. Thus Rodney disposed of the most telling precedent against dangerous tendency by reworking it into a support for the prosecution: impeachable offenses were not limited to criminal acts. Pickering's removal proved the same point. The "whole weight of American authority" was on the prosecution side. The "obscure dicta" of English cases, mentioned by Harper and discoursed on by Martin, was irrelevant.[51]

Rodney judged that the worst of all Chase's offenses were violations of the unwritten rules of public office. The judge had admitted the virulence of party into the "calm and tranquil" oasis of a court. Upon this line of reasoning, Rodney advanced into the dangerous tendency test: that the consequence of Chase's conduct was to deny justice to the people. This was the very argument used in *Addison*. Chase set a precedent for other judges as well, a model of partisanship and intemperance in the cause of party. No republic could withstand such body blows against the fair administration of its laws. Chase had to be removed.[52]

Randolph's closing words for the prosecution weakened its case, for just when the managers needed a succinctly reasoned summation, they got a harangue. He even admitted that he had lost his notes—though their absence did not prevent him from outlasting all his colleagues on the floor. Randolph restated dangerous tendency ably enough, but he confused its test with the popular will theory that he, personally, preferred. He assaulted Chase's character, waved English precedent about just enough to undercut the other managers' reliance on *Addison*, and then fell back upon rhetorical devices. He painted Chase as a Lord Jeffries, stalking the king's enemies through the bloody assizes. The danger of Chase's acts was now no longer framed within the scaffolding of a coherent legal doctrine but dumped upon a jerry-built analogy between the Federalist party and the Tories. In 1805 the menace of Federalism was less apparent than in 1799, and this species of bloody-shirt waving did not sway the Senate.[53]

On Friday, March 1, the court reassembled for the judgment of its members: "guilty or not guilty of a high crime or misdemeanor, as charged in the Article of impeachment." Even this formula had occasioned fierce debate behind closed doors. James Bayard plumped for the inclusion of this part of Article II, section 4, of the United States Constitution, while Wright of

Maryland wished to avoid any controversy the additional words might introduce. John Quincy Adams, one of the senators insisting on the inclusion of the formula, had in mind the verdict in Pickering's case. At that time, he had written that the vote, taken without the words *high crimes and misdemeanors*, permitted senators to avoid the reproach of *conscience*. "Some of them knew the *word* [guilty] would stick in their throats." This time, he was unwilling to let the Republicans off so easily. In a letter written after the trial he told his father that the issue was one of great constitutional significance. Forced to vote upon the sufficiency of the charge under the law, as well as on its factuality, senators had second thoughts about the prosecution brief. In particular, the "high crime and misdemeanor" formula underlined the need for proof of "evil intent," which, to Adams and presumably some Republicans, was never satisfactorily established. Giles, for the Republicans, conceded the amendment.[54]

When the vote was taken, it followed party lines—with a few significant exceptions. A handful of Republicans deserted their party on every one of the articles. The closest vote, as Chase's counsel had anticipated, came on article 8. Nineteen Republican senators voted against the judge, but Samuel Mitchell, a New York lawyer and doctor who had managed Pickering's impeachment; James Elliott, a Vermont lawyer; Israel Smith, a Yale graduate and lawyer from Connecticut; John Smith of New York and John Smith of Ohio, both former congressmen who had voted against Pickering at his Senate trial; Stephen Bradley, another Vermont lawyer who had weathered the Federalist seditious libel assaults and voted against Pickering; and John Gaillard of South Carolina, trained in the law in England, sided with the Federalists on every vote. Of the other charges, only articles 3 and 4 received majorities, 18 to 16. No one, not even Giles, voted guilty on article 5, the use of a *capias* against Callender. He also voted not guilty on articles 6 and 7. Abraham Baldwin, a Connecticut Republican who migrated to Georgia at the beginning of the century, also voted not guilty on 2, 4, 5, 6, and 7. Indeed, only Breckinridge of Kentucky, Jeffersonian whip in the upper house, William Cocke of Tennessee, and Benjamin Howland, a Rhode Island farmer, joined Pennsylvania radical "Billy" Maclay to vote guilty on seven of the eight articles.[55]

Undoubtedly a destitute, infirm, and bowed Chase was a more sympathetic figure than a Chase in full cry on the bench. His contribution to the winning of independence, added to the humiliation of the impeachment, might have seemed arguments against his removal. According to John Quincy Adams, Randolph had alienated many Republican senators by his bluster and incompetence. Cocke told Adams that Randolph cost the cause votes (though not his own). The Senate may also have noted that Chase never bullied another judge—merely those defendants, counsel, and the odd juror in his court.[56] The lawyers among the Republican defectors (all but one of them were practicing attorneys), must have recognized the great scope of judicial power in the courtroom. Although Chase was something of a throwback in his view of the judiciary, he was not unique in his manners. *Shippen* had left open the question of how much American judges might draw from common-law courts' procedure.

Richard Ellis has pressed for a political explanation of the Republican split. The moderates, he believes, simply could not permit Randolph and his faction to dominate the party—not with the divisive aftershocks of Yazoo, Louisiana, and neutrality still disturbing the party. The Republican victory was not yet assured for these men, and they feared that a Randolph triumph would leave the party prey to dissolution. Jefferson himself detested the spitefulness of the gangling Virginia congressman and made plain that he did not count the vote on Chase as a test of loyalty to himself. Randolph certainly did his part to alienate these moderates, insisting upon taking a leading role in the trial, which prudence (and lack of preparation) would have cautioned a wiser man against. The truth of Ellis's argument cannot be determined, for despite the split, some moderates voted guilty on some of the articles, and some virulent enemies of Federalism like Giles and James Jackson voted not guilty on some of the articles.[57]

Chase and Randolph staggered away from the trial, in different ways, both broken by the ordeal. Though his family and friends were exuberant at his vindication, Chase was humbled. He never again dashed off a vitriolic political charge for a grand jury or used a courtroom as a forum for his politics. After the trial, ill health and problems with his finances caused him to miss a number of sessions of the highest court, and even when he sat with his brethren, he lacked fire and determination. Randolph, angry and wild, returned to the House chamber with two amendments to the Constitution. He would, he proposed, have senators liable to recall by their legislatures in midterm. What was more, he wished to alter the Article IV of the Constitution to allow the president to remove judges upon a joint address of both houses of Congress. Although the ideas were neither new nor devoid of value—both would reappear in the House before the end of the decade—witnesses regarded his manner as vengeful. He knew that his chance for legislative leadership had slipped away.[58]

Eight days after the *Chase* verdict, John Quincy Adams informed John Adams that the Republicans' frontal attack upon Federalists in the judiciary was over. In its wake was the broken career of Pickering and the bloodied reputation of Chase, but Adams gloated that the precedent was now established that only crimes warranted impeachment. The Massachusetts senator's grandson, Henry Adams, extended the argument: "The acquittal of Chase proved that impeachment was a scarecrow." Both Adamses had erred.

While impeachment did not incorporate popular will or dangerous tendency—perhaps a wise limitation—Chase's acquittal did not erase the lessons of *Pickering, Addison*, and other state legislature removals for incompetence, maladministration, misuse of power, favoritism, and other noncriminal offenses.[59] *Chase* did not overrule *Pickering*, in which an incompetent official, in the absence of alternative forms of discipline and removal, was impeached, convicted, and removed. The cases were distinct. No crimes were alleged against Pickering, but the Senate ordered his removal nonetheless. Nothing in the Chase verdict mentioned *Pickering*; further, the formal record did not connect the two cases. They were related by political concommitance, not by law. The verdict in *Chase* thus distinguished the two cases, leaving *Pickering* in force. One must bear in mind that Chase was not charged with incompetence but with willful violation of his oaths and duties. The managers themselves were thus not asked to link Chase's case to Pickering's, nor was the defense team required to refute that charge. The prosecution knew that incompetence could not be proved, and the defense did not have to fall back upon it to explain Chase's conduct.

Contrary to what Henry Adams, Charles Warren, and other scholars have deduced from the two episodes, *Chase* did not limit impeachable offenses to crimes. That had never been the boundary of impeachment in America. Instead, *Chase* shifted the center of attention for impeachment back to where it had been before *Pickering* (and remained throughout the two federal cases): the state legislatures. While Republicans in Washington, D.C., thought through the meaning of the *Chase* verdict, state lower houses pressed on against suspected malefactors, misusers of power, and corruptionists. Taken together, Congress's hesitancy and the state houses' continued activity determined the real meaning of the *Chase* precedent.

EPILOGUE
AFTER *CHASE*

SEEN IN PROPER PERSPECTIVE, CHASE'S TRIAL CAME NOT AT THE END OF A BRIEF but passionate Republican flirtation with impeachment, but rather concluded a long, sober, and thoughtful process of constitutional experiment. In the former, foreshortened view, impeachment failed. In the latter, one doctrine—impeachment as removal upon any grounds—was rejected and another—dangerous tendency—was found wanting without evidence of malicious intent. Chase's case made an eddy in the law but did not deflect its course. Impeachment had built an impressive record in 170 years of American history, based largely upon its restriction to certain types of offenders and offenses. The measure of its reputation after Chase's acquittal was not Randolph's despairing demand for an alternative—removal by address—but the continuing success of state governments' experience with it in the years immediately following 1805. In these same years Republicans in Washington, D.C., chose not to pursue impeachments, for practical, rather than constitutional reasons.

Chase's acquittal hardly slowed the pace of impeachment for cause in the states. In lower houses the precedent of ferreting out wrongdoing did not die in the wake of the rejection of extreme doctrines. Under older but still vigorous rules of limited culpability, assemblies continued to investigate and impeach upon petitions and complaints from citizens and motions of their own members. Again, the proof that these proceedings followed constitutional rather than Republican doctrines is their dispatch, the relative unanimity of the voting (one way or the other), and the compelling nature of the evidence to the eyes of later scholars. That is, cases that seem flimsy to a modern eye were deemed unpursuable by the lower house, and cases supported by substantial evidence received large majorities for impeachment and conviction or induced the immediate resignation of the accused official.

A brief survey of a number of these cases confirms this conclusion. In 1806 the assembly of South Carolina voted an impeachment against Daniel Doyley, treasurer of the lower division of the state. While in office, Doyley allegedly embezzled and speculated with state funds, and used them to assist his friends' private projects. Doyley, though already voluntarily retired, was still tried for his offenses in 1807, found guilty, and disqualified. The *Blount* precedent was disregarded. Shortly thereafter, separate impeachment proceedings were initiated against Governor Paul Hamilton, William Hasell Gibbes, master in equity for Charleston, John Grimké, judge of the court of common pleas, and two other, lesser officials.[1] Over the same years, justices of the peace were impeached in Massachusetts, Kentucky, and Tennessee. All the cases came to trial, though all but one ended in acquittal. Political differences still led to demands for impeachment, but once again mere partisanship, unpopularity, or unpalatable policies could not be constructed into impeachable offenses.[2] In the Pennsylvania Assembly session of January 1807 there were cries for the impeachment of Governor McKean. He had stood by his judges, refused to make peace with Leib, Duane, and other influential radicals after *Shippen*, and appointed family friends and retainers to office. Leib submitted a resolution for impeachment to the lower house. At first, McKean was not impressed—he continued to veto house bills he thought improper—but by December, his tone had changed. His new conciliatory demeanor seemed to be what, after all, the lower house wanted from him. The house rejected impeachment as its first order of business in January 1808.[3]

Although its impact was not felt so keenly in the states, Chase's acquittal did end, abruptly, an era in national impeachment law. The months of maneuver and weeks of debate culminating in the not guilty verdict raised genuine questions about the limits of official conduct in a republic. One may view the trial as the close of a period of party-conflict-spawned adjustment in the federal government during which relations between the legislative and judicial branches of government had shifted noticeably. In the tug-of-war between Federalists and Republicans, the courts accommodated themselves to party realignment by accepting the repeal of the Judiciary Act of 1801 while the Senate did not succumb to the extreme position of Giles and Randolph.

In the heat of the battle, the language of many Jeffersonians smacked of a more thorough democratic commitment than they, as a party, had embraced in 1801. Misreading this rhetoric, one may easily overestimate how great an impact Chase's case had upon Republican ideology. The eyes of the nation were focused upon the Senate when Chase sat before its bar. The debate ranged widely beyond the confines of impeachment law to include the duties of republican magistrates and judges and the extent to which they might be held accountable to the will of the people. The independence of judges was contested as never before, even at the constitutional conventions. The demand that popular opinion be served was trumpeted—at times more loudly than in the presidential campaigns of 1800 and 1804. Nevertheless, a major obstacle to assigning impeachment a leading role in the rise of democratic politics is the vast diversity of ideology within the Republican congressional leadership. Disagreements among Republicans during the impeachment trials of the 1800s shows this diversity as well as any other area of their political activity. The distance in political opinion between McKean and Duane was far greater than that between McKean and some Federalists in his state. Jeffersonians did not have a unified position on impeachment in part because of this larger ideological diversity. For radicals like Boileau, Duane, Leib, Smilie, and their allies, impeachment of Federalist judges was a democratic step. That is, they intended to make government directly responsible to the people, and involve ordinary people directly in government. Men of this sort were not the leaders of the Republican impeachment campaign on the federal level, however. John Randolph, foremost of these leaders, cannot be called a democrat. Randolph and his conservative friends spoke for a localistic, corporate "voice of the people," not for the grass-roots politics of later years.[4] Somewhere between these extremes, Republican moderates in the Senate voted to acquit Chase, while others actually opposed the impeachment from its inception.

Equally important objections to regarding the impeachment campaign as a step toward democracy lie in the inconsistencies between Jeffersonian ideals and Republican impeachment policies between 1801 and 1805. During the Republicans' struggle for national power, they resisted the tyranny of intrusive government. Too much government, reversing popular votes and curbing the expression of popular sentiments, was supposedly characteristic of Federalist authoritarianism. Republicans preferred a simple and limited government, particularly on the national level. In addition, Jefferson often expressed his long-standing fear of the tyranny of legislatures; a multitude of tyrants was as bad as one. Finally, Jeffersonian Republicanism rejected the loose construction of the Constitution—preferring to utilize only those powers explicitly granted to the federal government. One would expect from them a literal and narrow interpretation of constitutional language such as "high crimes and misdemeanors." When they sought power, the Republicans relied not upon the assistance of overweening government but of responsive and representative local electoral parties. The Jeffersonians' adoption of broad impeachment powers violated these tenets and practices. Impeachment under dangerous tendency or popular will required a very active use of government to investigate, try, and remove officeholders. Impeachment and trial were never the most economical, simple, and limited uses of government, and sweeping impeachment campaigns gave to the legislative branch a mighty weapon against other branches, especially the judiciary. "Republican" impeachment doctrine enlarged the power of the legislature at the expense of every other part of government. Impeachment for dangerous or unpopular conduct was hardly strict construction of Article II, section 4, although with much twisting and turning a case was made for a connection between the two. It is true that Jefferson backed away from Chase's impeachment late in 1804—but, had it not been Randolph who grasped leadership of it, Jefferson might well have pushed harder for the judge's removal.[5]

If the Republicans' impeachment of Chase did not bespeak or grow directly out of a nascent democratization of their party, and in fact contradicted some elements of their notion of representative government, impeachment and democracy still had a distant concordance. The brute fact was that Republicanism was moving toward democratic practices. To defeat the Federalists, the Jeffersonian party had to organize at the local level. The Jeffersonians insisted that popular opposition was legitimate, dissent was beneficial, and rotation in office could be accomplished without overturning government. Competitiveness and publicity brought out the vote. Their party organization spread from office-seeking to demands for liberalization of suffrage laws. While their conduct of politics and their espousal of popular government did not always fit together, they appeared to come together more often as time passed. They portrayed themselves as a party of the people, while the Federalists maintained their image as a party of an aristocratic, arrogant few. Despite the adoption of Republican campaigning techniques by a number of younger Federalists, their party did not accept the democratization of politics. When they were safe from disgruntled voters in tenured judgeships, the Federalists continued to demand submission from those who came before them and independence from outside interference (including interference from other branches of government). Against this Federalist stance, Republican impeachment showed Republican voters that the voice of the people (of course, in reality a faction) was heard by their elected representatives. This was the same affective function—an expression of the accessibility of republican government—that had made impeachment cases popular in the new states. Placed in the context of a burgeoning democratic system, the message of impeachment shifted. The process had not changed but its implications seemed different: the common man could no longer be bullied and harassed by officials; misconduct would be punished and liberty preserved. Nothing had changed, but everything had changed, for impeachment now looked as though it were a democratic tool.

This consideration of the practical value of impeachment raises a practical question: Why did the Jeffersonians let their impeachment campaign against the Federalists falter with Chase's narrow escape? After all, he was not the only target to choose after Pickering. An old, sick patriot, surrounded by victorious Republican enemies, impeached for offenses done half a decade before, was not the best test case of Giles's and Randolph's ideas. And if the Jeffersonian Republicans derived any benefit (as we have suggested above) from "Republican" impeachment, why stop with Chase? Chase was unpopular, partisan, vituperative, and perhaps even guilty of very dangerous conduct on the bench, but sympathy, intraparty politics, and concessions to the discretion of a judge in his court undoubtedly swung opinion among some Republicans in his favor. Why did Republican impeachment not fall upon some other Federalist judge? Marshall oozed anxiety about this in testimony at the Chase trial. Tiptoeing among the political implications of his words, he gave cautious support of prosecution on the fifth and sixth articles (regarding Callender's trial). Harper thought the next victim would be Paterson. But the blow never fell.[6] In the late winter of 1808, Pennsylvania Republicans introduced motions to amend the Constitution to permit direct recall of senators by the states, and to allow Congress to address the president to remove judges but these proposals went nowhere.[7] Why?

In the eighteenth-century context of experimental republicanism, rather than in the early nineteenth-century context of a burgeoning political democracy, impeachment was a practical weapon of new-minted governments against self-interested, disorderly, and arbitrary officials. This interpretation of impeachment law had no place for parties and predated the evolution of standing national parties in this country. In the early 1800s the Republicans adopted impeachment, again for practical reasons. The Addison case, a culmination of earlier Republican thrusts, led to a much more ambitious lunge against the entire supreme court bench of Pennsylvania. While Shippen, Yeates, and Smith awaited their trial, the removal of Pickering gave fair promise that impeachment might shackle the Federalist judiciary. All this time, the late eighteenth-century constitutional doctrine was being stretched, further and further, as Republicans strained the law to reach their opponents. With Chase they simply overreached themselves. No one, and no act, was safe from impeachment, Federalists warned, and there was much truth in their words. Evidently, many Republicans listened. Their motivation—as Americans' had been through the eighteenth century—was practical as much as theoretical, and a glance back at the evolution of impeachment and trial between 1798 and 1805 did offer overwhelming practical reasons for abandoning the two "Republican" impeachment tests.

Impeachments and trials were becoming more spectacular. The unusual crowd at Greenleaf's trial, forcing the senators and the spectators to march from the state house to Faneuil Hall, was a harbinger of the future. Upper houses themselves were increasing in size and the physical distance between the senators and the defendant was growing. At Addison's trial, senators begged both sides to speak up when questioning witnesses. Teams of counselors represented the defendants in major cases. As lower houses began to add fourth and fifth men to the managerial side and to hire outside counsel, the crowd at the bar of the upper house began to overflow the tables and chairs available. In Chase's trial the United States Senate floor was so packed with extra seats that passage among them required acrobatic agility. New galleries were constructed to accommodate the mass of spectators. The sergeant-at-arms gave way to the marshal of the District of Columbia, who brought with him deputies to keep order.[8] Both sides demanded time and space to copy "every word of every witness," a staggering project in itself.[9] The printed record filled two 400-page volumes. In Shippen's case, defense and prosecution final arguments filled more than 300 pages of print. Newspaper coverage of impeachments became regular, and shorthand experts, preparing transcripts for pamphlet and book publication, jostled with newspaper editors in the halls.

The same characteristics that were coming to mark major electoral campaigns—hoopla, press coverage, popular rhetoric preached to the mass of voters—appeared at the trial of impeachments. Arguments to the jury not only resembled, but became, political addresses to the voters. Defenses of personal acts became statements of party principle. In the swelling tide of political orations at these trials, the issues relevant to guilt or innocence were washed away. Conviction was rare in such carnival cases because the objective of proving a charge became less important than the objective of discrediting an entire party. None of these problems arose in more restricted impeachment trials in which prosecution had solid evidence of wrongdoing, evidence the defense had to counter. There was little advantage in rhetorical display and grandstanding at such trials.

An additional practical reason for the fall of Republican impeachment was that trials were getting so long they interfered with normal legislative business. The average trial in the 1780s lasted a day or two. By the 1790s this increased to a week. Shippen's case cost the Pennsylvania Senate a month of mornings. Pickering's and Chase's trials just about immobilized the United States Senate for a similar period. As the basis of the charges became more and more political, the difficulty of proving evil intent, or even evil consequences, grew more complex. More and more witnesses were called. Evidence of all kinds on questions of partisanship and party politics became admissible. This simply could not go on. Impeachment was adopted by the first state governments because it accomplished a delicate task with dispatch. The political trials of the mid-1800s dragged on interminably.

The converse point was also telling: were every incident of bullying, badgering, and sloppy judicial procedure to lead to impeachment and trial, the judicial system would grind to a halt. For fear of impeachment, judges would bear an inhuman burden in every case before them. Delays, with or without removals, would deny justice to litigants. Some line had therefore to be drawn before which error and misdeed on the bench were excusable. Addison and Chase argued that willful error, that is, intentional misconduct, must be an element in defining an impeachable offense. To this, the United States Senate added incapacity, under the *Pickering* rule. Criminality—cause for trial in a regular court—was not a necessary condition. The strength of Chase's defense lay not in his misplaced analogy between impeachment and indictment but in the fact that under the pre-Republician federal guidelines, there was no impeachment without proof of an intention to not only do mischief, but in some way profit or gain by it. In accusations of bribery, corruption, and misuse of power, it was logical for the assembly to assume prior, malicious intent. Maladministration of an office was a gray area. *Chase* showed the difficulty of reading the motive for questionable judicial rulings from evidence of prior partisanship or presumed bias, and the unwillingness of the Senate to substitute tests based upon dangerous tendency or popular will. The motive for bullying a witness and reading incorrect law to the jury might be sincere conviction that the witness was holding back or lying, and that the law was as it seemed to the judge. Chase's acquittal laid down a rule of innocence until proved guilty in such cases. This rule freed the judiciary from the fear of intrusive, carping, and inexpert criticism from the legislature. It was not the "independence" that Chase demanded, but it was enough freedom of action to relieve other judges.

Third and finally, Republicans could see that Chase's was the latest in a progression of impeachments that were reaching higher and higher in government. The defendants of the 1780s were county justices and tax collectors; by 1805 they had been joined by chief justices, governors, and senators. No officeholder, whatever his status, was truly safe from impeachment. The Republicians, who steadily gained command of all three branches, now had the most to fear from impeachment, should their enemies, however momentarily, wrest control of state and federal legislatures. The Republicans' turn on the block might then come, as it did for Harley, Queen Anne's impeacher, when George I ascended. As the War of 1812 approached, Republicans increasingly saw peril in Federalist electoral efforts. Republican self-interest thus dictated a growing aversion to impeachment in Congress.[10]

The Republicans' abandonment of political impeachment—in effect their desertion of dangerous tendency and popular will—ought also to be viewed in a positive way. By acquitting Chase and dropping prosecution of McKean and other unpopular political leaders, moderate and radical Republicans reaffirmed their commitment to limited use of legislative powers. In a republican system, much depends upon the voluntary adherence of politicians to the rules of the game agreed to by the people. Without this, representation becomes meaningless.[11] It is tempting for a majority party in a republican system to seek to use its power to crush opposition. The Federalists had succumbed to this temptation. The Republicans were certainly attracted to it. The notion of impeachable offenses definable by popular will or dangerous tendency as constructed by legislative majorities did not fit the rules of the game laid out in the Constitution, except by tortured construction. Applied with fervor by a majority of sufficient size, such impeachment tactics had no limits. When the Republicans stepped back from impeachment-as-removal, they returned to fairer means of party competition—organization at the local level, publicization of party positions, discipline of party members in the legislature—and let the electorate decide on the removal of the Federalists. They accepted the rules of the game on judicial appointments—permitting those Federalist judges who held tenure for good behavior under the 1789 act to remain unmolested in office. By this decision they also saved impeachment, for, limited to solid cases of willful wrongdoing, it retained its character as a genuine expression of legislative concern for the public interest.

CONCLUSION

THIS BOOK TRACES ACCUSATIONS OF CORRUPTION, MALFEASANCE, INCOMPE-
tence, and criminality among those entrusted with public office. Among
those charged were giants and minor officials. Hamilton, Jefferson, Jay, and
Washington all faced the threat of impeachment, while others, governors,
justices, and scores of lesser officials, actually were brought to trial in upper
houses. Some defendants owed their exposure to the malice of their political
opponents or were sacrificed to public anxiety over events over which they
had no control: scapegoats such as Peter Oliver suffering for allegiance to old
masters. Other defendants probably extorted money or favors, and took or
gave bribes, as charged. Some exceeded their powers, claiming privilege or
justification. The question of the impeachability of their offenses remains
open to this day. Nevertheless, there are lessons we can derive from this
parade of guilty and innocent, prosecutor and defendant.

The first is just what constitutional theorists from the Commonwealthmen to the authors of the *Federalist* agreed: no form of government was safe
from the corruption of its officials, and no set of officers in whatever form of
government would be entirely free from official malfeasance and private
turpitude. In the heady years after the war for independence, Americans
relearned this lesson in impeachment after impeachment. We should remember it ourselves. Whether in a constitutional monarchy and its colonies,
in the republics that emerged from the Revolution, or in our own modern,
sophisticated system of checks and balances, our officeholders are not proof
from temptation. When they fall to it, the entire system of government is
endangered.

The second lesson is more important: under English tutelage and then the
genius of our own experience, the framers of American republicanism created
a tool for dealing with corruption—efficiently, fairly, within the system of
laws. Impeachment and trial did not replace prosecution in the regular courts
but provided an alternative form of investigation, confrontation, and punishment. While the boundaries of impeachable offenses swelled and then
contracted in the first years of our nation, certain acts were always impeachable and others were always protected by law or custom. The constantly
shifting distance between the former and the latter might coax unfounded
impeachment charges from partisans in a competitive two-party system but

never quite allowed parties to abuse the power of impeachment. In recent years we have seen two impeachment efforts that remind us of the uncertainty of these boundaries. The attempt to impeach Justice William O. Douglas for unpopular judicial opinions and unsavory conduct away from the bench failed. The impeachment of President Richard M. Nixon was well on its way to success when the president resigned. He was accused of a variety of misconduct, some criminal, some not indictable at all, which together amounted to a serious breach of his official powers. The lesson is plain: though corruption and malfeasance may be inevitable, they can be curbed. The framers intended to safeguard the republic against the misuse of power with impeachment and trial, and thus far their plan has succeeded.

APPENDIX

ENGLISH PRECEDENT, STATE CASES, AND THE ORIGINS AND EVOLUTION OF FEDERAL IMPEACHMENT LAW

IN HIS FORCEFULLY ARGUED ESSAY ON IMPEACHMENT, RAOUL BERGER TURNED TO English precedent to trace the development of federal impeachment law. His thesis was that the framers of the Constitution had English cases before them "inferably" and relied upon these cases to fashion our own law.[1] To be sure, the origins of this branch of constitutional law lie in the practices of English Parliaments, but the historian must determine those ideas and experiences which actually influenced American constitutionalists. In our preface we warn against the seductive perils of "omniscient" legal history. The danger is not merely academic, the risk of misreading the motivation of historical characters. Recovered legislative intent becomes part of living law, and misplaced attribution of precedent may alter the application of intent. Berger's transformation of the framers' scattered references to English cases into a body of ruling precepts is a tour de force of scholarly omniscience. In the course of it, he mistakes acquaintance for intimate knowledge and illustrations for arguments from authority.

Students of early federal jurisprudence agree that the common law was under fire during the revolutionary era.[2] Much of it survived the attacks of reformers, codifiers, and later realists, but it was never received into the federal Constitution. The drafters of that document were careful to distinguish their efforts from English precedents. When they borrowed from common law, they did so cautiously and explicitly, for example, in the creation of a nonelective judiciary. If they intended to adopt English case law as their guide for federal impeachment, they would have said as much. Did they?

Despite Berger's claim that the framers' basic notions of impeachment "were but reflecting English sentiment," a closer look at the Federalists' and anti-Federalists' words indicates that they used English cases as counterexamples and passing illustrations or miscited the English cases rather than holding them up as ruling law.[3] Typical of the first type of error of attribu-

266

tion was Berger's reference to James Iredell's promise at the North Carolina ratification convention that there would be no federal impeachments based upon charges of giving bad advice to the president.[4] This was a feature of a number of English cases but Iredell was not citing the English cases as precedent. Quite the opposite was true. He was defining by negation—a very different order of argument. He did not need to know much about the English cases to insist they would not be an example here, and he cited no specific English case. On the second mistake: Berger supported James Maclaine's contention to the North Carolina delegates that impeachment did not lie against "petty officers," and to strengthen the argument Berger noted that Maclaine derived his views from a thorough acquaintance with English cases.[5] He quoted Maclaine on the subject: impeachment of inferior officers was a "departure from the usual and well-known practice both in England and America."[6] But Berger, and Maclaine, were wrong about American precedent, as this book makes abundantly clear. They were also wrong about the English law, for fully half of the cases Parliament heard in the seventeenth and eighteenth centuries involved inferior officials or private citizens. Maclaine's notion of English law was mistaken, and reference to it does not support Berger's contention about the framers' knowledgeability in this area.

Berger's use of George Mason's views on "high crimes and misdemeanors" illustrates a third type of error. He noted that Mason borrowed the English formula, or at least had the English formula "in mind."[7] This, even if true, does not establish Mason's acquaintance with the detail of English cases. It will be remembered that Mason had written a very different formula for impeachment into the 1776 Virginia Constitution. Did he master and learn to love English impeachment law between 1776 and 1787—or merely reach for a conventional phrase in the heat of debate?

Fourth, Berger created the illusion of reception by juxtaposing similar English and American readings of the use and consequences of impeachment. He wrote that James Wilson, for example, hoped that impeachment "will seldom happen" and, then, on the next line, that 90 years before, Lord Chancellor Somers told Parliament that impeachment ought seldom to be used.[8] This does not prove that Wilson borrowed anything from Somers. It does suggest that Wilson, a judge, and Somers, a judge, did not care to see wholesale legislative impeachment of the judicial branch. As we have seen, their fears were well founded; Wilson had a brush with impeachment in 1792, and Somers was impeached and tried in 1701.

One final point throws doubt on Berger's thesis: impeachment had just about disappeared from the English constitutional horizon between 1718 and 1786. It was revived for a few treason cases, to prosecute Macclesfield for corruption, and to bring Warren Hastings to brook in 1786, when most of the framers were already versed in state cases and law. Hastings's trial did make an impression in America but it began in 1788, after the federal convention was over. For the framers to have had English cases "before their eyes," they would have had to look back, past their own Revolution and half a century without a noteworthy impeachment in England, to the early years of George I's reign.

The one case in which Berger's view of the influence of English precedent was advanced by counsel, Bayard's and Harper's advocacy of universal impeachment in *Blount*, also proves Berger's thesis wrong. The Senate accepted Dallas's and Ingersoll's argument that the Constitution did not remold English law but deviated from it. Uncertainties in constitutional language were not resolvable by reference to English practices. Although both sides cited English case books, the defense used them to establish the danger and arbitrariness in the English doctrine of universal impeachment. And they prevailed.

Our purpose in this appendix is not to file a brief against Berger's book. That would exacerbate the problem in it—for Berger has written a brief, not a history. Missing from his work is an appreciation of American colonial and state precedents, the latter of which were far more important in influencing federal law than English examples.

If American impeachment law did not depend upon the English experience, where did the framers, and equally important, the next generations of early Republican impeachment proponents, obtain precedent? Throughout the current book we read the story not of borrowing and dependence but of deliberate divergence from English law. After 1775 we find that this distinctiveness was a product of self-conscious republicanism: an attempt to fit parliamentary impeachment (that is to say, impeachment in the lower house and trial in the upper house of a mixed monarchy) into republican systems. As an abstract body of theory (for what experience did Americans have with republican government before 1775?) republicanism did not provide for impeachment. Madison did not find it in his catalogue of ancient republican precedents, and Paine did not uncover it in his ideal republic. The conclusion is inescapable that republican theory did not include impeachment. Colonial experience, however, did. Impeachment was grafted onto republican theory because the first state constitution writers wanted to incorporate impeachment. Their familiarity with impeachment as the tool of the Commons against the crown must have made it attractive in an era of antimonarchical fury, but this in itself was not enough to induce state conventions to adopt it. Pennsylvania, the first state to adopt impeachment, had its own colonial impeachment precedent, and the connection between the two was no accident. All except one state had some colonial brush with impeachment before they adopted it, and all but one state that did not adopt it were free of colonial cases. A mixture of earlier colonial experience and perceived British precedent led to American incorporation of impeachment law. The actual shape of that state law shows great and deliberate differences from British law which correspond precisely to the outlines of colonial experience. That is, when state law on impeachment differed from English law the difference always and easily could be explained by colonial precedent. We already have explored this point in some detail.

The impeachment law promulgated in 1787 at the federal convention copied and refined the state law; this is clear in chapter 6. English references were window dressing or illustration by negation. Once the federal government was established, its courts upheld the dictum that federal law was supreme over state law in cases of conflicting interpretation of the federal constitution,[9] but this was not held to mean that the federal lawmakers must close their eyes to effective state law, useful provisions of state constitutions, or state precedent on matters coming before Congress when the jurisdiction of the two governments was "corresponding." Corresponding concerns of both governments included impeachment. Both federal and state governments could remove their own officials. Neither government could deny the other the right to discipline its officeholders. They could, if they wished, borrow from each other relevant notions of impeachable offenses and procedure at trial without raising questions of delegated or reserved powers. This had been true in the series of cases leading to Chase's trial—cases unlike those in England and very close in time and place to the January 1805 session of Congress.

Berger overlooks the frequency and effectiveness of federal imitation of state law when the two governments regarded a subject common to both. The Judiciary Act of 1789 provided that criminal procedure in the federal district courts was to conform to the procedure of the state in which the district court happened to sit. This was an area of corresponding jurisdiction—for both federal and state courts had to establish court procedure—and Congress simply borrowed the states' existing rules.[10] When the federal courts were called to adjudicate questions which also interested states, and state supreme courts had already rendered decisions on these questions, the federal courts on occasion took the earlier state court rulings into account. One example of this sort of case involves the separation of powers. Disputes over the duties of the respective branches were common in both state and federal governments early in their history (and remain so). The reasoning in one crucial early decision on separation of powers, *Marbury v. Madison* (1803), probably rested in part upon earlier state decisions on similar issues.[11] State constitutions were early testing grounds for later federal constitutional amendments in areas of corresponding jurisdiction. The federal bill of rights was preceded by and modeled upon a number of states' bills of rights.[12] Madison, who wrote the original amendments, was primarily influenced by the Virginia

Declaration of Rights.[13] So, too, in later years, federal amendments on prohibition and female suffrage were influenced by earlier state laws and constitutional provisions on these subjects.[14] Finally, on numerous occasions, Congress sought information on the operation of state laws before framing its own programs on subjects of mutual concern.[15]

The borrowing of precedent on corresponding interests has benefited both state and federal government. There is nothing binding about this exchange of ideas; instead, their relative utility determined whether they would be adopted by the borrower.[16] This was particularly true in the earliest period of the federal government, for there was little substantive or procedural federal law to guide Congress, while the states had been in operation for a decade and a half and had learned much. The impact of the states' experience was felt to good purpose at the federal constitutional convention, and the first federal congressmen brought the influence of state practices with them to New York City. One must remember that state government was far more influential and commanded far greater loyalty in those days than it does today. John Jay, for example, resigned his chief justiceship to return to state government. When Oliver Ellsworth left, five years later, Adams had great difficulty finding a replacement. As the years have passed—especially since the ratification of the Fourteenth Amendment—the area of exclusive state jurisdiction has shrunk and the purview of the federal government has grown. The sizes of their corresponding jurisdictions have expanded, however, as the roles of both governments have grown. Both federal and state government exercise more intrusive powers today than ever before. Borrowing in this area has increased. The first Congresses' use of early state impeachment precedent, seen in the light of modern congressional borrowing in areas of corresponding jurisdiction, appears natural and legitimate. There is no reason to assume that seventeenth-century English precedents weighed more heavily with the impeachers of Pickering and Chase than the immediate effects of Addison's and Shippen's cases.

NOTES

Abbreviations and Short Titles

MANUSCRIPT AND RECORD DEPOSITORIES

Ct	Connecticut State Library, Hartford
G-Ar	Georgia State Department of Archives and History, Atlanta
GHi	Georgia Historical Society, Savannah
Gu	University of Georgia Library, Athens
Ky	Kentucky State Archives, Frankfort
LC	Library of Congress, Washington, D.C.
M	Massachusetts State Library, Boston
M-Ar	Massachusetts State Library, Archives Division
MHi	Massachusetts Historical Society, Boston
Me-Ar	Maine State Archives, Maine State Library, Augusta
Nh	New Hampshire State Library, Concord
Nh-Ar	New Hampshire State Department of Archives and Records, Concord
NhHi	New Hampshire Historical Society, Concord
Nc-Ar	North Carolina State Archives, Raleigh
Nj	New Jersey State Library, Archives and History, Trenton
PHi	Historical Society of Pennsylvania, Philadelphia
PPL	Library Company of Philadelphia
Sc-Ar	South Carolina State Archives, Columbia
ScHi	South Carolina Historical Society, Charleston
T-Ar	Tennessee State Archives, Nashville
V	Virginia State Library, Richmond

MANUSCRIPTS

Diary of Adams

L. H. Butterfield et al., eds., *The Diary and Autobiography of John Adams*, 4 vols. (Cambridge, Mass., 1961)

Papers of Adams

Robert J. Taylor et al., eds., *Papers of John Adams* (Cambridge, Mass., 1977-)

Works of Adams

Charles Francis Adams, ed., *The Works of John Adams*, 10 vols. (Boston, 1850-1856)

Memoirs of Adams

Charles Francis Adams, ed., *The Memoirs of John Quincy Adams*, 12 vols. (Philadelphia, 1874-1877)

Papers of Hamilton

Harold C. Syrett et al., eds., *The Papers of Alexander Hamilton*, 26 vols. (New York, 1961-1981)

Papers of Jefferson

Julian P. Boyd et al., eds., *The Papers of Thomas Jefferson* (Princeton, 1950-)

Writings of Jefferson
(ed. Ford)

Paul L. Ford, ed., *The Writings of Thomas Jefferson*, 10 vols. (New York, 1892-1899)

Writings of Jefferson
(ed. Bergh and Lipscomb)

A. E. Bergh and A. A. Lipscomb, eds., *The Writings of Thomas Jefferson*, 20 vols. (Washington, D.C., 1903)

Papers of Madison

William T. Hutchinson et al., eds., *The Papers of James Madison*, vols. 1-7 (Chicago, 1962-1971), and Robert A. Rutland et al., eds., *The Papers of James Madison*, vols. 8 and after (Chicago and Charlottesville, 1973-)

Writings of Madison

Gaillard Hunt, ed., *Writings of James Madison*, 9 vols. (Washington, D.C., 1900-1910)

Papers of Marshall

Herbert A. Johnson et al., eds., *The Papers of John Marshall* (Chapel Hill, 1974-)

LEGISLATIVE RECORDS

Annals of Cong

The Debates and Proceedings in the Congress of the United States, 42 vols. (Washington, D.C., 1834-1856)

CJ

Journals of the House of Commons (England)

Cont Cong

Worthington C. Ford et al., eds., *Journals of the Continental Congress*, 34 vols. (Washington, D.C., 1904-1937)

Elliot, *Debates*

Jonathan Elliot, ed., *Debates in the Several State Conventions. on the Adoption of the Federal*

	Constitution, 4 vols., 2d ed. (Philadelphia, 1836)
Farrand, *Records*	Max Farrand, ed., *Records of the Federal Convention*, 4 vols., rev. ed. (New Haven, 1966)
Ga House	Journal of the Georgia State House of Representatives, G-Ar
Ga Senate	Journal of the Georgia State Senate, G-Ar
Hatsell, *Precedents*	John Hatsell, comp., *Precedents of Proceedings in the House of Commons, with Observations*, 4 vols. (London, 1818)
Jefferson, *Manual*	Thomas Jefferson, *Manual of Parliamentary Practice for Use of the Senate of the United States* [1797] (Washington, D.C., 1828)
Ky House	*Journal of the Kentucky House of Representatives*
Ky Senate	*Journal of the Senate of Kentucky*
LJ	*Journals of the House of Lords* (England)
Md Arch	William H. Browne et al., eds., *Archives of Maryland*, 72 vols. (Baltimore, 1883–1972)
Mass Gen Ct	Journal of the Assembly of the General Court of Massachusetts Bay, M-Ar
Mass House	Journal of the Honorable House of Representatives of . . . Massachusetts Bay
Mass Senate	Journal of the Senate of Massachusetts Bay, M-Ar
Mass Sup Ct	Records of the Superior Court of Judicature and Supreme Judicial Court of Massachusetts, Suffolk County Court House, Boston
NH House	Journal of the House of Representatives of New Hampshire, Nh-Ar
NH Senate	Journal of the Senate of New Hampshire, Nh-Ar
NH Sess	Sessions Papers of the New Hampshire State Assembly, Nh-Ar
NHSP	Nathaniel Bouton et al., eds., *State Papers, Documents and Records Relating to the State of New Hampshire*, 33 vols. (Concord, 1874–1915)
NJ Council	*Journal of the Proceedings of the Legislative Council of New Jersey*
NJ Sess	Sessions Papers of the Assembly of New Jersey, Nj
NJ Assembly	*Votes and Proceedings of the General Assembly of New Jersey*

NCCR	William L. Saunders, ed., *The Colonial Records of North Carolina*, 10 vols. (Raleigh, 1886–1890)
NC House	*Journal of the House of Commons of North Carolina*
NC Senate	*Journal of the Senate of North Carolina*
NCSR	Walter Clark, ed., *The State Records of North Carolina*, 24 vols. (Goldsboro, N.C., 1892–1905) [includes *NCCR* as vols. 1–10]
Pa Arch	Samuel Hazard et al., eds., *Pennsylvania Archives* (Philadelphia, 1852–1935)
Pa Council	*Minutes of the Provincial Council of Pennsylvania from the Organization to the Termination of the Proprietary Government* (Philadelphia, 1852–1853)
Pa Assembly	*Minutes of the General Assembly of the State of Pennsylvania*
Pa Votes	Gertrude MacKinney et al., eds., *Votes and Proceedings of the House of Representatives of the Province of Pennsylvania*, in *Pa Arch*, 8th series (Philadelphia, 1931–1935)
Plumer, *Memorandum*	Everett S. Brown, ed., *William Plumer's Memorandum of Proceedings in the United States Senate, 1803–1807* (New York, 1923)
Sources and Documents	William F. Swindler, ed., *Sources and Documents of U.S. Constitutions*, 12 vols. (Dobbs Ferry, N.Y., 1972–1980)
SC House	Journal of the South Carolina State House of Assembly, SC-Ar
SC Senate	Journal of the South Carolina State Senate, SC-Ar
Stats at Large	Danby Pickering et al., comp., *The Statutes at Large* [G.B] 109 vols. (Cambridge and London, 1762–1869)
Tenn House	*Journal of the House of Representatives of Tennessee*
Tenn Senate	*Journal of the Senate of Tennessee*
Tenn Sess	Sessions Papers of the House of Representatives of Tennessee, T
Thorpe, *Constitutions*	Francis N. Thorpe, ed., *The Federal and State Constitutions*, 7 vols. (Washington , D.C., 1909)

US Stats · Richard Peters, ed., *The Public Statutes at Large of the United States of America, from the Origin of the Government in 1789 to March 1845* (Boston, 1850)

Va House · *Journal of the Virginia House of Delegates*

Vt Assembly · *Journal of the Proceedings of the Vermont General Assembly*

VtSP · *State Papers of Vermont*, 9 vols. (Rutland, 1918–1958)

Vt Council · E. P. Walton, ed., *Records of the Governor and Council of the State of Vermont*, 8 vols. (Montpelier, 1873–1900)

Trial Records

Hamilton, *Shippen* · William Hamilton, ed., *Report of the Trial and Acquittal of Edward Shippen, Chief Justice, and Jasper Yeates and Thomas Smith* . . . (Lancaster, Pa., 1805)

Hogan, *Trials* · Edmund Hogan, ed., *The Pennsylvania State Trials* (Philadelphia, 1794)

Howell, *State Trials* · T. B. Howell, comp., *A Complete Collection of State Trials* [of England] 33 vols. (London, England, 1816–1826)

Lloyd, *Addison* · *The Trial of Alexander Addison . . . On An Impeachment . . . Before the Senate of the Commonwealth of Pennsylvania, Taken in Shorthand by Thomas Lloyd* (Lancaster, Pa., 1803)

Smith, *Trial of Chase* · *The Trial of Samuel Chase . . . Before the Senate of the United States, taken in Shorthand by Samuel H. Smith and Thomas Lloyd*, 2 vols. (Washington, D.C., 1805)

Wharton, *Blount* · *The Impeachment of William Blount*, in Francis Wharton, ed. and comp., *State Trials of the United States during the Administrations of Washington and Adams* (Philadelphia, 1849)

JOURNALS

AHR · *American Historical Review*

MHM · *Maryland Historical Magazine*

NCHR · *North Carolina Historical Review*

PMHB · *Pennsylvania Magazine of History and Biography*

VMHB	*Virginia Magazine of History and Biography*
WMQ	*William and Mary Quarterly*, 3d series

SECONDARY SOURCES

Bailyn, *Ideological Origins*	Bernard Bailyn, *The Ideological Origins of the American Revolution* (Cambridge, Mass., 1967)
Berger, *Impeachment*	Raoul Berger, *Impeachment: The Constitutional Problems* (New York, 1974)
Blackstone, *Commentaries*	William Blackstone, *Commentaries on the Laws of England*, 4 vols. (Cambridge, England, 1759–1765)
Chapin, *Treason*	Bradley Chapin, *The American Law of Treason, Revolutionary and Early National Origins* (Seattle, Wash., 1964)
Ellis, *Jeffersonian Crisis*	Richard E. Ellis, *The Jeffersonian Crisis, Courts and Politics in the Young Republic* (New York, 1974)
Goebel, *Supreme Court*, 1	Julius Goebel, Jr., *The History of the Supreme Court of the United States*, vol. 1: *Antecedents and Beginnings to 1801* (New York, 1971)
Haskins, *Supreme Court*, 2, pt. 1	George Lee Haskins, *The History of the Supreme Court of the United States*, vol. 2: *Foundations of Power: John Marshall, 1801–1815*, pt. 1 (New York, 1981)
Haw, *Chase*	James Haw et al., *Stormy Patriot, The Life of Samuel Chase* (Baltimore, 1980)
Johnson, *Supreme Court*, 2, pt. 2	Herbert A. Johnson, *The History of the Supreme Court of the United States*, vol. 2, pt. 2 (New York, 1981)
Roberts, *Responsible Government*	Clayton Roberts, *The Growth of Responsible Government in Stuart England* (Cambridge, England, 1966)
Shipton, *Harvard Graduates*	Clifford K. Shipton, ed., *Sibley's Harvard Graduates*. 16 vols. (Boston and Cambridge, 1873–1975)
Smith, *Appeals*	Joseph H. Smith, *Appeals to the Privy Council* (New York, 1950)
Walters, *Dallas*	Raymond Walters, *Alexander James Dallas, Lawyer, Politician, Financier, 1759–1817* (New York, 1943)
Wood, *American Republic*	Gordon S. Wood, *The Creation of the American Republic, 1776–1787* (New York, 1972)

PART I, INTRODUCTION

1. Discussion of the earliest English impeachment precedents can be found in Colin G. C. Tite, *Impeachment and Parliamentary Judicature in Early Stuart England* (London, 1974); Berger, *Impeachment*, 1-102; Clayton Roberts, "The Law of Impeachment in Stuart England: A Reply to Raoul Berger," *Yale Law Journal*, 84 (1975), 1419-39; and, generally, Allen H. Horstman, "Justice and Peers: the Judicial Activities of the Seventeenth-Century House of Lords" (Ph.D. diss., University of California, Berkeley, 1977). Impeachment precedent from the journals of both houses is conveniently collected in Hatsell, *Precedents* (hereafter cited in this section as Hatsell).

Impeachment, involving the participation of the Lords in a trial, was distinct from a bill of attainder, a conviction by legislative fiat. In an attainder, the accused was "reputed, judged and taken, as guilty" in the lower house; the Lords had only to give their assent to the bill. The lands and goods of the accused were forfeited to the crown. There was no requirement that the accused participate in any way, and attainder often fell upon traitors already dead in the field. If present in Parliament, the suspect might be asked to exculpate himself, but nothing in law guaranteed him either the time or the ear of Parliament to make a defense. See, for example, Mortimer's case (Hatsell, 4: 85, and Blackstone, *Commentaries*, 4: 373 ff.). Unlike impeachment, whose punishment was determined and executed by order of the Lords, the king always had to agree to an attainder and his officers carried out its punishment. The lower house could also pass "bills of pains and punishments" augmenting the sentence given defendants already tried in regular courts. The defendant went unheard in these proceedings. In bills of attainders and bills of pains and penalties, the majority of the Commons, and the Lords, along with the king, all had to agree to the punishment of defendants. See T. F. T. Plucknett, *A Concise History of the Common Law*, 5th ed. (Boston, 1956), 205, and Hatsell, 4: 103.

2. Roberts, "Law of Impeachment," 1438-39. Berger and Roberts disagree on the liberties the seventeenth-century Parliaments took with the formulation of charges. Roberts denies that the Lords allowed the Commons to make an action treasonous retrospectively in some form of ex post facto legislation or that *high crimes and misdemeanors* merely meant political offenses. The accused was always suspected of an illegal act, if not in the treason statute of 25 Edw. III (*Stats at Large*, 2: 50-53) then at common law, and if not of a treason, then of some other illegal act signified by the term *high crime and misdemeanor*. The colonists seem to have understood the necessity that the charge be one of illegal action, not merely unpopularity or political activities contrary to their own preferences. In addition to *CJ* and *LJ* and Hatsell, references to the seventeenth-century English cases can be traced in Roberts, *Responsible Government*.

3. For example, Michael De la Pole's case, 1387, Hatsell, 4: 57-58.

4. George Petyt, *Lex Parliamentaria, or A treatise of the Law & Customs of the Parliaments of England* (London, 1689), 67-68.

5. Bennet's case, April 1621, Hatsell, 4: 131-32; *CJ*, 1: 580-88, especially the comment by Sir Francis Seymor, April 20, 1621, on 583.

6. Scroggs's case, 1681, Hatsell, 4: 128, 157-58; Howell, *State Trials*, 7: 488 and after.

7. The Bishops' case, 1641, Hatsell, 4: 146.

8. Mainwaring's case, 1628, Hatsell, 4: 136. On Sacheverell, see n. 21 below. Impeachments of commoners were almost always for misdemeanors (Matthew Hale,

The History of the Common Law of England [1713], ed. Charles M. Gray [Chicago, 1971], 35).

9. Drake's case, 1660, Hatsell, 4: 147–49.

10. Blair et al.'s cases, 1689, Hatsell, 4: 252.

11. Berkley's case, 1641, Hatsell, 4: 145–46, 163; Howell, *State Trials*, 1: 603.

12. As in Lord Mordaunt's case, 1666, Hatsell, 4: 224–27.

13. 12 & 13 W. c. 3, sec. 3 (1700), *Stats at Large*, 10: 362.

14. Howell, *State Trials*, 8: 236–337.

15. Tite, *Impeachment*, 7.

16. Roberts, "Law of Impeachment," 1433. On the 1620s, see Conrad Russell, *Parliaments and English Politics, 1621–1629* (Oxford, England, 1979), 103–18, 198–202. On Clarendon's case, see Howard Nenner, *By Colour of Law, Legal Culture and Constitutional Politics in England, 1660–1689* (Chicago, 1977), 133.

17. *Priviledges and Practice of Parliaments in England* (London, 1640), 45.

18. John Selden, *Of the Judicature in Parliaments* (London, 1681), 21–31.

19. Roberts, *Responsible Government*, 284.

20. Howell, *State Trials*, 14: 234–349.

21. Geoffrey Holmes, *The Trial of Doctor Sacheverell* (London, 1973), 88–89, 100–01, 112–13, 130–31, 144–45, 154–55, 214–15, 224–25, 228–29.

22. Oxford et al.'s cases, Howell, *State Trials*, 15: 993, 1007, 1013–44, 1048 (1715). Oxford's enemies did not rest with the Tory's near escape (see Richard West, *A Discourse Concerning Treasons and Bills of Attainder* [London, 1717], 2–8).

23. Lord Derwentwater et al.'s cases, Howell, *State Trials*, 15: 762–892 (1717); Lord Lovat's case, Howell, *State Trials*, 18: 529–857 (1746).

24. Lord Macclesfield's case, Howell, *State Trials*, 16: 767–1402 (1725).

25. For example, Mordaunt's case, 1666, Hatsell, 4: 224.

26. Mordaunt's case, 1666, Hatsell, 4: 167.

27. On "Will's" alehouse and other political gossip shops, see Robert Latham and William Matthews, eds., *The Diary of Samuel Pepys: New and Complete Transcription* (Berkeley and Los Angeles, 1970–76), 1: 5, n. 6; 4: 31–32. John Starkey's newsletter, an example of an unofficial parliamentary journal sent out from London during the winter of 1671–72, is periodically cited in Caroline Robbins, ed., *The Diary of John Milward, Esq., Member of Parliament for Derbyshire, September, 1666 to May, 1668* (Cambridge, England, 1938). Seventeenth-century written accounts of impeachment procedure appeared in John Rushworth, *Historical Collections*, 6 vols. (London, 1721 [orig. publ. 1659]), and Selden, *Of the Judicature in Parliaments*, 17–33, 63, 111. Rushworth and Selden could be found in libraries at Harvard and Yale, and in private libraries in Philadelphia, New York City, Charleston, and Cambridge, Massachusetts, as well as throughout Virginia, according to H. Trevor Colbourn, *The Lamp of Experience: Whig History and the Intellectual Origins of the American Revolution* (New York, 1974), 200–32, and William H. Bryson, *Census of Law Books in Colonial Virginia* (Charlottesville, 1978), 73, 74.

28. Giles Jacob, *A New Law-Dictionary*, 5th ed. (London, 1744); also L. Kinvin Wroth and Hiller B. Zobel, "Editorial Note on the Case of *Field v. Lambert*," in L. H. Butterfield et al., eds., *The Earliest Diary of John Adams* (Cambridge, Mass., 1966), 86, n. 15; Thomas Wood, *An Institute of the Laws of England*, 7th ed. (London, 1745), 475; Hale, *History of the Common Law of England*, 35.

29. Some warning on the analysis of the transmission of precedent in the seventeenth century is nevertheless in order. The modern scholar, with a brief glance at the *CJ* or Howell's *State Trials*, first published in the nineteenth century, will learn more about specific charges, procedures, and legal arguments in seventeenth-century En-

glish impeachments than any American legislator alive at the time was ever likely to know. Because knowledge of the details of English charges and defenses cannot with any certainty be traced into American jurisdictions, reference to English precedent in discussion of seventeenth-century American cases must be advanced with caution. On the other hand, there can be no doubt that oral transmission of the law, combined with transportation of fragments of written law, did begin as early as the first settlements. See Julius Goebel, Jr., "King's Law and Local Custom in Seventeenth-Century New England," *Columbia Law Review*, 31 (1931), 417, and George L. Haskins, "A Problem in the Reception of the Common Law in the Colonial Period," *University of Pennsylvania Law Review*, 97 (1949), 842–53.

30. For the Massachusetts law consult *An Abridgement of the Laws in Force and Use in Her Majesty's Possessions* (London, 1704), "New England," 14. On Pennsylvania see "Penn's Charter of Liberties (1682)," in Thorpe, *Constitutions*, 5: 3015. The meaning of impeachment in general (that is, as a synonym for indictment) is discussed in Mary P. Clarke, *Parliamentary Privilege in the American Colonies* (New Haven, 1943), 39–43, and *Black's Law Dictionary*, 4th rev. ed. (St. Paul, Minn., 1968), 886.

31. On the Cary affair, see *NCCR*, 1: 779–99. The assembly acts for preserving the peace and bonding Cary to the peace were enclosed in a message from Spotswood to the Lords of Trade in July 1711. The involved maneuvering of all the parties is briefly recounted in Hugh T. Lefler and William Powell, *Colonial North Carolina— A History* (New York, 1973), 195–97. The term *impeachment of high crimes and misdemeanors*, supposedly used by the lower house, was reported by Hyde in a letter to Spotswood requesting capture of Cary (*NCCR*, 1: 806–07). Despite the assembly's words, Hyde regarded its action as an address to him to imprison and then try Cary.

32. *East Jersie Governor and Councill Record, 1682–1703* (Jersey City, 1872), 96.

33. SC House, 482 (February 7, 1727), 561–62 (August 3, 1727), 569 (August 4, 1727). Middleton told the lower house that Allen could not issue a writ of habeas corpus to someone confined upon a charge of high treason as Smith had been—a correct reading of the habeas corpus statutes. The incident is mentioned in Jack P. Greene, *The Quest for Power, The Lower Houses of Assembly in the Southern Royal Colonies, 1689–1776* (Chapel Hill, 1963), 215–16, along with a number of other South Carolina assembly investigations. The assembly tried to arrest Allen for contempt while he sat in the council. In the melee that ensued, their messenger was thrown out of the room. See Richard P. Sherman, *Robert Johnson, Proprietary and Royal Governor of South Carolina* (Columbia, S.C., 1966), 67–68.

34. In 1692 Maryland Governor Lionel Copley suspended councillor Thomas Lawrence for diverse, unspecified "high crimes and misdemeanors" (David W. Jordan, "The Royal Period of Colonial Maryland, 1689–1715" [Ph.D. diss., Princeton University, 1966], 112–13). Another example: New York Governor Cosby "deposed" Chief Justice Lewis Morris in 1733; see William Livingston, *Review of the Military Operations in North America* . . . (London, 1757), 17. These were typical, if not common, occurrences.

35. Thomas Hutchinson, "Charge to the Grand Jury, 3 Geo. III (1768)," in Samuel H. Quincy, ed., *Reports of Cases* (Boston, 1861), 267–68. See also discussion in the text at chap. 3, n. 20, on Shinner's case. The "normal" channels for removal or punishment for royal officers were very often used, according to Chapin, *Treason*, 8 and passim.

36. Bernard Bailyn, *The Origins of American Politics* (New York, 1968), 63.

37. *Diary of Adams*, 3: 300. On early colonial assumptions about the rights of assemblies see Alden T. Vaughan, *American Genesis: Captain John Smith and the Founding of Virginia* (Boston, 1975), 116–17, and Richard S. Dunn, *Puritans and*

Yankees: The Winthrop Dynasty of New England (New York, 1971), 24.
38. Clarke, *Parliamentary Privilege*, 60.
39. Nenner, *By Colour of Law*, xiv, 23, 82-83, 88-89, 132-33, 136.

CHAPTER 1

1. Jon Kukla, "Political Institutions in Virginia, 1619-1690" (Ph.D. diss., University of Toronto, 1979), 81.
2. Bacon's case, 1620, *CJ*, 1: 554, 563, 594-95, 604; Buckingham's case, *CJ* 1: 835, 841, and after.
3. "The Mutiny in Virginia, 1635," *VMHB*, 1 (1894), 416-24, and Robert Beverley, *The History and Present State of Virginia*, ed. Louis B. Wright (Chapel Hill, 1947), 60, are anti-Harvey, while "Account of the Mutiny, etc., of the Virginians," *VMHB*, 8 (1901), 302-06, written by Harvey's secretary, excoriated the accusers of Harvey. William Keith, *The History of the British Plantations in America... Part I* (London, 1738), 144, first referred to the incident as an impeachment. J. Mills Thornton III, "The Thrusting Out of Governor Harvey," *VMHB*, 76 (1968), 22, and Thomas J. Wertenbaker, *Virginia under the Stuarts, 1607-1688* (Princeton, 1914), 65-68, as well as Kukla, discuss the political issues involved.
4. Kukla, "Political Institutions," 91-92.
5. "Declaration of Sir John Harvey," *VMHB*, 1 (1894), 425-30; "The Mutiny in Virginia, 1635," ibid., 416-24; H. R. McIlwaine, ed., *Minutes of the Council and General Court of Colonial Virginia, 1622-1632, 1670-1676* (Richmond, 1924), 481; "The Virginia Planters versus Governor General John Harvey" (1635), Sir John Bankes MSS, 54/23, Bodley Library, Oxford. Harvey reported that the dissidents physically abused him. In Mathews's account, it was Harvey who struck the first blow—a powerful thump upon the shoulder of Councillor Menefee (or Minifee) while the governor raged against the entire roomful of councillors. Both Harvey and Mathews were trying to convince the authorities in England that the other side had struck the first blow. The burgesses' official *Journal* for this year is lost.
6. Harvey was able to quash the indictment, and he returned to his Virginia office in 1636. See H. R. McIlwaine, ed., *Journal of the House of Burgesses of Virginia, 1619-1658/1659* (Richmond, 1915), xxxv, and Wertenbaker, *Virginia under the Stuarts*, 78-79. The concept of the "Ancient domain" of the king is discussed in Julius Goebel, Jr.'s introduction to Smith, *Appeals*. One might compare the actions of the burgesses, "without precedent" in this situation, to the actions of the First Continental Congress in 1774. See David Ammerman, "The British Constitution and the American Revolution: A Failure of Precedent," *William and Mary Law Review*, 17 (1975), 473-501.
7. Charles M. Andrews, *The Colonial Period of American History*, rev. ed. (New Haven, 1964), 2: 55.
8. *Records of the Colony of Rhode Island and Providence Plantations in New England*, ed. John Russell Bartlett (Providence, 1856-65), 1: 361, 363-64.
9. Carroll T. Bond, "Review of the *Archives of Maryland*, LVII," *MHM*, 36 (1941), 345; George B. Scriven, "Maryland Medicine in the Seventeenth Century," *MHM*, 57 (1962), 33; Louis Dow Scisco, "Captain Robert Morris of Ratcliffe Manor," *MHM*, 38 (1943), 332-34; *Md Arch*, 2: 166-67.
10. Spiller's case, *CJ*, 1: 550, 652. On Bristol's failure to impeach Clarendon in 1663, see Allen Horstman, "Justice and Peers" (Ph.D. diss., University of California, Berkeley, 1977), 355.
11. *Md Arch*, 2: 158-67. Mary Patterson Clarke, *Parliamentary Privilege in the American Colonies* (New Haven, Conn., 1943), 18-19, and Charles M. Andrews, *The*

Colonial Period of American History, 2: 325–76, discuss constitutional conditions in Maryland in this period.

12. *Md Arch*, 2: 169–72.

13. "Maryland Rent Rolls," *MHM*, 20 (1925), 185; Donnell MacClure Owings, "Private Manors, An Edited List," *MHM*, 33 (1938), 330; Henry Hollyday, "The Hollyday Family," *MHM*, 26 (1931), 167–68; Alice L. L. Ferguson, "The Susquehannock Fort on Piscataway Creek," *MHM*, 36 (1941), 3–5; Matthew Page Andrews, *Tercentenary History of Maryland* (Chicago, 1925), 1: 297–300.

14. *Md Arch*, 2: 485–86.

15. *Md Arch*, 2: 494, 503–04; Michael G. Kammen, "The Causes of the Maryland Revolution of 1689," *MHM*, 55 (1960), 324–25. Trueman's pardon is in *Md Arch*, 15: 182.

16. Louis Dow Scisco, "Baltimore County Records," *MHM*, 25 (1930), 258–61; 25 (1931), 228; 27 (1932), 123–27; *Md Arch*, 2: 490–91.

17. *Md Arch*, 7: 334. The political background of this episode is traced in Susan Rosenfeld Falb, "Advice and Ascent: The Development of the Maryland Assembly, 1635–1689" (Ph.D. diss., Georgetown University, 1976), 167–71.

18. *Md Arch*, 7: 335, 348, 354–55, 357, 370, 379. On the laws relating to riots and Indians see Joseph H. Smith and Philip A. Crowl, eds., *Court Records of Prince George's County, Maryland, 1696–1699*, American Legal Records Series (Washington, D.C., 1964), 9: xlii, liii, lx.

19. *Md Arch*, 7: 380, 386, 513, 558, 559, 564, 591.

20. On More, see Gary B. Nash, "The Free Society of Traders and the Early Politics of Pennsylvania," *PMHB*, 89 (1965), 147–64, and Lawrence Lewis, Jr., "The Courts of Pennsylvania in the Seventeenth Century," *PMHB*, 5 (1881), 161–65. On the First Purchasers see John E. Pomfret, "The First Purchasers of Pennsylvania, 1681–1700," *PMHB*, 80 (1956), 154–58.

21. *Pa Arch*, 8th serial, 1: lv, 65; Charter of Liberties, 1682, in Thorpe, *Constitutions*, 5: 3047; *Pa Council*, 1: 135–42.

22. "Penn's Charter of Liberties," article 5, in Thorpe, *Constitutions*, 5: 3048; *Pa Arch*, 1: 70–71; Lewis, "Courts of Pennsylvania," *PMHB*, 5 (1881), 165; Gary B. Nash, *Quakers and Politics: Pennsylvania, 1681–1726* (Princeton, 1968), 111, 166. The quotation is italicized in the original.

23. Harry Emerson Wildes, *William Penn* (New York, 1974), 225, speculates that Penn's response to the trial was one of pity for More. It may be noted that Penn's father had been impeached for naval defeats at the hands of the Dutch.

24. *Pa Arch*, 1: 68–69. Nash states that an attempt was made to impeach Robinson (*Quakers and Politics*, 111). In actuality there was to be no trial before the council; hence it was not an impeachment. The Commons had the privilege of keeping order within their own halls and compelling by law the compliance of officers of government with legal parliamentary commands. The Pennsylvania Assembly assumed this privilege.

25. Richard Beale Davis, ed., *William Fitzhugh and His Chesapeake World, 1676–1701* (Chapel Hill, 1963), 217.

26. "Genealogy of Fitzhugh Family," *VMHB*, 7 (1899), 199.

27. H. R. McIlwaine, ed., *Journals of the House of Burgesses of Virginia 1659/60–1693* (Richmond, 1914), 265–66, 268, 271.

28. H. R. McIlwaine, ed., *Executive Journals of the Council of Colonial Virginia, 1680–1699* (Richmond, 1925), 1: 509, 510.

29. Fitzhugh to Nicholas Hayward, April 5, 1687, in Davis, ed., *William Fitzhugh*, 217.

30. David S. Lovejoy, *The Glorious Revolution in America* ([1972], New York, 1974), 264; Richard L. Morton, *Colonial Virginia* (Chapel Hill, 1960), 1: 310-29.

31. *Journals of the House of Burgesses, 1659/60-1693*, 303, 306.

32. Lefler and Powell, *Colonial North Carolina*, 54.

33. Nicholson to the Lords of the Plantations (Board of Trade), June 10, 1691, *NCCR*, 1: 371.

34. Proprietors to Sothel, December 2, 1689, *NCCR*, 1: 359-60.

35. Proprietors to Sothel, May 12, 1691, *NCCR*, 1: 367-71.

CHAPTER 2

1. Despite the new king's intention to supervise the administration of the colonies, English domestic politics undercut the effectiveness of the Board of Trade he created. See Ian K. Steele, *Politics of Colonial Policy: The Board of Trade in Colonial Administration* (Oxford, England, 1968), 10 and after.

2. Roberts, *Responsible Government*, 383. Oxford (Harley) nurtured a political press, which then carried news of his impeachment (James A. Downie, *Robert Harley and the Press* [Cambridge, England, 1979], 186-88). By the late 1710s, news of English ministers' culpability was readily transmitted across the Atlantic. See, for example, David L. Jacobson, ed., *The English Libertarian Heritage from the Writings of John Trenchard and Thomas Gordon* (Indianapolis, Ind., 1965), xlviii-lx.

3. On the judicial powers of the General Court see Edwin Powers, *Crime and Punishment in Early Massachusetts, 1620-1692: A Documentary History* (Boston, 1966), 45-76. The activity of the "country party" is developed in T. H. Breen, *The Character of the Good Ruler: A Study of Puritan Political Ideas in New England, 1630-1730* (New York, 1974), 234. Everett Kimball, "The Public Life of Joseph Dudley, 1672-1715" (Ph.D. diss., Harvard University, 1904), 62, and Shipton, *Harvard Graduates*, 4: 43-45, describe the governor and his friends. Dudley's rapport with the General Court suffered from his involvement in the Andros government (Lovejoy, *Glorious Revolution*, 147-48 and passim).

4. This was but one form of the smuggling activities of New England's rising commercial entrepreneurs (Bernard Bailyn, *The New England Merchants in the Seventeenth Century* [New York, 1964], 127). On Vetch see G. J. Waller, *Samuel Vetch: Colonial Enterpriser* (Chapel Hill, 1960), 30-93.

5. Mass Gen Ct, 8: 1703-09, 212-13, 214.

6. Mass Gen Ct, 8: 216, 217-18, 219.

7. Mass Gen Ct, 8: 228-29, 230-31, 232-33.

8. Richard Bushman, "Corruption and Power in Provincial America," *The Development of a Revolutionary Mentality, Library of Congress Symposium on the American Revolution* (Washington, D.C., 1972), 74.

9. Entry for August 10-16, 1706, *The Diary of Samuel Sewall, 1674-1729*, ed. M. Halsey Thomas (New York, 1973), 1: 548-49.

10. Mass Gen Ct, 8: 233.

11. *A Memorial of the Present Deplorable State of New England* [1707]; *The Deplorable State of New England* [1708]: both in *Mass. Hist. Soc. Collections*, 5th ser. 6: 49-50, 65-95, 99-131.

12. Mass Gen Ct, 8: 240-49.

13. *The Acts and Resolves, . . . of the Province of Massachusetts Bay* (Boston, 1869), 1: 595. The hidden question was whether the intent itself was an act, or merely necessary to prove that the illegal trade was "voluntary" and malicious (James Willard Hurst, *The Law of Treason in the United States, Collected Essays* [Westport, Conn., 1971], 79-80).

14. Sewall, "the Reasons of My Withdrawing My Vote . . . ," November 25, 1707, Sewall Papers, MHi; November 20–21, 1707, *Diary of Samuel Sewall* 1, 576–77.

15. Smith, *Appeals*, 639.

16. Mass Sup Ct, November 30, 1708, vol. 1700–1714, 230.

17. The General Court's reply is cited in Lawrence H. Leder, *Liberty and Authority, Early American Political Ideology, 1689–1763* (New York, 1976), 112–13.

18. Thomas Hutchinson, *The History of the Colony and Province of Massachusetts-Bay*, ed. Lawrence Shaw Mayo (Cambridge, Mass., 1936), 2: 155.

19. On Logan, see Irma Jane Cooper, *The Life and Public Service of James Logan* (New York, 1921); Joseph Esrey Johnson, "A Statesman of Colonial Pennsylvania: A Study of the Private Life and Public Career of James Logan to the Year 1726" (Ph.D. diss., Harvard University, 1942); Frederick B. Tolles, *James Logan and the Culture of Provincial America* (Boston, 1957), 63–69; and Albright G. Zimmerman, "James Logan, Proprietary Agent," *PMHB*, 78 (1954), 143–76. On Lloyd see Roy N. Lokken, *David Lloyd: Colonial Lawmaker* (Seattle, Wash., 1959), 3–187.

20. *Pa Votes*, 1: 630–31, 714, 652; Cooper, *Life and Service of Logan*, 210.

21. Tolles, *Logan and Culture of America*, 65; *Pa Votes*, 1: 102, 660.

22. *Pa Votes* 1: 715–19; *Pa Council*, 2: 352, 346.

23. *Pa Council*, 2: 355–57; *Pa Votes*, 1: 751–56. Evans's hesitation may have been based upon his belief that the colonial upper houses, unlike the House of Lords, were never intended to be courts. American colonial precedent went against Evans's ruling, for the upper house in Pennsylvania, as well as those of her neighbors, acted as an appellate court in criminal cases.

For the denoument of the case see James Logan to William Penn, January 2, 1706/07, in Edward Armstrong, ed., *Correspondence between William Penn and James Logan, . . . and Others, 1700–1750* . . . (Historical Society of Pennsylvania, *Memoirs*, 10 [1872]) 2: 194–97; Johnson, "Statesman of Colonial Pa.," 349–85; and Lokken, *David Lloyd*, 186–87.

24. Edward McCrady, *The History of South Carolina under the Proprietary Government, 1670–1719* (New York, 1897), 627–80; W. Roy Smith, *South Carolina as a Royal Province* (New York, 1903), 12–13.

25. Francis Yonge, *A Narrative of the Proceedings of the People of South Carolina, In the Year 1719* . . .(London, 1726), in Peter Force, ed., *Tracts and Other Papers, Relating Principally to . . . North America* (Washington, D.C., 1838), 2, no. 10: 10–11. See also L. Lynn Hogue, "Nicholas Trott: Man of Law and Letters," *South Carolina Historical Magazine*, 76 (1975), 25–34; M. Eugene Sirmans, *Colonial South Carolina: A Political History, 1663–1763* (Chapel Hill, 1966), 72–79; David Ramsey, *History of South Carolina from Its First Settlement in 1670 to the Year 1808* (Newberry, S.C., 1858), 2: 275; and McCrady, *History of South Carolina*, 690–93.

26. On the 1707 episode see Clarke, *Parliamentary Privilege*, 42–43. The records of the assembly for the years 1718–20 are no longer in existence (Verner W. Crane, *The Southern Frontier, 1670–1732* [Durham, N.C., 1928], 217n).

27. Yonge, *Narrative of South Carolina*, 17–39; McCrady, *History of South Carolina*, 692–99; Hogue, "Nicholas Trott," 30–34. Recoiling from their actual impeachment of Trott for trial in the upper house, the newly established royal lower house contented themselves with a petition to the Board of Trade for the removal of Councillor Middleton in 1725. Two years later they imprisoned Chief Justice Smith for judicial irregularities. Both these men were "impeached," but not for trial by the upper house. The former had the force and form of an "appeal," and the latter of a censure. Of course, both actions were designed to demonstrate assembly feeling to George I's ministers in London. See George Chalmers, *An Introduction to the History of the Revolt of the American Colonies* (Boston, 1845), 1: 99–103, and pp. 11–12 of this

book. Roger Foster, *Commentaries on the Constitution of the United States, Historical and Juridical* (Boston, 1895), 1: 635, also incorrectly identifies these as impeachment precedents.

28. William K. Boyd, ed., *Some Eighteenth Century Tracts Concerning North Carolina* (Raleigh, N.C., 1927), 3–6; William D. Price, Jr., "'Men of Good Estates': Wealth among North Carolina's Royal Councillors," *NCHR*, 49 (1972), 75, 79; Hugh Williamson, *The History of North Carolina*, (Philadelphia, 1812), 2: 43; *NCCR*, 3: 342–43, 552, 600, 607; 4: 449–50, 457.

29. *NCCR*, 4: 1207–09; William S. Price, Jr., "A Strange Incident in George Burrington's Royal Governorship," *NCHR*, 51 (1974), 149–58.

30. *NCCR*, 4: 501–14, 459.

31. *A True and Faithful Narrative of the Proceedings of the House of Burgesses of North Carolina . . .* (n.p., 1740), in Boyd, ed., *Some Eighteenth Century Tracts*, 9–53; Julian P. Boyd, "The Sheriff in Colonial North Carolina," *NCHR*, 5 (1928), 151–80.

32. Jonathan Swift, *Examiner Numb. 39*, April 19, 1711, in Temple Scott, ed., *The Prose Works of Jonathan Swift* (London, 1902), 9: 248.

33. Henry St. John, Lord Bolingbroke, *Remarks on the History of England, Letter 2*, in Isaac Kramnick, ed., *Lord Bolingbroke, Historical Writings* (Chicago, 1972), 166–67; Thomas Gordon, "Preface," *Cato's Letters*, 3d ed. (London, 1733), xxiii; but see also Caroline Robbins, *The Eighteenth-Century Commonwealthman* (Cambridge, Mass., 1961), particularly 273–74, on the disorganization of protest during George II's reign.

34. Stanley N. Katz, ed., *A Brief Narrative of the Case and Trial of John Peter Zenger . . . by James Alexander*, 2d ed. (Cambridge, Mass., 1972), 6–7.

35. H. Trevor Colbourn, *The Lamp of Experience, Whig History and the Intellectual Origins of the American Revolution* (New York, 1974), 208–09; Bailyn, *Ideological Origins*, 36. It may be surmised that the colonial assembly leaders found the ideas of Cato attractive in the pre-revolutionary period for the same general reason they adopted "real Whig" arguments after 1763: Americans were as far from the center of power, as dependent and impotent, as the Commonwealthmen felt themselves to be in England.

CHAPTER 3

1. Bernard Bailyn, *The Origins of Colonial Politics* (New York, 1970), 75–91; Jack P. Greene, *The Quest for Power* (Chapel Hill, 1963), 3–18.

2. Bailyn, *Ideological Origins*, 95 and after.

3. Thus, in the final crisis, the colonists could reject the authority of Parliament (David Ammerman, "The British Constitution and the American Revolution; A Failure of Precedent," *William and Mary Law Review*, 17 [1975], 494).

4. On wartime politics in Pennsylvania see Lawrence Henry Gipson, *The Great War for the Empire: The Years of Defeat, 1756–1757, The British Empire before the American Revolution, VI* (New York, 1946), 66–69, and James H. Hutson, *Pennsylvania Politics, 1746–1770: The Movement for Royal Government and Its Consequences* (Princeton, N.J., 1972), 13–40.

5. The Smith–Franklin controversy is followed in Ralph L. Ketcham, "Benjamin Franklin and William Smith: New Light on an Old Philadelphia Quarrel," *PMHB*, 88 (1964), 142–63; Verner W. Crane, *Benjamin Franklin and a Rising People* (Boston, 1954), 78–97; and Horace W. Smith, ed., *Life and Correspondence of Rev. William Smith* (Philadelphia, 1879), 1: 167.

6. Depositions taken in August 1757 on Moore's case survive in Wyoming Controversy Files, Penn Papers, 5: 163, PHi.

7. Moore's Address to Governor Denny, October 19, 1757, Smith Family Papers, PHi.

8. Theodore Thayer, *Pennsylvania Politics and the Growth of Democracy, 1740-1776* (Harrisburg, Pa., 1953), 68-69; Ernest H. Baldwin, "Joseph Galloway, the Loyalist Politician," *PMHB*, 26 (1902), 174-76.

9. Edward Shippen, Jr. to Edward Shippen, January 28, 1758, Balch Papers, PHi.

10. A copy of the committal warrant is filed in the Penn Papers, 5: 153, PHi.

11. On these events, see Peter C. Hoffer, "Law and Liberty, In the Matter of William Smith of Philadelphia, 1758," *WMQ*, 38 (October 1981), 681-701.

12. Denny deposition to Assembly, January 20, 1758, Penn Papers, Wyoming Controversy, 5: 155, PHi.

13. Assembly Message to Denny, January 10, 1758, *Pa Votes*, 6: 4683-85.

14. Denny to Assembly, January 13, 1758, *Pa Votes*, 6: 4693-96.

15. Assembly to Denny, January 17, 1758, *Pa Votes*, 6: 4697-4703. Here the assembly referred to arguments made by Lloyd in Logan's case. See *Pa Votes*, 1: 753.

16. Moore's petition, August 25, 1758, Penn Papers, Wyoming Controversy, 255, 259, PHi.

17. Smith, *Appeals*, 646-49.

18. Thomas Penn to William Peters, May 26, 1758, Thomas Penn Letter Book, 6: 33, PHi.

19. Bernard Bailyn, *Origins of American Politics*, 159.

20. On this incident see Carl Vipperman, *The Rise of Rawlins Lowndes, 1721-1800* (Columbia, S.C., 1978), 115-23, and E. Stanly Godbold, Jr., and Robert H. Woody, *Christopher Gadsden and the American Revolution* (Knoxville, 1982), 64. The charges and Shinner's replies are in South Carolina Records in the Public Record Office, 31: 328-92. They were sent to the Board of Trade for the attention of the king and council on May 12, 1767.

21. *NJ Assembly*, 20 (June 18, 1767); 21, 22, 23, 24 (June 19, 1767); 18 (October 20, 1769); 25-26 (October 27, 1769); 38, 42-43 (November 3-4, 1769).

22. The accounts in Larry R. Gerlach, *Prologue to Independence, New Jersey in the Coming of the American Revolution* (New Brunswick, 1976), 178-85, and "Politics and Prerogatives: The Aftermath of the Robbery of the East Jersey Treasury in 1768," *New Jersey History*, 90 (1972), 151, on the composition of the Kinsey faction, show that they were politically astute in advancing their own legislative power at the expense of Skinner and Franklin. We are grateful to Thomas L. Purvis for assistance in identifying the lower house leaders.

23. *NJ Assembly*, 86, 89 (September 23, 1772); 32-58 (November 29, 1773); 84, 86 (December 18, 1773); 116 (December 21, 1773); 135, 139 (February 9, 1774); 165, 166, 167 (February 20, 1774); 176-77 (February 24, 1774).

24. William E. Nelson, *Americanization of the Common Law: The Impact of Legal Change on Massachusetts Society, 1760-1830* (Cambridge, Mass., 1975), 32-33. The three firsthand accounts of this era include sections on the judicial issue. See *Diary of Adams*, 3: 299-300; Thomas Hutchinson, *History of . . . Massachusetts-Bay*, ed. L.S. Mayo (Cambridge, Mass., 1936), 3: 314-28; and Douglas Adair and John A. Schutz, eds., *Peter Oliver's Origin and Progress of the American Rebellion: A Tory View* (San Marino, Calif., 1961), 107-12.

25. Shipton, *Harvard Graduates*, 6: 255. Lynde was so wary of political complications that he avoided mentioning his resignation in his diary (Edward Fitch Oliver, ed., *The Diaries of Benjamin Lynde and of Benjamin Lynde, Jr.* [Boston, 1880]). The description of Oliver comes from the Hutchinson-Oliver Papers, 3, MHi. Citations can be found in Natalie Hull Hoffer, "The Origin and Progress of Peter Oliver, Portrait of a Loyalist," sr. thesis, Ohio State University, 1974. See also Robert

286

NOTES TO PAGES 50-60

Calhoon, *The Loyalists in Revolutionary America, 1760–1781* (New York, 1965), 234–43.

26. Bernard Bailyn, *The Ordeal of Thomas Hutchinson* (Cambridge, Mass., 1974), 118, 127; *Mass House*, 206 (February 3, 1773); 224 (February 15, 1773); 275 (June 23, 1773).

27. *Mass House*, 86–88 (June 25, 1773); 94 (June 28, 1773).

28. Bailyn, *Ordeal of Thomas Hutchinson*, 26, 98, 211.

29. The first colonial impeachment study was Josiah Quincy, Jr., *Boston Gazette*, January 4, 1768, in Samuel H. Quincy, ed., *Reports of Cases . . .*, appendix IV, 580–84. For Adams's remarks, see *Diary of Adams*, 3: 298–302.

30. Hutchinson, "Charge to the Suffolk grand jury," in Quincy, ed., *Reports of Cases*, 268.

31. *Diary of Adams*, 3: 301. See also *Papers of Adams*, 2: 7–16.

32. John Adams to William Tudor, January 24, 1817, *Works of Adams*, 10: 239.

33. Adams's contributions to the dispute were printed in the January 11, 18, 25, and February 1, 8, 15, and 22, editions of the *Boston Gazette*. Adams summarized his case in the last piece (*Papers of Adams*, 1: 294–303).

34. Edmund Trowbridge, "Memorandum," September 1775 [?]1–2, original in Social Law Library, New Suffolk County Court House, Boston.

35. [Samuel Adams], The Committee of Correspondence of Boston to the Committee of Correspondence of Worcester, September 11, 1773, *Writings of Samuel Adams*, ed. Henry A. Cushing (New York, 1904–08), 3: 51.

36. *Boston Evening Post*, October 11, 1773.

37. *Boston Evening Post*, January 24, 1774.

38. *Mass House* 117–18 (February 2, 1774); 137–39 (February 8, 1774); 146–48 (February 11, 1774).

39. Peter Oliver to the General Court, February 3, 1774, Misc. bound MSS, MHi.

40. Oliver to Trowbridge, May 8, 1774, Trowbridge, "Memorandum," 4–5.

41. Hutchinson, "Reply to Remonstrance of February 12, 1774," February 15, 1774, Mass. Col. Papers, MHi.

42. Francis G. Walett, "The Massachusetts Council, 1766–1774: The Transformation of a Conservative Institution," *WMQ* 6 (October 1949), 622. The council's address was printed in the *Boston Evening Post*, February 14, 1774.

43. Order to Council, March 7, 1774, Mass. Col. Papers, MHi. See also Adair and Schutz, eds., *Oliver's Origin and Progress*, 112–15. The action of the Suffolk grand jury is reported in Force, ed., *American Archives . . . Consisting of a Collection of Authentick Records* (Washington, D.C., 1837), 4th ser., 1: 74.

44. John Adams to Abigail Adams, June 29, 1774, *Adams Family Correspondence*, ed. Lyman H. Butterfield (Cambridge, Mass., 1963–73), 1: 110.

45. "Resolutions and Instructions by County and Corporate Freeholders and Others, 1 June–28 July [1774]," William J. Van Schreeven and Robert L. Scribner, comp. and eds., *Revolutionary Virginia, The Road to Independence* (Charlottesville, 1973), 1: 109–68.

PART II, INTRODUCTION

1. Samuel Sherwood, "A Sermon Containing Scriptural Instructions to Civil Rulers and All Free-born Subjects" (1774), quoted in Jack P. Greene, ed., *Colonies to Nation, 1763–1789* (New York, 1976), 215.

2. The Administration of Justice Act, passed on May 20, 1774 (24 Geo. III, c. 39;

Stats at Large, 30: 367–71) provided for removal of colonial felonies into English courts.

3. Franklin to the Federal Constitutional Convention, July 19, 1787, Farrand, *Records*, 2: 65.

4. Wood, *American Republic*, 208–09.

5. Wood, *American Republic*, 157–59.

6. Adams to Warren, April 16, 1776, *Warren–Adams Letters [Collections of The Massachusetts Historical Society*, 52] (Boston, 1917), 1: 222. On the connection between civic virtue and republicanism see J. G. A. Pocock, *The Machiavellian Moment, Florentine Political Thought and the Atlantic Republican Tradition* (Princeton, 1975), 507–13, and Wood, *American Republic*, 107–24.

7. Pauline Maier, *From Resistance to Revolution, Colonial Radicals and the Development of American Opposition to Britain, 1765–1776* (New York, 1972), 278–84.

8. *Journal of the Votes and Proceedings of the New Jersey Provincial Congress* (New York, 1776), February 6, 1776, n.p.

9. *Pennsylvania Gazette*, September 25, 1776.

10. Georgia Act of Attainder, March 1778, *The Revolutionary Records of the State of Georgia*, ed. Allen D. Candler (Atlanta, 1908), 1: 326–30.

11. Edmund Randolph, *History of Virginia* [1809–13], ed. A. H. Shaffer (Charlottesville, 1970), 268.

12. Robert A. Rutland, *The Birth of the Bill of Rights, 1776–1791* (Chapel Hill, 1955), 24 and after.

13. Wood, *American Republic*, 453–63.

14. Constitution of Virginia, 1776, *Sources and Documents*, 10: 49; Constitution of Pennsylvania, 1776, *Sources and Documents*, 8: 278.

15. See discussion in text of chap. 5, at n. 28, in chap. 7, at n. 20, and in chap. 10, at n. 26.

16. Maryland Constitution of 1776, *Sources and Documents*, 4: 374.

17. John Adams, *Thoughts on Government* [April, 1776] (Philadelphia, 1776), in *Papers of Adams*, 4: 91. Adams's ideas spread rapidly through the colonies (see *Papers of Adams*, 4, ed. note, 65–73).

18. Adams to R. H. Lee, November 15, 1775, *Papers of Adams*, 3: 307–08.

19. *Papers of Jefferson*, 1, ed. note, 333.

20. *The Papers of George Mason*, ed. Robert A. Rutland (Chapel Hill, 1970), 1, ed. note, 303.

21. George Mason, Draft of Virginia Constitution, June 10, 1776, *Papers of Mason*, 1: 301.

22. Jefferson, "1st Draft of Virginia Constitution" [Before June 13, 1776], *Papers of Jefferson*, 1: 342. The impeachment clause was added to the original draft before it was revised and cleaned in a second draft. The editor's headnote, 330 and after, traces the course of Jefferson's preparation of the draft.

23. Wood, *American Republic*, 226–29; Elisha P. Douglass, *Rebels and Democrats* (Chapel Hill, 1955), 263–71.

24. Pennsylvania Constitution of 1776, *Sources and Documents*, 8: 281–82.

25. [Bryan], Demophilus, *The Genuine Principles of the Saxon, or English Constitution* (Philadelphia, 1776), 37. Attribution of this work to Bryan is made in H. Trevor Colbourn, *The Lamp of Experience: Whig History and the Intellectual Origins of the American Revolution* (New York, 1974), 191.

CHAPTER 4

1. The extent to which the federal convention delegates drew upon their experience in the states, as opposed to abstract theory and English precedent, cannot be overemphasized. Recent scholarship has recognized this debt and given it full weight (Wood, *American Republic*, 467). In similar fashion, Donald S. Lutz, *Popular Consent and Popular Control, Whig Political Theory in the Early State Constitutions* (Baton Rouge, 1980), finds that the period 1776-87 represented a connected whole in constitutional thought at the end of which Federalists transformed Whig revolutionary concepts of consent and representation (ibid., 218-38).

2. The Connecticut Constitution of 1818 discusses impeachment in article 9 (*Sources and Documents* 2: 151). The Rhode Island Constitution added impeachment in 1842 (ibid., 8: 394-95). Connecticut and Rhode Island impeachment provisions followed those in the United States Constitution.

3. Pennsylvania Constitution of 1776, in *Sources and Documents*, 8: 282; see J. Paul Selsam, *The Pennsylvania Constitution of 1776, A Study in Revolutionary Democracy* (New York, 1938), 191 and after.

4. Vermont Constitution of 1777, in *Sources and Documents*, 9: 493. The Vermont Constitution of 1786 retained the earlier impeachment rules (ibid., 502). Dr. Thomas Young was the radical Pennsylvania framer who acted as go-between (Pauline Maier, *The Old Revolutionaries, Political Lives in the Age of Samuel Adams* [New York, 1980], 122-24).

5. Lewis H. Meader, "The Council of Censors," *PMHB*, 22 (1898), 265-300.

6. See discussion in the text of chap. 5, at n. 21.

7. *The Constitution of New Jersey* (Burlington, N.J., 1776), 8.

8. See discussion in text of chap. 5, at nn. 7 and 18.

9. *Proceedings of the Convention of the Delaware State Held at New Castle... the 27th of August 1776* (Wilmington, Del., 1776), 31-32.

10. The quasi-judicial character of Parliament remained with that body through the revolutionary era. James Otis, Jr., for example, appealed to Parliament-as-a-court against the Sugar Act (1764) passed by Parliament-the-legislative-body. See Bailyn, *Ideological Origins*, 179-80.

11. *Journals of the Provincial Congress, ... of New York* (Albany, N.Y., 1842), 1: 878.

12. The final version of the New York court for the trial of impeachments and the correction of errors is in *Sources and Documents*, 7: 177. It is evident from the extent of amendments to it that the New York framers were more concerned with the court of trials than with the impeachment mechanism itself (Charles Z. Lincoln, *The Constitutional History of New York* [Rochester, N.Y., 1905], 1: 181-83, 538-39).

13. *Sources and Documents*, 7: 406.

14. One can trace the effort to establish a court for trials as it passed through the legislature in *NCSR*, 17: 374, 389, 390-91; 18: 114, 198, 340, 343, 355; and 20: 80, 205, 230, 239, 387. The discussion of Ashe's case begins in chap. 5, with the text preceding n. 44.

15. On the Mason plan, see discussion starting in part II introduction, 65.

16. As passed, the provision followed Mason's lead (*Papers of Jefferson*, 1: 382 [June 29, 1776]). See also A. E. Dick Howard, *Commentaries on the Constitution of Virginia* (Charlottesville, 1974), 1: 553.

17. Jefferson's draft's impact is discussed in *Papers of Jefferson*, 1, ed. note, 329-37; the first draft appears on 337-45.

18. Jefferson's 2d draft (June 1776), *Papers of Jefferson*, 1: 351-52.

19. *Statutes at Large . . . the Laws of Virginia,* ed. and comp. William W. Hening (Richmond, 1821), 9: 477–78. See also the discussion of *Posey* in chap. 5, 82–83.

20. Judges and executive officers were not lumped together in these provisions; the removal of judges holding nonelective tenure presented a different set of problems to the framers from the removal of elected officials. The provision for impeachment of judges came two paragraphs after the impeachment of the governor (*Sources and Documents,* 10: 55).

21. See also n. 28, below.

22. Jefferson, Proposal for Revision of the Virginia Constitution, 1783, *Papers of Jefferson,* 6: 301.

23. On the two-thirds rule, see discussion beginning in the text of chap. 6, at n. 40.

24. Wood, *American Republic,* 454; Berger, *Impeachment,* 122 and after. More modern cases are discussed in Robert Kramer and Jerome A. Barron, "The Constitutionality of Removal and Mandatory Retirement Procedures for the Federal Judiciary: The Meaning of 'During Good Behavior,'" *George Washington Law Review,* 35 (1966–67), 458–62, and Frank Thompson, Jr. and Daniel H. Pollitt, "Impeachment of Federal Judges: An Historical Overview," *North Carolina Law Review,* 49 (1970–71), 87–121.

25. Entry for January 5, 1804, in Plumer, *Memorandum,* 101.

26. On Madison's response, see the editorial note on Madison's "Observation on Jefferson's Draft of a Constitution for Virginia" (1788), *Papers of Madison,* 11: 281–85.

27. Madison, "Observation," *Papers of Madison,* 11: 291–92.

28. Madison collaborated with Jefferson on some of these proposed revisions, but no. 100 (1785) seems to be work of the former (*Papers of Jefferson,* 2: 591–92).

29. *Papers of Madison,* 11: 292.

30. Adams, *Diary of Adams,* 3: 298–300.

31. Article XX of the 1778 Draft, in Oscar Handlin and Mary Handlin, eds., *The Popular Sources of Political Authority, Documents on the Massachusetts Convention of 1780* (Cambridge, Mass., 1966), 198.

32. [Theophilus Parsons], *The Essex Result* (1778), in Handlin and Handlin, eds., *Popular Sources,* 325.

33. Handlin and Handlin, eds., *Popular Sources,* 236, 250, 256.

34. *An Address of the Convention For Framing a New Constitution of Government, For the State of Massachusetts Bay, to their Constituents* (1780), in Handlin and Handlin, eds., *Popular Sources,* 439. For the final version of the article, appearing in the *Frame of Government,* see *Popular Sources,* 453.

35. The struggle to increase the power of state governors was largely won by 1787; even Pennsylvania would accede to the principle of executive independence in 1790.

36. *Sources and Documents,* 5: 100.

37. *Journal of the Massachusetts Constitutional Convention of 1779–1780* (Boston, 1836), 136.

38. *Documents and Records Relating to Towns in New Hampshire, with an Appendix, Embracing the Constitutional Conventions of 1778–1779 [and] 1781–1783, New Hampshire Provincial and State Papers,* ed. Nathaniel Boulton (Concord, N.H., 1875), 9: 837–41, 851, 868, 865.

39. *Sources and Documents,* 8: 464 (1776 South Carolina Constitution).

40. *Sources and Documents,* 8: 472 (1778 S.C. Constitution), and see Robert L. Meriwheather, *Basic Documents of South Carolina History* (Columbia, S.C., 1953), 5, which notes the similarity between South Carolina's new provisions and those of the other states.

CHAPTER 5

1. A prime example was William Greenleaf's case, 1788 (see chap. 7, text following n. 22).

2. On intent and criminal culpability, see R. Bryce Young, *Criminal Law: Codes and Cases* (New York, 1979), 229, 230. Contemporaries understood this restriction on impeachment, though Thomas Jefferson, *Manual*, 206, was extreme in arguing that rules of evidence in impeachment trials were the same as in regular criminal trials.

3. *Lining v. Bentham* (1796), Elihu Hall Bay, comp., *Reports of Cases . . . In the Superior Courts of Law of the State of South Carolina* (New York, 1811), 2: 3, 7.

4. *State v. Johnson*, 385, (1802), Bay, *Reports of Cases*, 2: 388.

5. *Hardison v. Jordan* (1801), Walter Clark, comp. and annotator, *Cases Adjudged in the Superior Courts of Laws and Equity and in the Court of Conference of North Carolina, Reported by Francis X. Martin* (Raleigh, N.C., 1901), 576.

6. *NJ Assembly*, 19, 22 (November 17, 1778); *NJ Council*, 23–24 (November 24 and December 3–4, 1778). See, generally, Leonard Lundin, *Cockpit of the Revolution, the War for Independence in New Jersey* (Princeton, 1940), 286–93.

7. *NJ Assembly*, 26, 27, 29 (November 13–15, 1782); 30 (November 16); *NJ Council*, 17 (November 16, 1782).

8. *NJ Assembly*, 28–29 (November 16, 1782).

9. *Vt SP*, 3, pt. 1, 268–69 (June 28, 1781).

10. *Vt SP*, 3, pt. 3, 32 (March 2, 1784); 83 (October 21, 1784); 91 (October 26, 1784); 108 (October 29, 1784); 148 (June 16, 1785); 159 (June 18, 1785); *Vt Council*, 1: 70 (June 10, 1785); 89–90 (October 24, 1785).

11. Hopkinson, *Judgments in Admiralty* (Philadelphia, 1792), includes the cases he heard from 1779 to 1788, but not *Morris v. the Brig Charlotte*.

12. Hogan, *Trials*, Assembly, 3–30 (November 22–December 12, 1780); Supreme Executive Council, 33–38 (December 12–21, 1780).

13. Hogan, *Trials*, Council, 41–62 (December 22–26, 1780).

14. *Papers of Madison*, 6, ed. note at 347–48; *Calendar of Virginia State Papers*, ed. William P. Palmer (Richmond, 1884), 4: 95, 225, 376.

15. *NJ Assembly*, 151–52 (June 17–18, 1778).

16. *NJ Assembly*, 49 (November 26, 1779).

17. Shute "Petition, April, 1779," box 11, #42, NJ Sess.

18. *NJ Council*, 106 (October 6, 1778); 25 (December 3, 1779).

19. *NJ Assembly*, 123, 130 (August 21, 25, 1784); *NJ Council*, 14 (August 25, 1784).

20. *NJ Assembly*, 42–43 (June 7, 1787).

21. *Vt SP*, 3, pt. 3, 175 (October 15, 1785); *Vt Council*, 3: 81–84, 92–93 (October 17–21, 1785); Alein Austin, *Matthew Lyon, New Man of the Democratic Revolution, 1789–1822* (University Park, Pa., 1981), 27, 49–50, 57–58; *The Public Papers of Governor Thomas Chittenden*, ed. John A. Williams, *VtSP*, 17 (Montpelier, 1969), ed. note, 251.

22. For example, see Pauline Maier, "The Charleston Mob and the Evolution of Popular Politics in Revolutionary South Carolina, 1765–1785," *Perspectives in American History*, 4 (1970), 188–89.

23. *NJ Assembly*, 32, 33 (November 19, 21, 1782); Robert Lawrence, Petition for relief of his daughter, Mary Leonard, October 7, 1777, Misc. Calendar, #129, NJ Sess.

24. William Livingston to George Washington, November 9, 1777, *The Papers of William Livingston*, ed. Carl E. Prince and Dennis P. Ryan (Trenton, N.J., 1980), 2: 108.

25. *Vt SP*, 3, pt. 3, 271, 300 (February 19, 28, 1787).

26. *Vt Council*, 3, appendix F, 361–80.

27. *Vt SP*, 3, pt. 4; *Vt Assembly*, 277 (January 27, 1791).

28. *NJ Assembly*, 190, 203 (May 15–27, 1780); 25, 26 (November 11, 13, 1780); 94 (December 22, 1779).

29. *Vt SP*, 3, pt. 3, 206, 245 (October 25, 27, 1785).

30. Edmund Randolph to James Madison, June 1, 1782, *Papers of Madison*, 4: 306. See also Randolph, *History of Virginia*, (ed. Schaffer) 296, and Merrill Peterson, *Thomas Jefferson and the New Nation: A Biography* (New York, 1970), 238.

31. H. J. Eckenrode, *The Revolution in Virginia* (Boston, 1916), 221; Peterson, *Jefferson*, 236–37; Emory G. Evans, *Thomas Nelson of Yorktown, Revolutionary Virginian* (Charlottesville, 1975), 104–05.

32. *Va House*, 15 (June 12, 1781).

33. Evans, *Nelson*, 106; Peterson, *Jefferson*, 238.

34. Peterson, *Jefferson*, 238; *Va House*, 17 (November 26, 1781).

35. *Va House*, 23 (November 20, 1781).

36. *Va House*, 37 (December 12, 1781).

37. Edmund Pendleton to James Madison, December 21, 1781, *Papers of Madison*, 3: 337–38. One fallout of the near miss was Jefferson's sharp condemnation of the unchecked power of the lower house in his *Notes in the State of Virginia* [1781–87], ed. William Peden (Chapel Hill, 1955), 120–21.

38. John Harvie to Jefferson, November 27, 1781, *Papers of Jefferson*, 6: 133–34.

39. *NHSP*, 21: 79(June 27, 1787); 72–73 (June 26, 1787); 115 (September 18, 1787)—the first official mention of the investigation of Moriss.

40. Moriss's defense is a document written in his own hand, dated August 30, 1787 (NH Sess). Evidently forewarned of the coming storm, Moriss had his colleague on the bench, Timothy Ladd, examine witnesses in the Stickney case before Moriss penned his defense. The petitions, and the letters withdrawing names from the petitions, are also gathered in NH Sess.

41. The affidavits accusing Moriss were given by John Spafford, David Bailey, Joseph Little, and Benjamin Poor, the first three to Justice Ladd, and the last to Jonathan Gove, chairman of the assembly committee investigating the case (NH Sess).

42. These charges are contained in Assemblyman Gove's notes on the case and in the draft of the impeachment articles in his possession (but never formally submitted because Moriss resigned before the assembly met in December), NH Sess.

43. *NHSP*, 21: 244 (December 17, 1787).

44. William Hooper to James Iredell, July 8, 1784, in *The Life and Correspondence of James Iredell*, ed. Griffith J. McKee, Jr. ([1857] New York, 1949), 2: 105–08; Jackson T. Main, *The Anti-Federalists, Critics of the Constitution, 1781-1788* (Chapel Hill, 1961), 34; Iredell to Henry McCulloh, September 26, 1784, *Life and Correspondence of Iredell*, 2: 109–10.

45. Beth G. Crabtree, *North Carolina Governors, 1585-1958* (Raleigh, N.C., 1958), 55–56; Alice B. Keith, ed., *The John Gray Blount Papers* (Raleigh, N.C., 1952), 1, ed. notes at 38, 398; William Hooper to Iredell, July 6, 1785, *Life and Correspondence of Iredell*, 2: 125–26; Samuel A. Ashe, *The History of North Carolina*, 2 vols. (Greensboro, 1925), 1: 603.

46. Maclaine to Iredell, August 3, 1786, *Life and Correspondence of Iredell*, 2: 143–44.

47. Iredell to McCulloh, September 24, 1784, *Life and Correspondence of Iredell*, 2: 108–09.

48. Maclaine to Iredell, March 6, 1786, *Life and Correspondence of Iredell*, 2: 137.

Maclaine, a fiscal conservative, wanted hard-money redemption of the state debt (Norman K. Risjord, *Chesapeake Politics, 1781-1800* [New York, 1978], 104).

49. James R. Morrill, *The Practice and Politics of Fiat Finance* (Chapel Hill, 1969), 74, 86.

50. For example, in the session 1787–88 the two houses suspended Henry Spears and Travis Harper, justices of the peace, while charges against them were investigated. See *NC Senate*, 5, 21 (December 5, 15, 1787), and *NC House*, 38 (December 15, 1787); 31 (November 24, 1788).

51. A Citizen [Iredell], "To The Public," August 17, 1786, *Life and Correspondence of Iredell*, 2: 145–49.

52. *NCSR*, 18, Senate, 194–95 (January 1–2, 1786); 212–17 (January 3, 1786); House of Commons, 421–25 (January 1, 1786).

53. Alfred Moore to Iredell, December 14, 1786, *Life and Correspondence of Iredell*, 2: 153–54.

54. *NCSR*, 18, House, 427–28 (January 3, 1786).

55. Walter Clark, "Prefatory Note," *NCSR*, 18: vi–viii; Ashe, *History of North Carolina*, 2: 51–53.

56. [Archibald Maclaine], *The Independent Citizen*, no. 4, in William K. Boyd, ed., *Some 18th Century Tracts Concerning North Carolina* (Raleigh, N.C., 1927), 483; *Independent Citizen*, no. 2, in *Tracts*, 466; *Independent Citizen*, no. 5, in *Tracts*, 486.

57. Alfred H. Kelly, Winfred A. Harbison, and Herman Belz, *The American Constitution, Its Origins and Development*, 6th ed. (New York, 1983), 90; Wood, *American Republic*, 460–61. *Bayard v. Singleton* (1787), *North Carolina Reports*, Walter Clark, ed., 1: 5–9.

58. Risjord, *Chesapeake Politics*, 130–31. Risjord, 200–01, proposes that the assembly inquiry in January 1787 went forward because the Tory-baiters in the lower house were angry with Ashe for his refusal to uphold the confiscation laws (in the first, adjourned hearing of *Bayard v. Singleton* at the previous session of the court). The hearing would be a censure and a warning to the judges. A strange alliance would thus have temporarily formed between the defenders of the Tory claims and the Tory-baiters. Undermining this reconstruction of motives in the impeachment is the fact that *Bayard v. Singleton* was not mentioned in the attack upon the judges' conduct.

59. Maclaine, *An Address to the People of North Carolina . . . October 26, 1787* (Wilmington, N.C., 1787), 2; *NC House*, June 1, 1787; Courts Bill, 1787 session, *NC House*, appendix, 2; Samuel Ashe to James Iredell et al., August 30, 1787, in *NC House*, Additional Papers, 14.

60. James M. Varnum, *The Case, Trevett v. Weeden . . .* (Providence, 1787), 44–46.

61. John P. Lynch, Petition to New Jersey Assembly, October 27, 1782, box 5, #19, NJ Sess.

62. Bogart et al., Petition to New Jersey Assembly, November 12, 1783, NJ Sess.

63. "Charges Brought Before Assembly Against Dudley Pettibone, Justice of the Peace and Tax Collector," May 1785, Crimes and Misdemeanors, 6: 269–74, Ct.

64. *Public Records of the State of Connecticut, 1785-1789*, ed. Leonard Labaree (Hartford, 1945), 4: 149, 285, 401. There is no record of the memorial from Simsbury.

65. *Brown v. Oswald* is reported in *Pa Arch*, 1st ser., 11, Supreme Court (July Term, 1788), 348–49.

66. Robert Brunhouse, *The Counter-Revolution in Pennsylvania, 1766-1790* (Harrisburg, Pa., 1942), 126.

67. Leonard Levy, *Freedom of Speech and Press in Early American History: Legacy of Suppression* (New York, 1966), 176–248, argues that even after the Revolution, freedom of the press was equated with no prior censorship. Truth was not yet a

defense against either individual slander suits or seditious libel cases brought by the government. The entire issue was reviewed in Chase's case, discussed in chap. 12.

68. *Pa Assembly*, 203–15 (September 5, 1788). See also Levy, *Freedom of Speech*, 204–06.

69. *Respublica v. Oswald* (1788), in A. J. Dallas, *Reports of Cases Ruled and Adjudged in the Courts of Pennsylvania*, 3d ed. (Philadelphia, 1830), 1, n. 353–60. Addison's case is discussed in chap. 10.

70. *Pa Assembly*, 236–37 (September 16, 1788); 246–47 (September 22, 1788); 259 (September 30, 1788); 268–71 (October 3, 1788).

CHAPTER 6

1. Randolph, July 20, 1787 in Farrand, *Records*, 2: 67 (hereafter cited in this chapter as Farrand).

2. On Hastings's case, see the brief description in Keith Feiling, *Warren Hastings* (London, 1954), 343–71, and discussion in text of part III introduction, beginning at n. 14.

3. Mason, September 8, 1787, in Farrand, 2: 550.

4. *Constitution of the United States*, Article II, section 4.

5. *Constitution of the United States*, Article I, section 3.

6. Earlier commentators on federal impeachment have neither stressed these differences nor sought American precedents for them. For example, see Alexander Simpson, *A Treatise on Federal Impeachments* (Philadelphia, 1916), 7. Roger Foster, *Commentaries on the Constitution of the United States*, 1: 511–12, mentioned the state provisions but did not differentiate them, or the federal law, from English precedent. Berger, *Impeachment*, 87 and passim, and John R. Labovitz, *Presidential Impeachment* (New Haven, 1978), 1–25, may be criticized for the same oversight.

7. Randolph, May 29, 1787, Farrand, 2: 22.

8. Robert L. Hilldrup, *Life and Times of Edmund Pendleton* (Chapel Hill, 1939), 275.

9. Randolph, July 20, in Farrand, 2: 67.

10. Hugh Williamson, June 2, 1787, in Farrand, 1: 88.

11. William Paterson, June 13, 1787, in Farrand, 1: 231, 244.

12. See note on two drafts of New Jersey Plan in Farrand, 1: 245; 3: 613–14.

13. Wilson, June 16, 1787, in Farrand, 1: 252.

14. Hamilton, June 18, 1787, in Farrand, 1: 292–93. Hamilton tinkered with the court of trials in various versions of his address (Farrand, 4: 626). Nevertheless, he was a strong advocate of a separate court, at least according to Robert Yates, another New York delegate (Yates to New York Ratification Convention, in *Papers of Hamilton*, 5: 138).

15. Pinckney [?] to Committee of Detail, in Farrand, 2: 136, 159.

16. Madison [?] to Committee of Detail, in Farrand, 2: 145.

17. Journal of Convention, August 27, 1787, in Farrand, 2: 423.

18. Journal of Convention, September 4, 1787, in Farrand, 2: 493.

19. Labovitz, *Presidential Impeachment*, 6.

20. Mason, September 4, 1787, and Wilson, September 4, 1787, in Farrand, 2: 500–01.

21. Morris, September 4, 1787, in Farrand, 2: 501.

22. Journal of Convention, September 8, 1787, in Farrand, 2: 552–53.

23. James McHenry to Maryland House of Delegates, November 29, 1787, in Farrand, 3: 148; Luther Martin to Senate, as counsel for Supreme Court Justice Samuel Chase, February 23, 1805, *Annals of Cong.*, 8th Cong., 2d sess. (Senate), 436, (1805).

24. [Hamilton], *Federalist No. 65*, in Clinton Rossiter, ed., *The Federalist Papers* (New York, 1961), 396–97.

25. Hamilton to New York Constitutional Ratification Convention, July 15,1788, *Papers of Hamilton*, 5: 168–69. Although Hamilton dropped the issue after ratification, Egbert Benson, a New York Federalist congressman, reintroduced the "court of impeachments" plan as an amendment to the Constitution (*Annals of Cong.*, 1st Cong., 3d sess. [House], 1976–77 [1791]).

26. [Hamilton], *Federalist No. 65*, in Rossiter, ed., *Federalist Papers*, 400, 398–99.

27. [Hamilton], *Federalist No. 66*, in Rossiter, ed., *Federalist Papers*, 402–07.

28. See the discussion in chap. 4, following n. 26.

29. See the votes in convention during May and June, for example, Farrand, 1: 78, 236, 292.

30. Morris, July 19, 1787, in Farrand, 2: 53.

31. The debate is covered in Farrand, 2: 64–69.

32. Randolph and Madison spoke on July 20 (Farrand, 2: 67–69). Labovitz, *Presidential Impeachment*, regards this day's debate as the most important on the subject of impeachment. While their debates were equally significant, particularly on September 4, the July 20 debate was crucial for this issue. Even among those delegates who did not favor the impeachment of the president, there was support for impeachment of judges. King, for example, had no objection to the impeachment of judges (Farrand, 2: 66–67).

33. Committee of Detail, August 20, 1787, in Farrand, 2: 337.

34. James Wilson, "Lectures on the Law, No. 11, Comparison of the Constitution of the United States with that of Great Britain," April 1792, in James D. Andrews, ed., *The Works of James Wilson*, (Chicago, 1896), 1: 408.

35. Hamilton, *Federalist No. 65*, in Rossiter, ed., *Federalist Papers*, 396.

36. Journal of the Convention, September 8, 1787, in Farrand, 2: 545.

37. The debate occurred on September 8, 1787, in Farrand, 2: 550–51. Madison seems to have shifted his ground somewhat from his position on July 20. At that time, he used the words "incapacity, Negligence or perfidy" to describe impeachable offenses, in addition to "betrayal of trust" and "corruption"(Farrand, 2: 65–66). By September 8, Madison had agreed with the committee of eleven to narrow the grounds for impeachment. Thus, when the vote was taken on Mason's compromise, Madison appears to have consented to a formula very much like his first, July 20, position. Charles L. Black, Jr., *Impeachment: A Handbook* (New Haven, 1974), 27–33, argues that the framers feared subjective categories such as "maladministration," but the state laws and precedents, in fact, show the framers to be very comfortable with charges of maladministration.

38. Jefferson, *Manual*, 206.

39. Blackstone, *Commentaries*, 4: 5, defines misdemeanors as "smaller faults, and omissions of less consequence" than "crimes."

40. Williamson, June 6, 1787, in Farrand, 1: 140.

41. Madison, "Ancient and Modern Confederacies" [April–June 1786], *Papers of Madison*, 9: 7.

42. Charles Cotesworth Pinckney, "The Draught of A Federal Government . . ." reconstructed in Farrand, 3: 608.

43. July 12, 1776, *Cont Cong.*, 5: 546–47.

44. *Cont Cong.*, 5: 552.The word "nine" appears in the final draft in Dickinson's hand. See Paul H. Smith, ed., *Letters of Delegates to Congress, 1774–1789* (Washington, D.C., 1979), 4: 245, 255.

45. Merrill Jensen, *The Articles of Confederation, An Interpretation of the Social-Constitutional History of The American Revolution, 1774–1781* (Madison, Wisc.,

1943), 126–27; Josiah Bartlett to John Langdon, June 17, 1776, in *Letters of Members of the Continental Congress*, ed. Edmund C. Burnett (Washington, D.C., 1921–38), 1: 495.

46. Jensen, *Articles*, 126. The debate over the political intentions of these men is still heated.

47. Franklin, Draft of Objections to Articles, 1776, Franklin Papers, Library of Congress, in *Cont Cong.*, 5, note on 555–56.

48. David L. Jacobson, *John Dickinson and the Revolution in Pennsylvania, 1764–1776* (Berkeley, Calif., 1965), 114, 118.

49. *Cont Cong.*, 9: 849.

50. Jefferson, "Resolution Opposing Ratification of Definitive Treaty by Less than Nine States" [December 27, 1783], *Papers of Jefferson*, 6: 424. The complex maneuvering leading to ratification is discussed in the editor's note (see ibid., 425–26).

51. Madison to Jefferson, March 16, 1784, *Papers of Madison*, 8: 6–9.

52. Thomas A. Bailey, *A Diplomatic History of the American People*, 7th ed. (New York, 1964), 61–62; Merrill Jensen, *The New Nation: A History of the United States During the Confederation, 1781–1789* (New York, 1950), 171–72.

53. Dickinson, June 2, 1787, in Farrand, 1: 78, 89–90. Dickinson incorporated both impeachment and removal upon address in his "Plan of Government" of June 18, 1787. See James H. Hutson, "John Dickinson at the Federal Constitutional Convention," *WMQ*, 40 (April 1983), 269.

54. [Hamilton], *Federalist No. 75*, Rossiter, ed., *Federalist Papers*, 452–53.

PART III, INTRODUCTION

1. P. D. G. Thomas, *The House of Commons in the Eighteenth Century* (Oxford, England, 1971), 36–37.

2. R. H. Lee to Edmund Randolph, October 16, 1787, in Elliot, *Debates*, 1: 503.

3. Wilson to Pennsylvania Convention, December 4, 1787, Elliot, *Debates*, 2: 477; "Cincinnatus," no. 4, *New York Journal*, November 22, 1787.

4. McKean to Pennsylvania Convention, December 11, 1787, Elliot, *Debates*, 2: 534.

5. James Monroe to Virginia Convention, June 10, 1788, Elliot, *Debates*, 3: 220.

6. Madison to Virginia Convention, June 18, 1788, Elliot, *Debates*, 3: 516.

7. The exchange occurred in the North Carolina Convention, July 28, 1788, Elliot, *Debates*, 4: 117, 125–27.

8. The precise timing and ontology of the "first party system" are not so important here as its functional difference from earlier party systems. See Paul Goodman, "The First American Party System," *The American Party Systems*, eds. William N. Chambers and Walter D. Burnham (New York, 1967), 56– 89.

9. Richard Hofstadter, *The Idea of a Party System, the Rise of Legitimate Opposition in the United States, 1780–1840* (Berkeley, 1969), 4–5, 8.

10. Madison, "A Candid State of Parties" *National Gazette*, January 23, 1792; see also Lance Banning, *The Jeffersonian Persuasion* (Ithaca, N.Y., 1978), 177.

11. [Jefferson] "Draft of Kentucky Resolutions," in *Writings of Jefferson*, ed. Ford, 8: 458–79; Jefferson to Elbridge Gerry, March 1801, *Writings of Jefferson*, ed. Bergh and Lipscomb, 10: 254. On the collaboration between Madison and Jefferson on party ideology, see Adrianne Koch, *Jefferson and Madison, The Great Collaboration*, rev. ed. (New York, 1964), 174–211.

12. Pickering to Timothy Williams, in Octavius Pickering, ed., *Life of Timothy Pickering* (Boston, 1868–73), 3: 181; Fisher Ames, *An Oration on … General George Washington … 8th of February, 1800* (Boston, 1800), 17–18.

13. Burke, *Thoughts on the Cause of the Present Discontents* (1770), *Works of Edmund Burke* (Boston, 1839), 1: 375, 395, 383, 403, 428-29.

14. On Burke, the younger Pitt, the Whigs, and Hastings, see Robin Reilly, *William Pitt the Younger* (New York, 1979), 180-92. Pitt changed the position of the ruling party by voting with the opposition on the second impeachment article and thereafter. Without Pitt's support, the impeachment would never have occurred. Thereafter, Pitt remained neutral, refusing to lend administration support to the prosecution when the case went to trial. The prime minister had never liked Hastings and came to believe some of the charges against the governor general. One should note that Hastings resigned the governorship before he returned to England, and his impeachment and trial could not thus have been aimed at his removal from office.

15. Burke to Philip Francis, December 10, 1785, *The Correspondence of Edmund Burke*, ed. Holden Furber (Chicago, 1958-), 5: 241. Francis was a member of the East India Company Council in 1772, quarreled many times with Hastings, and left the colony a sworn enemy of the little governor general.

16. Burke, speech of February 16, 1788, *Works of Burke*, 7: 146. Burke almost became obsessed by Hastings's offenses in India, far more emotionally involved than simple partisanship would lead one to expect (Isaac Kramnick, *The Rage of Edmund Burke: Portrait of an Ambivalent Conservative* [New York, 1977], 126-42).

17. [Burke], "Report from the Committee Appointed to Inspect the Lords Journals . . . on the Trial of Warren Hastings," *Works of Burke*, 7: 496, 526, 530. On Burke, party, and impeachment see Harvey C. Mansfield, *Statesmanship and Party Government, A Study of Burke and Bolingbroke* (Chicago, 1965), 146-54.

18. Dallas, speech to Pennsylvania Senate, January 17, 1803, in Lloyd, *Addison*, 26; Francis Hopkinson, speech to Senate, February 21, 1805, in Smith, *Trial of Chase*, 2: 7. Neither Dallas nor Hopkinson made much of Hastings's case, if we assume they had any knowledge of its details.

19. For example, see Garry Wills, *Inventing America, Jefferson's Declaration of Independence* (New York, 1978), 268-71, and Wood, *American Republic*, 370-72, on the duties of representatives.

CHAPTER 7

1. James Willard Hurst, *Dealing with Statutes* (New York, 1982), 10, finds "general standards" here rather than vagueness.

2. *US Stats*, 1:93 (1789) linked federal procedure to state rules. The act did give the federal courts exclusive jurisdiction over crimes defined by the laws of the United States; Goebel, *Supreme Court*, 1: 473.

3. Jefferson to Gideon Granger, August 13, 1800, *Writings of Jefferson*, ed. Ford, 9: 139; [Madison] Report of the Resolution of the Virginia House . . . on the Alien and Sedition Acts . . . Session of 1799-1800, *Writings of Madison*, 6: 354-79.

4. *U.S. v. Worrall*, 2 U.S. [2 Dallas], 384 (1798).

5. But see Morton Horwitz, *The Transformation of American Law, 1780-1860* (Cambridge, Mass., 1977), 8, 25, for the attack on precedent.

6. Madison, July 18, 1788, Elliot, *Debates*, 3: 516.

7. Iredell, July 28, 1788, Elliot, *Debates*, 4: 126.

8. Madison in House of Representatives, June 16, 1789, *Papers of Madison*, 12: 226.

9. Madison in House, June 17, 1789, *Papers of Madison*, 12: 233, 235.

10. Madison in House, June 17, 1789, *Papers of Madison*, 12: 235.

11. Madison to Edmund Pendleton, June 21, 1789, *Papers of Madison*, 12: 252.

12. Georgia Constitution of 1789, *Sources and Documents*, 2: 452.

13. Delaware Constitution of 1792, Article V, section 2; *Deleware Code Annotated* (1953), 1: 100, 101–02.

14. Kentucky Constitution of 1792, *Sources and Documents*, 4: 146. The constitution of 1799 repeated these rules (*Sources and Documents*, 4: 159). See also Tennessee Constitution of 1796, *Sources and Documents*, 9: 145.

15. "Franklin" Constitution of 1784, *Sources and Documents*, 9: 132, duplicated the N.C. constitution of 1776, Article XXIII, *Sources and Documents*, 7: 406.

16. *Journal of the First Constitutional Convention of Kentucky ... April 1 to 19, 1791* (Lexington, Ky., 1942), 5–7 (April 13, 1792).

17. *Minutes of the Convention ... of Pennsylvania ... 1789–1790 ... Altering and Amending the Constitution of this State* ... (Philadelphia, 1790), 18, 40, 43, 47, 55, 156, 175.

18. Jay to Grand Jury of the Eastern Circuit (Federal), 1790, quoted in Stephen Presser, "A Tale of Two Judges: Richard Peters, Samuel Chase, and the Broken Promise of Federalist Jurisprudence," *New Law Review*, 73 (1978), 49–50.

19. This question is considered at length in Berger, *Impeachment*, 56–107. His chief source is English law, a mistake in emphasis discussed in the appendix. His conclusion, that "high crimes and misdemeanors" did not stop with indictable crimes (61), is correct but not correctly based upon English cases—even if the framers, as he assumes (79), knew the English cases and drew the right inferences from them.

   In fact, no one in these debates in the state or federal conventions spent much time on the meaning of *high crimes and misdemeanors*. Whether the acts had to violate some positive law or earlier ruling, or could be ex post facto, did not concern the Americans. Formulas like *high crimes and misdemeanors* sometimes outlive their precise earlier meanings, and through adoption take on new connotations. By 1787, *high crimes and misdemeanors* incorporated misconducts and maladministration which would not be censurable at all if done by a private citizen, with the result that impeachment was common and often commonplace. Lesser officials might be removed for any offense fitting Article II, section 4, no matter how insignificant.

20. *NC House*, 39 (December 5, 1789). Craig's case in Kentucky is traced in the text of chap. 9, preceding n. 34.

21. *Ky Senate*, 55 (December 20, 1794); 35 (December 15, 1795); Patricia Watlington, *The Partisan Spirit, Kentucky Politics, 1779–1791* (New York, 1972), 82–83, 172–73, 174, 178; W.E. Connelly and E. Merton Coulter, *History of Kentucky* (Chicago, 1922), 1: 310, 311.

22. William Greenleaf to Governor James Bowdoin, February 17, 1787, Bowdoin-Temple Papers, MHi; Octavius Pickering and William H. Gardiner, *Report of the Trial By Impeachment of James Prescott ... in the Year 1821, with an Appendix* (Boston, 1821), 212.

23. Mass House, 413 (March 7, 1788), M-Ar.

24. Mass House, 55, 58, 68 (June 4–5, 1788); 85, 88; (June 12, 1788). Biographical information on the legislators is from Shipton, *Harvard Graduates*, 12–17, Mass. State Library file, "Massachusetts Legislators," and David H. Fischer, *The Revolution of American Conservatism, the Federalist Party in the Era of Jeffersonian Democracy* (New York, 1965).

25. Expenses for the impeachment inquiry are listed in *Acts and Resolves of the Commonwealth of Massachusetts, 1788–89* (reprinted, Boston, 1894), 218, 268, 277. These include expenses for Greenleaf's trial.

26. Mass House, 98, 99, 101 (June 14, 1788).

27. Blackstone, *Commentaries*, 4: 302.

28. *Mass. Acts and Resolves* (Boston, 1866), 5: 620.

29. Mass House, 101 (June 14, 1788); 134 (June 20, 1788).

30. Diary of William Heath, Heath MS., November 5, 1788, MHi.

31. Mass. Senate File Papers, #73, has the writ to coroners, July 14, 1788, and Greenleaf's Plea, November 11, 1788.

32. Thomas C. Amory, *The Life of James Sullivan* (Boston, 1859), 1: 238–39. The senate file papers include drafts of agreements of managers with Greenleaf's counsel, November 12, 1788.

33. Bayard, speech to Senate, January 3, 1799, Wharton, *Blount,* 263; and see the discussion of Pickering's case in the text of chap. 11, following n. 4, as well as *Memoirs of Adams,* 1: 327–28, on *Chase.*

34. Mass Senate, 129 (November 5, 1788); 141 (November 11, 1788); *Massachusetts Centinel* (Boston), November 5, 17, 1788.

35. *Massachusetts Spy, or Worcester Gazette,* November 13, 1788.

36. *NHSP,* 21: 465, 467 (January 20, 1789); 599–600 (June 10, 1789).

37. Jere R. Daniel, *Experiment in Republicanism, New Hampshire Politics and the American Revolution, 1741–1794* (Cambridge, Mass., 1970), 84, 143, 144; William Plumer, MS Biography, 4: 305, NhHi.

38. *NHSP,* 21: 201–02, 393, 476, 676.

39. Josiah Bartlett and John Dudley, justices, to House of Representatives, September 17, 1789, Josiah Bartlett Papers, NhHi.

40. Woodbury Langdon to House of Representatives, December 23, 1789, NH Sess.

41. *NHSP,* 22: 76, 77, 81, 82, 85, 86, 90 (June 16–18, 1790).

42. *NHSP,* 22: appendix, Senate 751–55 (June 19, 1790).

43. William Plumer MS, Biography, 307, NhHi.

44. Plumer to Abiel Foster, June 28, 1790, Plumer Letterbook, 1: 1781–1804, NhHi.

45. Plumer to Smith, July 6, 1790, Plumer Letterbook.

46. Langdon to House of Representatives, June, 1790, NH Sess.

47. *NHSP,* 22: Senate, 117 (January 28, 1791); 135 (February 11, 1791).

48. Langdon to the Senate, January 17, 1791, NH Sess.

49. *NHSP,* 22: House, 172 (January 22, 1791); 177 (January 26, 1791).

50. *NHSP,* 22: Senate, 241–42 (February 17, 1791).

51. Langdon to Plumer, March 1, 1791, Plumer MS, NhHi.

52. NH House, 650 (December 10, 1798); Albert S. Batchellor, ed., "Biographical Sketch of Judge Woodbury Langdon" [taken from Plumer, MS Biography], *NHSP,* 20: 812–15.

53. NH House, 176 (February 16, 1791).

54. NH House, 250 (December 1, 1791); 308 (December 28, 1791); 70 (December 22, 1794).

55. Timothy Olcott and Timothy Farrar to John Dudley, October 8, 1794, John Dudley, Superior Court Papers, 1784–96, NhHi; NH House, 62–63 (January 8, 1795). On Pickering see biographical data cited in chap. 11, n. 4, below.

56. NH House, 69 (January 10, 1795); 365 (December 9, 1796); 398–99 (December 13, 1796); Governor J. T. Gilman Address to NH House, 163–65 (December 3, 1795).

57. This, despite Henry H. Metcalf, ed., *Laws of New Hampshire, 1784–1792* (Concord, N.H., 1916), 5: 845, ed. note: "It was generally considered that personal animosity was at the bottom of the procedure."

58. See discussion at chap. 11, n. 23.

59. Josiah Bartlett to his son, January 15, 1791, Bartlett Papers, NhHi; Daniel, *Experiment,* 226.

60. "Henry Osborne," Genealogical files, G-Ar; Camden County MS, G-Ar; Maguerite Reddich, comp., *Camden's Challenge, A History of Camden County, Georgia* (Camden County, 1976), 147.

61. Osborne to State Treasurer, January 1, 1788, Georgia Executive Dept. Incoming Correspondence, file II, G-Ar.

62. Osborne to Governor, December 15, 1790, Georgia Executive Dept., Incoming Correspondence, file II, G-Ar.

63. Harry E. Wildes, *Anthony Wayne, Trouble Shooter of the American Revolution* ([1947] New York, 1970), 335-47.

64. William O. Foster, *James Jackson, Duelist and Militant Statesman, 1757-1806* (Athens, Ga., 1960), 90-101.

65. [Savannah] *Georgia Gazette*, August 11, 1791; July 28, 1791.

66. *Augusta* [Georgia] *Chronicle*, September 24, 1791.

67. Ga House, Nov. 14, 1791, in *Augusta Chronicle*, November 24, 1791 [the original is lost].

68. Ga House, November 23, 1791.

69. Anthony Wayne to Thomas Gibbons et al., November 29, 1791, Wayne MS, PHi.

70. Ga Senate, November 24, 25, 26, 1791, in *Augusta Chronicle*, December 10, 1791.

71. Ga Senate, November 26, 1791, in *Augusta Chronicle*, December 10, 1791.

72. Ga Senate, December 3, 1791, in *Augusta Chronicle*, December 10, 1791.

73. Ga Senate, 251-52 (December 16, 1791), G-Ar.

74. Ga Senate, 227-28 (December 9, 1791).

75. Ga Senate, 10-13 (December 19, 20, 1791).

76. Ga Senate, 30-31 (December 21, 1791).

77. Ga Senate, 21 (December 20, 1791).

78. Ga Senate, 25 (December 23, 1791).

79. Foster, *Jackson*, 100-01; Petition of Augusta, Georgia, Citizens to "Restore Henry Osborne . . . to All the Rights," in Edward Telfair Papers, Telamon Cuyler Coll., Ga.

80. SC House, 55-56 (December 10, 1791).

81. SC House, 148, 149 (December 19, 1791).

82. SC House, 176 (December 20, 1792).

83. SC Senate, 86 (December 10, 1792).

84. SC Senate, Sessions Papers, 1792.

85. SC Senate, 86 (December 10, 1792).

86. SC Senate, Dec. 8, 1792, Sessions Papers.

87. SC Senate, 57-58 (December 10, 1793). Once the lower house proved earnest, the mere threat of impeachment was powerful enough to drive Chancellor Richard Huston, a drunkard, from office (see James W. Ely, "Judicial Incompetents and the Struggle for Democracy in South Carolina," *Vanderbilt Law Review*, 30 (March 1977), 171.

88. *Biographical Directory of the South Carolina House of Representatives*, ed. N. Louise Bailey and Elizabeth I. Cooper (Columbia, S.C., 1981), 3: 515-16.

89. C. Peter Magrath, *Yazoo, Law and Politics in the New Republic* (New York, 1967), 3-5.

90. Moultrie to Commissioners for Settling the Public Accounts, April 20, July 25, 1792, Alexander Moultrie Papers, Sc-Ar. Unknown to the commission, Moultrie was desperately trying to unscramble his speculations; a "Memorial to the Georgia Senate, December 12, 1791," signed by Moultrie, for himself and others, sought to close the Yazoo land deal (James Jackson Papers, Cuyler Coll., Ga.).

91. Commissioners to Moultrie, April 18, July 12, October 25, 1792, March 3, 1793, Moultrie Papers.

92. SC House, December 18, 1792.

93. Moultrie to Commissioners, endorsed by latter, November 13, 1792, January 12, 1793, Moultrie Papers.

94. Moultrie to Commissioners, February 25, 1793, SC House Sessions Papers.

95. SC House, "Committee for Preparing Articles of Impeachment," Report, December 19, 1792, House Sessions Papers.

96. SC House, Committee to Impeach, legal papers attaching Moultrie, in Court of Common Pleas, for debt of £85,104.3.10 to the state. Pringle, the attorney general, also asked damages of £85,108.11.0. The warrant was issued March 25, 1793, and the judgment given November 17, 1793.

97. This correspondence limns a sad tale in the land-speculative mania of post-revolutionary America. Moultrie was not alone in its grasp. James Wilson, Robert Morris, and William Blount, to mention but three of the many who also have parts in our story, were bitten by the bug. Moultrie to Commissioners, July 17, August 18, September 19, October 18, 1793; Commissioners to Moultrie, January 8, February 11, February 25, July 16, August 15, 1793, SC House Sessions Papers. The committee to impeach Moultrie also obtained depositions from the recipients of Moultrie's largesse—damaging admissions of financial manipulation by the defendant (Committee to impeach, correspondence, November 14-23, 1793, SC House Sessions Papers).

98. SC Senate Sessions Papers, December 10, 1793, has Moultrie's "Answer" to charges.

99. SC Senate, 58-61 (December 10, 1793).

100. SC Senate, 72-73 (December 11, 1793).

101. The party ramifications of Moultrie's activity are traced in George C. Rogers, Jr., *Evolution of a Federalist, William Loughton Smith of Charleston (1758-1812)* (Columbia, S.C., 1962), 254-58.

102. Robert D. Arbuckle, *Pennsylvania Speculator and Patriot: The Entrepreneurial John Nicholson, 1757-1804* (University Park, Pa., 1975), 39-60.

103. Nicholson to Jasper Yeates, June 20, 1792, Edward Hand Papers, PHi.

104. *Pennsylvania Statutes at Large*, 12 (Harrisburg, Pa., 1908), 264-66 (March 27, 1789); 14 (Harrisburg, 1909), 62-66 (April 7, 1791); 305-12 (April 10, 1792).

105. Hogan, *Trials*, 70-71, 77, 78-81 (December 4-5, 1793) (hereafter cited in this chapter as Hogan).

106. Hogan, 85-86, 91, 96, 100-01, 108 (April 3-11, 1793).

107. Hogan, 110-61 (Sept. 3, 1793); 195 (December 20, 1793).

108. Hogan, 203-06 (January 9, 1794).

109. Hogan, 196 (February 19, 1794).

110. Hogan, 270 (February 25, 1794).

111. Hogan, 270 (February 26, 1794); 277, 301 (March 5, 1794); 310-16 (March 8, 1794); 337 (March 9, 1794).

112. Hogan, 341-42 (March 10, 1794); 391-410, 414 (March 11, 1794); 438-40 (March 12, 1794); 509 (March 16, 1794).

113. Hogan, 531, 528, 534, 543, 557, 577 (March 21, 1794); 672-73 (March 22, 1794).

114. Arbuckle, *Nicholson*, 37. On the domino effect of speculative failure, see Alfred F. Young, *The Democratic Republicans of New York, The Origins, 1763-1797* (Chapel Hill, 1967), 298-99.

115. Hogan, 753-57 (April 5-9, 1794).

116. Arbuckle, *Nicholson*, 60.

117. Shipton, *Harvard Graduates*, 17: 46-48.

118. Mass House, 233 (January 20, 1794); 317 (February 11, 1794), 330 (February 13, 1794); Mass Senate File Papers, #160; Sullivan to House of Representatives, January 20, 1794, House File Papers, M-Ar.

119. Mass House, 330 (February 13, 1794). On the defense team, see David H. Fischer, *The Revolution of American Conservatism, the Federalist Party in the Era of Jeffersonian Democracy*, 254, and Samuel Eliot Morison, *Harrison Gray Otis, The Urbane Federalist, 1765-1848* (Boston, 1969), 75. On the two parties, see Paul Goodman, *The Democratic Republicans of Massachusetts, Politics in a Young Republic* (Cambridge, Mass., 1964), 121-22.

120. Mass Senate File Papers, #160, February 20, 1794; Mass Senate 233 (February 20, 1794).

121. Mass House, February 22, 1794; February 25, 1794; Mass Senate, February 22, 1794; February 25, 1794.

122. *Massachusetts Centinel*, February 22, 1794; *Massachusetts Mercury*, February 25, 1794.

123. Seven Petitions of Robert C. Walton, March 10–October 30, 1795, Box 16, NJ Sess; Report of Committee, November 2, 1795, 2656 AM, NJ Sess, Nj.

124. *Annals of Cong.*, 2d Cong., 1st sess. (House) 556, 557, 559, 573. (1792); Max Farrand, "The First Hayburn case, 1792," *AHR* 13 (1907-08), 281-85; Charles Page Smith, *James Wilson, Founding Father, 1742-1798* (Chapel Hill, 1956), 348-49.

125. *Papers of Hamilton*, 13, ed. headnote, 532-33; Dumas Malone, *Jefferson and the Ordeal of Liberty, Jefferson and His Time, III* (Boston, 1962), 32-33; Robert Hendrickson, *Hamilton, II: 1789-1804* (New York, 1976), 225-45.

126. *Annals of Cong.*, 2d Cong., 2d sess. (House), 753-61, 835-36 (1792-93).

127. *Annals of Cong.*, 2d Cong., 2d sess. (House), 840 (1793).

128. Hamilton, "Report on the Balance of All Unapplied Revenues...," February 4, 1793, *Papers of Hamilton*, 13: 546-47.

129. *Annals of Cong.*, 2d Cong., 2d sess. (House), 900 (1793).

130. *Annals of Cong.*, 2d Cong., 2d sess. (House), 959-66 (1793).

131. Hamilton to William Short, March 15, 1793; Edward Carrington to Hamilton, March 26, 1793, *Papers of Hamilton*, 14: 206-07, 247-48.

132. Richard Buel, Jr., *Securing the Revolution, Ideology in American Politics, 1789-1815* (Ithaca, N.Y., 1972), 94-97.

CHAPTER 8

1. Stephen G. Kurtz, *Presidency of John Adams, the Collapse of Federalism, 1795-1800* (Philadelphia, 1957), 22, 24.

2. *Annals of Cong.*, 4th Cong., 1st sess. (House), 426 (1796); see also Kurtz, *Presidency of Adams*, 44-49.

3. *Annals of Cong.*, 4th Cong., 1st sess. (House), 760-62 (1796).

4. "The Defense," no. 38 [New York, January 9, 1796], *Papers of Hamilton*, 20: 24-25.

5. Kurtz, *Presidency of Adams*, 51-52.

6. A. C. Quisenberry, *The Life and Times of Humphrey Marshall* (Winchester, Ky., 1892), 50, 56, 57.

7. Stuart S. Sprague, "Kentucky and the Navigation of the Mississippi, the Climatic Years, 1793-1795," *Register of the Kentucky Historical Society* 71 (October 1973), 388-91.

8. *Ky House*, November 21, 1795; December 16, 1795.

9. *Annals of Cong.*, 4th Cong., 1st sess. (Senate), 58-60 (1796).

10. Pickering to John Adams, November 5, 1798, *Works of Adams*, 8: 616. Gerry and Adams were close friends (see George Athan Billias, *Elbridge Gerry, Founding Father and Republican Statesman* [New York, 1976], 294, on this incident).

11. See discussion in the text of chap. 8 following n. 20.

12. On the plot against Randolph, see Albert Hall Bowman, *The Struggle for Neutrality, Franco-American Diplomacy During the Federalist Era* (Knoxville, 1974), 214-18.

13. Ga House, 2, 3, 6 (January 15-16, 22, 1796); Foster, *Jackson*, 114-23.

14. Foster, *Jackson*, 123-24; Ga House, 8-10 (January 25, 1796); C. Peter Magrath, *Yazoo* (New York, 1967), 6-7.

15. Foster, *Jackson*, 124; Jackson always felt this way; typically: "I have daily abuse poured on me from all quarters" (Jackson to John Milledge, April 11, 1796, *Correspondence of John Milledge, Governor of Georgia, 1802-1806*, ed. Harriet Milledge Smalley [Columbia, S.C., 1949], 42). His victims were equally plaintive: James Gunn reported that "infamous provocations appear every day" on December 23, 1796. (Gunn to W. Jones, Keith Reid Coll., Gu).

16. Clayton Family Genealogy File, Inventories of the County Archives of Georgia, no. 121: Richmond County, G-Ar. Minutes of the Executive Department, Georgia, 1794, 181, G-Ar, has Clayton's letter of resignation as court clerk.

17. Georgia Treasury Department, Clayton's Ledger, 1794-96, G-Ar.

18. Ga House, 77 (January 25, 1796).

19. February-March 1796, in Jackson's handwriting, reprinted in "Papers of James Jackson, 1781-1798," ed. Lilla M. Hawes, *Collections of the Georgia Historical Society* (Savannah, 1955), 11: 30-31.

20. Minutes of Exec. Dept., March 2, 1796, G-Ar, notes Clayton's resignation. The treasury ledger for February 10, 1796, p. 5, has Shepherd's expenses and reimbursement of $61. For 1794 he received $142, all on warrants from speaker Thomas Napier. This amount was about average for legislators.

21. William H. Masterson, *William Blount* (Baton Rouge, 1954), 298-99. A sample of the detailed and enervating complexity of these schemes appears in Blount to John Gray Blount, Nov. 7, 1797, *John Gray Blount Papers*, ed. William H. Masterson et al. (Raleigh, N.C., 1965), 3, particularly 176-86.

22. Robert Liston, the British ambassador, was the clearinghouse for this correspondence, nothing of which actually named Blount until after the congressional investigation was under way (Liston to [Lord Grenville], July 8, 1797, "Documents on the Blount Conspiracy, 1795-1797," ed. Frederick Jackson Turner, *AHR*, 10 [April 1905], 592-94). Before that, Blount was included among the unnamed "employers and partners" of the venture.

23. *Annals of Cong.*, 5th Cong., 1st sess. (House), 448-66, (1797); Masterson, *Blount*, 315-17; the Pickering to Liston correspondence is traced in Gerald H. Clarfield, *Timothy Pickering and American Diplomacy, 1795-1800* (Columbia, Mo., 1969), 133.

24. William Blount to J. G. Blount, Nov. 7, 1797, *Papers of Blount*, 3: 175. John Dawson, Jr., a Virginia congressman, reported Republican tactics to Madison (Dawson to Madison, August 13, 24, 1797, Madison Papers, LC).

25. John Adams to Atty General of the U.S. [Charles Lee], June 20, 1797; Adams Letter Book, March 1797-June 1797, Adams Papers, MHi; Masterson, *Blount*, 316; Wharton, *Blount*, 200 (hereafter cited in this chapter as Wharton).

26. *Constitution of the United States*, Article I, section 5, pt. 2.

27. Wharton, 202, 250-52. The holdout was Henry Tazewell of Virginia; *Annals of Cong.*, 5th Cong., 1st sess. (Senate), 40-41, 44 (1797).

28. Wharton, 202-03.

29. Blount to Romayne, February 9, 1797, in Wharton, 210-11.

30. Wharton, 216-17.

31. Wharton, 221-26.

32. Wharton, 252.

33. Wharton, 253-55.

34. Morton Borden, *The Federalism of James A. Bayard* (New York, 1955), 49–52.

35. Borden, *Bayard*, 60. Irving Brant, *Impeachment, Trials and Errors* (New York, 1972), 37, goes further: "The guilt or innocence of William Blount was reduced to insignificance; the issue at stake was the political rights of all Americans." Brant, as Borden, believes that the motive for the impeachment was partisan.

36. Wharton, 257–60.

37. Wharton, 262–63.

38. Wharton, 263.

39. Wharton, 266, 267–68, 270.

40. Wharton, 263–64.

41. Wharton, 271.

42. Wharton, 271.

43. Wharton, 271.

44. For example, Brant, *Impeachment*, 42–43, loses the force of the refutation of senatorial exemption.

45. Berger, *Impeachment*, 229–30.

46. See Brant, *Impeachment*, 28–29.

47. Jefferson to Madison, February 8, 15, 22, 1798, Madison Papers, LC.

48. Madison to Jefferson, March 4, 1798, Madison Papers, LC.

49. Wharton, 273–75.

50. Wharton, 281–83.

51. Wharton, 286.

52. Wharton, 289.

53. Wharton, 300.

54. Wharton, 301.

55. Wharton, 302–03.

56. Wharton, 316.

57. *Gazette of the United States,* April 14, 1800.

CHAPTER 9

1. Vt. Const. of 1793 (sections 23 and 24), *Sources and Documents,* 9: 512.

2. *Vt Assembly,* 551–52 (1799).

3. *Vt Assembly,* 587 (October 1799); 657 (November 2, 1799).

4. *Vt Assembly,* 29–31 (October 11, 1800).

5. *Vt Assembly,* 51, 54–55 (October 14, 1800); 72 (October 16, 1800).

6. *Vt Assembly,* 104 (October 20, 1800).

7. *Vt Assembly,* 119 (October 21, 1800); 130 (October 23, 1800).

8. *Vt Assembly,* 121, 129 (October 23, 1800).

9. *Vt Assembly,* 41–42 (February 1, 1804).

10. *Vt Assembly,* 66, 68 (February 3, 1804).

11. *Vt Assembly,* 32 (October 14, 1805).

12. But see discussion of seditious libel law prosecutions in the text of pt. IV, introduction, at n. 15.

13. [Philadelphia] *Aurora,* October 14, 1800.

14. Randolph J. Pasler and Margaret C. Pasler, *The New Jersey Federalists* (Rutherford, N.J., 1975), 42–43.

15. *NJ Assembly,* 21, 28, 89, 90–92 (November 4, 7, 18, 19, 1799); *NJ Council,* 12–13 (November 5, 1800).

16. Pasler and Pasler, *New Jersey Federalists,* 211; Carl E. Prince, *New Jersey's Jeffersonian Republicans* (Chapel Hill, N.C., 1964), 5.

17. *NJ Assembly,* 26–27, 70, 71, 73, 81–83, 95 (November 5, 11, 14, 18, 1801).

18. John Lacey Letter of Resignation to Assembly, November 24, 1801, Assembly Sessions Papers, Nj. A Republican majority in the lower house had refused to play politics with the case (see Prince, *New Jersey's Jeffersonian Republicans*, 105).

19. *NJ Assembly*, 130, 131 (November 30, 1801); 217, 223 (October 29, 1804).

20. *NJ Assembly*, 135 (November 30, 1801); 23 (November 3, 1802).

21. *NJ Assembly*, 405, 408, 410, 413, 419, 460, 462 (November 6, 7, 11, 12, 13, 1805); *NJ Council*, 454, 460, 471, 473 (November 15, 1805, February 7-19, 1806).

22. Copies of indictment, plea, and Supreme Court record, *Commonwealth v. Vinal*, August 1799, Massachusetts Senate File Papers # 228, M-Ar.

23. James Sullivan to Speaker of the House, Feb. 24, 1800, Mass. House File Papers; Mass. House, 339, 342, 348 (Feb. 24, 25, 26, 27, 1800); Report of the Committee to Prepare Articles, Feb. 25, 1800; House File Papers, M-Ar.

24. Senate to Speaker of the House, February 27, 1800. Mass. House File Papers; Senate File Papers # 228, Trial of William Vinal, March 1-3, 1800, M-Ar; [Boston] *Massachusetts Centinel*, March 5, 1800.

25. Ignatius Sargent, "Col. Paul Dudley Sargent of Sullivan, Me," *Bangor* [Me.] *Historical Magazine*, 2 (January 1887); Nathan Gould, "Col. Edmund Phinney's 18th Continental Regiment," *Collections & Proceedings of the Maine Historical Society*, 2d ser., 9 (1898), 48.

26. Edmund H. Bartlett, *Local Government in Penobscot County* (Orono, Me., 1932), 15-16; Petition of Justices of Sessions in Hancock County, to Mass. General Court, January 1790, *Documentary History of the State of Maine*, ed. James P. Baxter, *Colls of the Me. Hist. Soc.*, 2d ser., 22 (1916), 411-14.

27. *Sargent v. Maines and Kent* (May term, 1799), Hancock County, Maine, Court of Common Pleas Record, 3; *Portland* [Maine] *Eastern Herald and Gazette*, October 11, 1799.

28. *Woodman v. Booden* (May term, 1799), Hancock County Court of Common Pleas Record, 3; Hancock Cty. Court of Common Pleas, File Papers, May 1799, no. 131; Me-Ar.

29. Mass House, 28, 31-33, 79, 93, 101, 107 (June 1, 2, 8, 12, 13, 1801).

30. See discussion in epilogue, following n. 1.

31. Stephen A. Channing, *Kentucky, A Bicentennial History* (New York, 1977), 72-73; Joan Wells Coward, *Kentucky in the New Republic, The Process of Constitution Making* (Lexington, Ky., 1979), 153-59.

32. [Lexington] *Kentucky Gazette*, December 25, 1801; November 9, 1802.

33. Robert M. Ireland, *The County Courts in Antebellum Kentucky* (Lexington, Ky., 1972), 7, 10, 79, 100-01, 117-18.

34. *Ky House*, 18, 108-09 (November 6, December 16, 1801); *Ky Senate*, 78-79, 88 (December 14, 16, 1801).

35. *Ky Senate*, 23, 52-53, 58, 59, 60, 62 (November 22, December 5, 6, 7, 1803); [Frankfort] *Palladium*, December 10, 1803.

36. *Ky Senate*, 46, 54, 91, 109, 112, 123 (November 24, 30, December 18, 22, 23, 24, 25, 26, 1805).

37. Captain James Bentham, "Regimental Book," *South Carolina Historical and Genealogical Magazine*, 53 (1952), 13; *Directory for the District of Charleston*, ed. Richard Hrabousky [Charleston, 1809], 8, 135; *Journal of the House of Assembly*, *S.C., 1783-4* (Columbia, S.C., 1977), 98-99.

38. SC House, 120, 210, 214, 215 (December 10, 1803).

39. SC House, 100, 143, 166, 168, 171-72 (December 5, 10, 11, 12, 1804); SC Senate, 124, 136-37 (December 13, 14, 1804).

40. SC Senate, 10, 18, 23, 27, 39, 119, 279 (November 25, 26, 27, 28, 30; December 9, 19, 1805).

41. *Tenn House*, 407, 409, 416 (December 12–14, 1798); *Tenn Senate*, 305, 307, 308, 309, 311–12 (December 17, 1798); "Articles of Impeachment," December 17, 1798, Records Group (RG) 60, box 5, folder 26, T-Ar. See also Cortez A. M. Ewing, "Early Tennessee Impeachments," *Tennessee Historical Quarterly*, 16 (December 1957), 292–96.

42. Masterson, *Blount*, 324–28.

43. Masterson, *Blount*, 328–40; Carl S. Driver, *John Sevier, Pioneer of the Old Southwest* (Chapel Hill, 1932), 137–42.

44. Deposition of Hugh Lawson White, December 12, 1798, RG 60, box 5, folder 25, deposition of Doctor Thomas Claiborn, December 12, 1798; RG 60, box 5, folder 25; deposition of William Blount, December 12, 1798, RG 60, box 5, folder 26, T-Ar.

45. See text of chap. 10, following n. 40, and discussion in chap. 12, at n. 47.

46. Daniel H. Calhoun, *Professional Lives in America, Structure and Aspiration, 1750–1850* (Cambridge, Mass., 1965), 59–87.

47. Joshua W. Caldwell, *Sketches of the Bench and Bar of Tennessee* (Knoxville, 1898), 13–14; Andrew Jackson to George Washington, February 8, 1797, *Papers of Andrew Jackson*, ed. Sam B. Smith and Harriet C. Owsley (Knoxville, 1980), 1: 121–22.

48. Report on Arrest of Judge Campbell, March, 1798, RG 60, box 5, folder 44, T-Ar.

49. Jackson to President John Adams, March 5, 1798, *Papers of Jackson*, 1: 185–86.

50. White, "Deposition," RG 60, box 5, folder 25. Depositions from Edward Scott, a minister, Townsend W. Dade, and William Cocke, the United States senator from Tennessee, as well as from Blount, generally corroborated White (RG 60, box 5, folders 25 and 26, T-Ar).

51. Deposition of Col. J. P. Roddy, December 12, 1798, RG 60, box 5, folder 26, T-Ar.

52. Preamble to Articles of Impeachment against David Campbell, December 17, 1798, RG 60, box 5, folder 29, T-Ar.

53. Campbell, "Memorial to the Honorable the Senate," December 10, 1798, RG 60, box 5, folder 25, T-Ar.

54. *Papers of Jackson*, 1, ed. note, at 213; Masterson, *Blount*, 340–41.

55. Committee Report, "Mode of Proceeding in Cases of Impeachment," December 18, 1798, RG 60, box 5, folder 26; Summons to Witnesses, December 19, 1798, RG 60, box 5, folder 26, T-Ar.

56. *Tenn Senate*, 328–29 (December 24, 1798).

57. *Tenn House*, 39, 42–43, 52–53, 54 (September 28–29, October 3, 1803); Articles of Impeachment, October 3, 1803, RG 60, box 5, folder 25, T-Ar.

58. File Papers, *Hitchings v. Miller* (1801), RG 60, box 5, folder 27; *Tenn Senate*, 51, 58 (October 3, 1803), includes Hugh Lawson White's defense of his guilty vote.

PART IV, INTRODUCTION

1. Jefferson to Madison, February 15, 1798, Madison Papers, LC.

2. MS Draft of Inaugural Address [before March 4, 1801], Jefferson Papers, LC.

3. Noble E. Cunningham, Jr., *The Process of Government Under Jefferson* (Princeton, 1978), 165–70.

4. Jefferson to Giles, March 23, 1801, *Writings of Jefferson*, ed. Ford, 9: 25. Dumas Malone believes that Jefferson truly intended to follow this course (*Jefferson the President: First Term, 1801–1805, Jefferson and His Time, III* [Boston, 1970], 72–73).

5. Jefferson to William Findley, March 24, 1801, *Writings of Jefferson*, ed. Ford, 9: 225.

6. James Willard Hurst, *The Law of Treason in the United States* (Westport, Conn., 1971), 14–67.

7. *Rex v. Peter Messenger* (1668), cited in Chapin, *Treason*, 4.

8. Matthew Hale, *A Treatise of Pleas of the Crown*, 2 vols. (London, 1673), 1: 86. For a more modern confirmation of the link between constructive treason and bad tendency, see Robert F. Cushman, *Cases in Constitutional Law*, 4th ed. (Englewood Cliffs, N.J., 1975), 492–93.

9. Chapin, *Treason*, 87–90.

10. Chapin, *Treason*, 90–97; Jane S. Elsmere, "The Trials of John Fries," *PMHB*, 103 (October 1979), 432–45.

11. [Philadelphia] *Aurora*, March 12, 1799.

12. Walters, *Dallas*, 78–79.

13. Chase, Charges to Grand Jury, 1799–1800, quoted in Haw, *Chase*, 199–200.

14. Dangerous tendency did appear as a test of impeachable offenses as early as Strafford's case, in 1640–41. Thomas Wentworth, Earl of Strafford, was the king's strong right arm in the attempt to coerce money from the realm and obedience from Parliament. When the Commons rose up against the earl, John Pym framed charges of treason: "Other treasons are against the rule of the law: this is against the being of the law. It is the law that unites the King and his people, and the author of this treason hath endeavored to dissolve that union ... of protection and allegiance whereby they are, and I hope ever will be, bound together." Strafford's offense was to make the king appear to be arbitrary and tyrannous, "to bereave a king of the glory of his goodness," and, conversely, to "breed in his majesty an ill opinion of his subjects." Pym's charges were flimsy, for Strafford had the loyalty of the king and acted for the crown. Yet Pym and the other impeachers accused Strafford of intending and working to alienate and withdraw the hearts and affections of the king's "liege people" from him—by the bad tendency of his acts. In the body of the articles, the Commons alleged that Strafford had misruled in Ireland and had placed crown interests ahead of the law in the North country of England, but as Strafford replied in April 1641, there was no evidence of treason. In later and less troubled years, Strafford might have been charged with extortion, misuse of power, and corruption, but the Commons refused to budge from its charge of treason. For Pym, the treason law "doth entitle a king to allegiance and service of his people; it entitles the people to the protection and justice of the King." The bad tendency of Strafford's conduct was evident to the members of Parliament. When the impeachment effort began to flounder, both houses passed a bill of attainder, to which a beleaguered and confused Charles gave his assent. The bad tendency doctrine was thereafter attached to impeachment. See Pym's address and Charles I's reply in J. P. Kenyon, ed., *The Stuart Constitution, 1603–1688, Documents and Commentary* (Cambridge, England, 1966), 206–16.

15. *US Stats*, 1: 596–97; *Annals of Cong.*, 5th Cong. 2d sess., (House), 2171 (1798). The formal title of the act was "An Act, in Addition to the Act, Entitled 'An Act for the Punishment of Certain Crimes against the United States.'"

16. Leonard W. Levy, *Freedom of Speech and Press in Early American History: Legacy of Suppression* (New York, 1963), 241–48, 258; see also Goebel, *Supreme Court*, 1: 635–51.

17. Howell, *State Trials*, 14: 1129.

18. *CJ*, 29: 667 (November 15, 1763).

19. Howell, *State Trials*, 20: 895.

20. Lord Mansfield, c.j., ordering retrial of Woodfall, November 20, 1770, quoted in *A Letter to the Jurors of Great Britain, Occasioned by An Opinion of the Court of Kings Bench ... in the Case of the King and Woodfall* (London, 1771), vi; Hurst, *Law of Treason*, 33–34.

21. *Aurora*, January 19, 27, 1800.

22. *Annals of Cong.*, 5th Cong., 1st sess. (Senate), 67–96, 111–12 (1800).

23. James Morton Smith, *Freedom's Fetters, The Alien and Sedition Laws and American Civil Liberties*, rev. ed. (Ithaca, N.Y., 1966), 288–306.

24. Chase, Charge to Grand Jury, April 1801, in "The Trial of Cooper," [William Cobbett], *Porcupine's Works* (London, 1801), 12: 8.

25. Monroe to Jefferson, March 3, 1801, Jefferson Papers, LC; *Annals of Cong.*, 7th Cong., 1st sess. (House), 982 (1802).

26. Giles to Jefferson, March 16, 1801; June 1, 1801, Jefferson Papers, LC; *Annals of Cong.*, 7th Cong., 1st sess. (House), 579–602 (1801).

27. William C. Bruce, *John Randolph of Roanoke, 1773–1833*, 2 vols. ([1922] New York, 1970), 1: 140–200; Plumer to Theodore Lyman, March 17, 1804, Plumer Papers, LC; *Memoirs of Adams*, 1: 318. Randolph's supposed aims for Congress were disclosed by Timothy Pickering (a fervent Federalist), in a letter to Theodore Lyman, February 11, 1804 (Henry C. Lodge, ed., *Life and Letters of George Cabot* [Boston, 1878], 444). Pickering was hardly an objective observer, but the imputation was logical.

CHAPTER 10

1. Sanford Higginbotham, *The Keystone in the Democratic Arch: Pennsylvania Politics, 1800–1916* (Harrisburg, Pa., 1952), 25–76.

2. David H. Fischer, *The Revolution of American Conservatism: The Federalist Party in the Era of Jeffersonian Democracy* (New York, 1965), 328–32.

3. Russell J. Ferguson, *Early Western Pennsylvania Politics* (Pittsburgh, 1938), 138–54.

4. Higginbotham, *Keystone*, 37–38.

5. Ellis, *Jeffersonian Crisis*, 161–66.

6. Addison, introduction, *Reports of Cases in the County Courts of the Fifth Circuit* (Washington, Pa., 1800). On Federalist fears about Republican judicial reforms in 1801 and after, see Haskins, *Supreme Court*, 2, pt. 1, 165–67.

7. *Papers of Adams*, 1: 252–309.

8. Berger, *Impeachment*, 160–65.

9. Berger, *Impeachment*, 166–72.

10. Dana's charge to Grand Jury of Suffolk in 1804 brought forth "Sidney" in the [Worcester] *National Aegis*, October 24, 1804.

11. Ellis, *Jeffersonian Crisis*, 194–96.

12. *The Examination, No. XV* (March 3, 1802), *Papers of Hamilton*, 25: 558.

13. *The Examination, No. XV, Papers of Hamilton*, 25: 556, 558.

14. Brackenridge, *Modern Chivalry*, ed. Claude M. Newlin (New York, 1937), 449.

15. Fischer, *Revolution of American Conservatism*, 339–40, 341, 344. The full blossoming of the bar lay a decade or so in the future, however (Perry Miller, *The Life of the Mind in America* [New York, 1965], 109–10).

16. Ferguson, *Western Pennsylvania*, 115–16.

17. Addison, "Charge to the Grand Jury of the Fifth District, September sess., 1798," in Addison, *Reports of Cases in the County Courts of the Fifth District*, 280, 285; Addison, *Analysis of the Report of the Committee of the Virginia Association* (Philadelphia, 1800), 3, 8.

18. Washington to Marshall, December 30, 1798, *Papers of Marshall*, 3: 530–31; Ellsworth to Pickering, December 12, 1798, quoted in Goebel, *Supreme Court*, 1: 646–47.

19. Brackenridge, "Incidents of the Insurrection in Western Pennsylvania ...1794,"

in Daniel Marder, ed., *A Hugh Henry Brackenridge Reader: 1770–1815* (Pittsburgh, 1970), 279, 301, 325.

20. Elvert M. Davis, "The Bates Boys on the Western Waters, Part II," *Western Pennsylvania Historical Magazine,* 29 (September–December 1946), 128–30; Hugh C. Cleland, "John B. C. Lucas, Physiocrat on the Frontier," *Western Pennsylvania Historical Magazine,* 36 (September–December 1953), 146–52.

21. Brackenridge to Lucas, May 1, 1801, cited in Cleland, "Lucas," 149.

22. Lloyd, *Addison,* 5 (hereafter cited in this chapter as Lloyd).

23. Lloyd, 6.

24. Lloyd, 7.

25. Lloyd, 8–9.

26. Lloyd, 11–12.

27. McKean judged that Addison's actions were so rash that even his Federalist allies would refuse to come to his aid. Events proved this prediction partially correct (G. S. Rowe, *Thomas McKean, The Shaping of an American Republicanism* [Boulder, Colo., 1978], 360–89).

28. Lloyd, 16–17.

29. Lloyd, 31, 36.

30. Lloyd, 44.

31. Addison, "Charge to Grand Jury, Sept. sess., 1798," 285; *Analysis of the Report, 1800,* 30–33, 34.

32. [James Madison], "Virginia Resolutions," December 21, 1798, *Writings of Madison,* 6: 326–31.

33. Lloyd, 48.

34. Lloyd, 46, 52–53.

35. Lloyd, 50.

36. Lloyd, 48–49.

37. Lloyd, 55–60.

38. Lloyd, 69–70, quoting the March 1801, Supreme Court hearing.

39. Lloyd, 72.

40. Lloyd, 75–76, 80.

41. Quite true, but as Federalists dominated the bench in the 1790s these charges, by Justices James Iredell, William Paterson, and Samuel Chase of the United States Supreme Court, among others, were increasingly uniform and shrill in their anti-Jeffersonianism. On the practice, see Don Higginbotham, ed., *The Papers of James Iredell* (Raleigh, N.C., 1976), 2: ed. note at 24.

42. Lloyd, 98.

43. Lloyd, 105.

44. Lloyd, 110.

45. Lloyd, 119.

46. Lloyd, 119–20.

47. Walters, *Dallas,* 122–23, attributes the counselor's narrow argument to his "growing conservatism." On *Shippen's Case,* see chap. 11, discussion in text beginning at n. 34.

48. Lloyd, 73.

49. Lloyd, 101.

50. Lloyd, 105.

51. Lloyd, 122.

52. Lloyd, 129. Dallas knew all this and included part of the debate in the lower house over Oswald's petition in an appendix to his report on the contempt hearing (*Respublica v. Oswald* [1788], *Reports of Cases Ruled and Adjudged in the Courts of Pennsylvania,* 3d ed. [Philadelphia, 1830], 1: 358).

53. Lloyd, 137.
54. Lloyd, 151–52.
55. Lloyd, 153–54. Walters, *Dallas*, 128, argues that Dallas wanted this moderate punishment.
56. *Aurora*, January 12, 1804.
57. See chap. 12, n. 11.

CHAPTER 11

1. Jefferson to James Duane, July 24, 1803, Jefferson Papers, LC. Plumer obliquely showed his knowledge of the Addison case in his animosity to John Lucas, Addison's accuser (see Plumer, *Memorandum*, 130–31, 393).
2. Although the doctrine may appear to be a close cousin of "recall," the relation between the two is not so strong. Recall, a "populist" device to remove legislators as well as other officials, could be and often was aimed at corruption in the very branch whose powers Giles and Randolph wanted to expand.
3. Though the doctrine could be borrowed from "corresponding" state cases, the jurisdiction over persons was distinct.
4. "John Pickering, Class of 1761," Shipton, *Harvard Graduates* (Boston, 1970), 15: 91–96.
5. Plumer wrote on Pickering to John Hale, September 18, 1786, a letter reprinted in *Publications of the Colonial Society of Massachusetts, Transactions for 1906–1907* (Boston, 1910), 11: 389–90.
6. See discussion beginning at n. 55 in text of chap. 7. Timothy Olcott to John Dudley, Oct. 8, 1794, Dudley Superior Court Papers, NhHi.
7. Dumas Malone, *Jefferson the President: First Term, 1801–1805, Jefferson and His Time, III* (Boston, 1970), 410–61; *Annals of Cong.*, 7th Cong., 2d sess. (House), 460 (1803).
8. *Annals of Cong.*, 8th Cong., 1st sess. (House), 380, 790 (1803).
9. *Annals of Cong.*, 8th Cong., 1st sess. (House), 795, 797, 801 (1803–04).
10. *Annals of Cong.*, 8th Cong., 1st sess. (Senate), 346–47, 350–51 (1804).
11. Macon to Joseph Nicholson, July 26, 1803, Nicholson Papers, LC. Berger, *Impeachment*, 192, finds the verdict "a common-sense view."
12. *Annals of Cong.*, 8th Cong., 1st sess. (Senate) [*Trial of Pickering*], 315–18 (1803); *Memoirs of Adams*, 1: 283; Plumer, *Memorandum*, 97.
13. Plumer, *Memorandum*, 97–98; *Annals of Cong.*, 8th Cong., 1st sess. (Senate), 317, 319 (1804).
14. Plumer, *Memorandum*, 97–99.
15. *Annals of Cong.*, 8th Cong., 1st sess. (Senate), 319–26 (1804).
16. Plumer, *Memorandum*, 100–01.
17. Plumer, *Memorandum*, 101–02.
18. Jeremiah Mason to William Plumer, January 29, 1804; Plumer Papers, NhHi.
19. Plumer, *Memorandum*, 148–49; *Memoirs of Adams*, 1: 297–99.
20. *Annals of Cong.*, 8th Cong., 1st sess. (Senate), 328 (1804).
21. In the states that allowed removal upon an address to the governor, impeachment and trial were not necessary to oust an insane incumbent. Shortly before the Senate reached a decision on the admissibility of Jacob Pickering's affidavit, Jabez Bowen, Jr., a Georgia superior court judge, began to evidence mental instability. In his court he railed against the "wretched effects of party spirit" upon his political enemies and warned the grand jurors that his views alone were correct. He then publicly burned court records and committed the entire grand jury to gaol. Litigants and defendants faced the fury of the judge as well (see, for example, petitions to the

governor growing out of *State v. Bolton* [January 1804] in John Milledge Papers, box 45, Cuyler Coll., Gu). Both houses petitioned Governor John Milledge to remove the judge, which the governor did in May 1804 (Ga House, May 16, 1804; Ga Senate, May 17, 1804; [Savannah, Georgia] *Republican and State Intelligencer*, January 13, May 29, July 24, 1804). Bowen, a transplanted New Englander, returned to his home in the north for treatment but was later found to be incurably insane. Benjamin B. Carter to Huldah M. Carter, April 1, 1820, describes Bowen's conduct in a Philadelphia lunatic asylum (*Proceedings of the Rhode Island Historical Society, 1893–1894* [Providence, 1894], 249).

22. Plumer, *Memorandum*, 158–62.

23. *Annals of Cong.*, 8th Cong., 1st sess. (Senate), 328–30 (1804).

24. Plumer, *Memorandum*, 164–66, 167.

25. *Annals of Cong.*, 8th Cong., 1st sess. (Senate), 332 (1804).

26. Plumer, *Memorandum*, 168–72.

27. *Annals of Cong.*, 8th Cong., 1st sess. (Senate), 340, 342 (1804).

28. *Annals of Cong.*, 8th Cong., 1st sess. (Senate), 344, 345 (1804).

29. *Annals of Cong.*, 8th Cong., 1st sess. (Senate), 348, 349, 351, 353, 359–61 (1804).

30. *Annals of Cong.*, 8th Cong., 1st sess. (Senate), 362–63 (1804); *Memoirs of Adams*, 1: 302–03; Plumer, *Memorandum*, 174–76.

31. *Memoirs of Adams*, 1: 305–07; J. Q. Adams to Timothy Pickering, March 11, 1804 (2 letters and enclosure), *Writings of John Quincy Adams*, ed. Worthington C. Ford (New York, 1914), 3: 34–38.

32. *Annals of Cong.*, 8th Cong., 1st sess. (Senate), 364 (1804); *Memoirs of Adams*, 1: 309.

33. *Memoirs of Adams*, 1: 309; *Annals of Cong.*, 8th Cong., 1st sess. (Senate), 367–68 (1804).

34. Lynn W. Turner, "The Impeachment of John Pickering," *AHR*, 54 (April 1949), 505–06.

35. *Memoirs of Adams*, 1: 310.

36. Elizabeth K. Henderson, "The Attack on the Judiciary in Pennsylvania, 1800–1810," *PMHB*, 61 (April 1937), 113–26; Ellis, *Jeffersonian Crisis*, 157–80; Brackenridge, *Modern Chivalry*, ed. Claude M. Newlin (New York, 1937), 389.

37. *Aurora*, June 25; August 3, 1803. "Aratus" attacked the judges.

38. Hamilton, *Shippen*, 6–7, 9, 12.

39. Monroe to Breckinridge, January 15, 1802, cited in Haskins, *Supreme Court*, 2, pt. 1, 205; Hamilton, *Shippen*, 13–14.

40. James L. Anderson, "The Impact of the American Revolution on the Governor's Councillors," *Pennsylvania History*, 34 (April 1967), 138.

41. *Aurora*, January 9, 1804.

42. "Diary of the Hon. Jonathan Mason," *Proceedings of the Massachusetts Historical Society*, 2d ser., 2 (Boston, 1885), 12.

43. Richard Smith to Jasper Yeates, March 11, 1804, Dreer Coll., PHi.

44. Walters, *Dallas*, 129–30; Edward Shippen to Jasper Yeates, February 13, 1804, Legal Men of Pennsylvania Folio, PHi.

45. Shippen to Jasper Yeates, April 6, 1804, Simon Graatz Coll., PHi. The defense was originally broached in a letter to the lower house (Hamilton, *Shippen*, 12–13).

46. Thomas Smith to Jasper Yeates, March 28, 1804, Graatz Coll., PHi.

47. Jasper Yeates to Edward Burd, January 8, 1805, Addenda to Mrs. Burd, Shippen Papers, PHi.

48. Brackenridge, *Modern Chivalry*, 389.

49. Brackenridge, *Modern Chivalry*, 396.

50. Brackenridge, *Modern Chivalry*, 453-54. See Blackstone, *Commentaries*, 4: 280-81, on the law, and Bradley Chapin, *Criminal Justice in Colonial America, 1606-1660* (Athens, Ga., 1983), 29-30, and William E. Nelson, *Americanization of the Common Law: The Impact of Legal Change on Massachusetts Society, 1760-1830* (Cambridge, Mass., 1975), 38-39, on the American practice.

51. Brackenridge, *Modern Chivalry*, 454-55.

52. Hamilton, *Shippen*, 36-37, 59, 97, 112, 123.

53. Hamilton, *Shippen*, 178, 182, 185, 187, 188, 250, 282.

54. Hamilton, *Shippen*, 297, 305, 315, 321, 323.

55. Hamilton, *Shippen*, 326, 331-32.

56. Hamilton, *Shippen*, 334, 355.

57. Hamilton, *Shippen*, 370, 376.

58. Hamilton, *Shippen*, 378-79, 389.

59. Hamilton, *Shippen*, 491.

60. *Aurora*, January 28, 1805, but the issue was put to press before the verdict was returned.

61. A. J. Dallas to Thomas McKean, January 16, 1805, McKean Papers, PHi.

62. *Aurora*, January 29, 1805.

63. *Aurora*, February 9, 1805; March 3, 1805.

64. James Hopkins to A. J. Dallas, January 28, 1805, George M. Dallas Coll., PHi.

65. William Barton to Jared Ingersoll, January 28, 1805, George M. Dallas Coll., PHi.

66. Walters, *Dallas*, 131-32.

67. *Aurora*, January 28, 1805, citing an article in the Boston *Palladium*. The *Aurora*, January 24, 1805, used an article from the *Republican Argus*, to the same conclusion: no mere reform of the courts gave relief against the power of corruptly partisan or tyrannical judges.

CHAPTER 12

1. Samuel Chase, "Instructions to the Grand Jury," undated MS in Chase Papers, quoted in L. Marx Renzulli, Jr., *Maryland: The Federalist Years* (Rutherford, N.J., 1972), 237.

2. Haw, *Chase*, 191-208. District Judge Richard Peters's often quoted "I never sat with him without Pain," written in 1804, summed up Peters's view of a long association with Chase on the Eastern Circuit.

3. Chase's version appears in Smith, *Trial of Chase*, 1: 28-46 (hereafter cited in this chapter as Smith, *Trial*); Haw, *Chase*, 199-201. Evidence for the prosecution begins in Smith, *Trial*, 1: 127.

4. Smith, *Trial*, 1: 49-89; Haw, *Chase*, 202-06. See Stephen Presser, "A Tale of Two Judges: Richard Peters, Samuel Chase, and the Broken Promise of Federalist Jurisprudence," *Northwestern Law Review*, 73 (1978), 88-93, a sympathetic account of Chase's conduct of the trial.

5. Smith, *Trial*, 1: 89-93, and Haw, *Chase*, 206-07 exculpate the judge; the accusations appear in Smith, *Trial*, 1: 207-12.

6. For example, see Haskins, *Supreme Court*, 2, pt. 1, 171, on Chase's response to the repeal.

7. Smith, *Trial*, 1: 212-19; Haw, *Chase*, 214-16; Malone, *Jefferson the President: First Term, 1801-1805, Jefferson and His Time, III* (Boston, 1970), 465-69; William C. Bruce, *John Randolph of Roanoke, 1773-1833* ([1922], New York, 1970), 1: 214-15.

8. Fisher Ames to Timothy Dwight, January 25, 1804, in *Works of Fisher Ames*, ed.

Seth Ames, 2 vols. (Boston, 1854), 1: 337; Bayard to Robert Goodloe Harper, January 30, 1804, *Papers of James A. Bayard*, ed. Elizabeth Donnan, *Annual Report of the American Historical Association for the Year 1913* (Washington, D.C., 1915), 2: 160; Plumer, *Memorandum*, 101; *Memoirs of Adams*, 1: 323; [Adams], *Publius Valerius*, no. 1 (October 1804), *Writings of John Quincy Adams*, ed. Worthington C. Ford (New York, 1914), 3: 48–49.

9. Rodney to Joseph Nicholson, February 16, 1803, and Macon to Nicholson, August 6, 1803, Nicholson Papers, LC. For modern views of the case, compare Haskins, *Supreme Court*, 2, pt. 1, 238–45, which hedges its bets on Chase's guilt, with Berger, *Impeachment*, 234–62, finding for the prosecution, and Ellis, "The Impeachment of Samuel Chase" in Michal Belknap, ed., *American Political Trials* (Westport, Conn., 1981), 57–75, which finds for the defense. Charles Warren, *The Supreme Court in United States History*, 3 vols. (Boston, 1922), 1: 281–82, 289–97, regarded the case as little more than political harassment. Berger takes issue with this claim, focusing primarily upon Chase's "prejudgment" of Callender's guilt. One may properly ask if a state of mind was impeachable? The answer is—only if it resulted in impeachable acts. So we return to the question of the legitimacy of Chase's rulings in the courtroom. Here Berger singles out the exclusion of Taylor's testimony and the refusal to excuse Bassett from serving on the jury. Chase, Berger argues, was aware of the error of these rulings, but persisted in them—despite objection by counsel. There was precedent in English cases for impeachment and conviction upon charges of "browbeating" a witness (Berger cites Scroggs's case; [*Impeachment*, 280]). Chase also may have violated his oath of office under the Judiciary Act of 1789.

10. Marshall to Chase, January 23, 1804, Etting MS, PHi. Marshall made a much weaker version of this sentiment public at the trial (Smith, *Trial*, 1: 258–59).

11. *Annals of Cong.*, 8th Cong., 1st sess. (House), 806–07, 809–10, 814–15 (1804).

12. Ellis, *Jeffersonian Crisis*, 88–91; Haw, *Chase*, 218–22; Malone, *Jefferson: First Term*, 468–69.

13. *Annals of Cong.*, 8th Cong., 1st sess. (House), 819 (1804).

14. *Annals of Cong.*, 8th Cong., 1st sess. (House), 822–24, 828 (1804).

15. A minority view, but once expressed, it created a record on the issue of legislative intent. See appendix.

16. *Annals of Cong.*, 8th Cong., 1st sess. (House), 837 (1804).

17. *Annals of Cong.*, 8th Cong., 1st sess. (House), 842, 854, 863, 864–65 (1804).

18. *Annals of Cong.*, 8th Cong., 1st sess. (House), 857 (1804).

19. *Annals of Cong.*, 8th Cong., 1st sess. (House), 876 (1804).

20. *Annals of Cong.*, 8th Cong., 1st sess. (House), 1180, 1238, 1239 (1804).

21. Bushrod Washington to Edward Shippen, January 7, 1805, and Timothy Pickering to Theodore Lyman, March 14, 1804, quoted in Jane S. Elsmere, "The Impeachment Trial of Samuel Chase" (Ph.D. diss., University of Maryland, 1962), 128, 78; John Marshall to James M. Marshall, April 1, 1804, in Albert Beveridge, *Life of John Marshall* (Boston, 1916–19), 3: 176, 192–96; Fisher Ames to Thomas Dwight, January 20, 1805, *Works of Ames*, 1: 338; Chase to John F. Mercer, quoted in Elsmere, "Trial," 60–61.

22. Smith, *Trial*, 1: 5–8; *US Stats*, 1: 92. *Annals of Cong.*, 8th Cong., 2d sess. (House), 726–63 (1804), reported the debates on the articles and their transmission to the Senate.

23. On Martin's role, see Paul S. Clarkson and R. Samuel Jett, *Luther Martin of Maryland* (Baltimore, 1970), 206–28. On Harper's "moderation," see Joseph W. Cox, *Champion of Southern Federalism, Robert Goodloe Harper of South Carolina* (Port Washington, N.Y., 1972), 216.

24. *Memoirs of Adams*, 1: 318–19, 321; Plumer, *Memorandum*, 229; *Aurora*, January 8, 1805.

25. Haw, *Chase*, 228.

26. Smith, *Trial*, 1: 32–34, 37, 40, 43, 47, 48.

27. Chase to John Marshall, April 24, 1802, NyHi; Smith, *Trial*, 1: 56, 63, 85–86, 89.

28. Smith, *Trial*, 1: 95, 97, 98, 101.

29. Smith, *Trial*, 1: 109–24.

30. Smith, *Trial*, 1: 183; 2: 300.

31. Smith, *Trial*, 1: 192–99.

32. Smith, *Trial*, 1: 303.

33. Smith, *Trial*, 1: 326–27, 338, 343.

34. Smith, *Trial*, 1: 354.

35. Smith, *Trial*, 1: 367, 368. At this point Campbell or Early might have argued that there were strict liability crimes—sexual offenses, for example—in which the prosecution did not have to uncover *mens rea*. Chase tried to forestall this thrust by arguing that he had violated no law, but in fact the prosecution did not pursue this line.

36. Smith, *Trial*, 2: 6–7, 9–10, 11; Plumer, *Memorandum*, 297.

37. Smith, *Trial*, 2: 12, 13, 14, 17.

38. Smith, *Trial*, 2: 34–35, 50–51, 63–64, 72.

39. Smith, *Trial*, 2: 81..

40. Smith, *Trial*, 2: 82, 98.

41. Smith, *Trial*, 2: 111, 114, 119, 124, 130.

42. Clarkson and Jett, *Luther Martin*, 221; Smith, *Trial*, 2: 133, 135, 138, 141.

43. Smith, *Trial*, 2: 145.

44. Clarkson and Jett, *Martin*, 225–26; Plumer, *Memorandum*, 300.

45. Smith, *Trial*, 2: 249, 250.

46. Smith, *Trial*, 2: 254, 256.

47. Smith, *Trial*, 2: 258, 262, 316–17, 320, 326, 328–30.

48. Smith, *Trial*, 2: 332, 333, 335, 336, 339, 340, 364.

49. Smith, *Trial*, 2: 369, 371, 372, 374.

50. Smith, *Trial*, 2: 378, 381, 385, 386–87. The issue of other remedies for judicial misconduct is still open (Berger, *Impeachment*, 141–65).

51. Smith, *Trial*, 2: 393–94, 397, 399, 400.

52. Smith, *Trial*, 2: 447, 448, 450.

53. Smith, *Trial*, 2: 452–53, 474, 475; *Memoirs of Adams*, 1: 359.

54. Smith, *Trial*, 2: 484–92; *Memoirs of Adams*, 1: 308, 360–61; J. Q. Adams to John Adams, March 14, 1805, *Writings of John Quincy Adams*, 3: 115.

55. *Annals of Cong.*, 8th Cong., 2d sess. (Senate), 664–69 (1805).

56. *Memoirs of Adams*, 1: 364.

57. Ellis, *Jeffersonian Crisis*, 102–07.

58. Haw, *Chase*, 242–43; Bruce, *John Randolph of Roanoke*, 1: 216–17; *Annals of Cong.*, 8th Cong., 2d sess. (House), 1213, 1214 (1805); J. Q. Adams to John Adams, March 14, 1805, *Writings of J.Q. Adams*, 3: 117–18. On subsequent introduction of address and recall methods for removal, see epilogue, n. 7.

59. Henry Adams, *History of the United States: The First Administration of Thomas Jefferson* (New York, 1921), 2: 243–44; John Quincy Adams to John Adams, March 8, 1805, *Writings of J.Q. Adams*, 3: 108–14.

EPILOGUE

1. On Doyley's case: SC House, 77, 80, 81, 116–27, 131–34 (December 13, 15, 18, 19, 20, 1806); SC Senate (November 30, December 4, 5, 15, 18, 1807). On Hamilton, see SC House, 34 (November 29, 1806); 82–91 (December 15, 1806). For the other cases see James W. Ely, Jr., "'That No Office Whatever Be Held During Life or Good Behav-

ior,' Judicial Impeachments and the Struggle for Democracy in South Carolina,'' *Vanderbilt Law Review*, 30 (March 1977), 167–209.

2. In Tennessee, justices of the peace Isaac and John Philips were impeached and put to trial for criminal conspiracy. Isaac was found guilty and disqualified for two years (Cortez A. M. Ewing, "Early Tennessee Impeachments," *Tennessee Historical Quarterly*, 16 [December 1957] 300). On Moses Copeland, impeached in Massachusetts in 1807, see Pickering and Gardiner, *Report of the Trial By Impeachment of James Prescott* (Boston, 1821), 217–19.

3. G. S. Rowe, *Thomas McKean, The Shaping of An American Republicanism* (Boulder, Colo., 1978), 375–89.

4. Norman K. Risjord, *The Old Republicans of 1800, Southern Conservatism in the Age of Jefferson* (New York, 1965), 3–5, 35–36. The variety of this ideology is easily demonstrable; one need only compare the democratic Republicans of Lance Banning's *Jeffersonian Persuasion* (Ithaca, N.Y., 1978), 282, with the "minority of vocal critics" profiled in Risjord.

5. Ellis, *Jeffersonian Crisis*, 103–04; Malone, *Jefferson the President: First Term, 1801–1805, Jefferson and His Time, III* (Boston, 1970), 483.

6. See Leonard Baker, *John Marshall, A Life in Law* (New York, 1974), 432–38; Haw, *Chase*, 220; and John E. O'Connor, *William Paterson, Lawyer and Statesman: 1754–1806* (New Brunswick, N.J., 1979), 275.

7. For the 1808 proposals, see *Annals of Cong.*, 10th Cong., 1st sess. (House), 1680–1681, 1695–1696 (1808).

8. Smith, *Trial of Chase*, 1: 22–23.

9. Nahum Mitchell to Charles P. Greenough, February 12, 1805, Greenough Papers, MHi.

10. Richard Buel, Jr., *Securing the Revolution, Ideology in American Politics, 1789–1815* (Ithaca, 1972), 267; Roger H. Brown, *The Republic in Peril: 1812* (New York, 1964), 181.

11. V. O. Key, Jr., *Public Opinion and American Democracy* (New York, 1961), 538–39.

APPENDIX

1. Berger, *Impeachment*, 80.

2. See Perry Miller, *The Life of the Mind in America* (New York, 1965), 105–09, and Morton J. Horwitz, "The Emergence of an Instrumental Conception of American Law, 1780–1820," *Perspectives in American History*, 5 (1971), 299–308, both tracing aspects of what Lawrence Friedman has called the "Americanization" of the common law (*A History of American Law* [New York, 1973], 96).

3. Berger, *Impeachment*, 93.

4. Berger, *Impeachment*, 94.

5. Berger, *Impeachment*, 169.

6. Berger cited Elliot, *Debates*, 4: 43–44.

7. Berger, *Impeachment*, 80.

8. Berger, *Impeachment*, 93; quotes Wilson, in Elliot, *Debates*, 2: 513.

9. *Constitution of the United States*, Article III, section 2; on which *McCulloch v. Maryland*, 4 Wheaton 316 (1819) is based. One notes that the Supreme Court of the United States did not seek to overturn state supreme court rulings except in a few distinct areas of conflict, including the necessary and proper legislative powers of Congress, the "contract clause," and other constitutional matters. The United States Supreme Court heard appeals from the states' courts under section 25 of the Judiciary

Act of 1789 and acted with great "restraint" (Johnson, *Supreme Court*, 2, pt. 2, 624–25).

10. Section 34 of the Judiciary Act of 1789 was specifically upheld in *Resler v. Shekee*, 1 Cranch 109 (1801), a case coming out of Virginia, despite the fact that, at Callender's trial, Chase did not follow the Virginia procedure.

11. *Marbury v. Madison*, 1 Cranch 137 (1803), drew some of its inspiration from *Bayard v. Singleton* and *Trevett v. Weeden* (see discussion at chap. 5, nn. 55 and 58), at least according to Robert F. Cushman, *Cases in Constitutional Law* (Englewood Cliffs, 1975), 11, and Haskins, *Supreme Court*, 2, pt. 1, 189–90.

12. Bernard Schwartz, *The Great Rights of Mankind* (New York, 1977), 53–106; Robert Rutland, *The Birth of the Bill of Rights* (Chapel Hill, 1955), 24–189.

13. Irving Brant, *James Madison, Father of the Constitution* (New York, 1950), 164–75; Rutland, *Bill of Rights*, 194, 202.

14. On Prohibition, see Norman H. Clark, *Deliver Us From Evil, An Interpretation of American Prohibition* (New York, 1976), 107–39. Repeal of the Eighteenth Amendment was also preceded by action in the states. On women's suffrage, see Eleanor Flexner, *A Century of Struggle, The Women's Rights Movement in the United States*, rev. ed. (Cambridge, Mass., 1975), 159–81, 286–303.

15. One example was the Seditious Libel Act of 1798, which Congress modeled, among other precedents, upon understandings of seditious libel in various states (see Leonard W. Levy, *Freedom of Speech and Press in American History: Legacy of Suppression* [New York, 1963], 202–03). Levy's point is that in both the states and Congress, the concept of freedom of the press comprehended no prior censorship—the English common-law precept. In this episode the states' adoption of English rules bolstered the Federalists' drive to adopt them in Congress. Although not a typical subject of federal criminal law, the sedition law, when used, continued to parallel state prosecutions. Each party chose a different tribunal—the Republicans preferring the state courts, which they increasingly controlled after 1800. See Johnson, *Supreme Court*, 2, pt. 2, 638–39.

16. Criminal law has always been one area in which this borrowing is especially common. Federal procedure, through the incorporative features of the Fourteenth Amendment, has been enjoined upon the states, while certain substantive portions of state criminal codes have been absorbed by the federal government. A striking case in point is the Alien Registration Act, or Smith Act as it is commonly known, passed in from the 1940 Congress. The substance of the bill was taken state antisedition laws dating from the mid-1930s. Michal R. Belknap, *Cold War Political Justice, The Smith Act, The Communist Party, and American Civil Liberties* (Westport, Conn., 1977), 11–18, notes that the federal precursor of 1935 to the Smith Act was called, by its opponents to be sure, new "alien and sedition acts." On the state precedents for the federal bills, see "Federal Sedition Bills: Speech Restriction in Theory and Practice," *Columbia Law Review* 35 (1935), 917–27.

INDEX

Abbot, John: impeached in Vt., 80
Acton, Clement: investigated in N.J., 168
Adams, Henry: on Jefferson, 182; on
  impeachment, 254
Adams, John: on *Oliver*, 51, 52, 55, 56; and
  tenure of judges, 52, 193; on impeachment
  in republics, 60, 61, 64, 65, 66, 67;
  Thoughts on Government, 65–66; and
  Mass. const., 75; and *Blount*, 148, 152; and
  Fries, 184
Adams, John Quincy: and *Addison*, 206; at
  Pickering's trial, 211, 213, 214; on Chase's
  case, 231, 238, 252–53, 254
Adams, Samuel: on *Oliver*, 53; against
  Articles of Confederation, 104
Addison, Alexander: Pennsylvania state
  judge, 140, 187, 193, 195; impeached and
  tried, 187, 195–205, 260; as precedent in
  Pickering, 219; as precedent in *Shippen*,
  227; as precedent in *Chase*, 248, 249, 250,
  252, 254
"address" (assembly petition to governor): in
  colonies, 11–12, 35, 48; and republicanism,
  63–64; used in states, 122, 123, 172, 194,
  197, 198; proposed for U.S. Const., 254,
  260
Allen, Ira, 83
Allen, Richard: accused in S.C. Assembly,
  12, 279 (n. 34)
Allen, William, 43
Ames, Fisher: defends Federalist party, 111,
  124, 125, 143; and *Chase*, 231
Anne, Queen of England, 7, 39
Articles of Confederation, 103–05
Ashe, Samuel, 88; impeachment probed in
  North Carolina, 88–91, 123
assembly: colonial rights asserted, 9, 11, 26,
  27, 28, 39, 40, 41; judicial powers in state
  government, 62–63, 92, 103, 105–06, 144,
  146, 165, 167, 195; removal of officials
  without impeachment, 85, 122. *See also*
  "address"
Atlee, William, 93–94
attainder, 4, 30, 62, 277 (n. 1)

Bacon, Francis, Lord Verulam: impeached
  and tried in Parl., 6, 15
Baldwin, Abraham: and Gunn's case, 150; at
  Pickering's trial, 211
Bank of North America, 137
Bank of the United States, 143
Banks, David: impeached in N.J., 79
Barret, John: impeached in Vt., 80–81
Bartlett, Josiah: in *Langdon*, 127
Bayard, James: prosecutes Blount, 151,
  154–59; and *Pickering*, 208; and Chase's
  case, 231, 238, 252
Bayard v. Singleton (N.C.), 91, 92, 292 (n. 58)
Bedford, Gunning: on Chase, 230, 232
Bentham, James: sued in S.C., 79;
  impeached, 173
Berger, Raoul: impeachment of legislators,
  157, 158; impeachment of judges, 193; use
  of English precedent, 266–68; disputes
  Roberts, 277 (n. 2)
Bernard, Francis, 49
Bigelow, David, 123
"Bill of Rights" (first ten amendments to
  Const. of U.S.), 117, 232, 269–70
Blair et al. (Eng.), 5
Bland, Thomas, 21
Blount, William, 70, 88, 90, 151, 152;
  impeached, 151–62; prosecutes Campbell
  in Tenn., 174–77; *Blount* as precedent, 257
Blount v. Hall (Tenn.), 174, 176, 177
Boileau, Nathaniel: on Addison, 197;
  prosecutes Shippen, 224–26
Bolingbroke, Henry St. John, Lord:
  impeached in Parl., 8, 154; decries
  corruption, 39
Borland, John: impeached in Mass., 28, 29, 31
Boston Port Act, 56
Bowdoin, James, 123–24
Bowen, Jabez, Jr.: removed in Ga., 309 (n. 21)
Brackenridge, Hugh Henry, 192, 195; in
  Addison's case, 196, 200; defends common
  law, 220, 222–24
Bradbury, Thomas: removed by petition in
  Mass., 194, 197

Bradford, William, 81, 139

Brattle, William: on judicial tenure, 52, 193

Breckinridge, John: on Ky. const., 171; in attack on Federalist judiciary, 189; on Pickering trial, 211, 214; views common law, 221

Brown, Andrew: role in *Oswald*, 93, 94

Brown, John, 73, 74

Brunhouse, Robert, 93

Bryan, George, 67; *Genuine Principles of the Saxon, or English Constitution*, 67

Buckingham, George Villiers, Duke of: impeached in Parl., 6, 15, 19

Bull, William: role in *Shinner*, 46

Burke, Edmund, 113; and *Hastings*, 113–15

Burr, Aaron: presides at *Pickering*, 213, 216; presides at *Chase*, 238

Callender, James: prosecuted for seditious libel, 230; issue at Chase trial, 236, 239, 241, 250

Campbell, David, 174–75; impeached in Tenn. (*1798*), 174–77; impeached in Tenn. (*1803*), 177

Campbell, Dougal, 46

Campbell, George: prosecutes Chase, 243–44

Cary, James: witness against Blount, 152, 153

Cary, Thomas, 11

Cato's Letters, 39

Charles I, King of England, 4

Chase, Samuel, 117, 228–29, 255–56; presides at *Fries*, 184, 229–30; and Cooper's case, 187; impeached and tried, 189–190, 233–55; tries Callender in Richmond, 230; grand jury charge in Newcastle, 230, 236; address in Baltimore, 231, 237; *Chase* in retrospect, 259–60, 312 (n. 9)

Chipman, John, investigated in Vt., 165

Chiseldyne, Kenelm: counsel for Trueman, 19; and *Young*, 21

Chittenden, Thomas, 83, 84

Clarendon, Edward Hyde, Earl of: impeached in Parl., 17, 18, 19

Clarkson, Matthew: role in *Hopkinson*, 81, 82

Clay, Matthew: on Chase impeachment, 233

Clayton, Philip, 150; resigns from office in Ga., 150–51

Clayton, William: impeached in N.J., 83

Cocke, William: and *Blount*, 174; at Pickering's trial, 210, 211; vote in *Chase*, 253

Committee of Correspondence, Mass.: and *Oliver*, 33

common law, 117, 156–57, 159; and contempt of court, 95, 220, 223, 225, 226; and discretion of judges, 234; survives in America, 250, 266. *See also* judges; seditious libel; treason

Congress of the United States: Senate, 99–100, 102, 186–87; House of Representatives, 102, 142, 144, 251; and war v. France, 162–63. *See also* impeachment, trial on: in Congress

Connecticut: const. of *1818*, 92; impeachment in, 93

Constitution of the United States, 68, 96–106, 112, 118, 120, 121; convention to draft, 68, 96, 97, 98, 99–102, 105–06, 116, 119; ratification, 109, 110, 118, 157; Art. II, sec. *4*, 116, 118, 121, 154, 161, 219, 239, 245, 250–52; Art. III, sec. *1*, 118, 250; Art. I, sec. 3, 154–55; Sixth Amend., 156, 232; Art. II, secs. *2* and *3*, 159; Art. III, sec. *3*, 183; First Amend., 242; Art. II, sec. *1*, 245; Art. IV, 251, 254. *See also* impeachable offenses, high crimes and misdemeanors

constitutionalism, American: representative government, 8, 9, 12–13, 55–56; respect for law, 13–14, 78, 261–62; separation of powers in, 60–61, 70, 72, 76–77, 246, 269; role of elections in, 62–63, 119, 181–82, 189, 218, 250, 259; checks and balances in, 87, 100. *See also* republicanism

constitutionalism, English: received in colonies, 9–11, 26, 27. *See also* common law; impeachment precedent, English

contempt of court: charged in *Oswald*, 94–95; charged in *Passmore*, 220–21

Cooley, William: investigated in Vt., 165

Cooper, Thomas: prosecuted for seditious libel, 187

"corresponding powers," 269, 270; and impeachment, 269, 270

corruption, fear of, 39, 40, 46, 61, 62, 63, 80, 82, 113, 264

Cosby, William, 39

Coursey, Henry, 20

Court of the Star Chamber, 94

Craig, Elijah: impeached in Ky., 171–72

Dallas, Alexander James, 137; defends Blount, 155, 159–60; defends Fries, 184–85, 229, 236; prosecutes Addison, 200–05; defends Shippen, 222, 224, 225, 226

Dana, Francis, 194

"dangerous tendency," doctrine of, 139, 183, 188–89, 190, 206–07, 256, 262; in *Addison*, 199–205; in *Pickering*, 219; in *Shippen*,

226; in *Chase*, 228, 237, 241–52 passim. *See also* impeachment law, American

Davis, William: impeached in S.C., 133–34

Dayton, John: role in *Pickering*, 217

defendants. *See* impeachable offenses

Delaware: constitutional provisions for impeachment and trial, 69, 120

Denny, Thomas: impeached in N.J., 79

Denny, William: role in *Moore*, 42, 43, 44

DeSaussure, Henry: role in *Davis*, 133; role in *Moultrie*, 134, 136

de Tocqueville, Alexis, xiii

Dexter, Samuel: prosecutes Nicholson, 139–40

Dickinson, John, 103, 104, 105; and *Articles of Confederation*, 103, 104; and Const. of U.S., 105

disqualification, as legal penalty, 64, 149, 151, 161, 204

Douglas, William O., 265

Doyley, Daniel, 46; impeached in S.C., 256-57

Drake, William: impeached in Parl., 5

Duane, William: opposition to Federalists, 184, 186–87; and *Shippen*, 220, 226; and *Chase*, 238

Dudley, John: rebuked in N.H., 129

Dudley, Joseph, 28; role in *Vetch*, 29, 30, 31

Duer, William, 140

D'Yrujo, Carlos Martinez: and *Blount*, 153

Early, Peter: prosecutes *Pickering*, 208, 215; prosecutes *Chase*, 236, 242

East Jersey Colony, 11

Effingham, Francis Howard, Lord: and *Fitzhugh*, 23, 24

Elliott, James: speaks for Chase, 233

Eustis, William: and *Chase*, 236

Evans, John: and *Logan*, 33–34, 44, 45, 283 (n. 23)

Everard, Richard: and *Smith*, 37, 38

Fassett, Jonathan: impeached and tried in Vt., 84–85

Fauchet, Joseph, 148

Febiger, Christian: testifies against John Nicholson, 137

Federalist party (Hamiltonian): views of government, 111, 113, 117, 252, 259; takes sides in state cases, 122, 129, 136, 140, 141, 142, 143, 146–47, 148; uses *Blount*, 151, 155–56, 158, 161–63; and limited impeachment, 164, 166; resists Republican impeachment campaign, 181, 183, 184, 185–86, 193–94; maneuvers at Pickering's

trial, 210–17 passim, 218, 227; fears *Chase* outcome, 231

Federal Pension Act of *1792*, 142–43

Findley, William, 192; condemns Chase, 234

Fitzharris, Edward: impeached in Parl., 5

Fitzhugh, William, 23; impeached in Va., 23–24

Fordenir, Benjamin: censured in N.J., 83

Forman, David: forced to resign in N.J., 84

Forman, John: impeached in N.J., 47

Franklin (state of), 174

Franklin, Benjamin, 42, 60, 100, 103, 104

Franklin, William: defends Skinner, 47-48, 49

freedom of speech and press, 94, 205, 315 (n. 15)

French and Indian War, 41, 42

Fries, John, 184; tried and convicted for treason, 184, 185, 229–30, 234; discussed during *Chase*, 238–39

Gage, Thomas, 56

Gallatin, Albert: confutes Nicholson, 139; and *Pickering*, 208

Galloway, Joseph: role in *Moore*, 43, 44

Georgia: const. of *1789*, 119–20, 132; assembly, 131, 149–50; senate, 131–33

Gerry, Elbridge: at constitutional convention, 96, 101; as diplomat, 148, 154

Giles, William Branch, 143; attacks Hamilton, 143–44; espouses "popular will" doctrine, 188–89; role in *Chase*, 237, 238, 253, 254

Glorious Revolution of *1689*: in England, 7; in America, 27

Godfrey, Elijah: forced to resign in N.J., 167

Goodwin, F. L. B.: investigated in Mass., 171

Greenleaf, William: impeached and tried in Mass., 123–26, 260

Grimké, John, 79; impeached in S.C., 257

Griswold, Roger: and *Pickering*, 208; and *Chase*, 233, 235

Grundy, Felix: and Ky. courts, 171

Gunn, James: accused in Ga., 149–50

habeas corpus, writ of, 43

Hale, Matthew, 10

Hall, Prince: investigated in Vt., 165

Hamilton, Alexander: at constitutional convention, 96, 98, 99, 109; *Federalist No. 65*, 99, 100, 101, 106; and *Nicholson*, 137; defends against own impeachment, 143–44; on judicial independence, 194; and *Chase*, 238

Harper, Robert Goodloe: prosecutes Blount, 151, 161; defends Pickering, 213–15; defends Chase, 238, 249–50
Harris, William: impeached in R.I., 17
Harrison, Benjamin, 71
Harvey, John, 15; impeached and tried in Va., 15–17, 280 (n. 5)
Harvie, John, 86
Hastings, Warren: impeached and tried in Parl., 8, 97, 113–15; case as precedent, 109, 211, 235, 267
Henry, Patrick, 46, 85
Higginson, Nathaniel: prosecutes Nicholson, 139
Hobbes, Thomas, 73
Hodgson, John, 37
Hogan, Edmund: records *Nicholson*, 140
Hopkins, Peter: impeached in N.J., 83
Hopkinson, Francis, 81; impeached and tried in Pa., 81–82
Hopkinson, Joseph: counsel for Chase, 238, 245–46
House of Commons (England): and impeachment in England, 3–10 passim; as model for colonies, 26, 27, 28, 38, 44, 48; rejected as American authority, 60, 61, 67, 76, 97
House of Lords (England): as trial court, 3–10 passim, 44; incomparable to American senates, 60–61, 67, 97, 102; and *Hastings*, 114–15; allows counsel, 125
Humphrey, Reuben: impeached in Ky., 172
Hunt, William: impeached and tried in Mass., 141–42
Hutchinson, Thomas: on royal authority, 12, 50, 51; on *Vetch* as precedent, 32, 38, 49; defends Oliver, 52–55 passim, 59; as officeholder, 61

impeachable offenses: political error, 3, 5, 7–8, 13, 42, 112, 198; high crimes and misdemeanors, 3, 91, 97, 101, 119, 182, 189, 198, 217, 252–53, 277 (n. 2), 279 (n. 34), 297 (n. 19); crimes, 5, 20, 25, 78–79, 161, 169, 238–39; breach of public trust, 6, 18, 25, 49–56 passim, 87, 131, 141, 151, 200, 240, 250, 261–62, 294 (n. 37); bad advice, 8, 118, 267; misuse of power, 15–16, 18–19, 22, 25, 34, 38, 81–82, 84, 95, 166, 208–09, 240; high misdemeanor, 20, 29, 137, 152–53, 246; misuse of funds, 23–24, 25, 38, 47–48, 79–80, 134, 135, 136, 138, 158, 294 (n. 37); mal-administration, 68, 70, 97, 121, 142, 165; mal-conduct, 69, 121; misbehavior, 69, 127, 219; general

discussion of, 78–79, 112, 116–17, 119, 121, 122, 123, 255, 261–62; motivation in, 79, 118, 242–43; incompetence (incapacity), 85–86, 294 (n. 37); debated at constitutional convention, 101–02; misdemeanor, 102, 202, 203, 244, 250–51; "general" charges, 124, 132, 136, 145; "improper" conduct, 133; "error," 169; insanity, 208–19 passim; drunkenness, 216; in exigency, when removal necessary, 218–19, 234; "injustice," 236; partiality, 238, 242
impeachment, trial on: in England, 3, 4, 5, 7–8, 115; in colonies, 19, 20–21, 22, 30–31, 34, 35, 44, 54–55; alternative use of regular courts, 24, 30, 62, 85, 93, 97, 110, 148, 149, 155, 159, 248; procedural questions in, 60, 73, 148–49, 155–56, 203, 245, 260–61; Jefferson's views on, 70–75 passim, 103, 104, 111, 117, 119; two-thirds vote required to convict, 72, 75, 97, 100, 102–06, 120, 121; Madison's views on, 73–77 passim, 119; in states, 84, 124–26, 136, 138–40, 141–42, 200–04, 224–26, 257; in Const. of the U.S., 98–99, 100; in Congress, 155–61, 209–16, 238–54; common occurrence, 167; in absence of defendant, 219–20
impeachment law, American: basis in colonies, 12–14; develops in states, 64, 67, 68–77 passim, 80, 82; effect on state government, 78, 84, 92; and presidency, 100–01, 118–19, 294 (n. 32); and party system, 112, 113, 146, 148–61 passim, 177–78. *See also* impeachment precedent, American; parties, political
impeachment law, English, 3–10 passim, 264–65; modified in America, 60–61, 67, 114, 115
impeachment precedent, American: colonial, 55–56, 64; state, 96–97, 112, 116, 122, 140, 144–45, 158, 164, 193, 268–70, 288 (n. 1); *Blount* as, 162; Chase's view of, 239; *Chase* as, 255
impeachment precedent, English: recognized in America, 38, 47, 51, 52; distinguished from American cases, 60, 67, 96–97, 105, 112, 140, 234, 249, 252; Federalists use, 156, 235, 246; misattributed to American constitutionalists, 266–68
Indians: dispute over land, 153–54, 174–75
Ingersoll, Jared, Jr.: counsel for Hopkinson, 81, 137, 139, 140; defends Blount, 155, 160; defends Shippen, 222, 224, 226
Iredell, James: role in *Ashe*, 88, 91; on Const. of U.S., 110, 118; and *Vigol*, 184, 229; fears impeachment, 267

Jackson, Andrew: aids David Campbell, 175
Jackson, James, 130; and *Osborne*, 130–33;
    forces Clayton's resignation, 149–50, 161;
    at Pickering's trial, 211, 213, 217
James, Charles: impeached and tried in Md.,
    19
James II, King of England, 5, 24
Jay, John, 105; Jay-Gardoqui Treaty, 105;
    Jay Treaty with G.B., 112, 116, 146–47;
    Pension Act controversy, 142–43; fears
    impeachment, 147
Jefferson, Thomas, 60; and Va. const., 65–66;
    faces impeachment, 85–86; role in
    Hamilton's case, 143; presides at *Blount*,
    158; on executive removals, 181–82, 188;
    and *Pickering*, 208, 212; and *Chase*, 231.
    See also impeachment, trial on: Jefferson's
    views; parties, political; Republican party
Johnson, Nathaniel: role in *Trott*, 36
Jones, Seaborn: defends Osborne, 131–33
Jones, Thomas: impeached in Ky., 172
judges: tenure of, 52, 181, 193, 218, 263; and
    Revolution, 62–63, at trials, 72–73;
    independence of, 73, 91, 122, 128, 194, 195,
    217, 233, 239, 257; under attack, 206–07,
    212, 217–18, 259, 260; use of discretion,
    220–24 passim, 231, 232, 244–45, 246, 248,
    249. *See also* judicial reform
judicial reform: in Mass., 49, 50, 193–94; in
    N.H., 129; in Pa., 192–94, 220, 225;
    nationally, 193–94, 232; disputed in *Chase*,
    246
judicial review, 91, 92
Judiciary Act of *1801*, 188, 194, 215, 231
Judiciary Act of *1789*, 117; issue in *Chase*,
    237, 247
jury trial: after impeachment, 74, 148, 156,
    172, 211; as issue in impeachment cases,
    90, 95, 220, 223; bars impeachment, 160

Keith, William: on *Harvey*, 15
Kenton v. McConnell (Ky.), 122
Kentucky: const. of *1792*, 120; assembly, 122,
    147, 171, 172; senate, 122, 147, 172; const.
    of *1799*, 171; reform of courts in, 171; later
    impeachments in, 257
Key, Philip Barton: counsel for Chase, 238,
    246–47
King, Rufus: and constitutional convention,
    96, 106
Kinsey, James: and *Skinner*, 47, 48, 285 (n. 22)
Kling, John, 93
Kukla, Jon, 15–16

Lacey, John: impeachment threatened in
    N.J., 168

Langdon, John, 126, 161
Langdon, Woodbury, 126; impeached in
    N.H., 127–30
Lawson, Roger: impeached and tried in
    Mass., 28, 29
lawyers: adherence to rules of evidence,
    xiii–xiv, 254; and impeachment, 125,
    170–71, 214, 220, 224; and impeachment
    law, 191, 195; as defense counsel, 230, 233,
    247, 250
Leavens, Charles: investigated in Vt., 166
Lee, Charles: counsel for Chase, 238, 247–48
Lee, Richard Henry, 65, 85, 110
Leech, Thomas, 43
legal history: and case law, xii; pitfalls in,
    265, 278–79 (n. 29)
Leib, Michael: and *Fries*, 185; seeks
    impeachment of Richard Peters, 234; seeks
    impeachment of Thomas McKean, 257
Leigh, Egerton, 46
Lewis, William, 120; defends Nicholson,
    139, 140, 141; defends Fries, 229, 236
Lining v. Bentham (S.C.), 79
Liston, Robert; and *Blount*, 153, 154
Livingston, Edward: attacks Jay Treaty, 147
Livingston, William: in N.Y., 43; in N.J., 84
Lloyd, David: role in *Logan*, 32–35 passim
Logan, George: at Pickering's trial, 214, 216
Logan, James, 32; impeached and tried in
    Pa., 32–35, 45
Loyalists: prosecuted, 62; efforts to regain
    property, 79, 88, 89, 90
Lucas, John B. C., 196, 197; witness against
    Addison, 196, 198, 200, 201, 203
Lynde, Benjamin, Jr., 49
Lyon, Matthew, 80, 83–84; impeached and
    tried in Vt., 80, 83–84; prosecuted for
    seditious libel, 166

McClenahan, Blair, 81, 82, 94
Macclesfield, Lord Chancellor: impeached
    and tried in Parl., 8, 109, 267
McDowell, John: witness for Addison, 201
McIntosh, Lachlan: and David Campbell,
    174, 177
McKean, Joseph: prosecutes Addison, 196,
    199
McKean, Thomas, 93, 110, 120, 121, 192;
    accused by Oswald, 94–95; and *Addison*,
    204; faces impeachment in Pa., 257
Maclaine, Archibald: attacks judiciary in
    N.C., 88–91 passim; on Const. of U.S., 267
Macon, Nathaniel, 188, 209
Madison, James: on impeachment trials, 73,
    74, 75, 98, 100; on Jefferson's case, 86; and
    state precedents, 96; and impeachable

Madison, James (*continued*)
offenses, 101, 102, 111, 117, 118, 119, 120;
on two-thirds rule, 104
Maine, province of, 170–71
Mainwaring's case (England), 4
Marshall, Humphrey, 147; call for his
impeachment, 147–48; and Blount, 162
Marshall, John: and Chase, 231, 232, 241; as
potential defendant, 260
Martin, Daniel: impeached and removed in
Vt., 80
Martin, Luther: defends Chase, 230, 238,
248–49
Maryland: assembly, 17–20 passim; colonial
charter, 18; council, 18, 19, 20; const. of
1776, 63
Mason, George: and Va. const., 65–66, 70;
and Const. of U.S., 96, 97, 99, 101, 267
Massachusetts: council, 28, 29, 30, 31, 51, 54,
55; colonial charters, 28, 33, 50; superior
court of judicature, 29, 30, 31, 49–50,
52–55 passim; const. of *1780*, 75, 76, 103,
125; bill of rights, 171
Massachusetts General Court: as grand
inquest, 12, 13, 52–54; and impeachment,
28–33 passim, 49–55 passim; 123–26
passim, 141, 169
Mather, Cotton, 30
Messinger's case (England), 183
Middlesex, Lionel Cranfield, Lord:
impeached and tried in Parl., 6, 18
Mifflin, Thomas: and Nicholson, 137, 140
Miller, William: impeached in N.J., 83
Monroe, James, 110, 148, 188; on *Shippen*,
221
Montagu, Charles: and *Shinner*, 47
Montgomery, John: attacks Chase, 231, 240,
250
Moore, Alfred: and *Ashe*, 89
Moore, Maurice: lobbies against William
Smith, 36, 37
Moore, William, 42; impeached in Pa., 42–46
More, Nicholas, 21; impeached and tried in
Pa., 21–23, 33
Morecroft, John, 17; impeached and tried in
Md., 17–19
Morey, Israel, 126
Moriss, Moody: forced to resign in N.H.,
86–87, 291 (n. 40)
Morris, Gouverneur, 96, 98, 100
Morris, Lewis, 83, 166
Morris, Robert (of Md.): brings
impeachment against Morecroft, 17, 18
Morris, Robert (of Pa.), 82, 140
Moultrie, Alexander, 134; impeached and
tried in S.C., 134–36; and Yazoo lands,
135

Muter, George: censured in Ky., 122, 147, 198

New Hampshire: state const., 76; assembly,
86–87, 126–30 passim, 201; senate, 127,
128, 129; supreme court, 127, 128, 129
New Jersey: assembly, 47, 48, 49, 59, 62,
79–80, 83, 84, 85, 92, 122, 142, 166, 167,
168, 169; council, 48, 59, 69, 80, 83, 167,
169; const. of *1776*, 69
New Loan notes (Pa.): and *Nicholson*,
137–40 passim
New York: const. of *1777*, 69, 70, 71, 98, 103
Nicholas, George, 85, 86
Nicholas, Wilson Cary: at Pickering's trial,
216
Nicholson, John: impeached and tried in
Pa., 137–41, 200
Nicholson, Joseph: prosecutes Pickering,
208, 209, 215; and Chase, 231, 235, 237;
arguments in *Chase*, 250–51
Nixon, Richard M., 265
Norris, Isaac, 43
North Carolina: assembly, 11, 24, 25, 37, 88,
89, 90, 91, 122; proprietors of, 25, 26;
council, 36, 37, 38; const. of *1776*, 70, 120;
supreme court, 88, 91

Oliver, Andrew, 49
Oliver, Peter, 12, 49–50; impeached in Mass.,
12, 49–56, 59, 65
Osborne, Henry: impeached and tried in
Ga., 130–33
Osgood, Abner: investigated in Vt., 85
Oswald, Eleazer: sued for libel in Pa., 93;
accuses judges, 94, 95; and Nicholson, 137
Otis, Harrison Gray, 141
Otis, James, Jr., 46
Oxford, Robert Harley, Lord: impeached
and tried in Parl., 7, 8, 154

Parliament: and impeachment in England,
3–10 passim; as model for colonies, 13, 27,
28, 38, 39, 44; rejected as model during
Revolution, 59, 61. *See also* House of
Commons (Eng.); House of Lords (Eng.)
Parker, Oliver: investigated in Mass., 170
Parsons, Theophilus: on Mass. const., 75, 76;
defense counsel in impeachment cases,
124–25, 141
parties, political: Tory (Eng.), 7, 8; Whig
(Eng.), 7, 8; Federalist (pro-Const. of U.S.),
94; and impeachment, 109–15, 144, 146,
151–61, 162–63, 219, 249, 258–63; and two-
party system, 111, 146–49, 181–83, 191–92,
244, 257, 261–63. *See also* Federalist party
(Hamiltonian); impeachable offenses;
Republican party (Jeffersonian)

Passmore, Thomas: held in contempt in Pa., 220–21; calls for impeachment of judges, 221

Paterson, William: at constitutional convention, 96; and New Jersey plan, 98; and *Vigol*, 183, 184, 229; potential impeachment, 260

Peck, John: impeached in N.J., 79

Pendleton, Edmund, 86

Penn, Thomas: and *Moore*, 45

Penn, William, 21; and *More*, 21, 22, 281 (n. 23); and *Logan*, 32

Pennsylvania: colonial charters, 11, 22, 33, 34, 44, 102; assembly, 21, 22, 23, 32, 33, 34, 42, 43, 44, 45, 81, 94–95, 137, 138, 191, 196, 197, 198, 221, 257; council, 22, 34, 82, 94; provincial convention, 62, 66; const. of *1776*, 63, 66–67, 68, 71, 137; council of censors, 69; const. of *1790*, 120–21, 197, 224; senate, 138–39, 140, 203–04, 224, 225, 226; supreme court, 196, 201, 221–22

Peters, Richard: presides in *Fries*, 184, 229; on Chase, 232; investigated in Congress, 234, 236

Pettibone, Dudley: investigated in Conn., 93

Petyt, George, 4

Phillips, Josiah: tried for treason in Va., 62

Pickering, Jacob: defends John Pickering, 213–14

Pickering, John, 129, 207; impeached and tried in Congress, 208–19, 220, 227, 255

Pickering, Timothy, 111; and Blount, 148; demands prosecution of Gerry, 148, 154; and John Pickering, 216

Pinckney, Charles Cotesworth: at constitutional convention, 96, 100, 103

Pitt, William (the younger): and *Hastings*, 114, 296 (n. 14)

Plumer, William: and *Langdon*, 127, 128; and Addison, 200; and *Pickering*, 207, 212, 216; and *Chase*, 231, 238

"popular will," doctrine of, 189, 256, 262; used in *Pickering*, 219; used in *Shippen*, 225; discussed during *Chase*, 228, 237, 241, 246, 249, 251, 252

Posey, John Price: tried in Va., 82–83

Prescott, James: impeached in Mass., 171

Privy Council (England), 11, 13, 31–32, 38, 43–44, 45, 48, 63

Procter, Thomas, 93

public opinion: and impeachment, 144, 189

Quincy, Josiah, Jr., 51

Rabun, Thomas: accused in Ga., 149

Randolph, Edmund: at constitutional convention, 96, 97, 100; removed as secretary of state, 148; testifies at *Chase*, 241

Randolph, John, 188; and impeachment doctrine, 188–89; and Jefferson, 189, 233–34; and Pickering, 208; prosecutes Chase, 228, 231–52 passim, 259; after *Chase*, 254, 258

Rawle, William: and Nicholson, 139; prosecutes Duane, 184

Read, Jacob: role in *Blount*, 158, 161, 163

republicanism: and impeachment, 59–64 passim, 68, 72, 74, 76, 106, 116, 146, 268

Republican party (Jeffersonian): emerges, 111, 113, 117; role in state cases, 122, 141, 143, 144, 146–47; and *Blount*, 151, 154, 156, 158–59, 160; and Federalist judiciary, 193–94, 199, 205–06, 214, 244; and democracy, 257, 258, 259; and limited government, 258–59

Rhode Island: assembly, 17; state const., 91; supreme court, 92

Richardson, John: counsel for Bentham, 173

Roberts, R. Clayton: on parliamentary impeachment, 277 (n. 2)

Robinson, Patrick: censured by assembly in Pa., 23

Rodney, Caesar: prosecutes Pickering, 215; prosecutes Shippen, 225, 226; prosecutes Chase, 232, 251–52

Romayne, Nicholas: witness in *Blount*, 153

Ross, James, 186, 191

Rouse, William: impeached and tried in Mass., 28

Rush, Jacob, 93–94

Rushworth, John, 10, 51

Rutledge, Edward: manages impeachments in S.C., 134, 135, 136

Sacheverell, Henry: impeached and tried in Parl., 4, 7, 187

Sargent, Johathan D.: witness in *Hopkinson*, 82

Sargent, Paul Dudley: investigated in Mass., 170–71

Scroggs, William: impeached and tried in Parl., 4, 22

Sebastian, Benjamin: censured in Ky., 122, 147, 198

seditious libel: federal law of, 117, 161, 185, 186; common law of, 117, 185–88; "bad tendency test," 182–83, 186, 187, 199; Addison's views on, 195; Chase's views on, 228, 230, 231, 240; Chase verges on, 231, 237, 250

Selden, John, 7, 10, 51

Sevier, John: and *Campbell*, 174, 175

Sewall, Samuel: and *Vetch*, 29, 30, 31

Shays's Rebellion, 84
Shepherd, John: and *Clayton*, 150–51
Sherburne, John S.: complainant in
    Pickering, 209, 216
Sherwood, Samuel, 59
Shinner, Charles: forced to resign in S.C., 46
Shippen, Edward, Jr.: reports on *Moore*, 43
Shippen, Edward, Sr.: and Addison, 201;
    impeached and tried in Pa., 221–27, 261;
    case used in *Chase*, 252, 254
Sitgreaves, Samuel: prosecutes Blount,
    151–53, 154
Skinner, Stephen: forced to resign in N.J.,
    47–49
Smilie, John, 192; and *Chase*, 233, 234
Smith, James, 81
Smith, John: and *Pickering*, 214
Smith, Samuel: votes in *Pickering*, 213
Smith, Thomas: impeached and tried in Pa.,
    221–27
Smith, William (chief justice of North
    Carolina): impeachment vote fails in N.C.,
    36–38
Smith, William (Philadelphia minister):
    tried for contempt of assembly in Pa., 42,
    43, 46
Smith, William, Jr. (New York lawyer): aids
    William Smith of Phila., 43
Smith Act: and "corresponding powers," 315
    (n. 16)
Smyth, Frederick: investigated in N.J., 47
Somers's case (England), 8, 267
Sothel, Seth: impeached and driven out of
    N.C., 24
South Carolina: assembly, 12, 35, 46, 133,
    134, 135, 173, 257, 283 (n. 27); proprietors,
    35, 36; council, 35, 46; state const., 76;
    supreme court, 79; senate, 134, 136, 173
Spain: interest in *Blount*, 152, 153
Spencer, Samuel: impeachment inquiry
    target in N.C., 88–91; and ratification of
    Const. of U.S., 110
Spiller's case (England), 18
Sprague, John: role in *Greenleaf*, 125–26
Stickney, Mary: and *Moriss*, 87
Story, Joseph: and impeachment of
    legislators, 157
Strafford, Thomas Wentworth, Lord:
    impeached in Parl., 306 (n. 14)
Sullivan, James: and impeachments in
    Mass., 125, 141, 169
Supreme Court of the U.S., 142–43, 230–31
Swift, Jonathan, 39

Taylor, John (of Caroline): at Callender's
    trial, 230, 236; testimony in *Chase*, 241

Tennessee: const., 120; assembly, 176, 177;
    senate, 177; impeachments after *Chase*, 257
Tichenor, Isaac, 83, 84
Trevett v. Weeden (R.I.), 92
Trott, Nicholas: impeached and tried in
    S.C., 35–36
Tracy, Uriah: condemns Duane, 186–87; at
    Pickering's trial, 210–14 passim
treason: law of, 3, 124, 183; and
    impeachment in America, 20, 30–31, 230.
    See also Vigol, Philip; Fries, John
Trowbridge, Edmund: and *Oliver*, 51–54
    passim
*A True and Faithful Narrative of the
    Proceedings of the House of Burgesses of
    North Carolina*: tract in Smith's case,
    37–38
Trueman, Thomas: impeached and tried in
    Md., 18, 19, 21
Tucker, Samuel: investigated in N.J., 47

U.S. v. Brig Eliza: and Pickering's case, 208,
    213, 216
U.S. v. Goodwin and Hudson (1812), 117
U.S. v. Worrall (1798), 117, 229, 232

Vermont: const., 68–69; council of censors,
    69, 83, 165, 166; assembly, 80–81, 83, 84,
    85, 165, 166; council, 80, 81, 84, 85;
    supreme court, 165
Vetch, Samuel: impeached and tried in
    Mass., 11, 28–31, 32, 33, 38, 49, 50
Vigol, Philip: tried for treason, 183, 184, 229
Vinal, John: impeached and tried in Mass.,
    169–70
Vinall, William: investigated in Mass., 170
Virginia: assembly, 13–17 passim, 23, 24, 62,
    66, 71, 82, 83, 85–86; council, 15, 16, 17, 23,
    24, 71, 83; const. of 1776, 62, 65–66, 70, 71,
    86, 267; criminal procedure in, 247, 248

Wade, Robert: impeached in N.J., 79
Walett, Francis, 55
Walpole, Robert, 8, 39, 109
Wardwell, Jeremiah: Maine litigant, 120
Warren, Charles: on *Chase* verdict, 255
Washington, George: and Jay Treaty,
    147–48; pardons Vigol, 184
Wayne, Anthony: coconspirator in *Osborne*,
    130, 131, 133
Webster, David: investigated in N.H., 126
Whiskey Rebellion, 183
White, Hugh Lawson: and *Campbell*, 175
White, John: and *More*, 22
White, Samuel: at Pickering's trial, 216, 217

Whitehill, Robert: and *Addison*, 199; and *Shippen*, 226

Willard v. Hall (Vt.), 166

Williams, John: impeachment probed in N.C., 88–91

Williams, Roger: demands impeachment in R.I., 17, 93

Williamson, Hugh: at constitutional convention, 96, 97, 102

William III (William of Orange), King of England, 7, 27, 28

Wilson, James: counsel for Hopkinson, 81; at constitutional convention, 96, 99, 101, 110; revises Pa. const., 120, 121; and Pension Act controversy, 142–43; on contempt law, 224

Wilson, Robert: investigated in N.J., 168–69

Wood, Thomas, 10

Wythe, George, 65

Yazoo lands: and Moultrie, 135; and James Jackson, 149–50; and John Randolph, 189

Yeates, Jasper, 137; impeached and tried in Pa., 221–27

Yonge, Francis: and *Trott*, 36

Young, Jacob: impeached and tried in Md., 19, 20, 21